A History of Australian Tort Law 1901–1945

Little attention has been paid to the development of Australian private law throughout the first half of the twentieth century. Using the law of tort as an example, Mark Lunney argues that Australian contributions to common law development need to be viewed in the context of the British race patriotism that characterised the intellectual and cultural milieu of Australian legal practitioners. Using not only primary legal materials but also newspapers and other secondary sources, he traces Australian developments to what Australian lawyers viewed as British common law. The interaction between formal legal doctrine and the wider Australian contexts in which that doctrine applied provided considerable opportunities for nuanced innovation in both the legal rules themselves and in their application. This book will be of interest to both lawyers and historians keen to see how notions of Australian identity have contributed to the development of an Australian law.

Mark Lunney is a Professor in the School of Law at the University of New England in Armidale, Australia and a Visiting Professor at the Dickson Poon School of Law, King's College London. He has researched and published extensively in the law of tort and legal history including *Tort Law: Text and Materials* (5th edition with Ken Oliphant) and *The Law of Torts in Australia* (5th edition with Kit Barker, Peter Cane and Francis Trindade). He is a member of the World Tort Law Society.

The Law in Context Series

Editors: William Twining (University College London),
Christopher McCrudden (Queen's University Belfast) and
Bronwen Morgan (University of Bristol).

Since 1970 the Law in Context series has been at the forefront of the movement to broaden the study of law. It has been a vehicle for the publication of innovative scholarly books that treat law and legal phenomena critically in their social, political and economic contexts from a variety of perspectives. The series particularly aims to publish scholarly legal writing that brings fresh perspectives to bear on new and existing areas of law taught in universities. A contextual approach involves treating legal subjects broadly, using materials from other social sciences, and from any other discipline that helps to explain the operation in practice of the subject under discussion. It is hoped that this orientation is at once more stimulating and more realistic than the bare exposition of legal rules. The series includes original books that have a different emphasis from traditional legal textbooks, while maintaining the same high standards of scholarship. They are written primarily for undergraduate and graduate students of law and of other disciplines, but will also appeal to a wider readership. In the past, most books in the series have focused on English law, but recent publications include books on European law, globalisation, transnational legal processes, and comparative law.

Books in the Series
Ali: *Modern Challenges to Islamic Law*
Anderson, Schum & Twining: *Analysis of Evidence*
Ashworth: *Sentencing and Criminal Justice*
Barton & Douglas: *Law and Parenthood*
Beecher-Monas: *Evaluating Scientific Evidence: An Interdisciplinary Framework for Intellectual Due Process*
Bell: *French Legal Cultures*
Bercusson: *European Labour Law*
Birkinshaw: *European Public Law*
Birkinshaw: *Freedom of Information: The Law, the Practice and the Ideal*
Brownsword & Goodwin: *Law and the Technologies of the Twenty-First Century*
Cane: *Atiyah's Accidents, Compensation and the Law*
Clarke & Kohler: *Property Law: Commentary and Materials*
Collins: *The Law of Contract*
Collins, Ewing & McColgan: *Labour Law*
Cowan: *Housing Law and Policy*
Cranston: *Legal Foundations of the Welfare State*
Darian-Smith: *Laws and Societies in Global Contexts: Contemporary Approaches*
Dauvergne: *Making People Illegal: What Globalisation Means for Immigration and Law*
Davies: *Perspectives on Labour Law*
de Sousa Santos: *Toward a New Legal Common Sense*

Dembour: *Who Believes in Human Rights?: The European Convention in Question*

Diduck: *Law's Families*

Fortin: *Children's Rights and the Developing Law*

Ghai & Woodham: *Practising Self-government: A Comparative Study of Autonomous Regions*

Glover-Thomas: *Reconstructing Mental Health Law and Policy*

Gobert & Punch: *Rethinking Corporate Crime*

Goldman: *Globalisation and the Western Legal Tradition: Recurring Patterns of Law and Authority*

Haack: *Evidence Matters: Science, Proof, and Truth in the Law*

Harlow & Rawlings: *Law and Administration*

Harris: *An Introduction to Law*

Harris, Campbell & Halson: *Remedies in Contract and Tort*

Harvey: *Seeking Asylum in the UK: Problems and Prospects*

Hervey & McHale: *European Union Health Law*

Hervey & McHale: *Health Law and the European Union*

Holder and Lee: *Environmental Protection, Law and Policy*

Jackson and Summers: *The Internationalisation of Criminal Evidence*

Kostakopoulou:*The Future Governance of Citizenship*

Lewis: *Choice and the Legal Order: Rising above Politics*

Likosky: *Law, Infrastructure and Human Rights*

Likosky: *Transnational Legal Processes*

Maughan & Webb: *Lawyering Skills and the Legal Process*

McGlynn: *Families and the European Union: Law, Politics and Pluralism*

Moffat: *Trusts Law: Text and Materials*

Monti: *EC Competition Law*

Morgan: *Contract Law Minimalism*

Morgan & Yeung: *An Introduction to Law and Regulation: Text and Materials*

Nicola and Davies: *EU Law Stories: Contextual and Critical Histories of European Jurisprudence*

Norrie: *Crime, Reason and History*

O'Dair: *Legal Ethics*

Oliver: *Common Values and the Public–Private Divide*

Oliver & Drewry: *The Law and Parliament*

Picciotto: *International Business Taxation*

Probert: *The Changing Legal Regulation of Cohabitation, 1600–2010*

Reed: *Internet Law: Text and Materials*

Richardson: *Law, Process and Custody*

Roberts & Palmer: *Dispute Processes: ADR and the Primary Forms of Decision-Making*

Rowbottom: *Democracy Distorted: Wealth, Influence and Democratic Politics*

Sauter: *Public Services in EU Law*

Scott & Black: *Cranston's Consumers and the Law*

Seneviratne: *Ombudsmen: Public Services and Administrative Justice*

Seppänen: *Ideological Conflict and the Rule of Law in Contemporary China*

Siems: *Comparative Law*

Stapleton: *Product Liability*

Stewart: *Gender, Law and Justice in a Global Market*

Tamanaha: *Law as a Means to an End: Threat to the Rule of Law*

Turpin and Tomkins: *British Government and the Constitution: Text and Materials*

Twining: *Globalisation and Legal Theory*

Twining: *General Jurisprudence: Understanding Law from a Global Perspective*

Twining: *Human Rights, Southern Voices: Francis Deng, Abdullahi An-Na'im, Yash Ghai and Upendra Baxi*

Twining: *Rethinking Evidence*

Twining & Miers: *How to Do Things with Rules*

Ward: *A Critical Introduction to European Law*

Ward: *Law, Text, Terror*

Ward: *Shakespeare and Legal Imagination*

Wells and Quick: *Lacey, Wells and Quick: Reconstructing Criminal Law*

Zander: *Cases and Materials on the English Legal System*

Zander: *The Law-Making Process*

International Journal of Law in Context: A Global Forum for Interdisciplinary Legal Studies

The *International Journal of Law in Context* is the companion journal to the Law in Context book series and provides a forum for interdisciplinary legal studies and offers intellectual space for ground-breaking critical research. It publishes contextual work about law and its relationship with other disciplines including but not limited to science, literature, humanities, philosophy, sociology, psychology, ethics, history and geography. More information about the journal and how to submit an article can be found at http://journals.cambridge.org/ijc

A History of Australian Tort Law 1901–1945

England's Obedient Servant?

MARK LUNNEY

University of New England, Australia

CAMBRIDGE
UNIVERSITY PRESS

University Printing House, Cambridge CB2 8BS, United Kingdom

One Liberty Plaza, 20th Floor, New York, NY 10006, USA

477 Williamstown Road, Port Melbourne, VIC 3207, Australia

314–321, 3rd Floor, Plot 3, Splendor Forum, Jasola District Centre, New Delhi – 110025, India

79 Anson Road, #06-04/06, Singapore 079906

Cambridge University Press is part of the University of Cambridge.

It furthers the University's mission by disseminating knowledge in the pursuit of
education, learning, and research at the highest international levels of excellence.

www.cambridge.org
Information on this title: www.cambridge.org/9781108423311
DOI: 10.1017/9781108399609

First published 2018

Printed in the United Kingdom by TJ International Ltd. Padstow Cornwall

A catalogue record for this publication is available from the British Library.

ISBN 978-1-108-42331-1 Hardback

Contents

List of Figures   *page* x

Acknowledgements   xi

List of Abbreviations   xv

Table of Cases   xvii

Table of Statutes and Statutory Instruments   xxiii

1   Introduction   1

2   Historiography and the History of Australian Private Law in the First Half of the Twentieth Century: *Et in Arcadia Ego*?   10

3   Avoiding and Interpreting the 'Refinements of English Law': Defamation in Australia 1901–1945   32

4   Politics, Politicians, the Press and the Law of Defamation   51

5   Negligence and the Boundaries of Liability: Liability for Acts of Third Parties   84

6   Negligence and the Vexing Question of Shock-Induced Harm   111

7   Negligence and the Boundaries of Liability: Government and Quasi-Government Liability   147

8   In Defence of King and Country   166

9   Environment and Australian Tort Law: The Problem of Fire and Weeds   199

10   Sport and Recreation: Tort Law and the National Pastime 1901–1945   236

11   Conclusion   279

Index   283

Figures

5.1 Collapse of the verandah of Hoyt's picture theatre,
    24 July 1925   *page* 99
6.1 Flooded trench in *Chester v. Council of Municipality*
    of Waverley   130
8.1 Letter confirming intention of Shaw Savill and Albion & Co.
    Ltd to hold Commonwealth responsible for damage to
    MV *Coptic*   191
8.2 Note of meeting between Commonwealth's legal advisors,
    October 1940   192
8.3 Department of Navy Minute with handwritten annotation
    refusing to waive privilege   193
8.4 Map showing position of collision between *MV Coptic* and
    HMAS Adelaide   194
8.5 Minute of First Naval Member criticising Shower's conduct in
    relation to the collision   195
8.6 Department of Navy staff member note on effect of court
    martial on civil trial   196
8.7 Department of Navy staff member note on effect of court
    martial on civil trial   197
8.8 Handwritten comments of First Naval Member on Captain
    Showers' Noumea Mission   198
10.1 Charlie Spinks, Billy Lamont, Dick Smythe and Vic Huxley
    on the Davies Park Circuit in Brisbane   245
10.2 Len Jones   248
10.3 Rufe Naylor   250
10.4 A.B. Cowell   253
10.5 Victoria Park race course   268

Acknowledgements

This book could not have been written without the support, both personal and financial, of many people and organisations. My thanks is due first to the members of the Australian Research Council that supported the research on which the book is based with a three-year Discovery Grant commencing in 2013 (DP130103626). This allowed for the employment of research assistants, the purchase of rare materials, and travel and accommodation to archives and libraries without which the research could not have been completed. It also supported visits to collaborate with my partner investigator, Professor Paul Mitchell, of University College London. Paul's contribution to the book has been invaluable, including but not limited to his perceptive and helpful comments on the draft manuscript which he read in full. Thanks are also due to the College of Law at the Australian National University where I was a staff member when the grant application was submitted, and to the assistance of Karen Warnes and Katie Paterson whose expertise in the Research Office of the College added greatly to the quality of the application.

The book has been benefitted by the work of a number of research assistants and I would like to thank Michael Peterer, Sujini Ramamurthy and Alice Rumble for their help. But special praise must go to my final and longest serving research assistant, Peta Lisle, for her outstanding research assistance. Be it trawling through volumes of the *Australian Law Journal* or *Law Institute Journal*, burrowing into state and Commonwealth libraries and archives, or providing editorial assistance, Peta's remarkable competence and thoroughness have made this book immeasurably better than it would have been without her involvement and I thank her for her contribution.

I wish to acknowledge the support I or my research assistants have received from the various libraries and other repositories accessed during the research for the book. The staff of the National Archives of Australia in both Canberra and Melbourne ensured that relevant High Court files and associated departmental files were readily available when visited. The National Library of Australia and the State Library of Victoria willingly provided access to various sets of private papers they held. The Public Record Office of Victoria and the State Record Office of New South Wales assisted in locating case files and government files on state legislation. I am particularly grateful to Carole Hinchcliffe, Law Librarian at Melbourne Law School, for arranging access to manuscript copies of notes of tort lectures made by former students. Numerous other libraries provided books on inter-library loan and I thank them for that, and the ability to access the Australian Legal History Library through the Australian Legal Information Institute made accessing reported cases from the period much easier than it would otherwise have been. There are also numerous individuals who willingly gave their time to answer questions or provide snippets of information and I thank all of them for their help.

Various colleagues read parts of the book in draft and provided helpful comments. Professor Peter Cane kindly read a number of chapters and provided his usual penetrating and insightful comments. Professor David Rolph read the defamation chapters and provided important feedback. Many chapters of the book were presented when in draft at seminars and conferences both in England and Australia and I would like to thank the participants in those events for their comments and feedback. In particular, Professor Michael Lobban arranged for me to present twice to the London Legal History Seminar Series and Dr Matthew Dyson facilitated a seminar at the Faculty of Law at the University of Cambridge. In Australia, my thanks are due to Ron Levy for arranging a seminar at the College of Law at the Australian National University in April 2016 and to the organising committee of the Rare Books Lecture 2016 at Melbourne Law School for an invitation to present the lecture. I would also like to acknowledge the support I received from historians during the project. Among others, Professor Wilfrid Prest's enthusiasm for the approach adopted in the book provided much needed solace as did Professor Frank Bongiorno's comments on Chapter 2. Finally, I would like to thank my colleagues at the School of Law at the University of New England for their support and wonderful collegiality and congeniality.

This book was completed while I was receiving treatment for an ongoing serious back condition. I am grateful for the efforts of the specialists who attempted to fix the problem albeit with less success than we all had hoped. In Armidale, I must acknowledge the remarkable work of my physio Mary Sutherland whose efforts have thus far allowed me to work in a meaningful way despite the limitations. I must also thank the Australian Research Council who delayed the completion date of my research grant in recognition of the condition.

The idea for a book like this does not come out of thin air and I would like to mention the three academics most influential in its inception. The first is the late Professor A.W.B. Simpson whose work introduced a legally straight-laced Queenslander to the possibilities of interdisciplinary law and history research early in his academic career. The second is Professor Bruce Kercher, whose work demonstrated to me that there was a place for this kind of work in Australian legal history. His unfailing and infectious enthusiasm for Australian legal history has inspired a generation. Lastly, and by way almost of an apology, I want to mention my lecturer in Australian history in my first year at the University of Queensland, Dr Denis Murphy. This brilliant academic whose career was cut short the following year when he died of cancer planted a seed that lay dormant for many years. I may not have had the enthusiasm for Australian history then as I have now but I hope he would be pleased that in the end he had a convert!

On a personal note, the therapy provided by my Scottish and West Highland White Terriers, Duncan and Dennis, and my galah, Rosso, whose wise counsel got me through many a rough patch, is acknowledged. And it is impossible to do justice to the contribution of my long-term partner and now wife, Karen, who throughout her own troubles has provided wonderful support and companionship. The book could not have been written without her help.

Abbreviations

ACT	Australian Capital Territory
Adel L Rev	*Adelaide Law Review*
Age	*The Age*
AJC	Australian Jockey Club
ALJ	*Australian Law Journal*
Argus	The Argus
Australasian	*The Australasian*
CLJ	*Cambridge Law Journal*
Colum L Rev	*Columbia Law Review*
CTH	Commonwealth
GLR	*Griffith Law Review*
Harv L Rev	*Harvard Law Review*
Hous LR	*Houston Law Review*
ICLQ	*International and Comparative Law Quarterly*
Ill L Rev	*Illinois Law Review*
Imp	Imperial
IPQ	*Intellectual Property Quarterly*
J Soc Comp Legis	Journÿes de la sociÿtÿ de la lÿgislation comparÿe
JLH	*Journal of Legal History*
LHR	*Law and History Review*
LIJ	*Law Institute Journal*
LQR	*Law Quarterly Review*
LS	*Legal Studies*
MULR	*Melbourne University Law Review*
NAA	National Archives of Australia
NILQ	*North Ireland Legal Quarterly*
NLA	National Library of Australia
NSW	New South Wales
NT	Northern Territory
OJLS	*Oxford Journal of Legal Studies*
Qld	Queensland
RJC	Rockhampton Jockey Club

SA	South Australia
SALJ	*South African Law Journal*
SMH	*Sydney Morning Herald*
Syd LR	*Sydney Law Review*
Tas	Tasmania
TLJ	*Torts Law Journal*
U Tas LR	*University of Tasmania Law Review*
UNSW	University of New South Wales
UQLJ	*University of Queensland Law Journal*
UWALR	*University of Western Australia Law Review*
Vic	Victoria
WA	*The West Australian (newspaper)*
WA	Western Australia (legislation)

Table of Cases

Adelaide Chemical and Fertilizer Co. Ltd v. Carlyle (1940) 64 CLR 514

Aiken v. Kingborough Corporation (1939) 62 CLR 179

Alcock v. Chief Constable of South Yorkshire [1992] AC 310

Allen v. Flood [1898] AC 1

Anderson v. Commissioner of Railways [1910] WAR 10

Attorney General v. Adelaide Steamship Co. Ltd [1923] AC 292

Attorney General v. De Keyser's Royal Hotel [1920] AC 508

Bailey v. Truth and Sportsman Ltd (1938) 60 CLR 700

Baker v. Durack [1924] WAR 32

Baker v. Queensland Newspapers Pty Ltd [1937] St R Qd 153

Balmain New Ferry Co. Ltd (The) v. Robertson (1906) 4 CLR 379; [1910] AC 295 (PC)

Barker v. Herbert [1911] 2 KB 633

Barnes v. The Commonwealth (1937) 37 SR (NSW) 511

Bean v. Harper & Co. (1893) 18 VLR 388

Bennett v. Porter, Benalla Standard, 6 July 1923, 5

Bernina (The) (1886) 12 PD 36; (1888) 13 App Cas 1

Best v. Tasmanian Amateur Jockey Club, The Mercury (Hobart), 31 July 1925, 3; 1 August 1925, 7

Beyer v. Drews, The Courier-Mail (Brisbane), 27 May, 1937, 17

Black v. Christchurch Finance Co. [1894] AC 48

Blythe v. Birmingham Waterworks (1856) 11 Exch 781; 156 ER 1047

Boatswain v. Crawford [1943] NZLR 109

Bolton v. Stone [1951] AC 850

Borough of Bathurst v. Macpherson (1879) 4 App Cas 256

Bourhill (or Hay) v. Young [1943] AC 92

Bourke v. Butterfield and Lewis (1926) 38 CLR 354

Bradford Corporation v. Pickles [1895] AC 567

Britain Steamship Co. Ltd v. The King [1921] 1 AC 99

Brodie v. Singleton Shire Council (2001) 206 CLR 512

Brown v. Holloway (1909) 10 CLR 89

Brown v. The Mount Barker Soldiers Hospital Incorporated [1934] SASR 128

Browne v. McKinley (1886) 12 VLR 240

Buckle v. Bayswater Road Board (1936) 57 CLR 259

Bugge v. Brown [1918] VLR 413; (1919) 26 CLR 110

Bull v. Mayor of Shoreditch (1903) 19 TLR 64

Bunyan v. Jordan (1936) 36 SR (NSW) 350; (1937) 57 CLR 1

Burnie Port Authority v. General Jones Pty Ltd (1994) 179 CLR 520

Cambridge Water Co. Ltd v. Eastern Counties Leather plc [1994] 2 AC 264

Cameron v. Consolidated Press Ltd [1940] SASR 372

Canavan v. Syme & Co. [1918] VLR 540; (1918) 25 CLR 234

Carroll v. Nelson Park Pty Ltd, Argus, 6 September 1941, 3; 9 September 1941, 8

Cassidy v. Daily Mirror Newspapers [1929] 2 KB 331

Castle v. St Augustine Links (1922) 38 TLR 615

Chatterton v. The Secretary of State for India [1895] 2 QB 189

Chatwood v. National Speedways Ltd [1929] St R Qd 29

Chester v. Council of the Municipality of Waverley (1938) 38 SR (NSW) 603;
    (1939) 62 CLR 1

Chomley v. Watson [1907] VLR 502

Cofield v. Waterloo Case Co. Ltd (1924) 34 CLR 363

Collingwood v. Home and Colonial Stores Ltd [1936] 3 All ER 200

Collins v. Commonwealth of Australia (1945) 62 WN (NSW) 245

Cooke v. Midland Great Western Railway of Ireland [1909] AC 229

Cottrell v. Allen (1882) 16 SALR 122

Council of the City of Newcastle v. Australian Agricultural Co. Ltd (1929) 29 SR
    (NSW) 212

Cowell v. The Rosehill Racecourse Co. Ltd (1937) 56 CLR 605

Craig v. Parker [1906] WAR 161

Crowe v. Albany Road Board, Albany Advertiser, 22 October 1931, 3

Crowhurst v. Amersham Burial Board (1878) 4 Ex D 5

Crown of Leon (Owners) v. Admiralty Commissioners [1921] 1 KB 595

Daly v. The Commissioner of Railways [1906] WAR 125

Davidson v. Walker (1901) 1 SR (NSW) 196

Davison v. Vickery's Motors Ltd (1925) 37 CLR 1

Dawkins v. Lord Paulet (1869) LR 5 QB 94

De Libellis Famosis, Or of Scandalous Libels (1605) 77 ER 250

Dennis v. Victorian Railway Commissioners (1901) 27 VLR 323; (1903) 28
    VLR 576

Dickson v. Commissioner of Railways (1922) 30 CLR 579

Dominion Natural Gas Co. Ltd v. Collins [1909] AC 640

Donoghue v. Stevenson [1932] AC 562

Dougherty v. Smith, New Zealand Times, 29 July 1887, 3

Doyle v. McIntosh; Mutch v. McIntosh (1917) 17 SR (NSW) 402

Dulieu v. White [1901] 2 KB 669

Duncan v. Cammell Laird & Co. Ltd [1941] 1 KB 640 (CA); (1941) 69 Ll L Rep
    84 (CA); [1942] AC 624 (HL); [1943] 2 All ER 621 (KB)

E Hulton & Co. v. Jones [1910] AC 20

Eastern Asia Navigation Co. Ltd v. Freemantle Harbour Trust Commissioners (1951) 83 CLR 353

Enever v. R (1906) 3 CLR 969

Engelhart v. Farrant & Co. [1897] 1 QB 240

Entick v. Carrington (1765) 2 Wils KB 275; 95 ER 807

Esery v. North Coast National A and I Society, Northern Star (Lismore), 15 December 1938, 12

Evans and Wife v. Finn (1904) 4 SR (NSW) 297

Evans v. Municipality of Redfern, Sydney Morning Herald, 16 October 1907, 6

Ex Parte Marais [1902] AC 115

Filliter v. Phippard (1847) 11 QB 347; 116 ER 506

Flukes v. Paddington Municipal Council (1915) 15 SR (NSW) 408

Foley v. Hall (1891) 12 NSWR 175

Forrester v. Tyrrell (1893) 9 TLR 257

Fowles v. Eastern and Australian Steamship Co. Ltd [1916] 2 AC 556

Francis v. Cockrell (1870) LR 5 QB 501

Gibbons v. Duffell (1932) 32 SR (NSW) 31; (1932) 47 CLR 520

Gibbs v. Daily Examiner, Daily Examiner (Grafton), 25 September 1918, 2

Giles v. Walker (1890) 24 QBD 656

Givens v. David Syme & Co. (No. 1) [1917] VLR 418

Givens v. David Syme & Co. (No. 2) [1917] VLR 437

Godhard v. James Inglis & Co. Ltd (1904) 4 SR (NSW) 327; (1904) 2 CLR 78

Gold v. Essex County Council [1942] 2 KB 293

Goldsborough v. John Fairfax and Sons Ltd (1934) 34 SR (NSW) 524

Goodsell v. Moore (1915) 15 SR (NSW) 228

Gordon v. Young (1900) 21 NSWR 7

Gunter v. James (1908) 24 TLR 868

Hall v. Brooklands Auto Racing Club [1933] 1 KB 205

Hall-Gibbs Mercantile Agency Ltd (The) v. Dun [1910] St R Qd 333; (1910) 12 CLR 84

Hambrook v. Stokes Bros Pty Ltd [1925] 1 KB 141

Hanson v. Globe Newspaper Co. (1893) 159 Mass 293

Hargrave v. Goldman (1963) 110 CLR 40

Havelberg v. Brown [1905] SALR 1

Hawley v. Steele (1877) 6 Ch D 521

Hazelwood v. Webber (1934) 34 SR (NSW) 155; (1934) 52 CLR 268

Higgins v. Willis (1921) 2 IR 386

Hill v. Smith, The Daily News (Perth), 13 September 1938, 9

HMS Drake [1919] P 362

HMS Hydra [1918] P 78

Howe v. Lees (1910) 11 CLR 361

Hoyt's Pty Ltd v. O'Connor [1928] VLR 65; (1928) 40 CLR 566

Hughes v. Watson [1917] VLR 398

Hughes v. West Australian Newspaper Ltd [1940] WAR 12

Hurst v. Picture Theatres Ltd [1915] 1 KB 1

International News Service v. Associated Press 248 US 215 (1918)

Isaacs and Sons v. Cook [1925] 2 KB 391

Janvier v. Sweeney [1919] 2 KB 316

JC Williamson Ltd v. Lukey (1931) 45 CLR 282

Job Edwards Ltd v. Birmingham Navigation Co. Proprietors [1924] 1 KB 341

John Fairfax and Sons Ltd v. Punch (1980) 47 FLR 458

John Lamb's Case (1610) 77 ER 822

Johnson v. The Commonwealth (1927) 27 SR (NSW) 133

Jones v. Festiniog Railway Co. (1868) LR 3 QB 733

Joseph v. Colonial Treasurer (NSW) (1918) 25 CLR 32

Kellett v. Cowan [1906] St R Qd 116

Kelly v. Hayes (1903) 22 NZLR 429

Lang v. Willis (1934) 52 CLR 637

Lee v. Wilson [1934] VLR 198; (1934) 51 CLR 276

Lemmon v. Webb [1894]3 Ch 1

Lipman v. Clendinning (1932) 46 CLR 550

London Association for the Protection of Trade v. Greenlands [1916] 2 AC 15

London County Council v. Great Eastern Railway Co. [1906] 2 KB 312

Macintosh v. Dun (1905) 5 SR (NSW) 708; (1906) 3 CLR 1134; [1908] AC 390 (PC)

Mangena v. Wright [1909] 2 KB 958

Mansel v. Webb (1918) 88 LJKB 323

Mattinson v. Coote [1931] WAR 18

McCarty v. Leeming [1937] SASR 432

McCauley v. John Fairfax and Sons Ltd [1934] 34 SR (NSW) 339

McDonald v. Dickson (1868) 2 SALR 32

McDowall v. Great Western Railway [1902] 1 KB 618

McLoughlin v. O'Brian [1983] 1 AC 410

Meldrum v. Australian Broadcasting Co. Ltd [1932] VLR 425

Mentone Racing Club (The) v. The Victorian Railway Commissioner (1902) 28 VLR 77

Metropolitan Railway Co. v. Jackson (1877) 3 App Cas 193

Midland Railway Co. v. Connolly [1919] WAR 1

Miller v. McKeon (1905) 5 SR (NSW) 128; (1905) 3 CLR 50

Mitchellmore v. Salmon (1905) 1 Tas LR 109

Moody v. Municipality of Woollahra (1912) 12 SR (NSW) 597

Mowlds v. Ferguson (1940) 40 SR (NSW) 311; (1940) 64 CLR 206

Mulholland and Tedd Ltd v. Baker [1939] 3 All ER 253

Municipal Council of Sydney v. Bourke [1895] AC 433

Musgrove v. Pandelis [1919] 1 KB 314; [1919] 2 KB 43(CA)

Naylor v. Caterbury Park Racecourse Co. Ltd (1935) 35 SR (NSW) 281

Newspapers v. Bridge (1979) 141 CLR 535

Newstead v. London Express Newspaper Ltd [1940] 1 KB 377

Ormsby v. Douglass (1868) 37 NY Rep 477

Owens v. Liverpool Corporation [1939] 1 KB 394

Parisi v. Gallogly, The Telegraph (Brisbane), 2 December 1929, 20

Parker v. R (1963) 111 CLR 610

Patmoore v. Boon (1927) 22 Tas LR 75

Peatling v. Watson [1909] VLR 198

Peck v. Tribune Co. (1908) 214 US 189

Penfolds Wines Pty Ltd v. Elliot (1946) 74 CLR 204

Penton v. Calwell (1945) 70 CLR 219

Pett v. Sims Paving and Road Construction Co. Pty Ltd [1928] VLR 247

Pettingaudet (Owners) v. Warilda (Owners) (1920) 2 Ll L Rep 187

Piper v. Geary (1898) 17 NZLR 357

Piro v. W Foster & Co. Ltd (1943) 68 CLR 313

Pitts v. Hunt [1991] 1 QB 24

Polemis, Furniss and Withy, Re [1921] 3 KB 560

Powell v. Fall (1880) 5 QBD 597

Pratten v. The Labour Daily Ltd [1926] VLR 115

Prattis v. Council of Municipality of Bexley (1915) 15 SR (NSW) 232

Prout v. Stacey [1923] WAR 20

R (Ronayne and Mulcahy) v. Strickland (1921) 2 IR 333

R v. Allen (1921) 2 IR 241

Ratcliffe v. Evans [1892] 2 QB 524

Rea v. Balmain New Ferry Co. (1896) 17 NSWR 923

Read v. J Lyons & Co. Ltd [1947] AC 156

Richards v. Baker [1943] SASR 245

Richardson v. Mellish (1824) 2 Bing 229

Rickards v. Lothian [1910] VLR 425; (1911) 12 CLR 165; [1913] AC 263 (PC)

Ricketts v. Erith Borough Council (1944) 113 LJKB 269

Robins v. National Trust Co. [1927] AC 515

Robinson v. State of South Australia [1931] AC 704

Rohan v. Municipality of St Peters (1908) 8 SR (NSW) 649

Ruhan v. The Water Conservation and Irrigation Commission (1920) 20 SR
    (NSW) 439

Rylands v. Fletcher (1868) LR 3 HL 330

Savige v. News Ltd [1932] SASR 240

Sealey v. The Commissioner for Railways [1915] QWN 1

Sedleigh Denfield v. O'Callaghan [1940] AC 880

Sermon v. Commissioner of Railways (1907) 5 CLR 239

Shaw Savill and Albion Co. Ltd v. Commonwealth (1940) 66 CLR 344; (1953)
    88 CLR 164

Sheehan v. Park (1882) 8 VLR 25

Sinclair v. Cleary [1946] St R Qd 74

Slatyer v. Daily Telegraph Co. Ltd (1907) 7 SR (NSW) 488; (1908) 6 CLR 1

Smith v. Giddy [1904] 2 KB 448

Smith v. Jenkins (1970) 119 CLR 397

Smith v. Leurs [1944] SASR 213; [1945] SASR 86; (1945) 70 CLR 256

Smith v. London and South Western Railway (1870) LR 6 CP 14

Smith v. Ministry of Defence [2014] AC 52

Smith's Newspapers Ltd v. Becker (1932) 47 CLR 279

Sparke v. Osborne (1907) 7 SR (NSW) 842; (1908) 7 CLR 51

Strangways-Lesmere v. Clayton [1936] 2 KB 11

Subiaco Municipal Council v. Walmsley [1930] WAR 49

Sunday Times Publishing Co. Ltd v. Holman [1925] WAR 10

Telegraph Newspaper Co. Ltd v. Bedford (1934) 50 CLR 632

Thompson v. Gosney [1933] St R Qld 190

Thompson v. Truth and Sportsman Ltd (No. 1) (1931) 31 SR (NSW) 129

Thompson v. Truth and Sportsman Ltd (No. 4) (1930) 31 SR (NSW) 292

Tolmer v. Darling [1943] SASR 81

Trimble v. Hill (1879) 5 App Cas 342

Turberville v. Stamp (1697) 12 Mod 152; 88 ER 1228

Victoria Park Racing and Recreation Grounds Co. Ltd. v. Taylor (1937) 37 SR (NSW) 322; (1937) 58 CLR 479

Victoria Railway Commissioners v. Coultas (1886) 12 VLR 895; (1888) 13 App Cas 222 (PC)

Victorian Railways Commissioner v. Campbell (1907) 4 CLR 1446

Victorian Woollen and Cloth Manufacturing Co. Ltd (The) v. Board of Land and Works (1881) 7 VLR 461

Waghorn v. Waghorn (1942) 65 CLR 289

Wardle v. McInnes [1930] SASR 450; (1931) 45 CLR 548

Wason v. Walter (1868) LR 4 QB 73

Watego v. Byron Shire Council (1920) 5 LGR 82

Watson v. South Australian Trotting Inc [1938] SASR 94

Weld-Blundell v. Stephens [1920] AC 956

Wenbam v. Council of the Municipality of Lane Cove (1918) 18 SR (NSW) 90

Whinfield v. Lands Purchase Management Board of Victoria and State Rivers and Water Supply Commission of Victoria [1914] VLR 662; (1914) 18 CLR 606

Whitfield v. Turner (1919) 19 SR (NSW) 345; (1920) 28 CLR 97

Whitford v. Clarke [1939] SASR 434

Wilkinson v. Downton [1897] 2 QB 57

Winter Garden Theatre (London) Ltd v. Millennium Productions [1948] AC 173

Wise Bros Pty Ltd v. The Commissioner of Railways (1947) 47 SR (NSW) 233; (1947) 75 CLR 59

Wood v. Leadbitter (1845) 13 M&W 837

Woods v. Duncan [1944] 2 All ER 156 (CA); [1946] AC 401 (HL)

Wright v. Cedzich (1930) 43 CLR 493

Wright v. Wright (1948) 77 CLR 191

Yates; Ex Parte Walsh, Re (1925) 37 CLR 36

Young v. Tilley [1913] SALR 87

Zamora (The) [1916] 2 AC 77

Table of Statutes and Statutory Instruments

Imperial

Colonial Laws Validity Act 1865

United Kingdom

Fires Metropolis Act 1774
Law of Libel Amendment Act 1888

Australia

Commonwealth

Australia Act 1986
Australian Industries Preservation Act 1906
Broadcasting Act 1942
Broadcasting and Television Act 1956
Claims Against the Commonwealth Act 1902
Judiciary Act 1903
Statute of Westminster Adoption Act 1942
Wireless Telegraphy Act 1905–1919

Australian Capital Territory

Law Reform (Miscellaneous Provisions) Ordinance 1955

New South Wales

Careless Use of Fire Prevention Act 1866
Careless Use of Fires Act 1912
Compensation to Relatives Act 1897
Defamation (Amendment) Act 1909
Defamation Act 1912
Gaming and Betting Amendment Act 1938

Law Reform (Miscellaneous Provisions) Act 1944
Local Government Act 1906
Prickly-Pear Destruction Act 1901
Slander and Libel Act 1847

Northern Territory

Law Reform (Miscellaneous Provisions) Ordinance 1956

Queensland

Careless Use of Fires Prevention Act 1865
Criminal Code Act 1899
Defamation Act 1889
Prickly Pear Selections Act 1901
Prickly-Pear Destruction Act 1912
Racecourses Act and Other Amendments Act 1936
Rural Fires Act 1927

South Australia

Bush Fires Act 1854
Bush Fires Act 1913
Wrongs Act Amendment Act 1939

Tasmania

An Act for Regulating Buildings and for Preventing Mischiefs by Fire in the
   Town of Launceston 1853
Defamation Act 1895

Victoria

An Act to Restrain the Careless Use of Fire 1854
Railways Act 1890
Railways Act 1896
Victorian Railway Commissioners Act 1883
Wrongs Act 1932

Western Australia

Criminal Code Act 1902
Government Railways Act 1904
Ordinance to Diminish the Dangers Resulting from Bush Fires 1847

1

Introduction

This book discusses a heretofore unexplored area of Australian legal history by considering Australian contributions to the common law of tort in the first half of the twentieth century. To the extent that the issue has been considered in private law more generally,[1] almost by default it has been assumed that Australian law in substance mirrored developments of the English common law. This was so for both case law and for legislation even though the constraints attached to divergence were different. The common view held both by contemporaries and by later writers was, and is, that there was very little, if any, evidence of Australian exceptionalism in descriptions of private law during the period of this study. Australian courts, both through the rules of formal precedent and informal deference to the superior English courts, simply followed what was dictated in the mother country (the 'cultural cringe' argument).

The aim of this book is to subject this view to detailed critique by considering the evidence contained in Australian cases, and occasionally legislation.[2] Legislation was in theory constrained by the Colonial Laws Validity Act 1865 (Imp),[3] but by the beginning of this study, this legislation had imposed little constraint on legislative authority in private law. But with the Privy Council the superior court in the Australian legal hierarchy for all matters within its jurisdiction, and with decisions of superior English courts varying in the period

---

[1] There is very little historical analysis of Australian developments in private law and even less for the period of this study. For notable exceptions see P. Mitchell, 'The foundations of Australian defamation law' (2006) 28 *Syd LR* 477; A. Buck, *The Making of Australian Property Law* (Federation Press, 2006); J. Gava, 'Dixonian strict legalism, *Wilson v Darling Island Stevedoring* and contracting in the real world' (2010) 30 *OJLS* 519; J. Gava, 'When Dixon nodded: Further studies of Sir Owen Dixon's contract jurisprudence' (2011) 33 *Syd LR* 157. In intellectual property, see C. Bond, '"A spectacle cannot be owned": A history of the uneasy relationship between copyright and sport in Australia' (2013) 8 *Australian and New Zealand Sports Law Journal* 1; C. Bond, '"This is not a bill to legalize looting": Wartime regulation of enemy-owned intellectual property in Australia' (2015) *IPQ* 79. More generally see B. Kercher, *An Unruly Child: A History of Law in Australia* (Allen and Unwin, 1996) ch. 8.

[2] A. Castles, 'The reception and status of English law in Australia' (1963) 2 *Adel L Rev* 1.

[3] For the Commonwealth, this limitation remained until 1942 (*Statute of Westminster Adoption Act 1942* (Cth)) and for the states until 1986 (*Australia Act 1986* (Cth) s. 2): W. Gummow, 'The Australian Constitution and the end of Empire – a century of legal history' in K. Schultz (ed.), *Legal History Turns* (Federation Press, 2015) 74, 80–81.

of this study between being highly persuasive to virtually binding, the scope for judicial innovation appears limited.[4] At the heart of the book is the argument that Australian contributions to the common law cannot be understood without recognising not only the legal restraints but also the cultural and intellectual milieu in which members of the Australian legal community operated. Seen as part of a community of 'independent Australian Britons' – a phrase used by the historian Keith Hancock in his 1930 historical survey of Australia – a different story emerges as to Australian legal creativity. Australian lawyers had no difficulty in having equal but dual loyalties, loyalties that recognised a distinct kind of Australian patriotism which was not inconsistent with the maintenance of ancestral ties. A commitment to both the universality of the common law in the Empire/Commonwealth, and to the capacity of Australian lawyers to contribute to that common law for the greater good, underpinned their views as to how English legal authority was to be applied in Australia. Rather than hostility, the characteristic mode of engagement was progressive, recognising the limits that a colonial or dominion court had in making wholesale changes but equally careful to ensure that as far as possible the common law, in both theory and in its practical application, was suitable for a country with very different characteristics from England. This more nuanced approach does not reveal that assertions of uniformity with English law are wrong at a global level but by asking the wrong question they seriously undervalue the contribution made by this earlier generation.

This is a key insight in understanding the relationship between the English common law and the common law of the Empire. What to a modern generation of lawyers seems an impossible compromise between legal independence and legal subservience was not at all implausible to a group that had grown up with multifaceted loyalties. The compromise was not always convenient. Assertions that the common law was the same throughout the Empire hid the fact that in its application Australian lawyers and judges were adapting it to suit the needs of a quite different Australian society. At times this could be explained as simply the application of general principles to concrete facts but in some cases it seems as much a mantra as a critical evaluation of the nature of the relationship between English and Australian law. It was perhaps inevitable that the loosening of formal ties between Britain and its constituent Empire would lead to

---

[4] Privy Council decisions stressed the importance of uniformity in application of the common law to the effect that the decisions of superior English courts should be followed in colonial courts: see *Trimble v. Hill* (1879) 5 App Cas 342; *Robins v. National Trust Company* [1927] AC 515. In the 1940s the High Court of Australia accepted that it should consider itself bound by the Court of Appeal and House of Lords (as well as the Privy Council) if there was no local distinguishing feature (*Waghorn v. Waghorn* (1942) 65 CLR 289; *Piro v. W Foster & Co. Ltd* (1943) 68 CLR 313). This was more formalised than previous statements from members of the High Court, which held that House of Lords' decisions were binding by 'judicial courtesy' but that it was not bound to follow decisions of any other court albeit that Court of Appeal decisions would carry great weight: *Brown v. Holloway* (1909) 10 CLR 89, 102–103 (O'Connor J); *Davison v. Vickery's Motors Ltd* (1925) 37 CLR 1, 13–17 (Isaacs J).

greater normative acceptance of the value of divergence but this took time. By the late 1930s Hancock himself struggled to reconcile the inexorable logic of separation that greater independence would bring with his lived understanding that the collective ideal – now morphing to a Commonwealth – retained important practical meaning for each of the elements of the old Empire. As he put it, 'common sense seemed to be finding a middle way between dependence and disruption'.[5] While dependence was the dominant characteristic of Australian private law in the period of this study, that dependence was rooted in a shared understanding of the limits of divergence that was allowed without causing disruption.[6] For this reason it is worth looking at what Australian lawyers actually did as opposed to what they say they did. Only by a detailed critique of decisions made by Australian lawyers, made in light of the need to balance dependence and disruption, can we understand whether, and if so how, creativity and innovation took place within the wider societal constraints that operated to limit those attributes.

Why the Time Period?

There are a number of reasons why the first half of the twentieth century was chosen as the time period for this study. The creation of the Australian federation in 1901, and the High Court in 1903, provided for the first time a court that could speak with one voice for a 'new' country. While Australian nationalism was not born on 1 January 1901, the dynamics that influenced legal development were different after the creation of the Commonwealth than from the colonial period of the nineteenth century. Talk of an 'Australian' approach to a particular area of law had a new dimension when an Australian court could speak for Australian law as a whole. It also provided formal legal authority that bound the Supreme Courts of the Australian states, something that required the High Court to consider its own view on how cases from the mother country were to be interpreted. Despite the Commonwealth's limited legislative competence over private law,[7] the new federal structure provided the framework within which 'Australian' private law would need to develop.

While 1901 provides a convenient starting point for this study, it is more difficult to justify a specific date for its end. The process by which the political and cultural dynamic in which Australian lawyers operated changed was slow and subtle and historians argue over the point at which there was fundamental

---

[5] W.K. Hancock, *Survey of British Commonwealth Affairs Vol 1: Problems of Nationality 1918–1936* (Oxford University Press, 1937) 44.

[6] See, for example, Isaac Isaacs' view that, apart from decisions of the House of Lords, any English decision 'is sure to receive our traditional and unfeigned respect. But, short of emanation from a supreme source, every potion should at least be tasted and appraised before being swallowed': *Davison v. Vickery's Motors Ltd* (1925) 37 CLR 1, 14.

[7] There is no general power to legislate for private law in the enumerated areas of legislative power given to the Commonwealth in s. 51 of the Australian Constitution.

change in the Anglo-Australian relationship. Most place the date well after the Second World War.[8] It is not necessary for the purposes of this study to engage with these debates in any detail. The earliest period in which historians have recognised the potential demise of the traditional Anglo-Australian relationship is the end of the Second World War. By ending the study at the end of the war, it is possible to consider Australian legal development in the same broad context as applied at the beginning of the study. While that context was not static, it lacked the seismic changes in Australia's geopolitical relationships that characterised the second half of the twentieth century. The factors that led to the decline of British influence were largely in place by the end of the Second World War with the result that the normative force of the claim that Australian law should follow the English slowly diminished from this point.[9] How the post-war environment affected perceptions of Australian judicial independence in private law is a question that also requires detailed historical investigation[10] but that is another, quite different project from the one undertaken in the book.

Why the Law of Tort?

The law of tort is particularly suitable for the kind of bottom-up, finely-grained research which forms the basis of this book. The law of tort is the general law of the land (as opposed to contract law, for example, which depends largely upon the voluntary conduct of the parties). As a consequence, its subject matter reflects a wide variety of common situations. The way that the law responds to this variety of interactions between members of the community, frequently although not always unregulated, provides insight into both the role that law plays in a community and how that law is applied in practice. For this project, the law of tort was particularly suitable because it allowed for an examination of how this general law, created in England, was applied in very different Australian contexts. While this phenomenon was not captured in an indigenous Australian text published during the period of this study – perhaps because of its largely common law base[11] – the

---

[8] F. Bongiorno, 'Comment: Australia, nationalism and transnationalism' (2013) 10 *History Australia* 77, 79.

[9] A position formally reached in *Parker v. R* (1963) 111 CLR 610 when a unanimous High Court declared that it was free to depart from decisions of the Appellate Committee of the House of Lords.

[10] For differing views as to the effect of the Australian environment on the need to adapt the common law, see G. Barwick, 'Law and the courts' in A.F. Madden and W.H. Morris-Jones (eds.), *Australia and Britain: Studies in a Changing Relationship* (Sydney University Press, 1980); M. Lunney, 'Goldman v Hargrave' in P. Mitchell and C. Mitchell (eds.), *Landmark Cases in the Law of Tort* (Hart Publishing, 2010) ch. 8.

[11] There were a wide variety of general texts for non-lawyers (e.g. C.H. Chomley, *Law for Laymen: An Australian Book of Legal Advice and Information, Clear, Concise and Practical* (Fraser and Jenkinson, 1907) and specific texts on some areas of private law including real and personal property, hire purchase, banker and customer, landlord and tenant, marriage and divorce, principal and agent, insurance and intellectual property (especially patents). The Australian content in most of these works related to specific legislation passed in the various

reality of tort law litigation evidences the efforts of Australian lawyers to make their mark on the British common law they regarded as their own.

Whether this study is seen as a valuable insight into tort *law* or whether it is seen as a largely disassociated historical exercise will depend on the reader's views as to the inter-relationship between formal legal rules and their surrounding political, economic and social environments. Those scholars who see law in one form or another as self-contained may think this contribution has little to do with law, although it is hoped the wider contexts explored in the book will be recognised as valuable historical studies in their own right. Conversely, those lawyers who at varying levels see law affected by and affecting non-legal spheres of society will find abundant examples of that interaction detailed in the book.

While this is primarily a legal history of tort law, an important consequence of the research approach taken is that the book is at some levels accessible to a wider audience than lawyers. Because tort law frequently deals with the commonplace, the potential for its history to be explained to a wider audience is increased as the subject matter of disputes is intelligible to non-lawyers. Tort law's polymerous coverage – protecting interests in the person, land, and reputation from intentional, negligent and blameless conduct – allows the law's role to be explored in a diverse range of factual situations. By introducing a broader audience to this tentacled area of law, it is hoped that its potential value to other disciplines can be recognised and exploited. Tort law was intertwined with the important political, social and intellectual currents during the period covered by this book and by understanding how it operated we learn much more than mere insights into the legal rules themselves.

Approach

The approach adopted in this book is largely one of 'law in context' modelled (but never emulating as this is impossible) on work of a similar style by the late A.W.B. Simpson. The materials used in the research are largely Australian. Apart from primary legal sources (reported and unreported court cases, and legislation), a wide range of secondary literature, both legal and non-legal, informs the arguments in the book (although consistent with the approach of the book I have looked primarily to Australian literature to evaluate how these contributors saw their own contribution to the common law). The important and innovative features of the book are the extensive use of contemporary newspaper and periodical literature. The digitisation of large swaths of newspapers from

states and territories. In defamation, where there was statutory amendment to the common law, Australian texts too were published: see E.H. Tebbutt, *The Statute Law Relating to Defamation and Newspapers Etc.* (Law Book Co. of Australasia, 1909); J. Moriarty, *The Law of Actionable Defamation, Whether Spoken or Written in the State of New South Wales* (F Cunninghame and Co., 1909).

the period covered by the book opens up the possibility of contextual analysis of legal development in ways not (at least in practice) previously possible. At least one chapter (Sport and Recreation) draws on this source to access previously unknown litigation in this important facet of Australian life. The book also draws on court and government records.

The book is not 'the' history of Australian tort law from 1901 to 1945; it does not attempt to provide a comprehensive account of all possible tort law developments in the period under review. The research approach adopted made such a task impractical in both the time required and the length of any resulting book. Rather, the research proceeded by way of a comprehensive review of decided cases involving a tort issue. The choice of subject/theme for inclusion was based on what was found in the sources and inevitably involves some value judgements. For example, while there were literally thousands of cases on motor vehicle accidents, they have been largely ignored as a genre in this book because I thought they had little to add to an understanding of the way the Australian legal community interacted with English law. To a lesser extent the same is true of workplace accidents. The fact that other authors might perhaps reach different conclusions simply demonstrates the tremendous opportunities this kind of historical approach has for histories of Australian private law. I have also omitted any analysis of the impact of Australian law on its indigenous communities. This is a question of vital interest for many Australians and there is now a considerable literature on this question for legal developments both during the period of this study and outside it. This book in no way attempts to undermine or discredit this perspective on Australian legal development but it is not the only perspective and what makes this book unique is its attempt to explain tort law development through the quite different lens of British race patriotism.

The book is very much rooted in a national approach to the question of Australian legal identity. While there may be scope for transnational histories of private law based on this research methodology, there remains a dearth of core national histories of private law at the end of Empire. While British race patriotism played a role in the construction of identity in other old settler colonies, as the historian James Curran has written, 'the very novelty of Australia's response to the rise of mass nationalism is intellectually engaging in its own right'.[12] As part of the common law family, Australian lawyers were not insular: apart from developments in England, approaches in other common law jurisdictions of the Empire and Commonwealth, as well as in the United States, were absorbed and synthesised as thought appropriate.[13] But while references to the common law had their transnational dimensions, it was the special

---

[12] J. Curran, 'Australia at empire's end: Approaches and arguments' (2013) 10 *History Australia* 23, 29.

[13] 'In this court some trouble has been taken to preserve consistency of decision, not only with English courts, but also with those of Canada and New Zealand': *Waghorn v. Waghorn* (1942) 65 CLR 289, 297 (Dixon J). More generally, Isaac Isaacs' notebooks demonstrate a remarkable breadth of comparative common law learning ('Papers of Sir Isaac Isaacs, 1883–1969', NLA, MS2755, Series 3, Boxes 4 and 5, Items 10–360).

bilateral relation with the mother country's law that dominated Australian legal discourse and which is at the core of this book. While there have been some very good broad scale transnational histories of private law,[14] they do not replicate the kind of detailed critique and analysis of national identity and national law which is the subject matter of this study and which give it its core academic value as an exploration of an important aspect of Australian intellectual history.

The book is structured around an introductory framing chapter that attempts to place Australian lawyers within the intellectual and cultural environment in which they operated. The following eight chapters are based around a two-fold thematic approach. Some chapters have a relatively doctrinal classification (such as negligence and liability for nervous shock) while others are more abstract (environment, sport and recreation). Within that classification, some chapters consider a multitude of cases and other legal material while others consider considerably fewer legal sources (such as 'In Defence of King and Country' in which the focus is the remarkable *Shaw Savill and Albion Co. Ltd v. Commonwealth* litigation).[15]

Whatever the style, all of the chapters focus on a common question. In light of the existing law, to what extent could Australian developments be considered innovative? Writing in 1995, Bruce Kercher argued that it was too simple to state that in its first fifty or sixty years the High Court merely copied English law.[16] Using three tort law decisions of the High Court from the period of this study, Kercher noted that the High Court dealt with unwanted English precedents in three ways: deflecting legal principles by discovering new aspects of them, avoidance on the basis of factual distinctions, and head-on confrontation. As he notes, this led to a number of questions including whether the reason for avoidance was explicable in cultural, political, social or economic explanations, and that if a different rule was thought appropriate for Australia, how it would be justified within accepted common law methods.[17] The grand aim of this book is to attempt to answer in broad terms the profound questions Kercher is asking in one area of Australian private law. It is written in the belief that it 'is just as important to discover what the judges decided as the rules they apparently followed'.[18] If this study reveals that Australian law was more innovative than has previously been thought, this is not an attempt to create a hagiography around an earlier group of lawyers. Nor is it to reinforce any notion of the 'black armband' view of Australian history.[19] It is simply to affirm

[14] See, e.g., P. Karsten, *Between Law and Custom* (Cambridge University Press, 2002), esp. 363–450.

[15] Some well-known cases were excluded as 'stand-alones' not justifying a chapter: see, for example, *Penfolds Wines Pty Ltd v. Elliot* (1946) 74 CLR 204, and *The Balmain New Ferry Co. Ltd v. Robertson* (1906) 4 CLR 379; [1910] AC 295 discussed in M. Lunney, 'False imprisonment, fare dodging and federation – Mr Robertson's evening out' (2009) 31 *Syd LR* 537).

[16] Kercher, above n. 1, 171.

[17] Ibid.

[18] Ibid.

[19] A phrase brought to prominence by Prime Minister John Howard in the Robert Menzies Lecture in January 1996 where he said: 'The "black armband" view of our history reflects a

that Australian lawyers were part of a wider community that saw British race patriotism as core to its identity. As the common law was a component of that affinity it is hardly surprising that Australian law formally mirrored the common law of the mother country. But affinity was not subservience, and the legal independent Australian Britons recognised a place for Australian interests just as much as their colleagues in other fields. They sought to fashion a law that implemented those interests when the opportunity arose and this book is about recognising their efforts, however imperfect or misguided they might seem to a different generation. It is about rescuing this generation of lawyers 'from the enormous condescension of posterity'.[20]

As tort law in this period was largely the product of common law decision, the focus of the book is on judicial decisions. As appellate courts had greater scope for creativity than trial courts, more time is spent in the Banco Courts of the state Supreme Courts, and in the High Court, than at first instance in the Supreme Court or in lower courts. But given the greater availability of lower court decisions through easy and searchable access to many newspapers, it would be remiss to avoid all consideration of what was happening at 'grass roots' level and in several chapters the decisions of magistrate and district courts are included in the analysis.[21] While the book is not a history of judicial figures, it is impossible to write a book of this nature without making some assessment of the quality of the judiciary deciding the cases being discussed. These judgements too are personal and are reflected in the judges whose views are most discussed in the book: in the High Court, Griffiths, Isaacs, Dixon and Evatt, in New South Wales, Jordan, and in Victoria, Cussen. The reputations of these judges have lasted into modern times but this study allows a modern reader to see why they were respected in their own times. Legislators played a much less significant role in tort law in the period of this study (which postdates the introduction of the defamation code in Queensland) because legislative developments usually followed earlier English developments. The notable exception is the Law Reform (Miscellaneous Provisions) Act 1944 (NSW), which in its quest to end the shadow of *Victoria Railway Commissioners v. Coultas* over claims for nervous shock extended the law well beyond the pre-existing English common law, a development discussed in detail in Chapter 6.

Ultimately, the aim of this book is to challenge the reader to think differently about private law development in Australia in the first half of the twentieth century in two related ways. The first is to suggest that, the constraints imposed by judicial deference, formal and informal, to English and Privy Council decisions were not the straight-jackets that they might with hindsight have seemed. As discussed in Chapter 2, it is not that these limits were not real

---

belief that most Australian history since 1788 has been little more than a disgraceful story of imperialism, exploitation, racism, sexism and other forms of discrimination.'

[20] S. Macintyre, *A History for a Nation: Ernest Scott and the Making of Australian History* (Melbourne University Press, 1994) 211. The quote is originally from E.P.Thompson, *The Making of the English Working Class* (Victor Gollancz, 1963) 12.

[21] See, especially, 'Sport and Recreation', Chapter 10.

and did not impose boundaries, but rather that it required something other than outright conflict to avoid being 'dressed down' by an appeal to the Privy Council. But perhaps more important is that common law development took place in a political and social context that made outright conflict unthinkable, at least for a class that was an important part of the established order. Australian lawyers of the period were not interested in setting up their own independent legal rules or system. They saw themselves as part of a wider entity, the British race. Only by understanding this self-conception can we hope to understand both what Australian lawyers were doing and why they were doing it so as to fully appreciate the scope of tort law development in Australia between federation and the end of the Second World War.

2

Historiography and the History of Australian Private Law in the First Half of the Twentieth Century: *Et in Arcadia Ego*?

Introduction

At its broadest, this book is about the relationship between Australia and (primarily) England in the first half of the twentieth century. It aims to consider one aspect of that relationship – law – in a way that has not previously been explored in detail. The influence of British race patriotism has been explored in many aspects of Australian culture and society but not in relation to law (at least private law). Instead, the history of private law in Australia has been stuck in the historiography of the 1980s at the time when the dominant nationalist discourse identified a particular kind of anti-English Australian independence. As Australians became less reticent in proclaiming the virtues of their nationality and culture, Australian historians, in line with these greater assertions of self-confidence, began to see the flowering of a new nationalism born out of a period of deference (at best) or subservience (at worst) to the dominant Imperial culture. While Manning Clark's *History of Australia* is probably the best known example of this new history, it has a much longer genesis: Brian Fitzpatrick's critique of Australian economic history is an early example of the recasting of the narrative in terms of the exploitation of colonial labour by a remote imperial power.[1] It is no surprise too that 'cultural cringe' makes its first appearance shortly after the Second World War. The tale of Australia as a story 'of discovery as its people threw off the encumbering, derivative culture that they had brought with them in order to grasp the wisdom of what was distinctively Australian'[2] was particularly compelling in a world where Empire and Dominions had been replaced by the much more egalitarian Commonwealth. Whatever the merits of this argument historically,[3] it remains an important

---

[1] B. Fitzpatrick, *British Imperialism in Australia 1783–1833: An Economic History of Australasia* (George Allen and Unwin, 1939) and *The British Empire in Australia: An Economic History* (Melbourne University Press in association with Oxford University Press, 1941), described by S. Macintyre, 'Australia and the empire', in R.W. Winks (ed.), *The Oxford History of the British Empire: Historiography* (Oxford University Press, 1999) 172–173.

[2] Macintyre, above n 1, describing the final volumes of Manning Clark's *History of Australia*.

[3] The competing turns in Australian historical writing are traced in Macintyre, above n 1, 174–180. For recent critiques of the pervasiveness of British race nationalism see M. Lake, 'British world or new world?' (2013) 10 *History Australia* 36; C. Waters, 'Nationalism, Britishness and Australian history: The Meaney thesis revisited' (2013) 10 *History Australia* 12.

facet of the Australian psyche. As the historian Stuart Macintyre puts it, 'There is something in Australia's present disposition, it would seem, that resists the Imperial past.'[4]

Australian law has not been immune from this nationalist, or at least anti-Imperial, turn. The conventional view is that the recognition of an Australian law is of relatively recent origin.[5] This must be qualified depending on the area of law: there were clearly different views for different kinds of law. During the first half of the twentieth century no-one in Australia doubted that Australian constitutional law had genuinely indigenous components to it.[6] While much work remains to be done in that area,[7] this book is concerned with another area of law: private law, in particular, the law of tort and its development in Australia from federation to the end of the Second World War. That is not to say that studies of an earlier or later period are not worthwhile[8] but they do not address a core question of this period: to what extent was it true to regard the law of tort as applied in Australia as simply a mirror of the tort law that applied in England and Wales? A first step is to suggest that any attempt to answer the question must be rooted in the intellectual milieu of the first fifty years of the twentieth century. This analysis is not primarily concerned with legal materials – cases and statutes – but considers how a particular group of Australians viewed themselves and why this might have influenced the way in which views about matters such as the existence of Australian law were depicted.

The rationale for undertaking this analysis needs a little unpacking. One way to begin an historical analysis of law is by considering the current law and then looking for markers in the past which shed light on how we reached our present. This has been described as 'applied' legal history: 'deeply researched, serious scholarship that is motivated by, engages with, or speaks to contemporary issues.'[9] In terms of the Anglo-Australian legal relationship, this approach would consider the way we are now – a mature, confident legal system which has its own clear identity – and would look to the past to see any embryonic evidence of this system in place. In applied legal history this may work well but for

---

[4] Macintyre, above n 1, 164.
[5] See, for example, M. Ellinghaus et al., *The Emergence of Australian Law* (Butterworths, 1989); F. Trindade, 'Towards an Australian Law of Torts' (1993) 23 *UWALR* 74.
[6] On the international recognition of innovation in Australia's pre-1914 labour law see M. Lake, '1914: Death of a nation' (2015) 12 *History Australia* 7.
[7] For excellent examples see the studies of early cases in H.P. Lee and G. Winterton, *Australian Constitutional Landmarks* (Cambridge University Press, 2003).
[8] There are few studies of areas of private law in the Australian colonies. J.M. Bennett's *Lives of the Colonial Chief Justices* series usually contains a brief description of the decisions made by the judge the subject of the biography in a variety of legal areas including tort but the focus is primarily descriptive. For the law of property see A. Buck, *The Making of Australian Property Law* (Federation Press, 2006) and more generally, see J. McKenna, 'The Griffith opinion books' in J. McKenna and H. Jeffcoat (eds.), *Queensland Legal Yearbook 2013* (Supreme Court Library Queensland, 2014) and J. McKenna, 'The emergence of Australian common law in colonial Queensland' in A. Rahemtula and M. Sayers (eds.), *The Idea of Legal History: A Tribute in Honour of Dr Michael White QC* (Supreme Court Library Queensland, 2014).
[9] A. Brophy, 'Introducing applied legal history' (2013) 31 *LHR* 233.

other kinds of historical enquiry it can also be potentially misleading because the historical question to be answered is presupposed by the present. For example, it is easy to see the legal history of twentieth-century Australia as divided on a clear binary: an era of subservience and an era of independence. There is respectable academic support for doing so. In an essay published in 1997, the Canadian (former English) academic Gerald Fridman wrote the following:

> As far as the High Court of Australia was concerned, in 1938, the law in Australia was English law … It is perhaps not too strong to state that, certainly at that period of time, it would have been virtually unthinkable for courts in a Commonwealth country to adopt in relation to a given issue a view of the common law that differed from the way that issue was regarded and treated by courts in England. The mother country, it could be said, still knew best.[10]

Fridman's view was that it was only when Commonwealth courts were able to throw off the imperial yoke could an indigenous law develop, a process that (in 1997) he thought was well underway (but presumably not then complete).[11] Writing about the possibility of an Australian contract law, Ellinghaus is even less charitable to the earlier period: 'The essence of cultural cringe lies in its automatism… its first reaction, out of habit or routine, was that of self-deprecation, of an implicit concession that the foreign model was the natural point of reference, and that the native one was only too likely to suffer by comparison.'[12] Ellinghaus ascribes this behaviour to Australian judges in contract law, a position largely supported by Luntz's essay in the same collection on tort law.[13]

Both Fridman and Luntz's primary concern was to write pieces about changes in Commonwealth tort law from the 1960s so criticism of their historical methodology is in part beside the point. However, to reinforce their arguments have they set up a potentially straw past? The contention here is that the binary view of the history of private law in Australia leads to asking the wrong question. Within that dynamic, there is little evidence of an Australian private law in earlier periods, particularly the law of obligations, because the Australian legal fraternity simply did not think of the issue in that way. As Stuart Ward puts it, 'an analytical framework has become firmly entrenched in which independence is equated with defiance, self-assertion with divergence, autonomy with antagonism. Conversely, those Australian political or cultural figures deemed to have identified too closely with the British connection were looked upon as a national disgrace.'[14] A more fruitful approach may be to unpack the cultural

---

[10] G.H.L. Fridman, 'Judicial independence of a different kind' in N.J. Mullany (ed.), *Torts in the Nineties* (Law Book Co., 1997) 305. For a modern repetition of this view see S. Walpola, 'The Development of the High Court's Willingness to Overrule Common Law Prededent' (2017) 45 *Federal Law Review* 291, 294–298.

[11] Ibid., 331. For an English response see J.G. Collier, Review of 'The emergence of Australian law' [1991] *CLJ* 180, 181–182.

[12] Ellinghaus et al., above n 5, 47.

[13] The same comment can be made of H. Luntz, 'Throwing off the chains: English precedent and the law of torts in Australia', ibid., ch. 4.

[14] S. Ward, *Australia and the British Embrace* (Melbourne University Press, 2001) 6.

context in which these practitioners operated and in that context a different kind of innovation from that recognised by the binary view may be present. Viewed in this light, Australian legal innovation may have much greater continuity than previously recognised.

Australian Law and Australian Identity

It must be conceded there is good authority for the opinion that there was very little innovation in tort law in the period of this study. Writing in the Australian volume of the *The British Commonwealth, The Development of its Laws and Constitutions*, published in 1952, no less a figure than G.W. Paton, the Dean of the Law School at the University of Melbourne, noted that tort law was shortly treated in Chapter 1 'as there are few significant differences' between English and Australian law.[15] But Paton's comments must be read in light of other contributions to the book which included separate chapters on administrative law, real property, family law, succession, and procedure and pleading.[16] The chapter on administrative law, written by Wolfgang Friedmann, is particularly interesting because of Friedmann's background. German-trained, Friedmann had fled the Nazi regime in the early 1930s to settle in Britain before coming to Australia in 1948 (he stayed only three years before moving to Toronto and ultimately to Columbia where he spent the remainder of his distinguished career).[17] Commenting on an Australian administrative law (he wrote the first text on this subject in 1950),[18] Friedmann noted:

> The leading English authorities and principles of administrative law form the general basis of Australian administrative law but Australian courts and scholars have made many notable and original contributions to the science of administrative law well worthy of study and attention by British courts and lawyers.[19]

Friedmann highlights the distinctiveness of the Australian contribution to the generic area of administrative law. The contrast with the approach taken by Paton in the introduction is marked: 'One of the dangers of a general survey is that the writers, by stressing the differences, may obscure the fact that there is a basic uniformity with English law'.[20] While both authors are making

---

[15] G.W. Paton (ed.), *The British Commonwealth, The Development of its Laws and Constitutions: Vol. 2 Australia* (Stevens and Sons, 1952) xi.

[16] The omission of a separate chapter on criminal law, where codification in Queensland and Western Australia led to a significant structural difference from England, is explained by the publication of another book on the topic: ibid., 29fn.

[17] For Friedmann's influence on Australian tort law see M. Lunney, 'Legal emigres and the development of Australian tort law' (2012) 36 *MULR* 492. On Friedmann generally see J. Bell, 'Wolfgang Friedmann (1907–1972): with an excursus on Gustav Radbruch (1878–1949)' in J. Beatson and R. Zimmermann (eds.), *Jurists Uprooted: German-Speaking Emigre Lawyers in Twentieth Century Britain* (Oxford University Press, 2004).

[18] W. Friedmann, *Principles of Australian Administrative Law* (Melbourne University Press, 1950).

[19] Paton, above n 15, 80.

[20] Ibid., xii.

essentially the same point – that English and Australian law are largely similar – Friedmann is more enthusiastic about the contribution that Australian exceptionalism might make to overall common law development.[21]

Why might this be so? There is a clue in Friedmann's background. Friedmann's views about Australian law were from the position of an outsider, both to the common law and, perhaps more importantly, to Australia's historic relationship with England.[22] Friedmann's assessment that Australian administrative law was based on English law rested on an objective analysis of the data. Paton's analysis too was objective but it was mediated through the historical and intellectual connections between Australia and England. For Friedmann, the differences between English and Australian law were relevant only to the extent they contributed to legal science: what implications any dissonance might have for an understanding of Anglo-Australian relations were of marginal interest only. Conversely, for Paton – and for reasons explained below Paton can be considered as a stereotype of an engaged Australian lawyer – there could be important political and cultural undertones to proclaiming Australian judicial independence. It is unsurprising then that Paton was keen to emphasise the essential unity between English and Australian law.

A disarming possibility for this book is that statements like Paton's should be taken at face value. However, there are a number of reasons why the statement needs further interrogation. First, Paton never said that the laws were identical. That Australian law, especially case law, shared much in common with English law was not in doubt. The question is how one treats variations: as exceptions to be largely ignored or as nationally significant contributions to the development of the common law. Second, and more importantly, the shared cultural assumptions about the relationship between Australia and England, and Australia and Britain, shaped the way those lawyers of Paton's generation viewed Australian adaptation. What to a later generation of lawyers and academics might appear as an independent Australian legal development might be seen as a mere gloss on the law of the mother country a half-century before.

An important factor in understanding the comments about Australian law made in the first half of the twentieth century is the legal version of cultural cringe. This term is not used here in a derogatory way as has been the norm in Australia since the 1960s.[23] Rather, it is used as a potential lens with which to view how peculiar features of the legal system and views about Australia's place in the Empire played roles in conditioning how Australian lawyers viewed

---

[21] See also R.F.C. Heuston, 'The law of torts in Australia' (1959–60) 2 *MULR* 35, 37, who, writing at a slightly later date, provided an English observer's view that the High Court 'has never hesitated to reach a novel conclusion if it thinks it necessary to do so'.

[22] See Lunney, above n 17, and also M. Lunney, 'Fleming's law of tort: Australian-made or foreign import? Australia's role in making the 'king' of torts' (2013) 36 *Australian Bar Review* 211.

[23] L.J. Hume, *Another Look at Cultural Cringe*, Occasional Paper No. 45 (Centre for Independent Studies, 1993). This of course is an oversimplification: for more nuance see Macintyre, above n 1, 172–180.

Australian law. The term 'cultural cringe' dates to a surprisingly short essay by A.A. Phillips first published in 1950. It was not written about law or about Australian intellectual life more generally but was concerned primarily with how Australian literature was viewed by Australians. However, in a pertinent observation, Phillips wrote that one effect of cultural cringe was the estrangement of the Australian Intellectual:

> There is a certain type of Australian intellectual who is forever sidling up to the cultivated Englishman, insinuating: '*I*, of course, am not like these other crude Australians; *I* understand how you must feel about them; *I* should have been spiritually more at home in Oxford or Bloomsbury'.[24]

One explanation for the reticence of Australian lawyers to see anything different in Australian developments may lie in the fear of being marginalised. Those who might be considered the intellectual lawyers of the period were either born and/or trained in England or, more commonly as the century progressed, studied under lecturers trained in English law and used to thinking that English common law applied in Australia.[25] In this environment, an acceptance both of the existence and merit of Australian legal exceptionalism risked a charge of parochialism, a charge at the heart of cultural cringe. More prosaically, cultural cringe could operate in legal circles in a much more formal way. During the first half of the twentieth century, there was little recognition of the role of judicial discretion when applying legal rules to concrete fact situations.[26] To admit too openly Australian influences when applying legal rules might suggest professional incompetence at best and heresy at worst.[27] If there was seen to be a difference between English and Australian law, this might be because the judge(s) applying the law were not understanding, or worse, deliberately ignoring English law. To adopt such an approach suggested that the quality of the judge was not 'up-to-scratch', a view that entrenched the unequal relationship characterised in cultural cringe. By drawing a distinction between judicial and legislative approaches of 'old Australia' and the self-confident nationalism of a later period, the bifurcated view functions to 'distance the contemporary writer from the failures and inadequacies of the past'.[28]

While this version of cultural cringe has some explanatory value, it is unlikely it is the complete answer. It is hard to test the views of Australian judges as there

---

[24] (1950) 4 Meanjin 299, 300, reprinted in A.A. Phillips, *AA Phillips on The Cultural Cringe* (Melbourne University Press, 2006). Phillips' views in relation to literature were developed in his later writing: see 'The family relationship', ibid., 20, and the cultural cringe essay was updated in *The Australian Tradition: Studies in Australian Culture* (F.W. Cheshire, 1958).

[25] As Castles has pointed out, for case law this was assumed rather than required under the rules governing the reception of English law in Australia: A. Castles, 'The reception and status of English law in Australia' (1963) 2 *Adel L Rev* 1, 5–11.

[26] It was Julius Stone's *The Province and Function of Law* (Associated General Publications Pty Ltd, 1946) that gave this issue prominence in Australia.

[27] F.H. Lawson, 'Legal Orthodoxy' (1968) 6 *Hous LR* 1, 27.

[28] Hume, above n 23, 1.

is little evidence that they ever thought about the issue in the way understood by proponents of the cultural cringe thesis. There is, however, considerable evidence that Australian judges and lawyers did not see English law or English lawyers generally as infallible. There is relatively little judicial biography in Australia and even less in the period of this study but whatever there is suggests little evidence of extreme cultural cringe. For example, in 1913, during a visit to England, Chief Justice of the High Court Sir Samuel Griffith wrote that he was impressed by the camaraderie of the House of Lords but not its calibre.[29] Three years later he was more forceful. During the course of discussions over changes to the system of imperial appeals, Griffith deplored the old 'insular' doctrine of the essential difference in quality between English and colonial persons [which] was still regarded as axiomatic. It was never articulated but it was as truly present as 'the belief (in those who hold it) in ghosts haunting a churchyard or in original sin or any other inherited or instinctive sin of action'.[30] His biographer comments that this was Griffith writing as an Australian rather than as a man born in Wales[31] but Griffith was no nascent republican. His annoyance was rooted in the betrayal of his belief in the cultural unity of Empire by the derogatory connotations attached to colonial status and, by implication, to colonial judges.[32]

Australian judges could deprecate the ability of members of the House of Lords and Judicial Committee of the Privy Council and the decisions they reached while being firmly committed to the legal system they represented. Whatever the flaws, it was never contemplated that English law would not form the basis of Australian law. It was this belief that led Isaac Isaacs to reject 'loyalist' criticism that the 'bonds of empire' would be destroyed by restricting the right to appeal to the Privy Council as was proposed in the draft Constitution of 1898:

> We are bound to the empire by personal and corporate loyalty – loyalty to the traditions, loyalty to the future of the empire of which we are proud to form a part. But I cannot bring myself to believe that the links which bind us to the empire are in any way formed of a lawyer's bill of costs… I ask that we should have confidence in ourselves and in that High Court we hope to establish – confidence not only in its impartiality but also in its ability.[33]

As his leading biographer wrote, Isaacs was an ardent nationalist and imperialist. Only by recognising this can we understand why Isaacs was keen for

---

[29] R.B. Joyce, *Samuel Walker Griffith* (University of Queensland Press, 1984) 323. See also J. Hirst, *The Sentimental Nation: The Making of the Australian Commonwealth* (Oxford University Press, 2000) 28–30.

[30] Joyce, above n 29, 351. As Joyce details, Griffith objected to other aspects of the Privy Council, from its perception as inferior to the House of Lords to suggestions that colonies did not want other colonial representation on the Privy Council. Griffith discredited this latter suggestion – what he called the 'hierarchy of inferiority' view of the Privy Council.

[31] Ibid.

[32] Hirst, above n 29.

[33] Z. Cowen, *Isaac Isaacs* (Oxford University Press, 1967) 67.

there to be Australian representation on the Judicial Committee of the Privy Council while at the same time arguing that appeals on matters of peculiarly Australian interest should be restricted. This dual loyalty can be traced in many other Australian legal figures during period of this study. Owen Dixon's biographer notes that his love of England and things English was based on more than sentiment. Although Australian-born, his attachment represented an intellectual conviction as to the value to Australia of what was noblest and best in the British tradition, 'a matter of permanent institutional connection and cultural memory, and easy to understand'.[34] But Ayres also notes that Dixon's Anglophilia can be overstated. Apart from his dislike of Privy Council decisions – which increased throughout this judicial career – his experiences in Washington during the Second World War prevented him from holding too rose-coloured a view of English institutions and policy.[35] Yet in 1950 while visiting London after his stint as UN Mediator in Kashmir he wrote to his wife that they ought come and live in England.[36]

Independent Australian Britons

The reactions of these individual judges to England and things English reflect something deeper about the Anglo-Australian relationship that is captured by the historian Keith Hancock (who in fact knew a number of the judges referred to above). Hancock's own career represented the challenges of being attracted to the intellectual hub that was England whilst retaining a love for Australia. Hancock was born in rural Victoria, studied history at the University of Melbourne, won a Rhodes Scholarship and became a Fellow of All Souls College in Oxford before returning to Australia to take up a Chair at the University of Adelaide. It was during his time in Adelaide that he wrote his synopsis of Australia, published in 1930.[37] Here Hancock introduced the notion of Australia as a nation of 'independent Australian Britons'.[38] The chapter was the culmination of several years of thinking about the relationship between Australia and Britain and it reflected his comfort with the status quo.[39] Australians in this model did not want to be separate – 'the roots sent down in Australian soil by the transplanted British have only here and there struck deep beneath the surface' – but nor did they want to recreate England in the new country:

[34] P. Ayres, *Owen Dixon* (Miegunyah Press, 2003) 101.

[35] Ibid., 226.

[36] Ibid., 216.

[37] W.K. Hancock, *Australia* (Ernest Benn Ltd, 1930).

[38] The expression is not his own. It was used by Alfred Deakin in 1900 to describe himself and it was used in *The Bulletin* in the late nineteenth century.

[39] Not all his Melbourne contemporaries reacted to Oxford exposure with the same degree of comfort: J. Davidson, '"Home" becomes away: Melburnians in Oxford in the 1920s' in C. Bridge et al. (eds.), *Australians in Britain: The Twentieth Century Experience* (Monash University Press, 2009) ch. 9.

> It would appear that those writers exaggerate who paint such attractive pictures of the affection and trust subsisting between gentle and simple in the old country; for nothing is more evident than that the vulgar emigrants, having escaped from the gentry of England, vehemently resented the attempt of fortunate first-comers to establish themselves as gentry in Australia. And in resisting this attempt, they laid stress upon the difference, the uniqueness of Australia; on their own difference, their own uniqueness, as Australians.[40]

In this vision, Australians did not want to ignore their British traditions but rather wanted to improve on them. Hancock argued that all classes, even the conservatives, began to resent the connotation associated with the word 'colonial' and that 'when their children first visited England they were shocked at the poverty of London and the callousness of the rich towards the poor'.[41]

It is not necessary for the argument in this book to make the case for the truth of Hancock's views across the Australian population as a whole. As argued by Marilyn Lake and Christopher Waters,[42] there were no doubt different conceptions of identity and affinity throughout the period of this study, conceptions to which some members of the legal profession were attracted. But members of the legal profession, like Hancock, were largely establishment figures and it is to them that his biographer is referring when he notes that at the time of writing the book Hancock mixed in strongly Anglophile circles.[43] Moreover, there are examples from all spheres of life outside the political that can be identified within Hancock's characterisation.[44] It is this duality – in Hancock's words, the ability to love two soils[45] – that has something to contribute to our understanding of how Australian lawyers viewed Australian law. Leading judicial and academic figures of the period of this study were Anglophiles in the sense described above. Apart from the sentimental attachment to the institutions of the mother country – variously England or Britain – the formal constraints of the doctrine of precedent bound them in a more practical way than for other areas of civil society.

Yet that is not the complete picture. It was perfectly possible to try and improve the product of the mother country, or, less radically, to adapt it to Australian conditions, and in this way contribute something to the greater good. That greater good was wider than England or English law. Hancock's phrase is 'independent Australian Britons' and he argued that most stress was laid on the last word: 'It frequently occurs that those who are most intensely

---

[40] Hancock, above n 37, 61.

[41] Ibid., 63–64. Or in Manning Clark's more evocative phrase, 'England soon became one of my many lost illusions': C.M.H. Clark, *A Quest for Grace* (Penguin, 1990) 64 and see Lake, above n 6.

[42] Lake, above n 3; Waters, above n 3.

[43] J. Davidson, *A Three-Cornered Life: The Historian WK Hancock* (UNSW Press, 2010) 108–109.

[44] See, for example, the comments of the naturalist Charles Barrett in *Australia My Country* (Oxford University Press, 1940) 66–67, 118–120.

[45] Hancock, above n 37, 68. For a prominent contemporary political example see J. Connor, *Anzac and Empire: George Foster Pearce and the Foundations of Australian Defence* (Cambridge University Press, 2011).

British have a special dislike for the English; they will not, for example, extend the same tolerance to an English 'accent' as to a Scottish 'dialect'.[46] This commitment to Britain and the Empire, or Commonwealth, included a commitment to the common law. It was not to be jettisoned but was to be improved. This idea was certainly present in the mind of the Australian historians of the period: as Stuart Macintyre puts it,

> The earlier historians produced a colonial and later a national story within an Imperial framework. Australian civilisation was the product of a transfer of people, institutions, technology and culture from the metropolitan setting to a new setting; whether the preference was for faithful imitation of the original or for improvement upon it, the experiment was judged against received standards.[47]

One of those received standards was that the final decision on the common law rested with English courts. But this acceptance did not carry with it a requirement by English courts to see what the rest of the Empire made of the common law. As McPherson has noted, the Privy Council never attempted a synthesis of the decisions of the Empire on a particular point before deciding an appeal: it would have been practically impossible to do so given resource and time constraints.[48] The result was that the regulatory force of Privy Council decisions in ensuring compliance with the correct 'English' law lay largely in the prospective threat of appeal from an Empire court rather than in the actual decisions. But it was also unlikely that left to their own devices, the judges of the Empire and later Dominions would radically depart from what they knew.[49] Fragmentation, however, was different from incremental development and improvement – this was within the received standards for experimentation – and where it occurred it was not always rejected in the metropole. Mitchell has shown that the Privy Council, particularly in the nineteenth century, could be sensitive to local variations in tort law[50] which shows both some tolerance to regional variation and necessarily casts doubt on any empirical claim of the common law to universality in the Empire. Moreover, apart from the wide legislative competence of Australian jurisdictions to vary the common law, even accepted general principles required application to facts and this gave considerable scope for judicial creativity in applying the law to the facts or in determining which questions of fact could be left to a jury.[51] This process of interpretation and elucidation was part of a corporate project, the making of the 'best' common law, and if Australian judges understood their legal and cultural constraints, that did not

---

[46] Ibid., 6.

[47] Macintyre, above n 1, 163.

[48] B.H. McPherson, *The Reception of English Law Abroad* (Supreme Court Library Queensland, 2007) 28.

[49] Ibid., 28–29. See also G. Barwick, 'Law and the courts' in A.F. Madden and W.H. Morris-Jones (eds.), *Australia and Britain: Studies in a Changing Relationship* (Sydney University Press, 1980) 151.

[50] P. Mitchell, 'The Privy Council and the Difficulty of Distance' (2016) 36 *OJLS* 26.

[51] Stone, above n 26, ch. 7 pt. III. See also Barwick, above n 49, 150.

make them mere purveyors of mechanical jurisprudence. Judges, especially in the superior courts, thought that they could, and should, and perhaps for their own intellectual satisfaction and self-esteem, had to, do better than that.

Isaac Isaacs typifies this approach. The remarkable breadth of his comparative common law learning is evidenced by a series of notebooks he compiled over twenty years to organise his legal sources. While English case law dominates, there are references to a vast array of cases from other parts of the Empire (including a surprisingly large number from India, both Indian cases and Privy Council appeals). There are also extensive references to cases decided in the United States.[52] Although not numerically large, Australian cases, mainly from the High Court, are also included.[53] The same trend can be seen at the beginning of the period of this study, albeit with a primarily English and Australian focus, in the notes of lectures delivered on the law of torts by Woinarksi at the University of Melbourne in 1905[54] and also at the end of the period in the lecture notes on torts by G.W. Paton published by the University of Melbourne School of Law in 1948[55] although, as might be expected, Paton includes more Australian cases than in the earlier Woinarski lectures.[56]

There were also pragmatic reasons for adopting this incremental approach. As F.H. Lawson argued, deference to existing authority is part of legal orthodoxy, and in the Australian context this was based not just on general deference to the wisdom of the past (as represented by past cases) but also cultural deference to common law traditions. But Lawson perceptively noted that legal orthodoxy can be conducive to reform as 'a judge who has the reputation as a heretic arouses opposition, whereas, if an orthodox judge can be won over to the need for innovation, what he does is very likely to be accepted.'[57] This was important in an environment where the need for innovation was mediated through the dual notions of 'community of interest' and 'community of culture'. As Meaney points out, from an early period the Australian colonists realised that their community of interest did not always equate with those of the mother country and that, where there was conflict between the two, 'Australians, despite themselves, opted for the community of interest over the community of

---

[52] See Lake, above n 3, who argues that the reciprocal ties between progressive liberal thinkers in Australia and America contributed to an Anglo-Saxon race nationalism among that class. While Isaacs was certainly engaged with American legal materials, there is no suggestion he identified with this wider national identity.

[53] 'Papers of Sir Isaac Isaacs, 1883–1969', NLA, MS2755, Series 3, Boxes 4 and 5, Items 10–360.

[54] Notes of Lectures delivered on the law of torts by Mr Woinarski, during the year 1905, University of Melbourne Library, F6147 (manuscript). See also the student notes of Sir Keith Officer of lectures on the Law of Wrongs delivered by Mr Maguire in 1911, Melbourne University Law Library (rare books collection), 340 032 (manuscript), although the Australian references are more rare in the document (which does not cover all the lectures that were given in the course).

[55] G.W. Paton, *Lecture Notes – Torts* (University of Melbourne, School of Law, 1948).

[56] In large part due to the increased number of decisions of the High Court of Australia.

[57] Lawson, above n 27.

culture.'[58] While law, especially private law, seems to fit more neatly within the community of culture, the dividing line between the two categories was blurred. And even if law sat within interest, it was within a 'community' of interest in which Australian lawyers felt both sustained by law's affinity with their British roots and encouraged to maintain it by their best endeavours.

Even if the legal independent Australian Briton wanted to be taken seriously in his quest to improve the common culture, there is little evidence that the effort was appreciated 'back home.' It was only towards the end of the period of this study that Australian cases were cited in English cases and even then only rarely.[59] There was a failure to recognise that the communal development of the common law was in fact a reciprocal project. Yet it is striking how little criticism there was from the Australian judiciary of this snub from the metropole.[60] But E.A. Harney, a practising English barrister with previous experience in Western Australia, had no such reservations:

> It [Australian law] is deemed 'foreign'. Its laws must be proved like any other fact of which the Court is REALLY ignorant. The densest darkness is supposed to prevail at the set and centre of our United Empire of the legislative and judicial doings of one of its parts, and that the most distinctively British of the whole.[61]

While the malleability of the common law could allow outright conflict to be avoided, the lack of criticism has deeper roots in the importance of British race patriotism to Australian identity. Harney's concern was the exclusion of Australian contributions to the British common law and this was felt personally. As Curran comments, '...there is every reason to argue the case that the idea of "being British" had a far more compelling resonance in Australia than in the United Kingdom.'[62] This helps explain the turn of the High Court in the early 1940s towards greater conformity with English decisions that were not technically binding on Australian courts (although they had always been highly persuasive).[63] Looked at from the bifurcated view, this is cringe par excellence,

---

[58] N. Meaney, 'Britishness and Australian identity: The problem of nationalism in Australian history and historiography' (2001) 32 *Australian Historical Studies* 76, 85.

[59] J. Finn, 'Sometimes persuasive authority: Dominion case law and English judges' in H. Foster et al. (eds.), *The Grand Experiment: Law and Legal Culture in British Settler Societies* (Osgoode Society, 2008) 104.

[60] There were exceptions: Dixon J expressed his 'disappointment' that the English Court of Appeal had not considered an earlier High Court decision in reaching a contrary conclusion but he ultimately agreed that the High Court should follow the Court of Appeal decision: *Waghorn v. Waghorn* (1942) 65 CLR 289, 297–299. For a more robust academic criticism at the end of the period of the failure to engage with Australian authority see Peter Brett's review of Glanville William's *Joint Torts and Contributory Negligence* (1951) 2 *UWALR* 174.

[61] E.A. Harney, 'The law courts of England and Australia' in L.W. Matters (eds.), *Australasians Who Count in London and Who Counts in Western Australia* (Jas. Truscott and Son Ltd, 1913) 152.

[62] J. Curran, 'Australia at empire's end: Approaches and arguments' (2013) 10 *History Australia* 23, 28. See also N. Meaney, 'Britishness and Australia: some reflections' (2003) 31 *Journal of Imperial and Commonwealth History* 121, 126.

[63] *Waghorn v. Waghorn* (1942) 65 CLR 289; *Piro v. W Foster & Co. Ltd* (1943) 68 CLR 313. See further Barwick, above n 49, 149–153.

a weak submission to the dominant mother culture. While there is clearly some element of truth in this explanation, it must also be seen in light of the need to recommit to the imperial ideal – to the larger British family – when the Empire was under its greatest challenge.[64] It was a political as much as legal statement – in fact it actually complicated the legal position by equating Privy Council and House of Lords' decisions as binding on Australian courts[65] – but even its symbolic significance was questioned. As Parsons pointed out in a contemporary note on the case, the argument that this would strengthen 'our emotional links with the mother country' had little merit given that the independence already enjoyed by Australian legislatures had not weakened the Anglo-Australian relationship.[66] It would take some time before the realisation that the earlier dynamics of that relationship could not govern post-war Australia[67] but even a few years later, the changed circumstances brought about by the end of the Second World War meant that the High Court was already more circumspect in deciding when to follow English Court of Appeal decisions than at the height of the wartime crises.[68]

The idea of the Empire as the defining cultural identity has been taken up more recently by the historian James Curran when writing about John Curtin, Australia's Prime Minister during the Second World War. In critiquing the notion that Curtin was the epitome of anti-British Australian nationalism, Curran identifies a middle ground that he argues Curtin occupied which was based on equal partnership.[69] This equal partnership is the key to understanding at least one strand of Australian nationalism.[70] This was not the nationalism of narrow cultural cringe and was not characterised by lazy subservience or blind obeisance. Rather, in Curran's words, 'the problem of Australian nationalism can only be unravelled if it is appreciated that while "Australia's first response in terms of sentiment was to British race patriotism" rather than a distinctive national culture, Australians insisted they should maintain exclusive control over the direction of their political affairs.'[71] Although these comments are directed to politics rather than law, they have considerable explanatory value in unpacking attitudes to English law, even English private law. Australian lawyers saw themselves in sentiment as part of the wider family of the English common law. Paradoxically, that English common law was not formally part of the Britishness that characterised this sentiment – Scotland had its own legal

---

[64] For the post-war Labor governments' efforts in this regard see Meaney, above n 62, 125–132.
[65] Z. Cowen, 'The binding effect of English decisions upon Australian courts' (1944) 60 *LQR* 378.
[66] R. Parsons, 'English precedents in Australian courts' (1948–50) 1 *UWALR* 211, 212.
[67] Ward, above n 14.
[68] *Wright v. Wright* (1948) 77 CLR 191 (although note Barwick's view that this was only due to doubts as to whether the Court of Appeal decision accurately reflected English law: Barwick, above n 49, 152). It took until 1963 for the High Court to declare it should not automatically follow decisions of the House of Lords: *Parker v. R* (1963) 111 CLR 610.
[69] J. Curran, *Curtin's Empire* (Cambridge University Press, 2011).
[70] Meaney, above n 58, 83.
[71] Curran, above n 69, 21.

system – but informally the commitment to notions of the rule of law and fairness were embodied in the nebulous concept of a British common law. This is important as it allowed the anti-Englishness Hancock identified not to infuse views about English law. Throughout this chapter the terms 'England', 'English', 'Britain' and 'British' have been used relatively interchangeably because the relationship between the strictly legal English common law and more metaphysical British race patriotism was conveniently vague. Australian lawyers knew that the common law was English but in law as in identity they were happy to buy into the composite notion of 'Britishness'. The result was that the bilocationism of Australian lawyers was based on physical presence in Australia and emotional presence in the common law of Britain.

The Intellectual and Cultural Milieu of the Law

Apart from the broad claim that lawyers as members of the establishment were imbued with the values of that establishment, is there any direct evidence to suggest that lawyers thought of themselves in the way suggested above? Apart from the few judicial examples mentioned, the absence of detailed individual biography makes the claim hard to substantiate but in at least one important group – the academics at Australian law schools – there are good grounds for thinking they were at least in sympathy with an Australia of independent Australian Britons. In most of the period considered in this book, the Law School of Sydney University was run by Professor – later Sir – John Peden. Apart from his role in the law school, Peden was actively involved with the wider community, serving in the Legislative Council (over 10 years as president) as well being the inaugural law reform commissioner in 1921.[72] Part of his outside work was being secretary of the Sydney Round Table group between 1918 and 1935.[73] Founded in 1910, members of the Round Table believed in some form of imperial federation or, particularly after the First World War, a Commonwealth of Nations, as the political successor to the British Empire.[74] Apart from being a lecturer, Peden exerted influence on the legal profession as a whole through his close connections with the bar and judiciary; most of the lecturers at the law school were barristers employed on short term contracts, many of whom went on to become judges.[75] No doubt there were dissenters but it is unlikely that Peden could have been so central a figure in legal Sydney if his Round Table views were not mainstream.

---

[72] T. Bavin, 'Sir John Peden' in T. Bavin (ed.), *The Jubilee Book of the Law School of the University of Sydney* (Halstead Press, 1940) 29–33; J. and J. Mackinolty (eds.), *A Century Down Town* (Sydney University Law School, 1991).

[73] J. Ward, 'Sir John Peden', *Australian Dictionary of Biography*, Vol. 11 (Melbourne University Press, 1988).

[74] L. Foster, *High Hopes: The Men and Motives of the Australian Round Table* (Melbourne University Press, 1986).

[75] Mackinolty, above n 72, 57–85. Part-time lecturers during his period as Dean included six future High Court judges and 14 New South Wales Supreme Court judges.

Peden was not the only significant legal member of the Round Table. From its creation until the end of the period of this study, the list of members compiled by Foster in her history of the Australian Round Table reveals that over 35 members had involvement with the law or legal profession.[76] As the group as whole (including post-war members) numbered just over 270, the proportion of lawyers represented an important component of membership. Although details of membership of the Round Table during this period were restricted, it is now clear a number of judges, solicitors and academics, including senior judicial and academic appointments, were members for some time between 1901 and 1945.[77] Non-member correspondents included Henry Bournes Higgins, judge of the High Court of Australia between 1906 and 1929.[78] As Foster points out, the articles produced by the Australian Round Table of which they were all members 'reflected the primacy of the Australian national interest in the conflict between British and native loyalties…'.[79]

One lawyer-member of the Round Table with an intense interest in the issue of Anglo-Australian relations was Harrison Moore, the Dean of the Law School at Melbourne University from the commencement of the period of this study until 1927. English trained, Moore was a member of the Imperial Federation League of Australia, a forerunner to the Round Table and an organisation whose dual aims were to maintain the unity of the British Dominions and to strengthen it in the future by some form of federation.[80] In a speech he gave under the banner of the Imperial Federation League in 1905, Moore emphasised the importance of Empire 'as long as the individuality of component countries is recognised.'[81] The nature of imperial relations was a long-standing interest. In a series of four articles written in November 1912 ('The Empire and Dominions'),[82] Moore attempted to explain what notions of Empire and Dominion might mean in the early twentieth century; how there could be nationalism within the constituent parts while still retaining some common thread. Although the focus is primarily on foreign policy and international

---

[76] Foster, above n 74, Appendix A. On the British race patriotism of Australian judges during the First World War see T. Cuneen, 'Judges' Sons Make the Final Sacrifice: The Story of the Australian Judicial Community in the First World War' (2017) 91 ALJ 302, 304–5.

[77] These included Chief Justice of the High Court of Australia Sir John Latham, High Court judge Sir Victor Windeyer, Chief Justices of New South Wales Sir William Cullen and Sir Frederick Jordan, Chief Justice of South Australia Sir George Murray, New South Wales Supreme Court judge and Premier T.R. Bavin, South Australian Supreme Court judge Sir Herbert Angas Parsons, Challis Professor of International Law and Jurisprudence at the University of Sydney from 1920, Archibald Charteris and Dean of the Faculty of Law at the University of Melbourne from 1928, Kenneth Bailey.

[78] Foster, above n 74, 37–38. Cf. Lake, above n 3, 48, who argues that Higgins 'was not a British race patriot'.

[79] Foster, above n 74, 4.

[80] R. Campbell, *A History of the Melbourne Law School 1857–1973* (University of Melbourne, Faculty of Law, 1977) 115.

[81] *Colonial nationalism: an address delivered / by W. Harrison Moore, at the Town Hall, Melbourne, on Friday, 25th August, 1905* (Paul and Hewitt, 1905).

[82] *Argus*, 16 November 1912, 7–8; 20 November 1912, 15–16; 23 November 1912, 7–8; 27 November 1912, 12.

relations, Moore cited with approval the views of a Round Table author as well as those of Ramsay McDonald in which law was central to the bonds that gave Empire meaning. In McDonald's words:

> No State within the empire has the right to adopt a policy of administration or a standard of civil liberty contrary to or lower than the traditional policy of the empire itself. These imperial standards and traditions are in the main certain axioms regarding human liberty and the administration of justice. That no man can be a slave under the British flag, that the administration of justice shall not be prejudiced or tainted, and that every accused shall have a fair trial, conducted by certain clearly defined processes, that law shall rest ultimately upon the consent of the citizens, may, in summary, be laid down as the inheritance which past experience has taught the present generation of Britons to cherish.[83]

On one view, this has nothing to do with the common law of obligations: it is largely about minimum procedural safeguards in criminal law. But once the rule of law becomes central to conceptions of Empire, what that means takes on different meanings for different groups. As Moore commented, there was in the British Empire a consciousness that transcended material interests or even moral purposes.[84] This metaphysical relationship was increasingly important, if conveniently vague,[85] when Dominion status was both recognising and allowing for greater divergence from Westminster. In this increasingly confused constitutional conundrum,[86] the common law was an important unifying factor, something which could be common to the Empire or whatever community of nations that replaced it.

Moore's successor as Dean at Melbourne, Kenneth Bailey, was equally rooted in this tradition. Although Bailey had started at the University of Melbourne, he had broken his studies to enlist and upon returning to Australia he won a Rhodes scholarship and completed a Bachelor of Civil Law (BCL) in Oxford (where he met Keith Hancock who was at All Souls and was presumably exposed to Round Table thinking, as All Souls was a bastion of the movement).[87] He returned to Australia in 1923 to become Vice-Master of Queens College at the University of Melbourne, also lecturing in the History Department and briefly heading it when its long-term head and Round Table member Professor Ernest Scott took leave.[88] He was appointed the Dean of the Melbourne Law School in 1928, a position he held formally until 1946 although he was seconded to government appointments during parts of the Second World War. The author of his

---

[83] *Argus*, 23 November 1912, 8.

[84] Ibid.

[85] On the convenience of the vagueness of imperial citizenship see D. Gorman, *Imperial Citizenship: Empire and the Question of Belonging* (Manchester University Press, 2007) 211.

[86] F. Eggleston, 'Australia and the empire' in *The Cambridge History of the British Empire Vol VII, Part 1: Australia* (Cambridge University Press, 1933) 540. The Statute of Westminster was not ratified in Australia until 1942 although its operation was backdated to 3 September 1939.

[87] Davidson, above n 43, 128, describes Bailey as an old friend of Hancock.

[88] Campbell, above n 80, 124.

entry in the *Australian Dictionary of Biography* notes that the law school under his leadership was noted for its conservative, Oxford influence.[89] Paradoxically, this view may have been the result of attempts to reduce the influence of the practising profession in the curriculum[90]: although he does not appear to have taught in this way himself, Bailey was a supporter of teaching law against a social science background.[91] There is no suggestion, however, that these views led in any way to any kind of re-evaluation of the role of the English common law in Australian law.[92] Even his groundbreaking trip to the United States on a Carnegie Fellowship in 1937 seems to have been as much about styles of legal education as about the content of that education.

Other law academics in Australia are more difficult to categorise. There is little evidence that John Salmond, at Adelaide before really making his name in Wellington, was interested in any Australian legal development: the early editions of his tort texts contain little Commonwealth material.[93] More interesting is Jethro Brown, a native of South Australia who at various times in the 1890s had stints in Tasmania and Sydney. Brown later held chairs at University College London and in Aberystwyth before returning to Adelaide as Dean of the Law School, later taking a position on the South Australian Industrial Court.[94] His scholarship, although not concerned with private law, was a mix of Australian contributions to wider legal problems (particularly the solving of industrial disputes through conciliation and arbitration)[95] and more abstract theory (he wrote on John Austin's lectures on jurisprudence).[96] There is no or little sense of Australian legal independence in what these two academics wrote but, at least in the case of Brown, there is a sense of the distinctness of the Australian contribution to legal development. Moreover, Brown was at the centre of political discourse in both Britain and Australia. He mixed in establishment circles and had important establishment supporters.[97] As the First World War progressed, Brown became an increasing supporter of its prosecution, thereby 'following the patterns of bourgeois Australians of Protestant background and English

---

[89] J. Richardson, 'Sir Kenneth Hamilton Bailey', *Australian Dictionary of Biography*, Vol. 13 (Melbourne University Press, 1993).

[90] J. Waugh, *First Principles* (Miegunyah Press, 2007) 112–124.

[91] Ibid., 110.

[92] Manning Clark described Bailey as 'a fine flower of the Austral-British world': Clark, above n 41, 21.

[93] On Salmond's time in Adelaide see V. Edgeloe, 'The Adelaide Law School' (1983) 9 *Adel L Rev* 1, 12–15.

[94] See further O.M. Roe, 'Jethro Brown: the first teacher of law and history in the University of Tasmania' (1977) 5 *U Tas LR* 209.

[95] *The Underlying Principles of Modern Legislation* (John Murray, 1912) and *The Prevention and Control of Monopolies* (John Murray, 1914). He also wrote extensively earlier in his career about Australian federation: *Why Federate?* (Angus and Robertson, 1896); *The New Democracy* (Macmillian, 1899).

[96] *The Austinian Theory of Law* (John Murray, 1906).

[97] For example, Sir Samuel Way, Chancellor of the University of Adelaide and long-standing Chief Justice of the Supreme Court of South Australia: Roe, above n 94, 226–227.

connections'. Like many of that class, he did not see the war as the means of greater Australian independence from Britain:

> Finally, Brown claimed that since August 1914 there had overflowed long-welling streams of imperial patriotism, promising 'that the conclusion of the war will bring a great opportunity in the life of the Empire'. In terms of his 1890s ideas the pre-scription seemed to be that Australian federalism would give way to a closer union while imperial federation at last became a reality at a high level of 'great state-ness'.[98]

Many of these leading figures illustrate the interconnectedness of the Anglo-Australian relationship within law and legal education. They had studied and/or had spent time in English academic environments. But unlike the nineteenth century, where recent scholarship has shown the colonial history of Empire to be complicated and multi-dimensional,[99] twentieth-century Australian judges increasingly had careers which were based in Australia. This is not to suggest a lack of communication with the outside world – the movement of students, legal practitioners and academics between the metropolis and the Dominions may be one reason for the transnational appeal of the common law into the twentieth century – but the primary comparator for a Dominion remained the metropole rather than developments in other common law jurisdictions.[100] In the legal context it may be going too far to say, as Lester and Lambert argue generally, that 'the differences between places are the result of the trajectories intersecting in varied ways across the surface of the Earth'[101] but the regular interaction enhanced the ability of a certain class of Australians to happily maintain their dual loyalties.

Paton and Australian Tort Law Reconsidered

With this framework in mind, it is now time to return to Paton's – the Melbourne-born, Rhodes Scholar who accepted his Chair at the University of Melbourne when he was holding an Assistant Lectureship at the London School of Economics[102] – description of Australian tort law in 1952 discussed at

---

[98] Ibid., 237.
[99] See generally D. Lambert and A. Lester (eds.), *Colonial Lives Across the British Empire: Imperial Careering in the Long Nineteenth Century* (Cambridge University Press, 2006); C. Hall and S. Rose (eds.), *At Home with the Empire: Metropolitan Culture and the Imperial World* (Cambridge University Press, 2006), and more specifically for law, J. McLaren, *Dewigged, Bothered and Bewildered: British Colonial Judges on Trial 1800–1900* (Osgoode Society, 2011).
[100] Judicial decisions from other parts of the common law world were known and used and Sir Owen Dixon stated judicially that the High Court attempted to keep its decisions consistent with those of the courts not only of England but also New Zealand and Canada: *Waghorn v. Waghorn* (1942) 65 CLR 289, 297. Occasionally legislation from other common law jurisdictions was sought as a guide for reform: see, for example, Maurice Blackburn's 1940 request for a copy of the Libel Act 1939 from Georgia's Attorney General: Maurice Blackburn, 'Papers 1911–1971', State Library of Victoria, MS 11749, Box 4 Folio 6.
[101] Lambert and Lester, above n 99, 13–14.
[102] Waugh, above n 90, 111–112.

the beginning of the chapter. The Australian student, Paton said, could use the classic treatises of Salmond or Winfield (English tort texts) without embarrassment. He recognised that the student would need to know the state legislation affecting tort and that this generally re-enacted laws passed in England or even at times pre-dated them. There may be local decisions, he said, which reject a particular English precedent or cases dealing with points not yet decided in England. However, as he noted in the introduction to the volume, it was 'broadly true' that the most significant factor was the similarity of the law between Australia and England.[103] Paton spends the next five pages detailing a list of the most important Australian cases on the law of tort: *Victoria Park Racing v. Taylor*,[104] *Chester v. Waverley Corporation*,[105] *Aiken v. Kingborough Corporation*,[106] *Lipman v. Clendinning*,[107] *Penfolds Wines v. Elliot*[108] and number of defamation cases. There is also discussion of the fate of certain doctrines: *res ipsa loquitur*, the last clear chance doctrine, and the duty of occupiers to those on the land by right.[109]

There are two things that are striking to the modern reader. The first is the limited number of cases and statues actually mentioned. Even accepting the need for brevity, there are many more cases that could have been included.[110] The reference to statute is somewhat eclectic as well. After discussing *Chester v. Waverley Corporation*, Paton turned to *Victoria Railway Commissioners v. Coultas*[111] and noted that it had been abrogated by statute in Victoria.[112] He did not mention the much more recent and more extensive changes made legislatively in New South Wales in 1944.[113]

The second point to note is how limited a role Paton gives to the cases he mentions. Apart from the cultural limitations previously discussed, Paton had explicitly dealt with the question of deviation in an earlier section. Although no English court decision had bound an Australian court since 1828, 'special efforts are made to keep the common law decisions uniform with those of England'[114] and Paton cites the usual examples where Australian judges had stressed that generally decisions of English courts, in particular the House of Lords, should be followed.[115] Even here, however, the commitment to uniformity was not

---

[103] Paton, above n 15, 22.
[104] (1937) 58 CLR 479.
[105] (1939) 62 CLR 1.
[106] (1939) 62 CLR 179.
[107] (1932) 46 CLR 550.
[108] (1946) 74 CLR 204.
[109] Paton, above n 15, 22–29.
[110] Including the following High Court cases discussed later in the book: *Miller v. McKeon* (1905) 3 CLR 50; *Sparke v. Osborne* (1908) 7 CLR 51; *Lothian v. Rickards* (1911) 12 CLR 165; *Bunyan v. Jordan* (1937) 57 CLR 1; *Shaw Savill and Albion Co. Ltd v. Commonwealth* (1940) 66 CLR 344.
[111] (1888) 13 AC 222.
[112] *Wrongs Act 1932* (Vic) s. 4; Paton, above n 15, 24.
[113] *Law Reform (Miscellaneous Provisions) Act 1944* (NSW) ss. 3–4.
[114] Paton, above n 15, 11.
[115] *Waghorn v. Waghorn* (1941) 65 CLR 289; *Piro v. Foster & Co. Ltd* (1943) 68 CLR 313.

because English law as declared by English courts was inherently better law but because the common law was the law of the Empire/Commonwealth and there were benefits in a common law applying throughout that entity. Again, the loyalty is to the Britishness of the British Empire and its associated institutions and values. And as in the political sphere, that loyalty had a strong rhetorical component that could bend to other imperatives if required. Paton noted that 'uniformity should not be achieved at the cost of injustice' and that 'in spite of a laudable desire to preserve uniformity, there is no slavish adherence to English decisions'.[116]

From a different perspective, the mere fact that the roll call of names of tort cases decided by the High Court of Australia in this period jogs the memory of (at least) Australian tort lawyers suggests a greater contribution to the common law of the Empire than Paton allows in his survey. At the very least, the contention that there was relatively unthinking acceptance of English precedent is a premise that needs to be investigated. The aim of this chapter has been to frame the historical context in which comments about Australian law were made. It is not suggested that all lawyers, judges or academics were constrained in the same way by these cultural bonds but in the little available evidence there is considerable similarity of treatment. For example, Bernard Sugerman writing in the publication to commemorate Sydney Law School's 50th anniversary says both that writing the history of contracts, mercantile law and torts of New South Wales in the past 50 years was 'writing a history of English law' while also noting that divergence between English and Australian courts in the law of tort was to be expected more in this than in other areas of law.[117] Victor Windeyer's *Lectures on Legal History* begins by justifying the lectures not just as a series of abstract rules but as a history of the English people.[118] It finishes with a short chapter on the introduction of English law into Australia, a topic outside the remit of his lectures, but Windeyer makes the following comment:

> It must not be supposed, however, that the legal history of Australia is a mere appendix to the legal history of England. It has important lessons of its own. The British people in Australia have, during their comparatively short history, had their own peculiar problems to be met by the law. How the law has been developed to meet these problems will provide the student with much instructive material.[119]

Of course, not everyone was so forthright in admitting the Australian contexts. To take examples from the beginning and end of the period of this study, H.R. Curlewis' *The Mirror of Justice* assumes that the case summaries and analysis it contains (taken from his *Daily Telegraph* column) are about English law,[120]

---

[116] Paton, above n 15, 13–14.
[117] Bavin, above n 72, 202, 207.
[118] V. Windeyer, *Lectures on Legal History* (Law Book Co. of Australasia, 1938) vii.
[119] Ibid., 249.
[120] H.R. Curlewis, *The Mirror of Justice* (Law Book Co. of Australasia, 1906).

and in 1947 John Baalman's *Outline of Law in Australia* deals with Australian tort law as English law.[121] Even these works, however, resonate with some of the themes this chapter has discussed: Curlewis describes the law in the Australian cases he describes as the product of men whose genius and integrity are among the proudest traditions of England,[122] and Baalman happily cites Australian cases as part of his description of the English law that applied in Australia.[123]

It took an Englishman who became Foundation Professor of the Law School of the University of Canterbury outside the period of this study, Hamish Gray, to grasp what the Antipodeans were trying to do. Judges in Australia and New Zealand, he said, displayed 'to a marked degree an awareness … of the common law community'. When studying the law in Australia and New Zealand, one was 'continually struck with the presentation of the common law not as a collection of local rules, but as a series of principles of a largely universal validity.' These rules were assimilated in New Zealand and New South Wales not because they were English 'but because they exemplify the common law, a law which transcends its merely local manifestations in the jurisdictions in which it comes to be applied.'[124] He finished with what can be described as the plea of the legal independent Australian Briton:

> The common law, it has been said, is the common sense of the community crystallised and formulated by our forefathers. Let it be recognised that the community here referred to is the whole common law community; that is, above all, a contribution to the development of the law of tort in the twentieth century for which England might fairly look to Australia and New Zealand.[125]

Of course, too much may be read into these descriptions. The universality of common law principles was something of a myth, a myth created to perpetuate the existing social and political structures it supported.[126] Equally, however, comments must be read in context. The aim of this chapter has been to make a case for a more detailed study of the relationship between English and Australian private law by considering the wider context in which that law operated, and the constraints created by that context, than has previously been undertaken. More broadly, the argument is that Australian law and legal institutions should be given a more prominent place in Australian intellectual history. For many reasons, we have been accustomed to think of the Austral-Britain – that brilliant if limited creation of Manning Clark – as un-Australian. Perhaps Manning Clark was haunted by his past: in a memorable story he tells (in 1937–38) of being unable to articulate an Australian view when asked because

---

[121] J. Baalman, *Outline of Law in Australia* (Law Book Co. of Australasia, 1947).
[122] Curlewis, above n 120, iv.
[123] Baalman, above n 121, 266–267 (*Chester v. Waverley Corporation*).
[124] H.R. Gray, 'The development and function of the law of tort in the twentieth century in Australia and New Zealand' (1965) 14 *ICLQ* 390, 407.
[125] Ibid., 409.
[126] E. Hobsbawm, 'Introduction: inventing traditions' in E. Hobsbawm and T. Ranger (eds.), *The Invention of Tradition* (Cambridge University Press, 1983).

'I lacked the intellectual culture with which to give substance to my sense of being Australian'.[127] But we must be careful not to be taken in too much by Manning Clark's cathartic journey to his *History of Australia*: a journey in part to be free from the cultural cringe he associated with being an Austral-Britain. As Carl Bridge has reminded us, 'We read much about chips on shoulders, sensitive egos and colonial cringes or struts among Australians abroad, but it must be remembered that they fitted in, too, among their fellow Britons, and often even relished it.'[128] This was certainly the case for Keith Hancock: as Frank Bongiorno comments, it is 'the skill and even ease with which Hancock found his way into the highest echelons of the British civil and official society that now seems most marked'.[129] The focus of this chapter has been Keith Hancock rather than Manning Clark because his independent Australian Britons better capture the dominant grouping within the Australian legal fraternity. Sarah Burnside notes that 'conservatism' in an Australian context has often been conflated with Anglophilia and an attachment to Empire so that '[t]he English origins of the judicial system may render its practitioners unappealing to Australian historians.'[130] It is only when we understand a little more about how those practitioners saw themselves, and how they saw the relationship between Australia and the mother country, that we can hope to do justice to the development of Australian private law.

---

[127] Clark, above n 41, 38.

[128] C. Bridge, 'Australia, Britain and the British Commonwealth' in A. Bashford and S. Macintyre (eds.), *The Cambridge History of Australia Volume 2: The Commonwealth of Australia* (Cambridge University Press, 2013) 521.

[129] F. Bongiorno, 'Loving two soils', *Inside Story*, 29 September 2010, http://insidestory.org.au/loving-two-soils/.

[130] S. Burnside, 'Griffith, Isaacs and Australian judicial biography: an evolutionary development' (2009) 18 *GLR* 151, 161.

3

Avoiding and Interpreting the 'Refinements of English Law': Defamation in Australia 1901–1945

As in other areas of private law, the common law of defamation applied in the Australian colonies, and later states, was the English common law.[1] Unlike most areas of tort law, however, the common law was significantly altered in a number of Australian jurisdictions. The most radical alterations took place in Queensland, Western Australia, and Tasmania, where the common law was codified. In these jurisdictions, the governing law was the statutory code, and while the codes were based on the pre-existing common law, there were differences between that common law and the codes. The leading figure in this codification movement was Sir Samuel Griffith who drafted the Queensland Defamation Act 1889, which was included in the Criminal Code Act 1899 (Qld) and was later adopted in the Western Australian Criminal Code.[2] In Tasmania, the Queensland code was adopted in Defamation Act 1895 (Tas) although there remained doubt in the period of this study as to the extent the legislative changes altered the common law position in Western Australia and Tasmania.[3] Courts had a clear obligation to apply this Australian legislation and in these jurisdictions the judges were not obedient servants of English law.

Apart from the code states, Australian jurisdictions applied the English common law of defamation except where modified by legislation. In New South Wales this had a long history of dating back to 1847.[4] The Australian jurisdiction that most closely followed, at least formally, the English common law of defamation was Victoria. On numerous occasions there were statements in defamation cases that the law of Victoria was the same as the law of England and it is certainly true that Victorian judges cited many English cases as authority to

---

[1] The expression 'Refinements of English Law' is Sir Samuel Griffith's: *Hall-Gibbs Mercantile Agency Ltd v. Dun* (1910) 12 CLR 84, 92.

[2] Criminal Code Act 1902 (WA).

[3] The Western Australian provisions were later held to have only a limited application to civil claims: see *WA Newspapers v. Bridge* (1979) 141 CLR 535. Reported Tasmanian cases in this period rarely referred to the legislation but the language used suggests that it was understood to apply to civil cases: see, for example, the summing up to the jury in *Patmoore v. Boon* (1927) 22 Tas LR 75.

[4] Slander and Libel Act 1847 (NSW); Defamation Act 1901 (NSW); Defamation (Amendment) Act 1909 (NSW); Defamation Act 1912 (NSW). On the 1847 Act see P. Mitchell, 'The foundations of Australian defamation law' (2006) *Syd LR* 477.

support their judgments. As in other areas of tort law, however, English judicial voices were not the only opinions cited. High Court cases were binding and were increasingly cited as the leading authority. Cases from other state jurisdictions were cited but the different defamation laws in most other states limited their usefulness. And where case law was thought uncertain or unclear, academic texts were cited. Gatley, Odgers and Pollock were referred to frequently alongside a number of texts whose prominence has faded with time.[5] Where the law was uncertain – even if it was English law, or English law as mediated through Australian decisions – courts retained the usual flexibility of the common law in applying general principles to concrete fact situations.

The section on defamation is divided into two chapters, the second of which deals with political defamation. This chapter deals with some specific parts of the law of defamation where Australian judges had an opportunity to experiment with the common law either through explaining its amendment by local statute or by developing the common law to suit Australian conditions. In some cases this was due to a lack of English authority on a particular point, in others because the public policy orientation of the legal principle provided considerable scope for interpretation and innovation.

Libel and Slander, Trade Protection Societies and Australian Innovation

At the commencement of the period of this study the common law of defamation drew a clear distinction between two different kinds of defamation: libel and slander. The traditional distinction between the two was that libels were written and slanders were spoken. The distinction carried important procedural differences. If the defamatory communication constituted libel, damage to the plaintiff (the subject of the defamation) was assumed. In slander, however, special (i.e. actual) damage needed to be established unless the case fell into one of a number of exceptions, the most important being that a slander that affected a person in their trade or profession was actionable without proof of special damage.

The distinction was never without its problems as not every form of communication fitted neatly into a written/spoken divide and a number of Australian jurisdictions abolished the distinction by statute. Sir Samuel Griffith solved the problem as the draftsman of the Defamation Act 1889 (Qld) by simply recognising one category of defamatory publication.[6] Section 4 of the Act states:

> Any imputation concerning any person, or any member of the person's family, whether living or dead, by which the reputation of that person is likely to be

---

[5] E.g. H. Fraser, *Principles and Practice of the law of Libel and Slander*, seven editions between 1893 and 1936.

[6] Cf. the position in Tasmania where the traditional limits on bringing actions for slander were maintained: Defamation Act 1895 (Tas) s. 9.

injured, or by which the person is likely to be injured in the person's profession or trade, or by which other persons are likely to be induced to shun or avoid or ridicule or despise the person, is called 'defamatory', and the matter of the imputation is called 'defamatory matter'.

Once a defamatory imputation – as defined according to s. 4 – was communicated a person could be defamed. There was no special damage requirement for defamatory words or for any other type of defamatory publication but for defamatory words liability was, initially, kept within reasonable bounds by the defence of triviality.[7] Subject to overcoming this threshold, there was no special damage required for any defamatory imputation.

While the abolition of any substantive distinction between libel and slander in defamation caused few problems, the elimination of the special damage requirement for actions falling within the section was problematic. In *The Hall-Gibbs Mercantile Agency v. Dun*[8] the action arose out of the takeover of one trade protection business by another. T.M. Hall had carried on business in New South Wales and Queensland under a trade name but in 1894 sold all his interest in the Sydney business to a business partner and after various changes it was sold to the defendants in 1909. Hall retained control of the Queensland business, trading at the time of the alleged defamation as The Hall-Gibbs Mercantile Agency, Limited. Shortly after it acquired Hall's Sydney business, the defendant (which traded under its own name in Brisbane) published in its newspaper, *Dun's Gazette*, a statement suggesting that the business throughout Australia – including in Brisbane – had ceased to trade.

As *Dun's Gazette* circulated in Brisbane, the plaintiff alleged that as a result of the statement readers there would understand that the plaintiff's business had been taken over by the defendant. He also alleged readers would understand it was no longer in business on its own account, and that its managing director T.M. Hall had ceased to be involved in any trade protection business in Queensland, and that as a result the plaintiff company suffered loss. At trial in the Queensland Supreme Court Cooper CJ considered Griffith's provision, noting that before 1889 slander was not actionable without special damage. However, s. 4 (by 1910, s. 366 of the Criminal Code) had changed the law: the section made 'very remarkable and important changes directed towards an extension of the plaintiff's remedies.'[9] Although the section required an imputation, this did not carry with it a requirement of derogation or disparagement; the expression was wide enough to cover 'any intentional statement concerning a person which may result in an injury

---

[7]   Defamation Act 1889 (Qld) s. 20 – it was a defence to prove that the publication was made on an occasion and under circumstances when the person defamed was not likely to be injured thereby.

[8]   [1910] St R Qd 333; (1910) 12 CLR 84.

[9]   [1910] St R Qd 333, 336.

to him'.[10] Slander of title actions were expressly excluded from the Act which caused Cooper CJ some disquiet: if the other actions in which special damage had previously been required were included, 'there must have been some sufficient reason for it, though I confess my inability to discover what it is.' Judgment was awarded in the plaintiff's favour. Such a dramatic change from the common law was too great for the Full Court of the Supreme Court of Queensland to accept on appeal. As Shand J put it, the action in essence was an action for slander of title and that was excluded from the Act, and even if this was wrong s. 4 was not to be interpreted as extending the definition of defamatory matter to include statements previously only actionable upon proof of special damage.[11]

Two separate but related issues were discussed and sometimes conflated in these judgments, particularly in the views of Cooper CJ. The first was the relationship between defamation and other kinds of actions for damage to business reputation.[12] In 1892, in an analogous case to *Hall-Gibbs*, the English Court of Appeal in *Ratcliffe v. Evans*[13] considered that words which were not defamatory of the plaintiff but which had injured him in his trade or business were not actionable in defamation; they were actionable in a separate action on the case on proof of malice and special damage. The analogous action of slander of title also required malice and proof of special damage. It is not easy to follow the reasoning of Cooper CJ but he seems to have linked slander (as one form of an action for defamation) with the actions for damage to business reputation (the action on the case and slander of title): all required special damage to be proved.[14] As he thought the law had changed for all slander actions – which apparently included the action on the case and slander of title – by s. 4, he was confused why slander of title actions had been excluded from the 1889 Act. The second issue was what could amount to a 'defamatory' publication under the Act. This turned on the meaning of an imputation by which a person was likely to be injured in the person's profession or trade. The Full Court thought that the answer depended on the relationship between defamation and the other torts that protected business reputation and, in the Full Court's view, the 1889 Act did not reform this relationship. As Shand J put it, this would not have been an action for defamation prior to the Act – it would have been an action on the case for damages. So when Pring J stated that the 1889 Act 'did not alter the law

---

[10] Cf. *The Mentone Racing Club v. The Victorian Railway Commissioner* (1902) 28 VLR 77 where an incorrect statement that a race meeting had been postponed was held not actionable in the absence of malice even though it was alleged to have caused the plaintiff loss.

[11] [1910] St R Qd 333, 344.

[12] For the complicated early history and interconnectedness of these actions in the royal courts see R. Helmholz, 'Introduction' in R. Helmholz (ed.), *Select Cases on Defamation to 1600* (Selden Society, 1985) vol. 101, lxvi, esp. lxxxvi–cvi.

[13] [1892] 2 QB 524.

[14] It was also noted that various other actions that protected the plaintiff's goods or his reputation in his trade or profession required proof of special damage: [1910] St R Qd 333, 336–337.

in respect of actions wherein … damage was, before the Act, a necessary ingredient in the cause of action', he was not suggesting that the Act made no change to when slander was actionable. He was simply saying that what was a spade before 1889 remained so after the Act.

The appeal to the High Court of Australia gave the draftsman of the 1889 Act the chance to say exactly what he meant. In a robust judgment allowing the appeal,[15] Griffith CJ made it clear the question was what the Queensland statute meant, not how far it diverged from English law:

> … the question is not whether the action would lie in England, or, if it would, what it would be called, or on what conditions it could be maintained, but whether the publication complained of is within the words of the law of Queensland.[16]

Apart from 'the refinements of the English law', Griffith CJ thought there was good reason why an assertion made concerning a person likely to injure him in his profession or trade, and not justified or excused by law, should be actionable whether it imputed to him 'some small peccadillo or untruly alleges that he has ceased to carry on business altogether'.[17] Deference was required to the Queensland legislature: 'The English law may be defective on the point but that is no reason for limiting the meaning of the Statute law of Queensland.'[18] That law had now allowed the old action on the case to be actionable as defamation but had expressly excluded slander of title because the gist of the action was different. As Griffith CJ put it:

> There is in my opinion an essential distinction between disparagement of a man's title to property, by which he may be injuriously affected in his efforts to dispose of it, and the disparagement of a man with regard to his own conduct in respect of his property. In both cases, the man and the property are elements of the disparagement, but the nature of the wrong is quite different.[19]

Two points can be made about Griffith CJ's judgment. First, there was deliberate discrediting of the argument that Queensland law should by default be interpreted as aligned with English law. The legislatures of the Australian colonies had had extensive authority to depart from English law since 1865 and there was no reason to be wary of departing from English law where the statutory language required.[20] Second, there was no reticence to suggest that English law was in this area deficient. Whether there existed a general principle of liability for harm caused, subject to justification or excuse, had been highly topical when Griffith drafted the Defamation Act in 1889. Subsequently, the House of Lords came down against such a view in *Allen v. Flood* in 1898.[21] Griffith's

---

[15] Barton and O'Connor JJ delivered separate concurring judgments.

[16] (1910) 12 CLR 84, 92.

[17] Ibid.

[18] Ibid., 93.

[19] Ibid.

[20] The point was made more prosaically by O'Connor J who noted that the legislature 'sometimes thinks it expedient to extend the subject matter so as to take in an entirely new field': ibid., 103.

[21] [1898] AC 1.

comment that English law was defective in this area was not some colonial cocking a snoot at his imperial betters; rather it suggests an intellectual commitment to a widely supported view of a general theory of liability.

While *Hall-Gibbs* potentially extended the situations where plaintiffs could sue for damage to their trade reputation, trade protection societies – the class of defendants to which Hall-Gibbs belonged – had an alternative argument that reduced the incident of liability. Where the maker of a defamatory communication had a duty to make the statement and the recipient of the communication had an interest in receiving it, the common law allowed the defendant to plead that the communication was made on a privileged occasion and hence was protected. This qualified privilege was only defeated on proof of malice: broadly, that the communication was made for an improper purpose not within the reciprocal duties of provider and receiver of the communication that made the occasion privileged.

The scope of the defence in relation to trade protection agencies arose in the case of *Macintosh v. Dun*. The defendants, those involved in the management of the Australian arm of the American mercantile agency R.G. Dun, had published two reports about the creditworthiness of the plaintiffs' hardware business. The collapse of a large Sydney firm of contractors and builders, Dean and Sons, in October 1903 led to greater interest in the financial status of a business' potential customers. In December 1903, a representative of the defendant encouraged a third party, a subscriber to the defendant's business, to seek a credit report on the plaintiffs. He did so, and the subsequent report (and a following, unsolicited report) was equivocal, primarily because the business had passed from its original father owner to his two sons (the plaintiffs) who were not considered to have the same abilities or financial prudence as the father. All the information was obtained from third parties; the plaintiffs were not contacted. When the plaintiffs became aware of the reports, they commenced proceedings for defamation. At first instance in a jury trial in the Supreme Court of New South Wales they were successful, being awarded £800.[22] The defendants had applied for a nonsuit[23] but this was rejected by the trial judge, Cohen J, on the ground that he was bound by an earlier New South Wales decision, *Foley v. Hall*[24] to find that the occasion was not privileged. In *Foley*, Windeyer J held that the law 'would not recognise a joint-stock co-operative slander association limited'.[25]

The defendants' appealed successfully to the Full Court. Delivering the judgment of the Court, Pring J distinguished *Foley* on the basis that the defamatory communication in that case was a circular listing a group of people irrespective of whether they were of interest to any individual subscriber to whom the

---

[22] *SMH*, 27 June 1905, 7.
[23] *SMH*, 24 June 1905, 15.
[24] (1891) 12 NSWR 175.
[25] Ibid.,178.

circular was distributed. To the extent that Windeyer J's comments were meant to go further they should not be followed. Moreover, there were good pragmatic reasons why privilege should attach to a credit report delivered in these circumstances:

> Now it is obvious that it is for the common convenience and welfare of a trading community that a merchant should be able to make enquiries with respect to the financial standing and credit of another with whom he is dealing or about to deal, and that the answers to such enquiries, if given honestly and *bona fide*, should not subject the person giving them to an action for defamation. If the law were otherwise, the position of traders would be intolerable; their business would materially suffer, and the whole community would in turn feel the effects of the check thus imposed on trade and commerce.[26]

The plaintiffs' argument that privilege could not apply as the relationship between the defendants and the third party was contractual was also rejected. There was no direct English authority on point but Pring J felt no difficulty in citing a decision of the Court of Appeal for the State of New York[27] in support of the court's view: the case would be applicable in New South Wales as the reasoning 'must appeal to the common sense of everyone'.[28] Although an order for a new trial was granted on an evidentiary point (that need not concern us here), the principle that communications between a trade protection agency and a client were protected was clearly upheld. This view was emphatically endorsed on appeal to the High Court.[29] Citing the New York authority, Griffith CJ agreed entirely with Pring J's view that the reasoning in that case in favour of recognising the privilege appealed to common sense.[30] Barton J too held that the general interest of society required that the correct information should be obtained as to the business character of persons in whom others enquiring had a business interest.[31] As O'Connor J pointed out, it made no difference that the defendants were under a contractual obligation to provide the information. As the privilege would apply where the enquirer's employee was sent to make enquiries and the employee had a contractual duty under the contract of employment to divulge any information to the employer, the same privilege should apply if the task was delegated to someone else under a different contract.[32]

The two appellate court decisions in Australia represent a value judgement: in New South Wales in 1905 information as to the creditworthiness of potential trading partners was more valuable than the risk to an individual's reputation if incorrect information was supplied. Given the open-ended nature of the qualified privilege defence it was well suited to adapting to local conditions, and

---

[26] *Macintosh v. Dun* (1905) 5 SR (NSW) 708, 717.
[27] *Ormsby v. Douglass* (1868) 37 NY Rep 477.
[28] *Macintosh v. Dun* (1905) 5 SR (NSW) 708, 718.
[29] (1906) 3 CLR 1134.
[30] Ibid., 1149.
[31] Ibid., 1160.
[32] Ibid., 1165.

local conditions, as they had in New York, favoured legal rules that minimised financial risk to traders and avoided the economic uncertainty associated with commercial failure. When the case reached the Privy Council in 1908, however, a very different view of the appropriate balance was drawn.[33] Trade protection agencies were not seen, as is implicit in the Australian judgments, as acting in the public interest: they were bodies that profited by trading in the characters of others. There is a strong sense of moral self-righteousness in their Lordships' disapproval: profit-motive would reduce incentives for proper checking of the information obtained and the sources of information – gossip, discharged servants, disloyal employees – meant that it was 'only right that those who engage in such a business, touching so closely very dangerous ground, should take the consequences if they overstep the law'.[34] The balance drawn by the Australian courts was rejected because accurate information – and here is meant commercial information – was bought too dearly for the good of society.

The Privy Council's decision was controversial. It was recognised by *The Times* as significant in both England and the colonies, and the paper thought it disappointing that the law could not be extended to give protection to information clearly of interest to the business community.[35] In Sydney, the decision prompted a mixed but predominantly negative reaction but the tone was measured as initially the result and not the reasoning was available in Sydney.[36] When the reasoning was available, however, the displeasure with the decision was powerfully voiced in the *Sydney Morning Herald*. At the outset, the very structure of Privy Council decisions was criticised. It was unsatisfactory 'as are all the decisions of the Privy Council because being the composite result of the deliberations of the board we are not able to tell what were the individual opinions of the Judges who gave it, or what arguments had weight with them'. Moving to the substance, the paper noted that the decision would be criticised and that it would be said 'that for once it [the Privy Council] proved unable to adapt the principle of the common law to the changing needs of commerce'. In the paper's view, the decision was unacceptable:

> We have already given it as our opinion that such a decision cannot be final, and that the law will have to be altered to meet the situation just created. There is a demand for the information these societies supply and in legitimate ways the community will be served and not injured by their enterprise.[37]

There is no suggestion here that Australian public opinion, if not Australian courts, should passively accept a Privy Council decision that was perceived to

---

[33] [1908] AC 390; (1908) 6 CLR 303.

[34] (1908) 6 CLR 303, 307–308. For similar sentiments in a contemporaneous English case see *E Hulton & Co. v. Jones* [1910] AC 20.

[35] See reference in *SMH*, 8 June 1908, 7.

[36] *Evening News* (Sydney), 5 June 1908, 7; 9 June 1908, 6; *SMH*, 6 June 1908, 15; 8 June 1908, 6; 9 June 1908, 6; *The Newsletter: an Australian Paper for Australian People*, 13 June 1908, 1; 20 June 1908, 4; *Maitland Daily Mercury*, 2 July 1908, 2.

[37] *SMH*, 10 July 1908, 6.

be against Australian interests. The comments as to the nature of Privy Council opinions reveal a (not very) latent hostility to being told what to do in an area – the scope of the qualified privilege defence – which was explicitly based on public policy. Concerns over the decision were present in England too so the Australian reaction was not unique: it was not a case of singling-out Australia. But the Privy Council decision carried in Australia the extra connotation of being patronising. This is well-illustrated by the Judicial Committee's rejection of the use of American authority by Australian courts to support their conclusion: American authorities were, no doubt, entitled to the highest respect but the question had to be decided by English law.[38] As there was a dearth of English authority, recourse to the principle on which the law in England on this subject was founded was needed and, with the utmost deference to the judges of the High Court, they had (in my words) got it wrong! Little wonder that the decision raised hackles. The only 'principle' of English law applicable was one of public policy and Australian courts, informed by a decision in a comparable common law jurisdiction, had to be put in their place: only an English court could decide English public policy.[39] This putting of Australian courts in their place, as they were in *Macintosh v. Dun*, rankled. Writing in the *Commonwealth Law Review*, Leo Cussen, then a recently appointed Victorian Supreme Court judge, commented:

> We must all agree with the judicial committee that American decisions as such, although entitled to the highest respect, are of no authority in English courts, and questions must be decided by reference to principles of English law but it appears to me that in a case of this kind, where there is no direct English authority, to refuse the undoubted help it affords simply because it is labelled American, is like kicking away a ladder and then attempting to scale a wall with the meager help of one's fingers and toes.[40]

And in the end, Australians – at least in New South Wales – did not stand for the *Macintosh* decision. The Defamation (Amendment) Act 1909 (NSW) s. 6 provided that information provided pursuant to a contract for valuable consideration could attract the defence of qualified privilege if the publication was in answer to an inquiry made in pursuance of such contract, the matter published was relevant to the subject of the enquiry, the manner and extent of the publication did not exceed what was reasonably sufficient for the occasion, the person making the publication was not actuated by ill-will to the person defamed, or by any other improper motive, and the person making the publication had reasonable ground to believe the matter published to be true. The concern as to the profit-motive of the mercantile agency that underlay the Privy Council was

---

[38] (1908) 6 CLR 303, 307.
[39] On British concern over the growing American influence on Australia social and political life before 1914 see M. Lake, 'British world or new world?: Anglo-Saxonism and Australian engagement with America' (2013) 10 *History Australia* 36.
[40] (1908–9) 6 *Commonwealth Law Review* 105.

rejected but in return for a requirement that the mercantile agency had reasonable grounds for believing the communication to be true, making it difficult for defendants to rely on dubious sources where the reasonableness of a belief in truth would be hard to find.[41]

Even at common law, ways were found of avoiding the more extreme interpretations of *Macintosh*. In September 1910, the High Court was given the opportunity to revisit this area in *Howe v. Lees*,[42] a case involving an association of stock salesman in Bendigo. The defendant, a member of the association, had passed on information to the secretary that the plaintiff had not settled his account within four days after the relevant sale, as the rules of the association required him to do. This was incorrect and the plaintiff sued in respect of the defendant's communication. Another plaintiff had successfully sued a member of the Bendigo association of stock salesmen in similar circumstances in 1909, the Full Court of the Supreme Court of Victoria in part basing its decision on *Macintosh* in finding that the communication was not made on a privileged occasion.[43] Following this decision, the trial judge found for the plaintiff[44] but on appeal the High Court by a 4-1 majority overturned the decision and found the occasion privileged. Only Isaacs J, dissenting, thought *Macintosh* applied, and his judgment is heavily influenced by his view that the association was some kind of cartel.[45] The majority judges disposed of *Macintosh* in different ways. Higgins J, who had not been a member of the court that decided *Macintosh*, distinguished it on the basis that the request there had been procured by the defendant company and also that the defendant for its own self-interest was trading in the characters of other people.[46] O'Connor J agreed, stressing that it was the commercial purpose of the defendant's business in collecting the information that prevented the privilege from arising in *Macintosh*. The decision was not intended to lay down any new principles; it was an application of the general law to the special facts of the case.[47] The most telling comments are by Griffith CJ (with whom Barton J agreed). *Macintosh* laid down no new rule and was decided on a question of fact not law. Moreover, the Privy Council

> also thought, apparently, that the agreement under which the defendant was bound to make the communication was contrary to public policy, which as Burrough J said in *Richardson* v. *Mellish*, is a very unruly horse and when once

---

[41] On the innovation of this amendment see E. Descheemaekar, 'A man must take care not to defame his neighbour: the origins and significance of the defence of responsible publication' (2015) *UQLJ* 239.

[42] (1910) 11 CLR 361.

[43] *Peatling v. Watson* [1909] VLR 198.

[44] The trial judge was Madden CJ, who had given the leading judgment in *Peatling*.

[45] (1910) 11 CLR 361, 391. Isaacs had a long-standing interest in and opposition to anti-competitive conduct engaged in by cartels and monopolies and, as Attorney-General of the Commonwealth Parliament, introduced Australia's first competition legislation, the Australian Industries Preservation Act 1906 (Cth).

[46] Ibid., 398–399.

[47] Ibid., 373–374.

you get astride it you will never know where it will carry you … No question of public policy arises in the present case.[48]

There is no mention in *Macintosh* of the *contract* being void for public policy; the Privy Council simply pointed out that the nature of the business of which the contract formed part was not one that satisfied the public policy component of qualified privilege. Griffith CJ well knew that qualified privilege was based on public policy – he reiterated it in *Howe*[49] – but the sense here is that he wanted to both limit and discredit a decision that had overruled him. The future for the Privy Council decision in *Macintosh v. Dun* as a leading authority did not improve. Even at the time it was decided, there was academic support for the contrary conclusion[50] and it was later subject to academic critique[51] and judicial avoidance.[52] Later Australian cases were happy enough to accept the broad principle of the qualified privilege defence espoused in the case but the decision itself was largely confined to its own facts.[53]

The Problem of Radio Broadcasting

Whatever the uncertainties of amalgamating libel and slander for special damage requirements, the Queensland and New South Wales legislation avoided the difficult demarcation questions that arose when the distinction had to be determined outside the usual written/spoken divide.[54] Other jurisdictions were not so fortunate. While the academic question of the boundary between the two was raised in contexts outside the traditional divide, there was little practical concern as such cases were not the norm. The odd case, for example, might concern a sign or symbol, but these were relative oddities and could be left as cases decided on their own facts. The introduction of large-scale radio broadcasting, however, was a different story. This was a medium which had the capacity to transmit any defamatory imputation to a large audience almost instantaneously and the question of whether the subject of the imputation needed to prove special damage[55] (if it was considered slander) was of major practical significance. In answering the difficult question of whether a radio broadcast was libel or slander, Australian courts would have welcomed guidance from the mother

---

[48] Ibid., 371.

[49] Ibid., 369: 'The rule being founded upon the general welfare of society, new occasions for its application will necessarily arise with continually changing conditions.'

[50] W.B. Odgers, *A Digest of the Law on Libel and Slander*, 3rd edn (Stevens and Sons, 1896) 238–239.

[51] J. Smith, 'Conditional privilege for mercantile agencies. – Macintosh v. Dun' (1914) 14 *Colum L Rev* 187–210; 296–320.

[52] *London Association for the Protection of Trade v. Greenlands* [1916] 2 AC 15.

[53] See, for example, *Telegraph Newspaper Co Ltd v. Bedford* (1934) 50 CLR 632 (especially Evatt J).

[54] See Defamation Act 1889 (Qld) s. 5: Any person who, by spoken words or audible sounds, or by words intended to be read either by sight or touch, or by signs, signals, gestures, or visible representations, publishes any defamatory imputation concerning any person is said to defame that person.

[55] Assuming the imputation did not fall within the exceptions to this rule at common law or statute.

country but none was forthcoming: as Mitchell notes, there was virtually no authority on the point in England.[56]

The issue arose for decision in *Meldrum v. Australian Broadcasting Co. Ltd.*[57] The plaintiff's claim related to a radio broadcast by an employee of the defendant who had defamed the plaintiff. Conscious that the question remained unanswered in Australia, the plaintiff's pleading stated (in effect) that the defendant's employee wrote a script which was then read out and broadcast, and the defendant sought to have the whole pleading, or at least the part relating to writing or a script, struck out. Apart from some seventeenth-century cases of dubious value,[58] the plaintiff relied on the English decision of *Forrester v. Tyrrell*,[59] where the speaker read out from an obviously written script words defamatory of the plaintiff. This was held to be libel. At first instance, Cussen, ACJ of the Supreme Court of Victoria, noted that *Forrester* was not directly applicable as the listener of a radio broadcast had no idea whether the speaker was reading from a script or was ad-libbing. The question was one of first principle and after reviewing the history of the distinction he could not 'deduce from any recognized principle the rule which should be applied in the present case' with the result that he did what judges in the past had done in cases of libel and slander – 'give a decision which on the whole seems to be right when applied to the circumstances of the particular case'.[60] With this freedom, it was held that the publication was a slander, hence the references to 'script' and 'writing' were struck out. At this part of the judgment Cussen ACJ provided no support for his conclusion although he had noted earlier defendant counsel's argument that the author of Salmond thought this was slander as did a contributor to the *Harvard Law Review*. By contrast, when the case was appealed, counsel for both sides made their arguments from a variety of venerated English texts, texts both specific to defamation and more general tort texts.[61] The reason for this recourse was that the distinction between libel and slander, however workable it may have been in practice, was an accident of history, and in the absence of any theoretical justification for the distinction it was difficult to apply outside simple situations which could not have been anticipated when the rules was created.[62] The Full Court split in its reasoning. Lowe J agreed

---

[56] P. Mitchell, *A History of Tort Law 1900–1950* (Cambridge University Press, 2015) 165.

[57] [1932] VLR 425.

[58] The Case of *De Libellis Famosis, Or of Scandalous Libels* (1605) 77 ER 250 and *John Lamb's Case* (1610) 77 ER 822. Both were criminal cases from the Star Chamber and the holdings were not automatically transferable to civil cases.

[59] (1893) 9 TLR 257.

[60] [1932] VLR 425, 432.

[61] Including *Comyns Digest, Bacon's Abridgement, Viner's Abridgement, Halsbury's Laws of England, Gatley on Libel and Slander, Odgers on Libel and Slander, Roscoe's Evidence in Civil Actions*, W.S. Holdsworth, *History of English Law, Pollock on Torts, Addison on Torts, Clerk and Lindsell on Torts, Blackstone's Commentaries*. Lowe J referred to *Starkie's Law of Slander* in argument.

[62] [1932] VLR 425, 432, 440–441 (Lowe J).

with Cussen ACJ, a view he supported by reference to American authority.[63] But McArthur J did not accept that the result depended on whether the listener knew whether the words were read from a text or not. The differentiator was whether words were spoken or written and here the words were spoken. Any anomalies that resulted from the court's decision – that a communication to a blind person could not be libel a third party, for example – were the result of the difference between actionable libel and actionable slander, a distinction he accepted some writers thought unsatisfactory. Mann J agreed. Prosaically, he noted there was no discernible principle to apply and he based his decision on convenience and public interest: the simple rule that spoken words were slander gave certainty to ascertaining legal rights and to depart from this rule would open up a difficult field of enquiry, on both law and fact, as to relationship between spoken and written words in language, time and place.[64] The implication here is that the judicial role was to maintain certainty by not departing from the orthodox rules. If that approach yielded unsatisfactory results, it was a matter for the legislature.

Meldrum's case remained controversial in Australia. Writing shortly after the case, J.A. Redmond pointed out that the reasoning of all judges in the Full Court could not satisfactorily deal with technological changes that made it impossible to use a written/spoken distinction as the determinant of libel/slander.[65] In 1949, Sir John Barry, a judge of the Supreme Court of Victoria,[66] criticised the decision in the course of a wide-ranging survey of radio, television and the law of defamation.[67] In his view, it failed to take into account the social purposes of the law of defamation and failed to reform the law by enlarging the ambit of libel to overcome the injustices of the law of slander, to 'meet the state of affairs to which the new medium of mass communication by broadcasting has given rise'.[68] Other commentators on Barry's paper took a different view,[69] and Sir Charles Lowe (Lowe J) gave a thoughtful response (if not defence) in which it was clear the court was limited in what they could do consistent with the judicial function as he perceived it.[70] In the end the Commonwealth legislature did act shortly afterwards, adding s. 95A to the Broadcasting Act 1956 (Cth) which stated that 'for the purposes of the law of defamation the transmission of words or other matter by a broadcasting station or a television station shall be deemed

---

[63]   Albeit it was to a book review of a book rather than the book itself: see review of Stephen Davis, *The Law of Radio Communication* (1928) 41 *Harv L Rev* 814.

[64]   [1932] VLR 425, 435.

[65]   J.A. Redmond, 'Reading from script into broadcasting apparatus – libel or slander' (1933) 7 *ALJ* 257.

[66]   M. Finnane, *JV Barry: A Life* (UNSW Press, 2007).

[67]   J.V. Barry, 'Radio, television and the law of defamation' (1949) 23 *ALJ* 203.

[68]   Ibid., 213.

[69]   Professor K.O. Shatwell, Dean of the Law School at the University of Sydney, was more sympathetic: ibid., 218–219.

[70]   Ibid., 220.

to be publication in a permanent form',[71] albeit the amendment was inspired by the findings of the English Porter Committee[72] in 1948.[73] For present purposes, the importance of the *Meldrum* decision lies not in its legal merits, however they might be construed, but in recognising that the court had to deal with a novel situation which required more than passive acceptance of an English precedent. All the Victorian judges who heard the case refused to simply extend the only relevant, modern English authority to the facts of *Meldrum*, some by distinguishing it and some by simply declaring it was wrong. While this latter course did raise some eyebrows at the time, it demonstrates that the view that Australian judges demonstrated blind obeisance to English law is too simplistic.

Other Contributions to Defamation Law and Theory

In a number of other areas Australian courts made important contributions to the general law of defamation. Generally, these were not recognised in England. On the vexed question of fault in defamation there were important if ultimately conflicting views. In an early case from the period, *Godhard v. James Inglis & Co. Ltd*,[74] the issue was raised of whether a defamatory statement true of one person could give rise to an action to another who was objectively identified by the publication. Both Owen J in the New South Wales Supreme Court[75] and Griffith CJ in the High Court thought that intention to refer to the plaintiff was a necessary element in libel, the latter's analytical mind reasoning that '[i]f a man is doing a lawful act in speaking of A.B., that is to say, publishing defamatory matter of him which he is justified in publishing, it would be a very strange thing if his act could become unlawful because one of his hearers or readers misunderstood his reference'.[76] The legal landscape was changed when the House of Lords decided *Hulton v. Jones* in 1909.[77] After that case it was clear that an intention to refer to the plaintiff was no longer necessary – it will be remembered that in *Hulton* the defendant's (failed) argument was that he was writing about a fictitious character Artemus Jones rather than the plaintiff.[78] The musings of Australian courts were not cited in *Hulton*, and if evidence is

---

[71] Broadcasting and Television Act 1956 (Cth) s. 52. The Commonwealth had legislative competence under s. 51(v) of the Australian Constitution ('postal, telegraphic, telephonic, and other like services').

[72] Committee on the Law of Defamation (Cmnd. 7536/48), chaired by Lord Porter. For detailed discussion of the history and report of the Committee see Mitchell, above n 55, ch. 6.

[73] Hansard (House of Representatives), Broadcasting and Television Bill 1956, Second Reading Speech, 19 April 1956 (Mr Davidson, Postmaster General). The bill was amended and reintroduced a number of times subsequently before passing but this clause received no further mention after the second reading speeches in the House of Representatives and Senate for the first bill.

[74] (1904) 2 CLR 78.

[75] (1904) 4 SR (NSW) 327, 331–332.

[76] (1904) 2 CLR 78, 87. See also *Chomley v. Watson* [1907] VLR 502.

[77] *E Hulton & Co. v. Jones* [1910] AC 20.

[78] Note that this is unlikely to have been true: P. Mitchell, 'Artemus Jones and the Press Club' (1999) 20 *JLH* 64.

needed for why the judges of Empire sometimes felt angry that they were not considered as good as their British counterparts a comparison between Griffith CJ's judgment in *Godhard* and Lord Loreburn's speech in *Hulton* will provide it. But if *Hulton v. Jones* was to be applied in Australia, what exactly did it decide?

The issue arose in *AL Lee v. Wilson and Mackinnon; C Lee v. Wilson and Mackinnon*.[79] The *Lee* cases involved a newspaper report of proceedings of an inquiry held at Pentonville Gaol by a police magistrate involving allegations of corruption against police officers. It was reported that a member of the force, a Detective Lee, had accepted a bribe. The plaintiffs, one a Senior Constable and one a First Constable with the surname Lee, alleged that the words referred to them and were defamatory; the defence was, in effect, that the words were intended to be published of a third police officer called Lee whose name was mentioned at the inquiry.[80] This was rejected by the trial judge who gave judgment for £50 for each plaintiff. The defendants appealed to the Full Court of the Supreme Court of Victoria which unanimously allowed a new trial,[81] it being held by Lowe J that *Hulton* was only authority for the proposition that it was no defence for a defendant to say that 'in his breast' he did not intend to defame the plaintiff. The question was what the words meant considering the relevant surrounding circumstances. One such relevant circumstance was that the words were true of someone other than the plaintiff. Each member of the Full Court rejected an interpretation of *Hulton* that denied any role for intention in reference to the plaintiff. This fortified Lowe J to state that 'he was not able to accept the unqualified dictum of Russell LJ in *Cassidy v. Daily Mirror Newspapers* that 'liability for libel does not depend on the intention of the defamer; but on the fact of defamation'.[82]

An equally thoughtful, albeit opposite, reasoning process led a unanimous High Court to allow an appeal.[83] While Starke J agreed with the Full Court in theory, the role for intention recognised in *Hulton* was theoretical. Russell LJ's statement in *Cassidy* was 'accurate enough for practical purposes but is perhaps open to verbal criticism as a statement of legal principle: the judgment of Farwell LJ [in the Court of Appeal in *Hulton*] left the imputation of intent dependent in some degree upon proof, whereas the rule adopted in the House of Lords is definite and rigid in its terms'.[84] A different approach was taken by Dixon J: once *Hulton* made 'actual disparagement of the plaintiff's reputation'

[79] G. Fricke, *Libels, Lampoons and Litigants: Famous Australian Libel Cases* (Hutchison, 1984) 175–185.

[80] The alternative defence – that the word 'Detective' if erroneous was published without malice and as a result of a bona-fide mistake of the defendant's reporter – does not seem to have been seriously argued and was not commented on by the trial judge: *Argus*, 3 March 1934, 25.

[81] [1934] VLR 198.

[82] Ibid., 208.

[83] (1934) 51 CLR 276.

[84] Ibid., 285. Cf. an Australian commentator who thought liability in situations like *Lee* and *Cassidy* depended on the publisher's fault: R. Martin, 'Defamation – the relation of negligence to liability' (1939) 13 *ALJ* 217.

the gist of defamation, an inevitable consequence was that if more than one plaintiff was referred to in a defamatory statement each had a prima facie cause of action. That this consequence was inevitable was not supported by anything the House of Lord said in *Hulton* but by a judgment of Oliver Wendall Holmes in an American case – in Dixon's words – 'long before' *Hulton v. Jones*.[85] There was no reticence to cite an American jurist in support of his view: if Oliver Wendall Holmes had something of value to say, that could and should inform the Australian contribution to the common law.[86] English judges did not return the compliment. When this issue came before the English courts in *Newstead v. London Express Newspaper Limited* six years later,[87] there was only a bare reference to the existence of the *Lee* case in A.T. Denning's arguments for the plaintiff.

Another area where Australian courts ventured into uncharted waters was the attempt to extend absolute privilege to reports made within the police force. In *Gibbons v. Duffell*, the plaintiffs were three police officers who sued their former police inspector for defamation in respect of defamatory comments he had made to the Metropolitan Police Commissioner as part of a request they had made for a transfer away from the defendant's station. The report was extremely negative, including against the plaintiff allegations of untruthfulness and lack of discipline and that he was part of a conspiracy to cause annoyance to their superior officers. The nature of the report suggests considerable hostility to the plaintiffs, conduct which lead the Police Association to support the actions.[88] The trial was suspended by consent for the Full Court of the Supreme Court of New South Wales to consider whether a report of the kind made by the defendant to the Metropolitan Superintendent of Police attracted absolute privilege.[89] Outside of proceedings in Parliament, there had been very few examples of common law absolute privilege recognised by the courts and those that were generally dealt with communications between or to high-ranking government officials.[90] There was one authority – *Dawkins v. Lord Paulet*[91] – where absolute privilege was granted to a report made by a general to an adjutant-general to be put before the Commander-in-Chief of the British Army and a leading defamation text used this as authority for the proposition that no action in defamation lay for

---

[85] Ibid., 290–291. The case is *Hanson v. Globe Newspaper Co.* (1893) 159 Mass 293.

[86] Apart from Dixon J, a different judgment of Holmes J (this time in the United States Supreme Court: *Peck v. Tribune Co* (1908) 214 US 189) was also cited in Evatt and McTiernan's joint judgment: (1934) 51 CLR 276, 298.

[87] [1940] 1 KB 377.

[88] *Barrier Mining* (Broken Hill), 2 October 1930, 2. It may also explain why absolute as opposed to qualified privilege needed to be argued (as malice would have excluded a qualified privilege defence).

[89] (1932) 32 SR (NSW) 31.

[90] *Chatterton v. The Secretary of State for India* [1895] 2 QB 189; *Isaacs and Sons v. Cook* [1925] 2 KB 391.

[91] (1869) LR 5 QB 94.

reports in the course of military of naval duty.[92] No member of the Full Court accepted this statement but they did accept the widest rationale for the privilege in *Dawkins v. Lord Paulet*: that it was in the public interest that reports made by one person in the army or navy to another with reference to government or discipline should be absolutely privileged, the public interest lying in the importance of the armed forces to the preservation of the State. The Full Court saw an analogy: 'the police force in NSW is a State force organised on a semi-military basis for preservation of the safety of the State from internal enemies, as the army and navy are for its preservation from external enemies.'[93] Hence the report was the subject of absolute privilege: abuse by an individual officer was a matter for internal police rules and not the law of defamation. Harvey CJ's comments were made in the midst of a parlous political situation of New South Wales where the state Lang Labor Government was in conflict with Scullin's Federal Labor Government over the response to the Great Depression.[94]

Shortly after arguments closed in the appeal to the High Court, Lang was dismissed by Governor Philip Game and by the time the judgments were handed down the subsequent election had seen Lang defeated and a conservative premier elected. The plaintiff's appeal was unanimously allowed by the High Court.[95] None were impressed with the analogy of the police and armed services: in the words of Gavin Duffy CJ, Rich and Dixon JJ, it was unsafe.[96] Police discipline could survive an investigation of the motives by which a police officer was actuated in detracting from the character of a subordinate and arguments that police efficiency might be impaired were not found persuasive. In the absence of legislative intervention supporting the efficiency argument there was no warrant for extending the common law to provide this level of protection. Evatt J too was concerned with the military analogy: the police were 'seldom engaged in operations of a military character'. While recognising the importance of their principal duty in fighting crime, they did much other routine work – such as registering dogs – that was 'not different in kind' from that done by many of the departments of the Executive Government.[97]

Apart from the immediate political context, debate over the appropriate defamation liability of the police in carrying out their functions remained live throughout the 1930s. A major scandal involving police who allegedly 'set-up' victims of SP (starting price) betting offences in the early 1930s resulted in two internal police enquiries and two Royal Commissions and led to a number of defamation actions against the investigating officer and the media outlets

---

[92] H. Fraser, *Principles and Practice of the Law of Libel and Slander*, 3rd edn (Butterworths, 1901) 168. While the Supreme Court library did have one later edition of Fraser 6th edn (1925) it may have omitted this discussion as a new editor was responsible for this edition.

[93] (1932) 32 SR (NSW) 31, 39.

[94] F. Cain, *Jack Lang and the Great Depression* (Scholarly Publishing, 2005).

[95] (1932) 47 CLR 520.

[96] Ibid., 527.

[97] Ibid., 533.

that published and commented on the findings. The details are unnecessary for present purposes[98] but in one of the appeals to the Full Court of the Supreme Court of New South Wales, Jordan CJ, with the concurrence of the other members of the court, expressed his concern over the position of police officers who had to make reports about the conduct of others.[99] Ordinary citizens rarely were under any obligation to make statements or express opinions on whether a person had been guilty of misconduct. Police who had to do this performed their duty 'at the risk of financial ruin'.[100] Jordan CJ's judgment reveals considerable sympathy towards police and considerable scepticism towards witnesses in police investigations. In his view, if a police officer made an adverse finding in a report, all it took for a case to be left to the jury was for one of the informants to go into the witness box and deny he gave some or all the information. Similarly, if a person charged with a crime made a confession to the policeman who arrested him and later denied it, the communication by the policeman to his superior might subject him to liability. The reason was that in both of these situations the evidence of the informant or the person charged would be evidence of malice and the 'policeman's fate' depended on the jury's view of the evidence.[101] The problem, as Jordan CJ saw it, was that the privilege was only qualified and not absolute. He concluded:

> The question whether such a state of things can be regarded as satisfactory is one of public policy as to which it would not be proper for this Court to make any recommendation or to offer any advice. We think it desirable, however, to draw attention to the matter in order that the Legislature may realise what the position is, and may take action if it should think that any change is necessary.[102]

Jordan CJ can be accused of false modesty: the view of the court was clear and the suggestion that the court should not offer any advice to the legislature, a very formal approach to the separation of powers, seems incongruous in light

---

[98] In brief, there was an initial internal police enquiry exonerating the accused officers in 1934 carried out by an Inspector Fergusson. A Royal Commission in 1936 was highly critical of Fergusson's initial report and Fergusson was directed to review his initial findings. He did so and maintained his original finding was proper. A further reference was made to the same Royal Commissioner to examine Fergusson's conduct and in the course of that enquiry Fergusson admitted that he thought his initial findings were incorrect. One of the police officers involved in the initial prosecution sued the *Truth* newspaper for defamation for its report of the findings of the 1936 Royal Commission (*Bailey v. Truth and Sportsman Limited* (1938) 60 CLR 700) and the original complainant, whose evidence was disbelieved in the two internal police enquiries, sued Fergusson for the defamatory statements in the reports. He was successful at a jury trial but a new trial was ordered by the Full Court (*Mowlds v. Ferguson* (1940) 40 SR (NSW) 311), leave to appeal being refused by the High Court. At the second trial the plaintiff succeeded again but was awarded only one farthing damages. He appealed to the Full Court on the basis that one communication made by Fergusson held to be covered by qualified privilege was not but this appeal, and his subsequent appeal to the High Court (*Mowlds v. Ferguson* (1940) 64 CLR 206), was rejected.

[99] *Mowlds v. Ferguson* (1940) 40 SR (NSW) 311.

[100] Ibid., 335.

[101] Ibid., 335–336.

[102] Ibid., 336.

of the preceding argument. More broadly, however, underlying the judgment is a particular view of the role of the police in civil society and where the balance between wider welfare considerations and individual reputation should be drawn. But the vexed history behind *Mowlds v. Fergusson* suggests why the legislature did not take up the Full Court's suggestion: there were clearly corrupt policeman as well as corrupt informants and accused. As with most of the issues in this chapter, these issues were not unique to Australia but their very existence required judicial decisions that were at least sensitive to local context even if that local context, as might be expected, sent no clear signal in this contested area of public policy.

Conclusion

The law of defamation requires the balance between interests in free speech and interests in reputation to be drawn in an almost infinite variety of factual situations. The aim of this chapter has been to provide a sample of the situations that allowed Australian courts at all levels to interact with the formal legal rules applying to this tort. Sometimes this required an engagement with something explicitly at the core of the common law, such as whether something was libel or slander. At other times, the legal rule was clear but was so broad that new law was made in applying the general rule to a concrete fact situation. And occasionally it required courts to determine just how much statutory innovation was to be constrained by deference to the older common law rules.

In all these situations, Australian judges could not simply follow 'existing law': in a very real sense they had to make it. That they did so within the confines of the common law tradition and Australia's historic and contemporary links to Great Britain should not detract from the originality of their work. If their contributions were not always valued, or even noticed, by English judges, that was not because they had nothing to say.

4

Politics, Politicians, the Press and the Law of Defamation

From the earliest times, Australian politics and politicians have been leading subjects in defamation law. Reported actions for political libel were rare in England during the period of this study[1] but important questions on defamatory meaning, fair comment and qualified privilege arose for discussion by Australian courts amidst a complex and at times poisonous political environment. Sometimes Australian courts had to make decisions on novel or at least unanswered legal questions, such as whether a fair comment could be founded on facts set out in a report of parliamentary proceedings that itself was the subject of absolute privilege. More often, established legal principles had to be applied in the Australian context. Questions involving defamatory meaning, group defamation, whether politics was a trade and profession, and the limits of qualified privilege when discussing or reporting political matters all feature in the case law of this period. By answering these questions, the courts set the boundaries on the limits of political discourse imposed by the law of defamation and hence played an important role in defining acceptable conduct in Australian political society.

Many of the legal questions were raised in the context of reports and comments by the popular press. The second part of the chapter considers how the media fared, both in its reporting of political events and on wider matters of public interest, when it came before the courts. Two important but conflicting attitudes underlie judicial approaches to the media in defamation cases in the period of this study. The first was the fact that the press played a pivotal role in disseminating information, including political information to the general public.[2] While courts consistently denied that the press occupied any special position in defamation actions, there is evidence that juries may have been more sympathetic. Operating against any argument for a special place, however, was the rise of the mass media – the gutter press – which offended judicial notions

---

[1] But such actions existed even if they did not make it to the law reports: see the *Telegraph* (Brisbane), 2 September 1911, 6 on the spate of actions arising out of the 1909 British general election.

[2] A. Atkinson, *The Europeans in Australia. Vol. 2: Democracy* (Oxford University Press, 2004) 244–247.

of propriety and taste. As Mitchell has noted in the English context, there was considerable scepticism and hostility demonstrated towards the new mass media that emerged with the introduction of the tabloid press.

Context and Meaning in the Political World

There were many significant political controversies in Australia throughout the period of this study but none were greater than the division over conscription. The law of libel was the battleground for many of these intractable political problems and in deciding these cases Australian courts faced some difficult issues relating to the basic elements of the cause of action. Some of the cases involved internecine strife that arose out of the bitter dispute and subsequent split of the Labor Party over the attempted introduction of conscription in Australia during the First World War. The detail is complex and unnecessary for present purposes but in brief the Federal Prime Minister, W.M. Hughes, after a trip to Britain in 1916, became convinced that conscription was necessary in Australia and he declared that a referendum would be held to gain support for its introduction. The difficulty for Hughes, a Labor Prime Minister who had convinced a bare majority of federal parliamentary Labor members to support him in holding a referendum, was that this view was not the view of the labour movement in Australia.[3] Hughes pressed on with a referendum which was held in October 1916 and, after a bitterly fought campaign, was narrowly defeated. In November 1916, at the first meeting of the Federal Labor Caucus after the referendum, Hughes walked out of the party room taking twenty-five members with him. Similar fissures appeared in other state Labor governments in the wake of the referendum, including in New South Wales where the former Labor Premier William Holman was expelled from the party in November 1916. Shortly afterwards, a strike by coal miners took place in Newcastle, which forced Hughes – now head of a coalition non-Labor government – to make significant concessions to the miners to end the strike.[4]

The plaintiffs in *Doyle v. McIntosh; Mutch v. McIntosh*[5] were important players in this high drama. Doyle was the President, and Mutch a member of the executive of the New South Wales Political Labour League (PLL), the organisational arm of the Labor Party in New South Wales. In November 1916, the *Sunday Times*, owned by Hugh McIntosh, theatre entrepreneur and long-time friend of William Holman, now New South Wales Premier in a coalition government, published a scathing attack on the Political Labour League, 'as swayed

---

[3] V.G. Childe, *How Labour Governs: A Study of Workers' Representation in Australia* (Labour Publishing Co. Ltd, 1923) 33.

[4] Apart from the political controversy, Hughes' actions were criticised by Henry Bourne Higgins, High Court justice and sole judge of the Federal Court of Conciliation and Arbitration, as degrading the authority of the court: H.B. Higgins, 'A new province for law and order II' (1919) 32 *Harv L Rev* 189, 206–207.

[5] (1917) 17 SR (NSW) 402.

and directed by Doyle, Mutch & Co.' Most of the article was clearly comment (if vitriolic) but it also included the following: 'And they have, to make the crisis of their Party's fate end in disaster more irretrievably, engineered a great and calamitous strike at a time when industrial peace is essential to the integrity of the Empire as it has never been essential before.' Doyle and Mutch brought actions in defamation, claiming the allegation they had 'engineered a great and calamitous strike' was defamatory. The main arguments were in Doyle's case. The defence vacillated between truth and fair comment. The fact that no active steps had been taken to stop the strike was stressed because 'was it not the duty of the leading body of the labour movement to have done all it could to stop a strike which was paralysing industry at a time when such a condition of things was most dangerous to the solidarity of the Empire and the welfare of Australia?' The plaintiffs had been '*criticised merely for their public actions* as leaders of the PLL?' (italics in original).[6] Apart from conveying a sense that the plaintiffs got what they deserved for doing what they did, it is hard to discern to what defences the arguments were specifically addressed.

Cullen CJ's brief summing up did not add clarity.[7] After saying that all political prepossessions must be disregarded, he stated that the question was whether the article went further than ordinary comment on the acts of a public man in regard to public affairs. What the jury had to find for this defence to be established was not explained. Cullen CJ noted that Doyle had denied the serious charge of instigating a coal strike and that the defendant had not gone into the box to contradict him. However, counsel for the defendant had contended that such an interpretation (that he did not engineer a strike) was not justified. As the plaintiff had given uncontradicted evidence that this had not happened it is hard to see what else plaintiff's counsel needed to do to contradict any allegation that this was true. Cullen CJ then turned to damages where he noted that despite the defendant's denial that he had engineered the strike 'neither he nor the association, apparently, took any steps to stem a tide which would bring about the calamity of a strike at a time when the protection of the Empire from its enemies depended on the supply of coal'. Perhaps this was relevant to damages as going to the plaintiff's reputation although it is hard to see this as politically neutral. The jury retired for about fifteen minutes and returned a verdict in favour of the defendants. Mutch's case was tried immediately afterwards, and the same arguments were raised. The jury 'had scarcely entered the jury room'[8] when the Chief Justice was advised they had reached a verdict in the defendant's favour.

The plaintiffs appealed to the Full Court. For whatever reason, the ambiguity of the arguments at trial was left behind and the issue morphed into whether

---

[6] *Evening News* (Sydney), 7 June 1917, 5.
[7] Details are taken from *Evening News*, 7 June 1917, 5; *SMH*, 8 June 1917, 4.
[8] *Newcastle Morning Herald and Miner's Advocate*, 8 June 1917, 4. The *Barrier Miner*, 8 June 1917, 1, reported the jury recessed for less than a minute.

the expression 'engineered a calamitous strike' was necessarily defamatory.[9] Pring J held that it was: 'engineer' could have no other meaning than its popular one of promoting or instigating an act[10] and Gordon J agreed.[11] Despite the high threshold to overcome to overturn a jury verdict in a libel case, a new trial was ordered.[12] Dissenting, Sly J found that the words could bear an innocent meaning. As 'engineered' primarily meant something to do with an engine or engineer, the defamatory meaning had to be a secondary meaning. Sly J's reasoning skipped between defamatory meaning and fair comment:

> Why should not an individual or newspaper comment upon that action of a man in the public position of Mr Doyle? And if he comments upon it is it not libellous unless there is some defamatory meaning in the article. But surely when a man is in that position fair criticism of his conduct is not libellous because his actions are subject to all free comments on the part of newspapers without being libellous at all.[13]

While this argument – that because this was comment there could be no defamatory meaning – appears odd to modern readers, Sly J's judgment may reflect older views that the fair comment defence operated by rebutting the presumption of malice that would be inferred from a defamatory statement.[14] By 1917, this was already an outdated view[15] but it was preserved in part by New South Wales pleading practice and this may explain the form of argument at trial and the judgment of Sly J.[16]

Whatever the legal basis for Cullen CJ's summing up and Sly J's judgment, their distaste for the plaintiffs' actions is palpable. Sly J noted that if a labour league like the PLL 'did not act in the interests of the State' it could be legitimately criticised. It is impossible to divorce the legal issues in the case from the wider political context involving the split in Labor ranks and the conscription debate. At trial, Doyle revealed in cross-examination that he had been an

---

[9] The defendant pleaded 'not guilty' (the general issue) and such a plea 'admitted the falsity of the allegations complained of, whilst denying their defamatory character': *Goldsborough v. John Fairfax and Sons Ltd* (1934) 34 SR (NSW) 524, 534 (Jordan CJ). As defamatory meaning was in issue it could clearly be raised on appeal.

[10] (1917) 17 SR (NSW) 402, 406–407.

[11] Ibid., 412 (Gordon J).

[12] The actions later settled: *Sunday Times*, 16 September 1917, 3.

[13] (1917) 17 SR (NSW) 402, 408.

[14] Cf. Gordon J who clearly attached some significance to a finding that the statement was fact and not comment: (1917) 17 SR (NSW) 402, 412.

[15] On the confusion surrounding the nature of the fair comment defence see P. Mitchell, *The Making of the Modern Law of Defamation* (Hart Publishing, 2004) ch. 8. Cf. the comments in a contemporary New South Wales hand-book (E. Tebbutt, *The Statute Law Relating to Defamation and Newspapers e.t.c.* (The Law Book Company of Australasia Ltd, 1909) 21), that while privilege was a defence, 'fair comment implies that no actionability exists'.

[16] The practice of the New South Wales Supreme Court, maligned by Jordan CJ but recognised by the Privy Council, was that fair comment could be raised under the general issue: *Goldsborough v. John Fairfax and Sons Ltd* (1934) SR NSW 524, 535. But in the same case Jordan CJ also affirmed that truth and public benefit needed to be specially pleaded (535).

active opponent of conscription although newspaper sources differ on whether he called those who voted in favour of conscription 'renegades, derelicts and traitors'.[17] To many the actions of Doyle and Mutch were unpatriotic at best and seditious at worst. And, in truth, there was much that was unseemly about the politics of the left in New South Wales in 1917. During the trial, Doyle revealed that after his election to the Legislative Assembly in March 1917, he had indirectly contacted the Premier, William Holman, to see if he could be given a seat in the Upper House. He also said that McIntosh – the publisher of the *Sunday Times* – had approached him with a suggestion that if £1000 could be given to the Parliamentary Labor Party (led by Holman) from the Eight-Hours Committee this would facilitate his appointment and he (Doyle) said the law had to be observed and he would have to consult his committee. In his summing up, Cullen CJ expressed his astonishment that persons should coolly discuss what amounted to nothing less than the purchase of a seat in the legislature and that they did not think there was anything to be ashamed of in that conduct.[18] It is impossible to know whether Cullen's surprise was entirely genuine or calculated to discredit Doyle in the trial but it does demonstrate the high political intrigue and skulduggery of the period. In that setting it is hardly surprising that the law of defamation should find it difficult to satisfactorily mediate these differences.[19]

Conscription was also important in a case involving the ambiguous law that surrounded group defamation. If a defamatory statement was made about a group, could any individual member of the group not specifically named argue nonetheless that the publication referred to him or her and sue in defamation? The issue was ostensibly raised in *Canavan v. Syme & Co.*, the defendant being the publisher of *The Age* newspaper in Melbourne. In December 1917, there were a large number of pro- and anti-conscription meetings in Melbourne in the lead-up to the second conscription referendum on 20 December. The action arose out of *The Age's* report of two of these meetings. In the first, a pro-conscription meeting (described as a 'loyalist' meeting) in Aspendale, on the outskirts of Melbourne, one speaker, Sergeant Wallish Distinguished Conduct Medal (DCM), was reported as saying that the Returned Soldiers No-Conscription League was only about 100 strong, and these individuals had been sent back to Australia as undesirables.[20] In the second, the newspaper reported an anti-conscription meeting held in South Melbourne. One speaker had 'indignantly refuted' an allegation that the returned soldiers belonging to the

---

[17] *SMH*, 8 June 1917, 4, has Doyle saying that he remembered saying this but that he did not individualise and the remarks were general. *Evening News*, 7 June 1917, 5, records Doyle as denying that he described his opponents in this way.

[18] *SMH*, 8 June 1917, 4.

[19] In August, the defendant sought unsuccessfully leave from the Full Court to appeal to the Privy Council ((1917) 17 SR (NSW) 402, 412–418). The actions were settled the following month: *The Sun (Sydney)*, 14 September 1917, 4.

[20] *Age*, 12 December 1917, 10.

anti-conscription movement had been returned on disciplinary charges where-upon a member of audience shouted 'So they were.'[21] The plaintiff, Canavan, was a returned serviceman who was wounded at Gallipoli and lost a leg, and he alleged he was a member of the Returned Soldiers No-Conscription League and that the articles referred to him and were defamatory.[22] At the trial before the County Court in February 1918, it became clear that Canavan's action was the equivalent of a 'test' case. At the close of the arguments, Canavan's counsel advised the court that there was another member of the League suing in respect of these publications and that both parties had agreed to accept the result in Canavan's case as applying to this case as well.[23] Two issues were argued in defence: that the publications were not defamatory, and that they did not refer to the plaintiff. The jury found in favour of the defendants on both publications, the first because it did not refer to the plaintiff and the second on both issues raised by the defence. After the verdict, Canavan made an application for a new trial before the trial judge and was successful in respect of the first article, Judge Wasley holding as a matter of law that it did refer to the plaintiff.[24]

The Age appealed to the Full Court of the Supreme Court of Victoria where the appeal was dismissed by a 2-1 majority. The defendant's argument is not entirely clear, as its primary aim was to say the jury's verdict was reasonably open to it, but one strand was that the membership of the League was, according to the evidence, 400–1000 and that the reference to 100 should be construed as a reference to 100 out of a membership of 400–1000 hence the plaintiff was not sufficiently identified. This convinced the avid pro-conscriptionist Irvine CJ,[25] dissenting, but Cussen and Hood JJ found for Canavan. Hood J pointed out that the number of members of the League was irrelevant: the only fair meaning of the statement was that it applied to all individuals in the League and there was nothing on the face of the article to limit the statement or to make it apply to the bulk only, or to show any exaggeration or mistake.[26] In a similar vein, Cussen J explained why the mistake as to the number was irrel-evant: 'If the paragraph could be read to mean that only one hundred out of a much larger number of members were sent back as undesirables defendants

---

[21] *Age*, 13 December 1917, 8.

[22] *Argus*, 26 February 1918, 6.

[23] *The Age's* counsel, summing up to the jury, said it was 'within the jury's province to treat Canavan's suit as a pioneer in a campaign of libel actions to be brought by members of the league, for there was already another suit, and Bott, the secretary, had said in the witness box that he did not know whether he would bring an action and was waiting the upshot of this case to see what he would do': *Age*, 27 February 1918, 8.

[24] See also *Gibbs v. Daily Examiner*, *Daily Examiner* (Grafton), 25 September 1918, 2, where the plaintiff alleged he was defamed by a reference to the president of the Returned Soldiers' Anti-Conscription League. The jury found against him.

[25] After a long career in state and federal politics he was appointed Chief Justice a month before the trial: J.M. Bennett and A.G. Smith, 'Sir William Irvine', *Australian Dictionary of Biography*, Vol. 9 (1983).

[26] [1918] VLR 540, 546–547.

should succeed. But I do not think it capable of such meaning.'[27] A statement referring to a group could be defamatory of individual members of the group, a proposition Cussen J supported by reference to Pollock's notes on his Indian Civil Wrongs Bill.

Undeterred, *The Age* appealed to the High Court where the judges unanimously upheld the appeal. Only two reasoned judgments were given. Both relied on introducing matters extrinsic to the publication to support their conclusions. It is not easy to follow their reasoning. Barton J thought it was open to the jury to find that Sergeant Wallish 'was thinking of a number of men who had been sent back to Australia as undesirables; that he was saying that there were about 100 of them, and that they were members of the so-called league, whatever that body (which seems to have been shadowily described in evidence) might be. If that were so, then the question would be at large – which were the hundred men that had been sent back?'[28] This argument is seriously flawed. Since *E Hulton v. Jones*[29] the intention of Sergeant Wallish was irrelevant. The question, as Cussen J noted in the Full Court, was who was hit, not who was targeted. Moreover, Barton J completely reversed the order of the words: Wallish (as reported) did not say there were about 100 undesirables and that they were members of the League: he said there was a League of around 100 members and that these were sent back to Australia as undesirables. It was surely impermissible to redraft the defamatory statement in this way so that it could raise the problem of group defamation (that not every member of the class would fall within the defamatory imputation). Isaacs J reached the same result by an equally dubious method. Because the plaintiff had referred to the League as having one thousand members, and this was reported in *The Age* (on 4 December), the public 'had been told' that the League consisted of 1000 members and that readers of the 12 December report would have knowledge of the earlier article. More remarkably, the jury were, apparently, able to note that the words were said by Sergeant Wallish, a man in military service, and that when he said that 100 men had been sent back as undesirables he was more likely to know of 100 being sent back than to know the numbers of members in the League. The jury might conclude that Wallish was wrong in thinking that 100 constituted the whole league, and therefore that he did not mean by the words 'these individuals' to include any but about 100.[30] Put simply, in other words, the jury could simply disbelief everything Wallish had said! On the most generation interpretation, Isaacs J engaged in verbal gymnastics to interpret the statement in a way favourable to the defendant.

It would be too simplistic to say that those judges in favour of dismissing the case were simply showing their dislike of the anti-conscription movement.

---

[27] Ibid., 548–549.
[28] Ibid., 552–553.
[29] [1910] AC 20.
[30] [1918] VLR 540, 555.

A jury verdict always required appellate judges to respect the constitutional right, as Barton and Isaacs JJ put it, to decide facts when the law allocated that function to the jury. But was there a more convincing legal argument that the newspaper could have run? What *The Age* would have liked to have argued was that there was qualified privilege attached to the fair and accurate reporting of public events but there were two problems with this. First, there had been no such privilege recognised at common law or by statute in Victoria[31] so this would have required the recognition of a new category. An equally intractable problem was that even if such a privilege had been recognised it may not have been applicable. In evidence at the trial, Wallish himself said that 95 per cent had been returned as undesirables; another witness had him saying 90 per cent.[32] This important factual inaccuracy meant that while the matter was clearly one of public interest, it may not have been a fair and accurate report. Counsel for *The Age* was acutely aware of this problem and tried to avoid it by framing the issue as going to damages: a '"Defendants" Notice of Facts in Mitigation of Damages' was tendered, noting that (1) the public was 'greatly interested' in all matters relating to the referendum and conscription; (2) the plaintiff was unknown to the defendant; and (3) the words complained of were a true and accurate report of what the speakers had said at the meeting.[33] The context in which the publication was made was clearly relevant to damages but here too counsel had nailed his colours to the mask of an accurate report. When the discrepancy between the report and the witnesses as to the correct percentage became apparent, counsel was forced to argue, rather desperately, that this meant that 'the chances were "The Age" reporter correctly reported what Wallish did say' and that the jury 'had to consider whether the report was inaccurate'.[34] In truth, what *The Age* wanted to argue was that although it had made an error, it was a small error and it should not be punished for it. This was made clear in counsel's summing up to the jury:

> If the jury gave broad consideration to the case they would find that all 'The Age' had been doing was the performing of a public duty in reporting on a campaign of great public interest and they would agree that language ought not to be strained in order to enable plaintiff to succeed in his action for libel.[35]

As a matter of law, any alleged public benefit of the defendant's conduct was irrelevant to the reference to the plaintiff question; it went to damages. But

[31] As it had in England: Law of Libel Amendment Act 1888 (UK) s. 4. The position varied in Australian jurisdictions but during the period of this study no such privilege was recognised in New South Wales or Victoria, a matter that attracted pleas for reform: see for example *SMH*, 21 October 1907, 6, and the comments of Pring J noted in *Newcastle Morning Herald and Miners' Advocate*, 1 May 1913, 4.

[32] *Age*, 26 February 1918, 6. A local paper, *Seaside News*, 15 December 1917, 4, reported him as saying 95 per cent.

[33] NAA, A10074, 1918/17, *David Syme v. Canavan*.

[34] *Age*, 26 February 1918, 6.

[35] Ibid., 8.

in cross-examining the secretary of the League, counsel semi-jocularly commented that if Canavan won an award for £2000 it 'was going to cost us a couple of million'.[36] This brought home to the jury the practical consequences of finding for the plaintiff. By stating that *The Age* had given the League a 'fair deal' even though it was editorially in favour of conscription,[37] counsel was able to play on the inherent unfairness the severe punishment a verdict in favour of the plaintiff would have.

There is little doubt that the conscription context affected perceptions about what would be fair treatment of *The Age* for its mistake[38] and, as the law stood, this could only be mediated through the law on group defamation. Although not frequently cited, *Canavan* is still referred to as an authority on this topic. But perhaps its real legal significance lies not so much in the strained attempts to deny liability through the application of the rules on group defamation as in its exposure of the limits of the defence of qualified privilege at that time.

The Evils of Socialism

Perhaps the most overtly political defamation case in the period of this study is *Slatyer v. Daily Telegraph*.[39] Hampton Slatyer[40] was an independent candidate for the then Federal electorate of Parkes based in Sydney suburbs. He had stood in the 1903 federal election and was described as an Independent Free Trader. In that election he received 90 votes out of 21,110 formal votes and ran last of the five candidates. Slatyer was also a candidate for the 1906 election.[41] In the run-up to the election, the *Daily Telegraph* newspaper took a strong anti-socialist line (primarily against the Labor Party). Slatyer declared himself an independent candidate but the *Daily Telegraph* in an article leading up to the election referred to the 'Socialistic candidate' polling 90 votes in the last election. As the *Daily Telegraph* had in a series of contemporaneous articles been hostile to socialism, Slatyer sued, arguing that the reference to him as a socialist was defamatory.

---

[36] Ibid., 6. In the *Bendigo Advertiser*, 26 February 1918, 3, and *Ballarat Star*, 26 February 1918, 4, he was reported as saying they 'may have to go into liquidation over this'.

[37] Counsel was guilty of some hyperbole here: although there was some reporting of the League's manifesto, the secretary of the League stated it was 'reduced a great deal' whereas other papers published it in full, and other papers report him as saying *The Age* gave the manifesto 'a par' score: *Age*, 26 February 1918, 6, *Bendigo Advertiser*, 26 February 1918, 3, and *Ballarat Star*, 26 February 1918, 4.

[38] See the headline in the *Geelong Advertiser* reporting the trial: 'Two "no" returned soldiers sue The 'Age' for libel – for reporting that some Antis in Khakis were undesirables!': *Geelong Advertiser*, February 26 1981, 5.

[39] (1907) 7 SR (NSW) 488.

[40] Slatyer had a long history of political activism. He had been a member of the Australian Natives' Association and had been a candidate previously in local council and state elections.

[41] He did considerably better than in 1903, primarily because there were only two candidates. He received 21.8 per cent of the vote, losing to Bruce Smith, who held the seat from federation until 1919.

Slatyer's claim succeeded at first instance but failed before the Full Court of the Supreme Court of New South Wales and before the High Court. It seems there were two distinct claims although it is not clear how far the first – that it was defamatory to be called a 'socialistic' candidate – was argued. In the Full Court Cullen CJ noted that plaintiff's counsel had conceded this was not of itself libellous.[42] Street J agreed, noting that any misdescription of a person's political allegiance as such (e.g. by calling a Protectionist a Free Trader and vice versa) may cause damage but could not lower the character or reputation of the person in the eyes of reasonable and right-thinking men.[43] Slatyer's second argument was more complex. Because of the vitriolic criticism of socialists contained in the *Daily Telegraph's* columns – and he placed 12 of these in evidence – he argued that the right-thinking person would think less of him for being a socialist. This argument was rejected in the Full Court for reasoning that is not easy to follow but seems to be as follows. As all or at least most of the articles introduced in evidenced were simply fair comment on a matter of public interest, they could not be defamatory of the plaintiff.[44] Somewhat incongruously, there is also the suggestion that if the evidence had indicated the newspaper said that all socialists were in favour of confiscating property, this might be actionable: why this was so was not articulated. But to focus too narrowly on technical defamation law may miss the point. Even if it was not expressed as clearly as it might have been, the gist of the decision is that political comment was not defamatory at all – that right-thinking people should not think less of a person because of their political views or comments on those views. There were two possible limits. The first was that there was no malice in the publication. The absence of malice was stressed by the Cullen CJ[45] and although not mentioned by Street J his reliance on fair comment authorities would suggest a similar limitation. The second was that it must be political comment and not fact. This would explain the possible exception for the confiscation allegation: this was a fact and hence could be defamatory if it referred to the plaintiff (but, presumably, could be proved to be true).

Slatyer appealed to the High Court where his appeal was unanimously rejected.[46] Only Griffith CJ and Isaacs J delivered judgments, both short. Griffith

---

[42] (1907) 7 SR (NSW) 488, 490.

[43] Ibid., 498.

[44] This seems to be the reasoning of Street J. Cullen CJ held both that there was no evidence to support the innuendo and that the articles were 'fair comment upon a system and in no way attack the individual' – both these seem to go to defamatory meaning rather than a defence: [1907] 7 SR NSW 488, 495.

[45] (1907) 7 SR (NSW) 488, 492.

[46] (1908) 6 CLR 1. Slatyer's state of mind is revealed in a handwritten letter to the Registrar of the High Court in October 1908 objecting to the *Daily Telegraph* recovering the £50 he had paid as security for costs for the appeal. Among other claims, he wrote that his claim had not been decided, that the High Court had made an 'error of judgement' and that its judgment of 18 May 'being undecided' should prevent the defendant from accessing the funds: NAA, A10071, 1907, 27.

CJ treated the appeal as one of fact, noting only that he reserved his opinion as to whether it could ever be actionable to impute to a candidate on the eve of an election that he belonged to a party to which he did not in fact belong.[47] But Isaacs J articulated a version of the argument made above:

> But I think that in a community like ours it is impossible to regard epithets of that kind as anything but a mere strong expression of opinion as to the nature of that policy, not as imputing, taken in conjunction with the facts upon which the opinion is based, any moral turpitude to those who favour that opinion.[48]

Viewed in isolation, this seems clearly to relate to political opinions. But either side of this passage the difficulty of the fact/comment distinction is ignored. One of the epithets to which Isaacs J refers is the imputation 'to the whole of the socialistic party the platform of nationalisation'[49] but is this a fact and not a comment? And after this passage Isaacs J considers that an allegation of social-ist's 'stealing property' could be defamatory[50] but does not explain why this political expression was not a comment.

Slatyer is an important decision. The way the case was pleaded required the courts to consider not just the narrow question of whether a political label was defamatory but the much larger question of the boundaries of political criti-cism. If there were flaws in how the judges reached their results, the sentiment was progressive and in favour of free criticism. In terms of defamation law, the basis of the protection – whether it be by depriving a comment of a defamatory meaning or as a separate defence – was fair comment and not privilege (which would have protected statements of fact as well). It is noteworthy that there was no English authority cited dealing with this question: this was an Australian court grappling with what protection the law should give to political speech in Australian society. But if we are to give credit for how the issues were settled in *Slatyer*, we must also recognise its dark side. The freedom of political speech recognised was a freedom to criticise socialists and in the Full Court decision there is ample evidence of suspicion and distaste for socialism (and both Cullen CJ and Street J doubted the plaintiff's statement that he was not a socialist).[51] As an opponent of Bruce Smith, the sitting member in Parkes, Cullen CJ thought a socialist would think he (Slatyer) had a leaning for Communism but would vote for him over an anti-Socialist; Street J thought it was not a surprise that anyone against individualism and in favour of advanced legislation should be declared a socialist.[52] And while recognising that an opponent of socialism would not think less of a supporter in terms of character or reputation, Street J

---

[47] (1908) 6 CLR 1, 7.
[48] Ibid., 8.
[49] Ibid.
[50] Ibid., 9.
[51] Similar views were expressed in the press after the High Court decision: *Brisbane Courier*, 20 May 1908, 4.
[52] (1907) 7 SR (NSW) 488, 495, 497.

thought it would no doubt be a matter of regret to an opponent that the plaintiff 'should advocate such alterations to the social fabric of the State.'[53] There is a real sense that socialism presented a challenge to the established order and it is no surprise to see the right of the conservative *Daily Telegraph* to pour opprobrium on the nascent labour movement protected.

Protection of Political Reputation

While criticism of the substance of a political view might receive protection, as evidenced in *Slatyer*, a different strand of case law was working in the other direction. In *Pratten v. The Labour Daily Ltd*[54] the plaintiff was the Minister for Customs in the Federal Parliament. Shortly after his appointment, the defendant published an article critical of the plaintiff for allegedly repudiating an agreement relating to the Australian Dairy Council. He sued for defamation. The case was run by plaintiff's counsel on the basis that it was defamatory of the plaintiff in both his personal capacity and also in his 'official' capacity. This second charge was based on the idea that it was defamatory to lower someone's reputation in their trade, profession, calling or office. This arm of defamation had taken on special importance in slander where it was an exception to the general rule that special damage needed to be established before it was actionable but it was also actionable as libel. At the end of the trial, Irvine CJ directed the jury that to be defamatory the statement must hold a man up to hatred, ridicule or contempt and the jury by majority found for the defendant. After the jury had retired, Dixon KC, counsel for the plaintiff, argued for a redirection along the lines that if the words imputed impropriety or incompetency as a Minister they could be actionable even if they would not affect his personal reputation. This was opposed by counsel for the defendant, Menzies: in argument only damage to the plaintiff's personal reputation had been contended. Irvine CJ refused to redirect: the trade, calling, profession or office line of cases had not been expanded to a Minister exercising ordinary administrative functions or exercising judgement in administering his office and he would not on his own extend them to where there was no allegation of impropriety or corruption to support the claim.[55]

Pratten appealed to the Full Court where by a 2-1 majority he was successful. Cussen J gave the leading judgment. In his view, there was no difficulty in extending 'trade, office, profession or calling' to a politician. At the very least, the roles of parliamentarian or minister were analogous to the 'offices' with which the early cases in Star Chamber were concerned.[56] Moreover, to exclude politicians from suing for damage to their professional reputation was objectionable; if this was the case then:

---

[53] Ibid., 505.
[54] [1926] VLR 115. See also G. Fricke, *Libels, Lampoons and Litigants: Famous Australian Libel Cases* (Hutchison, 1984) 70–72.
[55] [1926] VLR 115, 117–118.
[56] Ibid., 125–126.

In relation to the public conduct of a member of Parliament or Minister of the Crown (or any other person holding public office), anyone, provided that there is no reflection on personal character, may, without any legal liability, make mis-statements of fact relating to such public conduct even though they show incompetence or unfitness in such office, and may also make comments thereon for the purpose of supporting a conclusion that there is general incompetence or unfitness in such office. If we laid down any such rule, there are many who would not be slow to take advantage of it, and (without suggesting anything worse) to assert and publish misstatements without taking any, or sufficient trouble, to verify them. The statement might be prefaced or accompanied by an assertion that the private character of the person attacked was the highest. We cannot think that any such immunity from liability is necessary on grounds of public policy or otherwise.[57]

Perhaps a modern audience would give greater weight to free speech than is recognised in the judgment but Cussen J was well aware that, even in 1925, concerns might be raised that this extension would unduly affect free speech. Free speech in the political context, however, was protected by the defence of fair comment: the conduct of Ministers and members of Parliament was a matter of public interest and defamatory statements in that context could avoid liability if the defence of fair comment succeeded.[58] The appropriate balance was explained pithily by McArthur J (who agreed with Cussen): 'He is not obliged to put up with criticism which is defamatory and is admittedly not fair comment.'[59]

A similar issue was raised in Queensland in a case that caused great controversy at the time. The plaintiff, Francis Baker, was the Federal member for Griffith, then as now a constituency in suburban Brisbane. In late May 1935 he attended a Labor party fund-raiser for the Cannon Hill branch of the Labor Party. Several days later, the *Courier Mail* published a report of the speech Baker gave at that meeting. The report of the speech suggested, among other things, that Baker was highly critical of the State Labor government in Queensland as to how it handled unemployment and also suggested that the finances of the nation should be centralised under the control of elected parliamentarians. While it was Labor policy to nationalise banks and centralise financial control this was to be done through an independent body and not politicians. Whatever the merits of these arguments, the problem for the *Courier Mail* was that the speech as reported was not the speech that had been given by Baker. Baker sued for defamation, alleging that the publication meant that he was disloyal to the Labor Party, and that he was not a fit and proper person to be a Federal member of the Labor Party or to hold the endorsement of the party.

In many ways, the trial that took place before Macrossin J and a jury was extremely unusual because the *Courier Mail*'s error did not arise as a result of

[57] Ibid., 128–129.
[58] Ibid., 127.
[59] Ibid., 130.

misreporting by an employee but because it published an edited version of the speech that had been delivered to it under cover of a letter purportedly signed by Baker. Much of the trial was taken up with evidence as to who might have signed the covering letter and whether the newspaper believed the report of the speech to be genuine. The detail is not important here but what was revealed was a bitter division between factions of the Labor Party in Griffith and some kind of alleged conspiracy to replace the plaintiff with a state Labor member (with whom Baker had previously worked). It was in this context that the question of whether a politician could practise a profession arose; this was necessary to consider because the statutory definition of defamation (Queensland had a statutory regime) covered situations where a person was likely to be injured 'in their profession or trade'. In neither the trial court nor the Full Court was *Pratten* cited, probably because it had relied on a politician holding an 'office' and the Queensland legislation did not refer to offices, but it is still surprising that some of the general comments were not referred to as the balance between political reputation and free speech was as relevant in Queensland as in the non-Code states. When counsel for the defendant asked for a non-suit on the ground that a politician did not practice a trade or profession, Macrossin J noted that 'queer things' had been held to be professions and that there was a term in common usage 'professional politician'.[60] In summing up to the jury he maintained this view: a public man could be a professional politician and 'trade or occupation' covered a man's occupation, his means of earning a living. It was admitted that Baker's sole source of income at the time was his parliamentary salary. On appeal to the Full Court, although there was criticism of other parts of the trial, this ruling was upheld: as Henchman J put it, the words profession or trade were intended to be all encompassing and the object of the Code must have been to protect the reputation and the means of livelihood of all classes of the community, not of privileged persons only, against unjustified attack by defamatory imputation.[61]

The strict legal ruling – that a professional politician could be defamed in that profession – did not answer the question of how this question was to be judged. Clearly Baker could claim that fellow members of the Labor Party would think less of him but were they the appropriate yardstick? Despite counsel for the defendant suggesting that only 'political fanatics' would find it defamatory,[62] the Full Court upheld the jury's verdict: reasonable fair-minded readers, whether political friends or foes, might think the plaintiff was unstable in character, untrue to his promises and not to be trusted to do in office what was expressed as a candidate.[63]

---

[60] *Courier Mail*, 29 September 1936, 19.
[61] [1937] St R Qd 153, 179.
[62] *Courier Mail*, 1 October 1936, 20.
[63] Ibid.

What is particularly noteworthy about *Baker* is that the party political dimension, present but muted in many of the other cases discussed in this chapter, was never far from the surface. Counsel for the defendant, Alec Douglas McGill KC, had been President of the Country and Progressive National Party between 1925 and 1935 and during his submissions on who was the reasonable fair-minded person Henchman J reminded him that he was 'not an unprejudiced observer of the activities of the Labor party'.[64] When discussing whether the jury might have legitimately rejected the evidence of newspaper staff, Henchman J remarked there was evidence that the *Courier Mail* was a Nationalist paper and that paper might have wanted to have published it for Nationalist purposes.[65] More broadly, the tension between the dirty laundry of the party political process and the judges was evident in the discussion of politics as a profession. In the course of that discussion Henchman J commented:

> Before professional politicians came, members were men of strength, expressing their own views, but now Parliamentarians do not express their own views except on rare occasions. They do what others decide they must do.[66]

He later pointed out that there were a 'number of men living on the game' and that he did not know what they get out of Parliament.[67] This prompted a response from the Speaker of the Legislative Assembly: the first statement was incorrect and the second was undignified and unwarranted and came in bad taste from a judge of the Supreme Court.[68] He pointed out that the office of a member of Parliament was 'quite as honourable' as that of a judge and was 'of at least equal importance to organised society' and that he frequently protected the judges in his capacity as Speaker to ensure their independence. Judges needed to show equal respect to the Legislature, the 'highest tribunal in the State', and any departure from this position of mutual respect 'would be fraught with serious consequences for the community'.[69] The Full Court decided that discretion was the better part of valour: Henchman J issued a statement, with which Webb and Douglas JJ concurred, that the words were said in response to counsels' argument and that he said nothing insulting to the dignity of Parliament or reflecting on the integrity of its members.[70] But there is little doubt that the comments did reflect a distaste for the modern politics of organised parties, something that can only have been reinforced by the revelations in *Baker*.

A different approach to this kind of political criticism was taken by Angas Parsons J in the South Australian case of *Cameron v. Consolidated Press*

---

[64] *Courier Mail*, 19 November 1936, 20.
[65] *Courier Mail*, 20 November 1936, 18. The exchange is interesting: Douglas J interjected that the paper was independent but counsel for the plaintiff, Hart, responded 'Definitely National'.
[66] *Courier Mail*, 19 November 1936, 20.
[67] Ibid.
[68] *Townsville Daily Bulletin*, 23 November 1936, 2.
[69] Ibid.
[70] *Courier Mail*, 21 November 1936, 16.

Limited[71] in 1940. The plaintiff here was Archie Cameron, leader of Federal Country Party and then Minister for Commerce and Minister for the Navy. The defendant, the owner of the *Daily Telegraph* newspaper, published an article relating to the alleged rejection by the Federal Coalition parties (the United Australia Party and the Country Party) of a plan to have Edward Theodore, a high-profile former Labor politician and Federal treasurer, appointed to a Commonwealth position. In the course of an article on the topic it was said:

> How much more is it a comment on the petty-mindedness of the little group of obstructionists which Mr Cameron leads that they should turn their spleen on to a man merely because he has been chosen to do the nation a service it urgently needs by those whose expert knowledge qualifies them to understand best what is required.[72]

Among other imputations, the plaintiff alleged the publication suggested a betrayal of trust as a Minister and a subordination of the national interest to his personal malice making him unfit to be a Minister or member of Parliament. In light of the cases discussed above it might be thought the plaintiff would make some argument about being injured in his trade or calling but none was. Although the plaintiff was a farmer – and Angas Parsons J noted that this was his occupation – it is still surprising that this line of argument was not pursued by plaintiff's counsel. Instead, the argument was that the terms used in the article were of themselves defamatory.

The evidence presented in the case revealed the complex political background in which this question needed to be answered. The suggestion that Theodore[73] – 'Red Ted' Theodore as he was popularly known – be appointed caused uproar in the rank and file of both the United Australia Party and the Country Party.[74] Although disputed, Angas Parsons J found that Cameron had threatened to pull the Country Party from the Coalition if the appointment went ahead. In the judge's words, the political atmosphere was 'charged with electricity'.[75]

The judgment of Angas Parsons J reveals a different approach to political comment to that in *Pratten* and *Baker*. In remarks that did not make it into the authorised reports, he said: 'I confess I am somewhat puzzled by plaintiff's objection to the article. He admits that he calls a spade a spade and it surely

---

[71] [1940] SASR 372.

[72] Ibid., 373.

[73] Apart from Theodore's history in the Labor Party, he was also the Chairman of Directors of Consolidated Press Limited, the company owned by Frank Packer that published the *Daily Telegraph*.

[74] The case excited considerable interest in the Adelaide press: see *News* (Adelaide) 14 November 1940, 7; 15 November 1940, 5; 16 November 1940, 3; 18 November 1940, 5; 19 November 1940, 5; 6 December 1940, 5. See also *Adelaide Advertiser*, 15 November 1940, 15; 16 November 1940, 21; 18 November 1940, 10; 19 November 1940, 9; 20 November 1940, 17; 7 December 1940, 21; *The Mail,* 16 November 1940, 2.

[75] *News* (Adelaide), 6 December 1940, 5.

cannot be said of him he is too squeamish to bear plain words.'[76] As people looked to the Government to govern the nation's affairs 'with the wisdom and energy' the present situation required, the actions of Ministers was watched by the people and press with increasing vigilance. As there was no consensus on what should be done 'it might be expected that criticism as well as approval would be expressed; criticism that might be as devastating as approval might be enthusiastic.'[77]

This sentiment underlay the judgment in the authorised reports. Whether something was defamatory was context-specific, including time, and any change in manners had to be taken into account. 'All this criticism, or abuse, is directed against the political conduct of public men. There is nothing new in the statement that those who oppose a reform are regarded by its advocates as being petty-minded and obstructionists.'[78] Even if 'vent their spleen' could be regarded as importing some malice against Cameron, this was irrelevant as it would not lower the plaintiff in the estimation of right-thinking persons generally: 'whatever its source, hostility would be resented by Theodore's friends and approved by his opponents. Ill-will is no new feature of political life.'[79] But he doubted whether the use of the term did import any malice. Any anger vented by Cameron and his party was political anger. The article did not attack private character or good name; at worst it was an exhibition of bad manners or discourtesy but not an attack on the plaintiff's character.[80]

In many respects, Angas Parson J's judgment is a departure from earlier cases. Defamation actions were not excluded in the political context but the imputations, whether in fact or comment, would need to affect private character. If it did, the defendant would need to prove the truth of the imputation (and in some jurisdictions the public benefit of the publication) or prove that any comment was fair.[81] However, as a matter of law – whether words were capable of bearing a defamatory meaning – the threshold that political criticism had to cross to reach private character was high. In practice, this was a significant extension of the protection given to political criticism as it was irrelevant whether the imputation was one of fact or comment. It would have made no difference to the reasoning if defamation in trade/calling/office had been argued: Angas Parsons J held (very briefly) both that the words were not defamatory of the plaintiff and that the defence of fair comment applied. The overwhelming sense of the judgment, however, is that this kind of political hot-air should be left to the political and not legal arena. This is also evident in the

---

[76] Ibid.

[77] Ibid.

[78] [1940] SASR 372, 378.

[79] Ibid.

[80] Ibid., 379.

[81] For Australian commentary on the uncertainties as to whether a comment imputing evil motives had to be honest and/or honest and reasonable see G.W. Paton, 'Fair comment' (1944) 18 *ALJ* 158, 159–160 and more generally Mitchell, above n 15, 179–182.

slightly earlier case of *Lang v. Willis*[82] in which a majority of the High Court upheld a jury verdict in favour of the defendant Jack Lang for vitriolic criticism made of a political opponent because of a statutory defence that allowed a finding for the defendant where in the circumstances the words spoken were unlikely to cause injury. While *Willis* was affected by the statutory context, the sentiment was similar to *Cameron* and both cases represent the political example of the general common law rule that 'mere' vulgar abuse was not actionable.

Two final comments can be made about damage to political reputation as the subject matter of defamation as discussed in these cases. The first is the varying treatment of the value of political criticism – the free speech interest – in the cases. It features, if at all, only (very) obliquely in *Baker* in the discussion as to what the reasonable person would consider to be defamatory. By contrast, Cussen J's judgment in *Pratten* and Angas Parson J's judgment in *Cameron* address the issue head-on albeit with different emphases. The second point raised by these cases is the dividing line between professional and personal reputation. Looking at *Pratten* and *Baker* today, it seems clear that defamatory imputations that reflected on personal as opposed to professional characteristics of the plaintiffs could have been pleaded. Hence these cases relate to the very small category of cases where only professional political reputation was damaged and have limited practical significance.[83] This should not mask their importance as examples where the competing interests of free speech and defamation law potentially collide, even if these issues were not seen in quite the same way as in modern law. But *Cameron* cannot be treated in this way. Although the distinction between personal and political reputation is recognised, the dividing line is not static but fluid and is determined by the political context itself. In effect, if not strict legal logic, it is a step to the recognition of the special status of political speech in Australia.

Political Speech and Defences in Defamation

As noted above, the effect of judicial decisions in this area was that free speech interests in political discussion was protected through the defence of fair comment. As Napier J said in *Whitford v. Clarke*,[84] a libel action by a member of the South Australian Legislative Council towards the end of the period of this study: 'It must often happen that observations are made upon public men which they know to be undeserved and unjust. Yet they must bear with them, as

---

[82] (1934) 52 CLR 637. For further background see G. Fricke, above n 54, 89–99.
[83] The cases have rarely been cited. In *John Fairfax and Sons Ltd v. Ashton* (1980) 47 FLR 458, words indicating a loss of confidence in a party political leader were held to be capable of bearing a defamatory meaning. The majority appear to have based the decision on damage to personal reputation (competence) while Brennan J based his judgment on damage to trade/profession reputation.
[84] [1939] SASR 434.

a matter of public policy. Freedom to criticise is the best security for the proper discharge of public duties.'[85]

But fair comment had its limits. For a comment to be fair, it had to have a base in true facts. But what if the facts were not true but were published on a privileged occasion? The issue was raised in *Givens v. David Syme & Co.* Givens was the President of the Federal Senate. At the end of 1916, as discussed above, the Australian Labor Party split over the conscription issue and the case arose out of the attempts by the new Nationalist government formed in the wake of the split to improve its position in the Senate (where it did not have a majority) by convincing Labor members of that chamber to change allegiance. On 3 March, 1917, the defendant's newspaper, *The Age*, published a report of a speech made in the Senate by Senator Watson, a New South Wales senator, part of which read:

> It was in the Senate that the storm first broke. After preliminary business had been disposed of, Senator Watson of New South Wales, made a long statement, in which he alleged that he had been approached by the President of the Senate (Senator Givens), the Minister for Defence (Senator Pearce) and the Prime Minister (Mr Hughes), with a view to resignation in return for another position and monetary consideration.[86]

The article was in the form of a short summary (of which the passage above formed part) of a series of Parliamentary speeches in both the Senate and House of Representatives; a much fuller report of the Senate proceedings followed, including the speeches of Senator Watson and Senators Givens and Pearce in reply. The accusations caused a political uproar and as *The Age* put it in an editorial several days later, 'Either Senator Watson has not spoken falsely or he is a reckless slanderer who deserves to be expelled from Parliament and hounded out of public life. His charges must either be fully vindicated or fully disproved without delay.'[87] The political acrimony continued: it was suggested that the resignation of a Tasmanian Senator the day before Watson's speech had been arranged so that a new appointment could be made who would support the government[88] and in reply Hughes charged the Labor Party (with some justification) that the whole issue had been stage-managed.[89] But even on their own admissions there was no doubt that some discussions had taken place about the possibility of Senator Watson changing allegiance[90]; as Hughes put it: 'Well, I say that an attempt has been made – several attempts – to persuade Senator Watson to vote in the way in which his conscience and his convictions lead.'[91] On 6 March 1917 Hughes declared in the House of Representatives that

---

[85] Ibid., 439.

[86] *Age*, 3 March 1917, 10–11.

[87] *Age*, 5 March 1917, 6.

[88] See *Age*, 6 March 1917, 8.

[89] *Age*, 5 March 1917, 6.

[90] Senator Pearce gave details of his role in his Senate reply to Watson's charge: *Age*, 3 March 1917, 10–11.

[91] *Age*, 3 March 1917, 11.

he would be issuing a writ against Watson and 'unless he pleads privilege it will be for him to make out his case.'[92]

In fact, both Hughes and Givens brought action, Hughes against Watson (for a different part of Watson's Senate statement of 3 March) and Givens against *The Age*.[93] Both actions attracted considerable publicity and there were a number of rulings and appeals on procedural matters. Hughes' action never went to trial; after Watson successfully appealed to obtain a ruling that he need not answer interrogatories that might incriminate him,[94] the case was settled in October.[95] But it is the procedural matters in *Givens'* case that were of greater significance for the law of defamation. The pleadings are complex but *The Age* seemed to have pleaded two defences: fair and accurate report of parliamentary pleadings and fair comment. The latter defence was based on a version of the rolled-up plea used when a defendant wanted to plead the defences of both truth and fair comment: that defence stated that so far as the publication related to facts they were true and so far as the publication contained expressions of opinion they were fair comments made in good faith and without malice upon the said facts, which were a matter of public interest. The narrow procedural issues related to striking out parts of the defence and particulars relating to those parts and much of the discussion focussed on whether the publication was capable of being construed as comment. But in answering this question some of the judges had occasion to consider the wider question of whether fair comment could be based, not on statements of fact which were true, but on statements of fact which were privileged. On appeals from Cussen J and Madden CJ on pleading questions,[96] Hood J felt some unease at the idea that fair comment could be based on privileged facts:

> It seems harsh to say that dishonourable motives may be imputed to a man simply on what is stated in Parliament, apart from any acts or words of his own, and apart from any evidence of the truth of the statements made.[97]

The proposition that privileged facts could found a fair comment defence was supported by *Odgers* on *Libel and Slander* and by the landmark English

---

[92] *Age*, 7 March 1917, 9–10.
[93] Without going into detail, Hughes attempted to avoid the parliamentary privilege defence by arguing that the allegations were also made outside Parliament.
[94] *Hughes v. Watson* [1917] VLR 398.
[95] Hughes paid Watson's costs in return for a statement from Watson that he did not intend to say of or impute to the Prime Minister an intention to bribe or corrupt anyone: *Truth* (Melbourne), 13 October 1917, 6. While Hughes had wanted a statement exonerating him from any suggestion Watson believed Hughes was trying to bribe him (*Age*, 29 January 1918, 8) *Truth* reiterated its earlier view that Hughes brought the action to silence discussion of the matter during the 1917 election which was called in part in response to Watson's allegations and was held in May 1917 (which the Nationalists won): it 'served its purpose in gagging the press and platform on the subject of the Senate scandals during the electioneering campaign and it was cheap at the price Hughes paid for it'.
[96] *Givens v. David Syme & Co. (No. 1)* [1917] VLR 418.
[97] Ibid., 436.

decision of *Wason v. Walter*,[98] the case whose primary importance lay in its recognition of qualified privilege for reports of events in Parliament. However, it also upheld a fair comment defence based on the report of events in Parliament but Hood J was troubled by the reasoning on this aspect of the case: it was 'fully' reported but it appeared no evidence was given beyond the fact that the report was accurate. 'Other facts' were admitted and 'the dates were material' but it is clear Hood J could not really see why the fair comment defence was successful. As this was still a preliminary matter he held simply that the authority of the case was enough to let the particulars in question go forward (and he also thought it could ultimately be distinguished).[99] When the case came on for trial before Cussen J, though, some resolution was needed. On fair comment, *Wason v. Walter* was in effect limited to its own facts by Cussen J. That case was primarily concerned with the importance of the privilege point and 'it was not very clear upon what ground the Court decided the minor question of comment'.[100] It was explained by certain admissions of the plaintiff and the remarks of Cockburn J during the argument of plaintiff's counsel. Rather than follow *Wason v. Walter*, Cussen J instead upheld the statement of Holroyd J in *Browne v. McKinley*, a Victorian Supreme Court decision from 1886:[101] if a man chooses to assume that anything said in Parliament is true, and on that assumption defames his neighbour, not by a report of what was said, for that is privileged, but by comments of his own upon it, he does so at his own risk.[102] Cussen J argued:

> No one, I think, suggests, at all events I do not suggest, that a person or a newspaper cannot comment upon what is said in Parliament but, of course, there is a marked distinction between commenting upon what is said in Parliament on the basis of what in fact was said, and commenting on the basis that what is said by every member of Parliament may be taken to be true. In such a case if a defendant relies on the truth of the statements as an answer to an action for defamation, he must be prepared to prove them to be true, either on a plea for justification or as foundation for comment.[103]

There was no sense of defiance in Cussen J's treatment of *Wason v. Walter* but neither was there any lack of self-confidence. *Wason v. Walter* was given the respect warranted of a leading English authority but on balance it should not be followed where there was an alternative, more persuasive authority, even if that authority was from colonial Victoria. Moreover, a rule that allowed character assassination based on what was said in Parliament was unlikely to appeal when the poisonous politics of the Federal Parliament of early 1917 was only

---

[98] (1868) LR 4 QBD 73.
[99] [1917] VLR 418, 436.
[100] *Givens v. David Syme & Co. (No. 2)* [1917] VLR 437, 445.
[101] (1886) 12 VLR 240.
[102] Ibid., 243.
[103] *Givens v. David Syme & Co. (No. 2)* [1917] VLR 437, 445.

too clearly on display. Seen at its least controversial, this is an excellent example of Cussen J contributing to the wider 'common law', the common law of the Empire. A slightly more nationalist perspective might see the deliberate crafting of a rule for Australian conditions that recognised cultural differences from England. But in neither explanation is there any sense of subservience.

Cussen J's comments were given in the course of a jury trial and ultimately the jury gave a verdict in favour of *The Age*.[104] Cussen J's clear statement of the scope of the fair comment defence seems to have been muddied in his address to the jury where he did not advert to the distinction his earlier judgment recognised. The only limit he noted was that the comment had to be reasonable (oral summing up) or fair and honest (written question to jury).[105] The jury struggled with the questions left to them: for example, they found (by a 9-3 majority) that the words were both fact and comment, an option that, with the agreement of both counsel, had not been left to the jury.[106] This lack of understanding is evidenced by the jury's need to add a resolution, in addition to their answers, that the report appearing in *The Age* was a substantially fair and accurate report of the proceedings in the Senate held on 2 March 1917.[107] In the end, the subtleties over the scope of the fair comment defence was thus avoided: the report was the subject of qualified privilege.

But there is another factor that may well have influenced the jury. In the course of defence counsel's (McArthur) address to the jury, plaintiff's counsel (Maxwell) interjected, referring to the 'lying charges' of *The Age* against the plaintiff. McArthur retorted: '*The Age* is merely a scapegoat.' This was correct: when, in the course of this exchange, Maxwell queried whether Givens should have sued Watson, McArthur said no – Watson would plead privilege.[108] When McArthur later included in his summing up a reminder of how valuable newspapers were – which mentioned both the value of comment upon and reporting of Parliamentary speeches – the danger of the newspaper 'carrying the can' for the real culprit was effectively brought home to the jury. The legal niceties of the relationship between privilege and fair comment played little role in this appeal to reach a fair and pragmatic outcome.

Even when the legal niceties were important, not everyone agreed with Cussen J's view of the privilege/fair comment relationship. The matter came up for discussion in the High Court of Australia in *Bailey v. Truth and Sportsman Ltd* in 1938.[109] This involved an 'immoderate and vulgar account' by the

---

[104] Details can found, among other sources, in *Argus*, 17 July 1917, 4; 18 July 1917, 13; 19 July 1917, 5; 20 July 1917, 5.

[105] *Age*, 19 July 1917, 7–8. Public interest was also mentioned as a requirement but this was clearly satisfied on the facts. On the ambiguities surrounding the meaning of 'fair' in fair comment at the time see n 81, above.

[106] *Age*, 20 July 1917, 6; [1917] VLR 437, 448 although in hindsight the question left to them was unclear on this point.

[107] *Age*, 20 July 1917, 6.

[108] *Age*, 19 July 1917, 7–8.

[109] (1938) 60 CLR 700.

defendant's newspaper of the findings of a Royal Commission into police in New South Wales for framing persons for SP (starting-price) betting offences. The plaintiff was one of a number of police officers referred to in the report who sued alleging they had been defamed. One defence was that some of the defamatory imputations were not actionable because they were fair comment on a matter of public interest. As the defendant led no evidence that any of the findings of the Royal Commission were true, fair comment would only be available if the facts as stated in the Royal Commission's report were a sufficient basis in law for the comment. At trial, the judge held they were, and the matter was not raised before the Full Court of the Supreme Court of New South Wales. In the High Court, by majority, Cussen J's view was supported. After citing *Givens*, Dixon J commented:

> It would enlarge greatly the carefully guarded privilege for fair and accurate reports of parliamentary and judicial proceedings if it were allowable to superadd to such a report statements reflecting on individuals actually made by members of parliament, or by witness, counsel and judges, a writer's own comment containing further and perhaps more damaging defamation of the same individuals, notwithstanding that the facts stated or assumed in parliament or in court and by the writer as his basis of comment were quite wrong.[110]

This did not mean that no comment could be made:

> Such difficulties [when fair comment could be a defence] must be solved upon a consideration of the character of the comment in the given case. If the comment is directed to the antecedent state of affairs and is a criticism, moral judgment, or expression of opinion thereon, it will not ordinarily be enough that the member of parliament, witness, counsel, judge or commissioner expressed his belief in that state of facts. But, in discussing public statements, it must often occur that statements are made of a hypothetical or contingent character, that is, made on the avowed assumption that what has been stated is or may be well founded and made in such a way that the hypothesis forms a part of the comment. In such cases, the comment may well be excused as a fair comment upon the debate, report, or judicial statement.[111]

The problem was that, as Starke J pointed out, the very distinction, no matter how expressed, was elusive at best (in truth, an argument assisted by Dixon J's somewhat elliptical prose). Taking a different line, he thought there was much to be said for allowing facts stated as a result of formal investigations commissioned directly or through a legislative act of parliament to be used as the basis for comment. Although this formally allowed for *Givens* to be distinguished – as there the facts were simply stated in debate – the general distinction made by both Cussen and Dixon (and which Starke as junior counsel had argued against in *Givens*) – was problematic:

[110] Ibid., 721–722.
[111] Ibid., 722–723.

[I] may say that the proposition that comment is permissible if introduced by the hypothesis that the facts found by the tribunal may be but are not necessarily true is attractive as an academic theory but not particularly practical. It might not trouble a man accustomed to the use of words such as the fluent journalist who sets the court so many nice problems in the law of libel. But the man struggling with words and yet desiring to comment upon a matter of considerable public importance and interest to him might easily be silenced or mulct in damages.[112]

Neither Dixon nor Starke felt constrained by undue deference to English authority. There was relevant English authority: in *Mangena v. Wright*[113] the Court of Appeal held that parliamentary or judicial statements of facts could be used as the basis of a fair comment defence. The case was not cited or argued in *Givens*, perhaps because it concerned a fact in a published parliamentary paper, although its omission is still surprising and if deliberate suggests great confidence in ignoring analogous English authority. The case was cited in *Bailey* and dealt with at some length by Dixon J: he attempted to distinguish it but suggested, implicitly, that if it did stand for the wider proposition for which it had been cited as authority (in *Salmond*[114] for example) then it was wrong. And, as Cussen J had done before him, *Wason v. Walter* was distinguished as all depended on the type of comment that was made. More generally, the debate as to the correct legal rule was not simply based about views of English authority. The disagreement between Starke and Dixon went to fundamental issues about the balance between free speech and protection of reputation and they argued over the appropriate balance in the Australian context they knew. If they assumed that context was the same as in England, that simply meant that the Australian experience would help develop the common law for the mutual benefit of all parts of the common law world.

Political Self-Defence

Another situation in which the law had long recognised the existence of qualified privilege was where the defendant was acting in the defence of his or her own reputation – in effect, a plea of self-defence. The existence of this privilege was not controversial in England hence not in Australia but on at least one occasion Australian courts were confronted with an unresolved issue in a political context. In *Penton v. Calwell*,[115] a government minister sued a newspaper contributor for defamation. The background to the case it set out below but the gist of the defence was qualified privilege based on self-defence. The response of the newspaper, however, took a particular form. After the defamatory statements had been made, the article continued:

---

[112] Ibid., 717–718.
[113] [1909] 2 KB 958.
[114] W.T.S Stallybrass, *Salmond on Torts*, 8th edn (Stevens and Sons, 1934) 439.
[115] (1945) 70 CLR 219. See Fricke, above n 54, 19–25.

And we invite him to take action against us.

The statement should be worth £10,000 at least – if the Court will give him a verdict.

Any suggestion that he might be taking action for profit, he can escape by offering the proceeds of the action to a good charity in his own electorate.

Surely that should be a good incentive to issue a writ at the earliest possible moment.

Otherwise we will gladly stand him the cost of a handsome yellow flag.

Calwell was being challenged to sue the paper/author for the defamatory state-ments made on pain of being called a coward if he did not. When Calwell took up the challenge, the defendant pleaded privilege. At first instance, Dixon J rejected the plea. In his view, the basis of the privilege allowed for self-defence was on the mutual understanding that the judgement of the rights and wrongs between the parties was to be left not to the courts but 'to the public or a section of the public or other body'. The challenge had ameliorated the usual scope of privilege because, in effect, the privilege only applied if the courts were to be kept out of it:

> To make a charge and invite the plaintiff to invoke the judgment of the courts of law is to depart from the course around which protection is thrown. The defen-dant cannot say in his libel, 'This is my charge against you; I make it so you may submit the issue to the courts and if you refuse the challenge you are branded' and then, when the plaintiff accepts the challenge, set up a privilege which, if well founded, intercepts the issue and defeats the action.[116]

Dixon J's judgment was based not on authority – he thought there was none – but on principle: the form of the libel took it outside the privilege claimed for the occasion. On appeal, only McTiernan J agreed with him. Starke J seems to have thought that too much was being read into the challenge for it to operate as a formal denial of a defence that would otherwise be open. Rich J agreed – 'it was a challenge to substitute for methods of unregulated and desultory com-bat a duel to be fought in legal form with every weapon the law allows, and as involving no promise that if it is accepted the challenger will fire into the air'[117] – and Latham CJ and Williams J seem to have thought the same although their reasoning is not entirely clear.[118] This is not the place to debate the merits of Dixon J's exception[119] but what is instructive is how much 'on his own' he

---

[116] Ibid., 234.

[117] Ibid., 248.

[118] Ibid., 245.

[119] Dixon may well have felt that there was considerable hypocrisy in Penton's approach. After the judgment, Calwell announced he was discontinuing the action as privilege could be pleaded (*SMH*, 29 August 1945, 5). Penton replied that privilege was only pleaded to throw on Calwell the onus of proving the statements that he made in Parliament were true (*SMH*, 29 August 1945, 5). Legally, this was nonsense – at best, Calwell's proving the truth of his statements might have been some evidence of malice to defeat the privilege – but it was good politics. And Penton knew it. Compare the report in the *Wingham Chronicle and Daily River Observer*, 4 September 1945, 1, where the newspaper reported what Penton had said above, with its report on 7 September 1945, 1, of Penton's later editorial where Penton said – correctly – that

was in reaching his decision. On appeal, defendant's counsel, apart from simply saying that Dixon was wrong, could only add that the issue would not be intercepted by a plea of privilege because 'the defendant has taken it upon himself to prove that the plaintiff was a liar and the plea of privilege does not mean he is going to fight the case on this issue'.[120] The plea of privilege 'may assist greatly in proving justification; the onus lies on the plaintiff to prove malice and this may force him into the box where he may be proved to be a liar'.[121] This was the last resort of the desperate: privilege was pleaded not because it may operate itself but for the ulterior purpose of assisting justification. But counsel for the plaintiff had little more concrete to offer: the general principle behind qualified privilege stated in Holmes' *The Common Law* features twice in his argument.[122] There was no point appealing to English cases because they said nothing on the matter.

The Press and Politics

Throughout the period of this study, newspapers (through their counsel) consistently argued that they served an important public function in the dissemination of political information. The results of the cases suggest that this argument had at least some traction with juries. But these successes should not encourage the view that any unique position newspapers held in this regard entitled them to special consideration when defending libel actions. The defences they had to defamation actions were strictly curtailed: apart from truth, qualified privilege for fair and accurate reports of parliamentary and judicial proceedings, and fair comment were the common law defences. When any suggestion of a special position was raised, it was robustly rejected.[123] In *Holman v. Sunday Times*,[124] Holman was the Secretary of the Australian Timber Workers' Union and a candidate for the Federal seat of Fremantle. The newspaper made an allegation that he was a Communist candidate and a member of a group affiliated to the Moscow revolutionaries and he sued for defamation alleging damage to both personal and professional reputation. At a somewhat confusing trial, the judge held that the occasion was privileged although the plaintiff was awarded damages on the basis of jury findings both that the writer believed the words to be true and that the words exceeded the bounds of what was reasonable comment! On appeal to the Full Court, the decision that the occasion of the

---

all Calwell had to do was to prove that his allegations were not bona-fide to defeat the privilege defence. See also *Truth* (Sydney), 2 September 1945, 20 and more generally Penton's later book, *Censored!* (Shakespeare Head Press, 1947).

[120] (1945) 70 CLR 219, 236.

[121] Ibid.

[122] Ibid., 237–238.

[123] In both common law and Code jurisdictions: A. Kenyon and S. Walker, 'The Cost of Losing the Code: Historical Protection of Public Debate in Australian Defamation Law' (2014) 38 *MULR* 554, 568.

[124] *Sunday Times Publishing Co. Ltd* v. *Holman* [1925] WAR 10.

publication was privileged was challenged and was overturned. Indeed, counsel's argument seems to have been treated as so fantastic as to encourage mirth. Nothing turned on the fact that the publication was in the course of an election campaign: if privilege attached to this circumstance, one judge noted that 'the man who entered politics would be a fool' and another commented 'if you can establish that [the privilege] I think you would be entitled to a leather medal for it'.[125] The argument, as counsel ultimately admitted, was that the newspaper was privileged when it writes anything on a matter of public interest. In argument, Justice Northmore thought this would be 'a tremendous extension of the law of libel'. There is also a hint of displeasure in his observation that when the law of fair comment was extended to the press he thought that would satisfy them but 'they wanted more than that'.[126] There is a concern here as to the power of the press, a sense of the exercise of power without accountability. This sense of getting too big for their boots was reinforced in the judgment of McMillan CJ:

> In the present case the defendant is not clothed with greater immunity than the rest of the public. The writer in the *Sunday Times* is only entitled to write about another person things which any other person would be allowed to write. A newspaper possesses no legal or social duty in the nature of a private right as opposed to the right of the community at large to assert what it believes. It has the right which belongs to everyone to comment freely on of public matters but the comment must be fair.[127]

As illustrated in other cases throughout this period, it was fair comment that protected any free speech interest in political discussion.

A similar result was reached in *Baker v. Queensland Newspapers Pty Ltd* (discussed above at 63ff) under the Queensland Code. In the Full Court, Henchman J held that the publication did not attract privilege as a publication in good faith for the public good under s. 377(3): in the absence of a duty on the newspaper to make the statement – the common law basis for qualified privilege – s. 377(3) did not cover the giving of general publicity to a defamatory statements, even in the case of a public man, apart from exceptional circumstances of which this was not one.[128] Nor did s. 377(5) apply (publication in good faith for the purpose of giving information to the person to whom it is made with respect to some subject as to which that person has, or is believed, on reasonable grounds, by the person making the publication to have, such an interest in knowing the truth as to make his conduct in making the publication reasonable under the circumstances). At first glance this seems appropriate for a newspaper publishing information of general political interest and

---

[125] *The Daily News*, 29 April 1924, 8. See also *Lang* v. *Willis* (1934) 52 CLR 637 where, obiter, both Dixon J (667) and Evatt J (672) rejected an argument that qualified privilege attached to statements made at public election meetings.

[126] Ibid.

[127] *Sunday Times Publishing Co. Ltd v. Holman* [1924] WAR 10, 14.

[128] [1937] St R Qd 153, 191.

Henchman J accepted that all readers in the Commonwealth might have an interest in knowing the views of a public man in Australian politics on public matters of great importance and that the *Courier Mail* might reasonably believe its readers to have such an interest. But the fact that the paper circulated in New Zealand and other parts of the world and the defendants did not argue any belief that these readers had an interest in the information prevented the defence from applying.[129] This effectively stopped this section operating in any meaningful way as a general privilege defence for newspapers unless their circulation precisely matched an interested readership, a limitation that practically excluded it for major newspapers.

The final attempt to argue a special status for newspaper publications was in *Penton v. Calwell*,[130] a case at the end of the period under study. The plaintiff, Arthur Calwell, was Minister for Information in the wartime Labor government of John Curtin. The defendant was the editor of the *Daily Telegraph*, a leading Sydney newspaper owned by Frank Packer, and there was long history between the defendant and the newspaper, and Calwell.[131] In the aftermath of the Cowra breakout in 1944,[132] Calwell, under cover of Parliamentary privilege, accused some Sydney newspaper proprietors of disregarding the safety of Australia and the lives of prisoners in Japanese hands by what they were publishing. In an article written by the defendant, the newspaper replied with a series of charges against Calwell, accusing him of being 'maliciously and corruptly untruthful' and a 'dishonest, calculating liar'. Calwell sued in the original jurisdiction of the High Court and the defendant pleaded privilege among other defences. The case never went to trial but in preliminary proceedings the scope of any privilege defence was discussed. Penton had argued[133] that the matter 'was published in defence of newspapers published and circulated in the Commonwealth against attacks on them, particularly in respect of their right to publish in accordance with the law matters of public interest'. While it was true that some of Calwell's comments – as in the specific publication in issue – had gone beyond individual newspapers, Dixon J at first instance rejected the argument:

> No case has yet gone so far as deciding that attacks upon an institution, such as the press, the theatre or the Bar, or a section of the community, create a privileged occasion in each person belonging to or concerned in the institution or the section of the community so that he is enabled in the exercise of a qualified

---

[129] Ibid.

[130] (1945) 70 CLR 219.

[131] K. Mason, *Old Law New Law: A Second Australian Legal Miscellany* (Federation Press, 2014) 169–173.

[132] Japanese prisoners of war were held in the southern central New South Wales town of Cowra. In August 1944, over 1100 attempted to escape. Four Australian and over 200 Japanese soldiers were killed.

[133] This was Dixon J's disentangling of what he thought was a confused pleading but he proceeded as if this had been pleaded.

privilege attaching to him personally to publish any defamatory matter by way of defence or counter-attack.[134]

On appeal, four of the five members of the High Court agreed that a privilege framed this widely should be struck out.[135]

At common law, newspapers also had a very limited protection for fair and accurate reports of certain proceedings and courts firmly rejected any non-statutory extensions of these situations. In *McCauley v. John Fairfax and Sons Ltd*[136] derogatory statements about the plaintiff, a candidate for election, had been made by another candidate in a speech that was reported by the defendant. Apart from a futile attempt to depart from the repetition rule,[137] the defence that the article was a true report of what was said by the candidate, and it was in the public interest that this be reported, was rejected. According to Halse Rogers J, this was an impermissible attempt to extend qualified privilege to fair and accurate reports of public meetings. This could be done by statute – as had been done in England – but the failure to include this situation in the list that attracted qualified privilege in the New South Wales legislation placed the responsibility on newspapers for statements reported at public meetings unless they were true.[138] Moreover, courts scrutinised the 'fair and accurate' component of the privilege carefully. The reporting of a defamatory interjection by a bankrupt in bankruptcy proceedings was not covered by the privilege protecting the report of court proceedings: what was covered was the processes of law, not things said that had no relationship to the proceedings or by persons having no connection with the proceedings.[139] And the insertion of anything that looked like comment was fatal to this defence. In *Thompson v. Truth and Sportsman Ltd (No. 1)*[140] the report of a Small Debts Courts case failed to attract the defence both because some aspects of the report were comment (the plaintiff 'did not answer the question directly') and because some key elements of the trial were omitted (e.g. the critical comment of the presiding Magistrate to defence's counsel about his questioning of the witness (the plaintiff in the defamation case)).

But there was another factor at play in preventing judicial expansion of any kind of privilege to newspapers. Mitchell has documented the suspicion of and hostility towards the commercialisation of the media exhibited by the judiciary in England in this period[141] and there is evidence of similar sentiment

---

[134] (1945) 70 CLR 219, 231–232.

[135] Ibid., 246 (Latham CJ and Williams J), Rich J (248), Starke J (251). McTiernan J did not consider the issue.

[136] [1933] 34 SR NSW 339.

[137] That it is no defence to a libel action to argue that the defendant was merely repeating what someone else had said.

[138] Ibid., 348.

[139] *Hughes v. West Australian Newspaper Limited* [1940] WAR 12.

[140] (1931) 31 SR (NSW) 129.

[141] P. Mitchell, *A History of Tort Law 1900–1950* (Cambridge University Press, 2015) 150–158.

in Australia. An extreme example is the remarks of Macrossan J in *Baker v. Queensland Newspapers Ltd*, discussed above. Macrossan was well known for his sharp tongue and nowhere is this better illustrated than in his treatment of the *Courier Mail*. During argument, he had mused that if two innocent parties were involved in a transaction that injured one of them, 'the person whose commercial business it is to make publications of this kind may have to put up with the risk'.[142] But he saved his ammunition for the summing up to the jury.[143] The duty of a newspaper when it had unwittingly caused injury to another was the same obligation of decency as an individual: in this case their equivocal attitude to printing a reply was a 'monstrous impudence'. Some newspapers 'go in' for libels and while not suggesting the *Courier Mail* was one, they were a powerful corporation that could afford to take risks that an individual could not afford. A newspaper could adopt a policy that if it made a mistake in publishing a libel it would not apologise but would 'stick to its guns and fight the other fellow to the last ditch'. He saw no value in appeals to the liberty of the press; that was no greater than the liberty of the subject. 'You might think I hold strong views on this matter. I do', he said, noting he had similar things in an earlier trial.[144] Perhaps most remarkably, he drew attention to a comment ('Social') made by *Courier Mail* staff on the letter containing the false report. Neither counsel had made anything of this annotation but for Macrossan J it was good evidence that a conscious choice had been made to change the initial editorial judgement (social pages) to publish this controversial report because of its news and hence commercial value. The distaste for commercial news practices and the consequent (in his view) disregard for individual reputation is evident, as it is in the more restrained comments of Webb J in the Full Court.[145]

An even greater concern about modern newspaper practices can be noticed in cases involving those outside of politics. In *Savige v. News Limited*,[146] a number of Australian officers, including the plaintiff, were defamed by the defendant newspaper's report that they were accused of deserting native wives in Persia at the end of the First World War. This was erroneous and caused by a misreading of a number of cables from London. 'All I need say', noted Angas Parsons J, 'is that if any reasonable care had been exercised in reading the cables received, it would have been apparent there was no basis for the belief. The fact is that an inexcusable blunder was made by the newspaper which has entailed serious consequences to the plaintiff.'[147] *Savige* involved a relatively respectable paper – not the 'gutter press' as the judge remarked – but the strongest language was reserved for the 'sensationalist' papers, the two most common of which before the courts were *Truth* and *Smith's Weekly*. An example of judicial distaste for

---

[142] *Courier Mail*, 30 September 1936, 21.
[143] What follows is contained in *Courier Mail*, 3 October 1936, 13.
[144] This was in a defamation case heard in Cairns in 1930: see *The Northern Herald*, 5 July 1930, 22.
[145] [1937] St R Qd 153, 170.
[146] [1932] SASR 240.
[147] Ibid., 249.

the former is found in *Thompson v. Truth and Sportsman Ltd No. 4*[148] where Jordan CJ mentioned the 'discreditable and sensational report' of proceedings in a Small Debts Court and that the case was one where the jury 'ought to mark in no uncertain terms their disapproval of the publication in a newspaper of a wholly unjustifiable and grossly improper defamatory article of that character.'[149] *Smith's Weekly* was the subject of a case involving the defamation of a German-qualified doctor who practised unregistered in South Australia where Dixon J expressed indirectly his distaste for the sensationalism of the newspaper:

> Among the judicious the credit of the allegations contained in the article would be much weakened by the intemperance and boisterous irresponsibility of its style. But among the large classes of uncritical readers who are attracted by such 'revelations', exuberance of denunciation is understood to produce a confused confidence that villainy has been unmasked.[150]

A subtly different approach was taken by Evatt J in the same case: 'Streamer headlines, the intermingling of facts with actual or possible expressions of opinion and screaming posters are features of this age of industrialism, and praise or blame is no concern of ours.'[151] Evatt's views may have been influenced by his representation of *Smith's Weekly* early in his career at the Bar[152] but for whatever reasons the tone was much less judgemental and patrician than many of his judicial brethren. But in his view the new mode of journalism attracted no special treatment from the law of defamation: fair comment would rarely protect defamatory matter in such journalism 'not because the motives of the proprietors are mercenary (resembling those of all other industries), but because of the impossibility of achieving sensations, and still effecting a clear separation of facts from the defamatory expressions of opinion.'[153] It is not hard to find traces of the Labor politician in these remarks. In a capitalist system it smacked of hypocrisy to single out the commercial practices of the mass media. Moreover, there is implicit criticism of the class bias of those who decried the gutter press; as evidenced by Dixon's comments it was the working classes who read this lower class of journalism. And perhaps also it was easier to make the case for *Smith's Weekly* than for similar papers as it had a reputation: as its historian wrote, *Smith's* was a 'pure Australian mechanism that ever pursued the loftiest ends in the national interest with what its critics considered to be the zest and tactics of a larrikin.'[154]

---

[148] (1931) 31 SR (NSW) 292.

[149] Ibid., 294, 298. Ferguson J also noted that *Truth* had not relied on a report from anyone in court but merely on the solicitor who had engaged in the disreputable cross examination implying that the paper was a joint participant in what was regarded as a scandalous trial.

[150] *Smith's Newspapers Ltd v. Becker* (1932) 47 CLR 279, 296.

[151] Ibid., 303.

[152] G. Blaikie, *Remember Smith's Weekly* (Rigby, 1966) 237.

[153] *Smith's Newspapers Ltd v. Becker* (1932) 47 CLR 279, 304.

[154] Blaikie, above n 152, 1.

While there was no case for special disadvantage, however, neither was there one for special treatment and, reflecting the long tradition of Australian courts in this period, any protection for these publications for public comment was through the neutral application of the fair comment defence. This is evidenced in Evatt J's approach in *Telegraph Newspaper Co Ltd v Bedford* several years later.[155] The defendant newspaper – not from the gutter press – had published a letter to the editor which alleged impropriety in the management of a mining company. In rejecting the newspaper's defence under ss. 377(3) and (5) of the Queensland Code, Evatt J emphasised both the primacy of fair comment and the limits of privilege as a public interest defence. In an impressive analysis of the English case law, the restrictive 'interest' requirement of common law qualified privilege was held to underlie the Code requirement that the publication be for the 'public good' in s. 377(3) and there was no evidence that the newspaper had that requisite interest in publishing.[156] Moreover, a belief that its readers would be curious about the private or business affairs of others would not found a s. 377(5) defence (which required a belief that the recipients had an interest in knowing the truth). While it might be interesting to readers to know of a suggestion of impropriety by a director or directors of a company, the 'interest' referred to in the section was far more limited.[157] In the result, commercial gossip in serious newspapers was no more entitled to protection through qualified privilege than lower forms of journalism for the masses.

Conclusion

Politics in Australia has always been played hard and the prevalence of defamation cases in this area simply reflects that fact. By bringing the courts into political disputes, important questions about the relationship between reputation and free speech had to be answered. A number of points emerge from this discussion. First, the primary protection for political speech was achieved through the defence of fair comment. Attempts to enlarge privilege defences, mainly argued or suggested by newspapers, largely failed. This reflected the concern that providing too great a protection for statements of fact would be too tempting in an environment where political passions and political instrumentalism were features of the body politic and where the rise of the mass media gave little reason to think the media might self-regulate to prevent abuse. It perhaps too represented a view that changes to the free speech/reputation balance in political discourse were best left to the legislature.

The cases discussed in this chapter suggest that Australian judges at times struggled to overcome political bias or to apply legal rules as clearly as they

---

[155] (1934) 50 CLR 632.

[156] Ibid., 654–662.

[157] 'But the "interest" to which the sub-section relates is a real and direct personal, trade, business or social concern': ibid., 662. See further Kenyon and Walker, above n 123, 568–569.

might have in less controversial contexts. But the fact that there were times when they might, perhaps, have done better is not surprising given the environment in which many of the judgments were given. What is more surprising is not that they were not perfect but that in most of the cases a consistent approach to the law was taken (even if juries sometimes took matters into their own hands). In a very real sense Australian judges were determining the boundaries for the protection of political speech in Australia.

5

Negligence and the Boundaries of Liability: Liability for Acts of Third Parties

This and the following two chapters are concerned with the outer limits of recovery in the tort of negligence. During the period of this study, the tort of negligence was generalised and its structure better understood. These conceptual advances, important as they were, must not blind us to the fact that fault as the basis for recovering damages for personal injury was commonplace at the beginning of the period of this study. The law reports are replete with references to accidents at work and increasingly accidents on the road where negligence was the cause of action. In most of these cases, it was never doubted that the defendant owed the plaintiff an obligation, a duty, to exercise reasonable care and the issue usually turned on whether the defendant had exercised reasonable care on the facts. However, there were a number of areas where the action did not take the paradigm form of a private defendant acting carelessly so as to directly inflict physical injury on the plaintiff. Later chapters consider situations where the defendant was the state or a governmental entity where courts were asked to consider the status of the defendant in determining whether liability in negligence should be imposed, and where the damage for which the plaintiff was claiming was shock-induced harm. These cases fell outside the run-of-the-mill and required courts to articulate rules about the boundaries of recovery in the tort of negligence.

This chapter considers the question of liability in negligence where the alleged fault was the failure to control or to prevent damage caused by the independent and wrongful act of a third party. Two important High Court cases, one well known for different reasons and one largely forgotten, demonstrate a level of judicial analysis of the problems that went beyond the sometimes confused jurisprudence of the English courts on this issue at the start of the period of this study. As always, Australian courts engaged with the English authorities that comprised the common law but in doing so set the rules for recovery by reference to Australian conditions.

Lavatories and Free Will: The Problem of the Overflowing Lavatory in *Lothian v. Rickards*

Harry Rickards, one of Australia's leading vaudeville promoters in the thirty years between 1880 until his death in 1911,[1] was the owner of a four-storied building at 226 Little Collins Street in Melbourne (called Rickards Buildings). The building formed part of an entire block that Rickards owned, the northern end containing the Tivoli Theatre (originally the Melbourne Opera House and rebuilt as the Tivoli in 1901).[2] Rickards Buildings was a commercial building and the various floors and parts thereof were let to tenants. A part of the second floor was leased to John Inglis Lothian, the founder of what was to become the well-known publishing company Lothian Books in Melbourne.[3] The remainder of the building was let to other commercial traders and organisations. The top floor also contained a number of toilets, the number being increased from the time the building was completed in 1906 until the date of the events in question in August 1909.[4] On the evening of 18 August, there was an overflow from a wash basin in the men's toilet which caused damage to the property of a number of tenants of the floors below, including some books of John Lothian.

Although not mentioned in any of the authorised reports, tenants on the second and third floor of the building had complained previously about water leaking from the bathrooms on the fourth floor.[5] Although there was a dispute about whether there had been a previous leak of water from the men's toilets, there was no dispute that water had leaked from the women's bathroom before August 1909. The damage had been minor and the manager of the building had arranged for precautions to be taken to avoid any damage from leaking water. The precaution that was adopted was to 'lead' the floor (to make it waterproof). This was a common safety precaution alongside the provision of a lead safe and, in most cases, an outlet pipe for the collected water from the safe. By the time of the events of August 1909, the men's lavatories had been leaded but not the basins which also formed part of the bathroom.

Why did the water overflow? This was the subject of some dispute but at a general level the cause was clear: the basin tap had been left running fully open with the result that the basin overflowed. Although the basin did have some holes which took away the water when it reached a certain height, evidence established that this was not sufficient to prevent an overflow when the plug

---

[1] See Martha Rutledge, 'Harry Rickards 1843–1911' in *Australian Dictionary of Biography,* http://adb.anu.edu.au/biography/rickards-harry-8207.

[2] Ibid.

[3] See further S. Sayers, *The Company of Books: A Short History of the Lothian Book Companies* (Lothian, 1988).

[4] Information obtained from the transcript of evidence of witnesses and trial judge's summing up contained in the NAA, A10074, 1910/28, Lothian v. Rickards, Appeal Book, Transcript of Evidence.

[5] See details of the evidence provided by witnesses when the case was first heard in the County Court, A10074, above n 4, Appeal Book, 9–19.

hole was blocked. What was not clear was how the plug hole was blocked. It was agreed that the blockage was caused by soap but there was a dispute over whether the soap had been deliberately inserted into the plug hole to block it or whether it might have been blocked by someone accidentally leaving some soap in the basin, the water forcing the soap in the plug hole. There was also evidence that the S-Bend had been blocked by a variety of items (pen nibs, some nails, a pen holder and some pieces of string matted together) and there was evidence that this also had been done deliberately. It is the possibility that the overflow was caused deliberately that presented the main legal issue in the case.

Lothian brought an action against Rickards in the County Court of Victoria. A number of causes of action were alleged, the most relevant for present purposes being the 'carelessness of yourselves or your servants or agents in the construction maintenance management and control of a certain lavatory basin'. But the relationship between this allegation and the possibility that the overflow had been caused maliciously played out not before a judge but before a judge and civil jury. And it was the particular way that the judge chose to use the jury that raised the role of a deliberate wrongful act which had intervened between the defendant's negligence and the plaintiff's harm.

The witnesses called for the parties addressed two main issues: first, whether it was careless not to have installed lead floors or lead sinks under the basins in the men's toilets, and second, how the blockage was caused.[6] Most of the evidence related to the first question – what we might describe as the carelessness question. The judge then summed up for the jury and here the troubles began. First, he described the relevant (for our purposes) allegation of negligence as being negligence 'in not providing a reasonable escape for water in the case of an overflow from those top lavatories arising from *accident or negligence*' (my italics).[7] This was incorrect, because nowhere was the negligence described as limited to overflows caused by negligence or accident. But the reason for stating the case in this way becomes clear later on in the summing up, where the judge said: 'Of course if this were a deliberate mischievous act by some outsider unless it was instigated by the Defendant himself the Defendant would not be responsible. He would not be responsible for a malicious act under those circumstances because he cannot guard against malice.'[8] The same point is made later on in the summing up: 'If it was [malicious] then the Defendant would not be responsible because the person who deliberately tried to flood the place could overcome the precautions.'[9]

It is clear that the judge's summing up gave the intention with which the basin was blocked considerable importance. But this was not reflected in what

---

[6] See evidence of witnesses at the trial: A10074, above n 4, Appeal Book, 9–18.
[7] Judge Chomley's summing up to the jury: A10074, above n 4, Appeal Book, 26.
[8] Ibid.
[9] Ibid., 31–32.

followed. After summing up, he gave the jury three questions to answer, two of which are relevant for our purposes:

1. Was the Defendant or any of his servants or agents guilty of negligence in not providing a reasonably sufficient escape for water in case of an over-flow resulting from accident or negligence having regard to the nature of the use of the rooms below?;
2. Was such negligence the cause of the injury to the plaintiff's goods?[10]

No question as to whether the interference was deliberate was left to the jury, a surprising omission given the summing up.[11] The jury did the best it could: it found that the defendant had been negligent as a lead safe was necessary to minimise the risk from overflow, and it found that the negligence was a cause of the plaintiff's damage. But it also took matters into its own hands and answered a question that had not been asked: it said that it was of the opinion that this (not specified but presumably the blockage) was the malicious act of some person. The judge was somewhat flummoxed by these findings and gave leave to move for judgment to both parties which they both did. Fourteen days later the judge found for the plaintiff and the short reasons need to be stated in some detail to explain why the case raised an important legal issue:

> The difficulty here arises from the peculiarity of the findings of the jury. The first two findings amount to a verdict for the plaintiff. But the jury add a sort of rider as follows 'We are of the opinion that this was the malicious act of some person'... It must be observed however that the jury do not say that this act was the cause of the injury to the plaintiff's goods. What they say amounts to this: There was a malicious act but the cause of the injury was the negligence of the defendant.[12]

The difficulty, which the judge, perhaps unwittingly, recognised, was brought about by the fact that the question of legal responsibility was treated at least partly as a question of causation. Broadly, the law took into account the inter-vention of a deliberate wrongful act between the defendant's negligence and the plaintiff's injury in two, possibly three, different ways. First, it could say that the nature of the intervening act meant that the defendant's negligence was not a sine qua non, or necessary condition, for the harm to the plaintiff. There are elements of this reasoning all throughout the courts that heard the case: because nothing can prevent damage caused by someone who was intent on causing it, any failure to take precautions was not a necessary condition of the harm.[13]

---

[10] Ibid., 34.
[11] As noted by the Privy Council: *Rickards v. Lothian* [1913] AC 263, 271.
[12] A10074, above n 4, Appeal Book, 19.
[13] See, for example, Hood J in the Full Court of the Victorian Supreme Court, Appeal Book, Ibid., 43; *Lothian v. Rickards* (1911) 12 CLR 165, 193–194 (Isaacs J); *Rickards v. Lothian* [1913] AC 263, 273 (PC).

The second way that deliberate wrongful intervention could be taken into account was through the notion of remote or proximate cause. This explanation did not deny that the defendant's negligence was a necessary condition of the plaintiff's harm but denied liability because the negligence was not the real, or effective, or proximate cause of the plaintiff's harm. This was the ground preferred by A'Beckett J in the Supreme Court of Victoria[14] and seems to have been the view adopted in the contemporary edition of *Clerk and Lindsell on Torts*, although the reference is very brief.[15] One problem with the use of proximate cause, as American legal realists were shortly to point out, was that it lacked any explanatory value. Denying liability on the basis that damage was not the effective, real or proximate cause effectively masked the broader reasons for the denial of liability.[16] The realist's scepticism as to the utility of proximate cause was increasingly shared among academics and even some members of the judiciary; in 1937 Sir Owen Dixon gave a lecture to law students at Melbourne University where he said that causal expressions such as 'immediate', 'direct' and 'proximate' were all illusory, 'broken links' or 'worse'.[17] In a case like *Lothian v. Rickards*, to say that the deliberate and malicious act of a third party was the effective cause did not elucidate why that was the case.

The final way in which the deliberate and wrongful intervention of another could be taken into account in a negligence action was by considering whether that intervention was a foreseeable result of the defendant's negligence. Analytically, this is a very different way of dealing with the question of wrongful intervening acts than through causal concepts[18] albeit this was not always recognised by the judges who used it. In part, this was because foreseeability was used not as an independent criterion for determining liability in cases of third party intervention but as the means of determining the proximate cause question. It was also because the same foreseeability reasoning can determine several elements of a negligence action. Forseeability is a device that is associated with the risks that are created by a defendant's conduct. As a limiting device, it can be used to cap the defendant's liability to only those risks the conduct created. In the case of deliberate and wrongful third party intervention, if the intervening conduct of the third party was not foreseeable then the defendant had created no legally-relevant risk and could not be liable for failing to take precautions against such an intervention. In legal terms, on the facts Rickards would not have been careless because the risk of deliberate wrongful

---

[14] See A10074, above n 4, Appeal Book, 39.

[15] See Wyatt Paine, *Clerk and Lindsell on Torts*, 7th edn (Sweet and Maxwell, 1921) 465.

[16] See, for example, L. Green, *Judge and Jury* (Vernon Law Book Co., 1930) chs. 6 and 7.

[17] Dixon's lecture was not published but notes of it were taken by a student, John Kinnear, who was present. 'Papers of Sir Owen Dixon 1886–1986', NLA, MS Acc09.166, Box 8, Paper to University of Melbourne Law Students' Society on 'Causation and the law'. See also P. Ayres, 'Owen Dixon's causation lecture: radical scepticism' (2003) 77 *ALJ* 692.

[18] See H.L.A. Hart and T. Honore, *Causation in the Law* (Oxford University Press, 1st edn, 1959, 2nd edn, 1985) ch. IX.

intervention was not a risk that was a foreseeable result of Rickards' conduct in failing to seal the floor with lead. This is a distinct question from both the existence or otherwise of necessary condition causation between the defendant's negligence and the plaintiff's injury and the question of the limits if any that should be placed on harm for which the defendant's negligence was a necessary condition. In modern law it is conventionally thought that foreseeability also plays a role at the remoteness of damage (now scope of liability) phase but even today the relationship between foreseeability at the duty of care, breach of duty and scope of liability elements of the cause of action is fluid. Whatever the merits of this breakdown, it requires a reasonably sophisticated understanding of the role that foreseeability, and through foreseeability, risk, plays in all three elements. This distinction is not always recognised today (and even if recognised, not accepted) and was certainly not articulated in 1911. This explains the otherwise cryptic defence that was pleaded to the plaintiff's action: 'a denial of negligence – a wilful and malicious act on the part of some person unknown to Defendant'.[19] This is best understood as saying that as the intervention of the third party could not have been foreseen there is no way Rickards could have been careless in failing to take precautions against *that* risk.

The English Texts – Help or Hindrance?

That there was considerable uncertainty surrounding the relationship between foreseeability, breach and intervening acts at the time of *Lothian v. Rickards* is graphically illustrated by the discussion of the issue in contemporary textbooks. A good example is Pollock's *The Law of Torts*, where he devotes eleven pages to 'Proximate or Remote Cause'.[20] He begins by stating that the doctrine of 'natural and probable consequences' – terminology associated with limiting liability for negligent conduct – was illustrated in the law of negligence by the rule that carelessness depended on a failure to take precautions against a foreseeable risk (citing Baron Alderson's well-known definition of breach of duty in *Blythe v. Birmingham Waterworks*).[21] This is followed by paradigmatic breach of duty reasoning: unforeseeable risks cannot give rise to legal liability and the likelihood of the risk materialising is a key factor in determining breach of duty: as he put it, in terms instantly recognisable in *Bolton v. Stone*[22] fifty years later: 'the reasonable man, then, to whose ideal behaviour we are to look as the standard of duty, will neither neglect what he can forecast as probable, nor waste his anxiety on events that are barely possible.'[23] Pollock was aware, however, that this was breach of duty reasoning:

---

[19] A10074, above n 4, Appeal Book, 9.
[20] F. Pollock, *The Law of Torts*, 7th edn (Stevens and Sons, 1904) 39–50.
[21] (1856) 11 Exch 781; 156 ER 1047.
[22] [1951] AC 850.
[23] Pollock, above n 20, 39–40.

It is suggested by an author [Beven, *Negligence in Law*] whose opinions are always deserving of attention that this rule applies only 'in determining what is negligence,' and 'not in limiting the consequences flowing from it when once established:' and the learned author works out this position in an ingenious and elaborate argument.[24]

Although Pollock expressed his disagreement with this view, 'the scale of this book forbids me to say more…'[25] The remaining part of the section is devoted to giving examples 'on either side of the line' – which simply meant stating which party won when the harm was caused in some indirect way. Nowhere did Pollock explain how to distinguish the results of the cases or to explain whether claims that failed did so because there was no breach of duty or because the harm was not the natural and probable consequence of the negligence.[26] The resulting analysis was somewhat cryptic. In *Engelhart v. Farrant & Co.*,[27] the driver of a tradesman's cart had instructions not to leave the cart with a youth he had with him, the youth being inexperienced in driving. When the driver was away the youth carelessly drove the cart and damaged the plaintiff's carriage. Pollock noted that the driver's original negligence in leaving the cart was held to be the effective cause of the harm. However, it is clear that the driver would not have been negligent unless the youth's intervention was foreseeable. If it was, then on Pollock's reasoning the harm would *have* to have been the natural and direct consequence of the breach. This was the connection made by Lord Esher:

> Now, if it is necessary to draw any inference about the probability, if Mears had done what he ought to do and had thought what was the probable result of his going away and leaving the cart with the lad in it, I think it is inevitable to come to the conclusion that he would have thought he was doing a dangerous thing. *Leaving that lad in the cart with the means of driving off at any moment makes what Mears did an effective cause of what happened afterwards.*[28] (my italics)

In reality, once the driver's conduct was negligent because of the risk created by the foreseeable actions of the third party, there was no separate issue relating to effective cause.

---

[24] Ibid., 40.

[25] Ibid., 41. Pollock was responding to comments made in Beven's 2nd edition (*Negligence in Law*, 2nd edn (Stevens and Haynes, 1895) 101, 105. By the 3rd edition (in 1908) he was more circumspect, not referring to Pollock by name, although the thrust of this argument did not change.

[26] A particularly confusing example is his discussion of *Metropolitan Railway Company* v. *Jackson* (1877) 3 App Cas 193. Pollock notes, correctly, that the House of Lords found there was no evidence of negligence that could go to the jury – a breach point. However, after arguing that the case 'was in truth of this [proximate and remote cause] class, he states: 'It was an accident which might no less have happened if the carriage had not been overcrowded at all'. As he had assumed the negligence lay in failing to prevent the overcrowding, his argument goes to factual causation rather than remoteness or proximate cause.

[27] [1897] 1 QB 240.

[28] Ibid., 244.

Pollock's opponent, Thomas Beven, took a quite different view but like Pollock he too did not seem to be entirely consistent. Broadly, Beven saw the limits of liability as depending on at least two factors: the presence of a responsible agent and a requisite causal connection. In Beven's view, as long as the injurious agency (i.e. the thing alleged to be responsible for causing the harm) was operating through 'the direct and undiverted impulsion of a responsible agent', the liability of the responsible agent continued.[29] In a complicated fact scenario, it was the last responsible agency that needed to be identified for the purpose of determining liability. For Beven a responsible agency was defined as 'all those with capacity to exercise moral choice, that is… all human beings, and none but them'.[30] This appears to exclude any notion of foreseeability of consequences as relevant to responsibility in the cause of an intervening deliberate wrongful act but the broad statement is almost immediately qualified. Where an 'extraordinary' cause was the primary means of setting in motion an injurious agency and the defendant's negligence co-operated with the extraordinary cause, any resulting injury was not the defendant's responsibility. In this case, the 'negligent act is not followed by injurious results in natural and probable sequence, but only by the occurrence of something abnormal and not to be anticipated'.[31] At least in this context, it seems, foreseeability was relevant. When discussing causal connection, however, Beven made it clear that it was no defence for a defendant to claim that the plaintiff's injury was not the natural and probable consequences of the negligence. In reasoning that was later to be adopted in *Re Polemis, Furniss and Withy*, the anticipated consequences of the defendant's conduct went only to determining whether that conduct was negligent.[32] The defendant was liable for the consequences of the negligence whether they be greater or less until 'the intervention of some diverting force or until the force put in motion by the negligence had become exhausted'.[33] Although not acknowledged by Beven, there was considerable overlap between responsible agency and causal connection: on facts like *Lothian v. Rickards*, Harry Rickards could not have been considered a responsible agent once the deliberate conduct had intervened nor could any negligence have been considered the cause of Lothian's harm. More problematic for its practical utility, by the third edition, in 1908, it was becoming clear that not all the cases could be reconciled with Beven's approach.[34] *Engelhart v. Farrand*, for example, was

---

[29] T. Beven, *Negligence in Law*, 3rd edn (Stevens and Haynes, 1908) 45.

[30] Ibid., 81.

[31] Ibid., 81–82.

[32] Ibid., 85–86.

[33] Ibid., 88.

[34] Ibid., 96–97 where he discusses *Bull v. Mayor of Shoreditch* (1903) 19 TLR 64 and in particular the first instance judgment of Kennedy J in *McDowall v. Great Western Railway* [1902] 1 KB 618. While the Court of Appeal decision ([1903] 2 KB 331) overturned this judgment (which Beven thought did not go far enough in rejecting the reasoning), Kennedy J's reasoning was effectively adopted by the House of Lords in *Cooke v. Midland Great Western Railway of Ireland* [1909] AC 229.

placed in the 'Responsible Agency' section but as noted above the judgment dealt with causation. In attempting to reconcile the case with this theory, Beven acknowledged that negligence of the servant 'may be admitting the intervention or affording facilities to it'[35] but this seems to admit responsibility (and perhaps causal connection?) could be based on some degree of foresight of consequences even if an independent agency intervened. Despite its superficial attraction, it is not surprising that Bevan was only cited in passing in the appellate courts in *Lothian*.[36]

While Pollock and Beven's approaches had their difficulties, they did at least provide a way to approach cases of this kind. Other contemporary textbooks were much more obscure. In *Addison's Law of Torts*, 8th edn (1906) the issue of intervening acts was identified as a remoteness of damage issue. Beyond this, however, the authors found it difficult to set out a general rule other than by collecting the various Delphic expressions used in the cases. The result was not felicitous:

> Whoever does an illegal or wrongful act is answerable for all the consequences that ensue in the ordinary course of events, though those consequences be immediately and directly brought about by the intervening agency of others, provided the intervening agents were set in motion by the primary wrong-doer, or provided their acts causing the damage were the necessary or legal and natural consequence of the original wrongful act. If the wrong and the legal damage are not known by common experience to be usually in sequence and the damage does not, according to the ordinary course of events, follow from the wrong, the wrong and the damage are not sufficiently conjoined, as cause and effect, to support an action, unless it is shown that the wrong-doer knew, or had reasonable means of knowing, that consequences not usually resulting from his act were, by reason of some existing cause, likely to intervene so as to cause damage to another.[37]

One can only wonder what guidance was given to practitioners by this menagerie of causal language. Although this general principle was illustrated by references to cases, as with Pollock there was no real analysis of why a particular result was reached. Confronted with the general rule as set out above, anyone consulting the text must have had a sense of foreboding when the authors later added that cases where the act complained of would not have occasioned any injury but for the immediate act of some third party caused 'considerable difficulty'.[38]

---

[35] Ibid., 79.

[36] In the High Court, only Isaacs J made reference to Beven but the citation is to the pages dealing with responsible agents rather than causation: (1911) 12 CLR 165, 192.

[37] W. Gordon and W. Griffith, *Addison's Law of Torts*, 8th edn (Stevens and Sons, 1906) 51. For an equally ambiguous explanation see H. Smith, *A Treatise on the Law of Negligence*, 2nd edn (Stevens and Sons, 1884) 19–20.

[38] Ibid., 57.

As is evident from the above, the limited analysis in contemporary textbooks did not assist in determining the relationship between foreseeability, breach and remoteness in relation to deliberate conduct that intervened between a defendant's negligence and the plaintiff's injury. This lack of clarity means that it is not easy to discern whether findings on foreseeability went to breach or proximate causation. In *Lothian*, Hood J in the Supreme Court of Victoria seemed to treat it as going to breach: there was no evidence that the basin might be interfered with in this way so there could be no negligence in not taking steps to prevent that risk materialising.[39] A similar approach, although a contrary view, was taken by Cussen J, the dissenting judge in the Supreme Court: a properly instructed jury might have come to the conclusion that 'a reasonable man would, in a building like this, anticipate and provide against an overflow which might be expected to happen occasionally from carelessness and occasionally from design'.[40] In both judgments, in determining the foreseeability question the relevant risk was the risk that the basin might be blocked by deliberate wrongdoing.

Lavatories in the High Court

The majority judgments in the High Court (Griffith CJ and O'Connor J) allowed an appeal in favour of Lothian. As with all the previous judgments in the case, the reasoning contains elements of all the three ways in which deliberate intervening acts effected liability in negligence but the main focus was on the foreseeability of the risk. However, unlike Hood and Cussen JJ in the Supreme Court, Griffith CJ and O'Connor J considered foreseeability at a high level of abstraction. As Griffith CJ put it:

> The real question for determination in the present case is whether, when the act which is likely to occur and cause injury is one that may be done either carelessly or mischievously or deliberately, the mental attitude of the person who does the act qualifies the nature of the act itself, or whether it is sufficient that the injurious consequence is likely to occur from a physical act of that kind, under whatever circumstances it is done?[41]

Griffith CJ adopted the second possibility: whether the act was foreseeable referred 'to the physical nature of the act, and has nothing to do with the motives of the actor'.[42] Applying this to the facts of *Lothian v. Rickards*, what needed to be foreseeable was an act (of any kind) that would result in the basin plug hole being blocked when the tap was running. Such an act was clearly foreseeable and the jury had found that the failure to take steps against this risk was careless and had caused the harm. A similar approach was taken by O'Connor

---

[39] Ibid., 42–44.
[40] Ibid., 52.
[41] (1911) 12 CLR 165, 173.
[42] Ibid., 177.

J: whether the choking arose from accident or from negligence or from mischief, the mode of preventing injury to the floors below would be precisely the same, namely the laying down of the lead floor. The duty would be a duty 'to take precautions, not against individual acts, but against the arising of a certain condition of things – the choking of the plug hole or waste pipes by foreign substances brought there by third parties using the lavatory'.[43]

There are a number of points to note about this approach. First, as was recognised by Griffith CJ, there was no English decision which directly concluded the question and very little discussion of this kind of issue in any English cases.[44] The confused state of the English authorities allowed him to dismiss ones that did not support his rationale. For example, in the contemporaneous Privy Council decision of *Dominion Natural Gas Co. Ltd v. Collins* Lord Dunedin made the following apparently definitive statement: 'On the other hand, if the proximate cause of the accident is not the negligence of the defendant, but the conscious act of another volition, then he will not be liable. For against such conscious act of volition no precaution can really prevail.'[45] However, this was said after recognising that this rule did not apply where the negligence related to a thing 'dangerous in itself'. Griffith CJ was nonplussed: the argument that this case established that in all cases the liability of the defendant for negligence is excluded if the conscious act of another volition intervenes would 'flatly contradict' what had immediately preceded it in the speech. Moreover, Lord Macnaugton, a member of the Judicial Committee in *Dominion Gas,* had only several months earlier expressed a different view in a House of Lords' case.[46] It was too much for Griffith CJ and he simply ignored Lord Dunedin's comments:

> Much has been said as to the inconvenience of the co-existence of two final and independent Courts of Appeal for the Empire, but it is inconceivable that the Judicial Committee should have intended, in July, by a statement which was merely obiter (since the point did not arise for decision) to declare the law for the British Dominions overseas in a contrary sense to that which had been declared in March by the House of Lords for the United Kingdom.[47]

There was even less discussion in the English textbooks[48] (and that little could be equivocal; hence both Griffith CJ and Isaacs J (dissenting) found support from Pollock's *Law of Torts*).[49] This is an example of an Australian court

---

[43] Ibid., 182.
[44] Ibid., 171.
[45] [1909] AC 640, 646–647.
[46] *Cooke v. Midland Great Western Railway of Ireland* [1909] AC 229.
[47] *Lothian* v. *Rickards* (1911) 12 CLR 165, 176.
[48] As noted earlier, there is only a brief discussion in Clerk and Lindsell (Paine, above n 15). The only reference in the then current edition of Salmond (J. Salmond, *Law of Torts* (Stevens and Haynes, 1907) to cases discussed in *Lothian v. Rickards* is in a section on breach of duty (p. 29) although some of the cases discussed were decided after this edition was published. The references in Pollock, Beven and Addison are discussed earlier in the text.
[49] (1911) 12 CLR 165, 176, 191.

considering relatively unsettled areas of the English common law of torts and making a contribution to it. Moreover, the majority in the High Court demonstrated the malleability of the foreseeability concept as a tool for limiting liability that flowed from a negligent act. The result of applying a foreseeability test for remoteness of damage – of which *Lothain v. Rickards* is an early example – depends upon the level of generality with which the relevant risk is described. There is no correct way of describing whether the risk that should have been foreseen in *Lothian v. Rickards* was the risk that the basin would be blocked and overflowed or whether it was the risk that the basin would be blocked by the malicious act of a third party and overflow.[50] The broader the description of the risk, the more likely it was that a defendant would be held liable for failing to take precautions against that risk and the more likely it was that, if foreseeability was the test for proximate cause, the harm was not too remote. By taking the focus away from causation and on to the level at which the risk needed to be foreseeable the approach of the majority of the High Court in *Lothian v. Rickards* potentially allowed for a significant expansion of liability.

In the end, the approach of the majority did not prevail. It did not command the assent of Isaacs J in the High Court who found that the deliberate and wrongful intervention was not foreseeable and, in effect, held that it was not permissible to generalise the risk in the way the majority had. As he put it, the results of the act 'might or might not prove to be similar to those of an event for which the defendant would be responsible, had it happened, but the two events, one to be foreseen and guarded against, and the other not, are still essentially distinct'.[51] The Privy Council agreed in result although the reasoning is not entirely clear: the fact that the intervening act was deliberate was crucial because, first, no precaution could have been taken to prevent harm caused in this way; second, the proximate cause of the damage was the malicious act of the third party; and third, such an act could not have been foreseen by the defendant. The appeal was thus allowed and the defendant successful, although Harry Rickards did not live to see his ultimate victory.

There are a number of reasons why a study of the Australian courts' decisions in *Lothian v. Rickards* is important. Although the cases were relatively rare, this was not the first case to consider the question of the effect of intervening acts, even deliberate intervening acts, on liability in negligence. Moreover, the judgments are far from uniform in their reasoning: identifying common themes is difficult. But for the judges who decided against Lothian, one theme is discernible: the fact that the damage was caused by the independent and

---

[50] Cf. Hart and Honore, above n 18, 257–258 (2nd edn) who argue that the means of determining the class of harm or accident which must be foreseeable can be determined by reference to the generalisations which one would have recourse to in describing conduct as negligent. As Nolan pithily puts it, 'And when it comes to identifying the risk or risks that made the defendant's conduct negligent, consensus is often hard to come by' (D. Nolan, 'Risks and wrongs – remoteness of damage in the House of Lords' (2001) 9 *Tort Law Review* 101, 104).

[51] (1911) 12 CLR 165, 194.

wrongful act of the third party made a difference. Earlier cases may well have considered this an important point but when jury trials predominated a general instruction about the need to take precautions against foreseeable risks could mask decisions based on a genuine lack of foresight as well as on the nature of intervening act. When courts began to consider the issue in more detail in the second half of the nineteenth century, it is no surprise they articulated the limit in the same terms as judges had instructed juries: the foreseeability of the intervening act. What made *Lothian v. Rickards* different was the unusual finding by the jury: Rickards had been negligent and that negligence had caused the damage. Some of the appellate judges, in effect, simply dismissed this latter finding as misguided given the inappropriate summing up[52] but for Cussen J in the Supreme Court of Victoria and the majority in the High Court it allowed for a more nuanced treatment of a deliberate intervening act.[53] In particular, it allowed the judges to consider the question as one related solely to the risk associated with the negligent conduct. As the majority judgments in the High Court demonstrate, the application of these tests could lead to a wide range of outcomes, including deliberate wrongful conduct, as being risks associated with the defendant's conduct. Moreover, the jury finding allowed the court to consider this question apart from the question of negligence. It allowed for a differentiation of the various risks created by the defendant's conduct and in doing so clearly differentiated a boundary between breach and proximate cause/remoteness. Rickards was negligent because the risk of overflow from a basin was a risk that was foreseeable and against which precautions ought to have been taken. If liability was to be restrained (other than by denying factual causation), it had to be because the damage was too remote. But if foreseeability was also the test for proximate cause, the scope of liability could be greatly extended. This was well understood by Isaacs J: this possibility gave rise to the 'vast and far reaching importance of this case'.[54] Proximate cause might achieve the desired results where it remained inscrutable but to apply a generalised foreseeability approach to remoteness could not exclude liability in all cases where it might be thought liability should be avoided. As Pollock wrote in his *Law of Tort* (7th edn) (quoted by Griffith CJ), albeit in the context of contributory negligence:

> A wrongful or negligent voluntary act of Peter may create a state of things giving an opportunity for another wrongful act or negligent act of John, as well as for pure accidents. If harm is then caused by John's act, which act is of a kind that Peter might reasonably have foreseen, Peter and John may both be liable; and this whether John's act be wilful or not, for many kinds of negligent and wilfully

---

[52] See, e.g., the comments of A'Beckett, A10074, above n 4, Appeal Book, 39; and of the Privy Council: [1913] AC 263, 272.

[53] Although both Griffith CJ and O'Connor J saw some difficulties with the trial judge's decision: (1911) 12 CLR 165, 177–178 (Griffith CJ) 165, 186 (O'Connor J).

[54] Ibid., 190.

wrongful acts are unhappily common, and a prudent man cannot shut his eyes to the probability that somebody will commit them if temptation is put in the way.[55]

Whether there was a risk could be manipulated by the flexibility that attaches to findings of foreseeability but this could go both ways. Hence if it was thought that there should be no liability for the deliberate, wrongful intervening acts of third parties, risk was an inadequate tool to achieve this result. Rather, the focus needed to be on the reasons *why* it was inappropriate to impose liability for harm caused in this way. In fact, Beven's analysis, with its focus on responsible agency, went to the core concern with imposing liability in this category of case (albeit one that if adopted would have resulted in a different view than that taken by the majority of the High Court in *Lothian v. Rickards*). We should not be critical of the judges for not engaging with these more normative arguments: appellate courts rarely did at that time. But they did adopt a mode of reasoning that made explicit the limits of foreseeability-based approaches to remoteness of damage. At least in part, this was due to the fortuitous circumstance that the jury finding on causation gave some scope to explore other reasons for preventing liability. Once the question had moved to foreseeability and risk, it also moved to the related question of responsibility, even if only in the muted form allowed for in judicial reasoning of the period. This was a considerable advance on contemporary judicial discussions on the point in England.

Foreseeability and Deliberate Wrongful Conduct

The scope of a defendant's liability for deliberate and wrongful conduct of a third party was rarely raised after *Rickards* during the period of this study, but when it was it demonstrated why using foreseeability as a criterion of responsibility was unsatisfactory and could produce results that were socially unacceptable. A case shortly after *Lothian*, *Prattis v. Council of Municipality of Bexley*,[56] is a good example. It was one thing not to saddle a defendant with liability where the third party intervener was the obvious party to blame for the injury but not all third party interveners, even those who acted deliberately and wrongfully, attracted approbation. In *Prattis* the plaintiff was a thirteen-year-old boy who was injured when he was playing on a crane in the control of the defendant council. The defendant had constructed a quarry adjoining the highway and the crane was located in the quarry. It had not been in use for some period and during that time it was secured using a padlock and chains to ensure that it could not be used. At some period between when the chains and padlock were checked (which was disputed at trial but was at a minimum some weeks before the accident), the precautions were removed and children were able to play on the crane which resulted in the plaintiff's injury. In a jury trial the plaintiff was successful and was awarded £350 and the verdict was upheld on appeal to the

---

[55] Pollock, above n 20, 462.
[56] (1915) 15 SR (NSW) 232.

Full Court of the Supreme Court of New South Wales. Assuming that any failure to regularly check the precautions was careless, the defendant, understandably, relied on the *Rickards v. Lothian* argument. As Cullen CJ noted:

> But the contention for the defendants is that no-one could reasonably be
> expected to guard against the use of force by some malicious or mischievous
> person in undoing the protection which they had applied in the first instance.
> And there is no doubt, on the authorities, that in considering what precautions
> are required to avoid a change of negligence, one is not expected to anticipate the
> very varied forms in which malice, or mischief, may undo the work even of the
> most careful person.[57]

But Cullen CJ, somewhat obliquely, rejected this approach on the facts of
Prattis. The cases cited to support the proposition in the quote – including
Rickards – were distinguished apparently on the basis that the malicious act of
the third party occurred very shortly before the plaintiff's injury whereas here
there was some considerable gap.[58] This approach moves away from any blanket
denial of liability but controls liability simply through breach of duty, a position
Cullen CJ defended forcefully: 'But you cannot negative responsibility simply
by putting questions that emphasise the difficulty, such as, Is inspection to be
made once a month or once a week, or how often?'[59] But on the wider issue
of why there was any responsibility Cullen CJ uses a nuisance case – *Barker
v. Herbert*,[60] where liability for failing to rectify a dangerous situation caused by
a trespasser was recognised although denied on the facts – by noting that liability could be established for a dangerous state of things for which a defendant
was not originally responsible. Although this was a case of nuisance, 'it has a
distinct bearing on the case where the gist of the action is negligence'[61] but the
exact bearing is left very much to be inferred by the reader.

Whatever the merits of the distinction based on the period of time between
the intervening act and the damage, one cannot escape the conclusion that the
case was heavily influenced by the fact that there was a child plaintiff. There was
evidence that the intervening acts that destroyed the security arrangements for
the crane was carried out by children.[62] This was not perhaps the same as the
deliberately wanton act that was assumed to have taken place in *Rickards*. At
least where children were involved, then, there was certainly no general rule
that liability in negligence would not extend to taking precautions to prevent
injury where the deliberate act of a third party had created a dangerous situation
on land in the occupation of the defendant. Liability would depend, as in other
negligence cases, on the reasonableness of the defendant's response to the risk.

---

[57] Ibid., 232, 240.
[58] Ibid., 241. During argument, Cullen CJ also noted that in *Rickards* the accident happened
immediately after the interference.
[59] Ibid., 242.
[60] [1911] 2 KB 633.
[61] (1915) 15 SR (NSW) 232, 242.
[62] Ibid., 240.

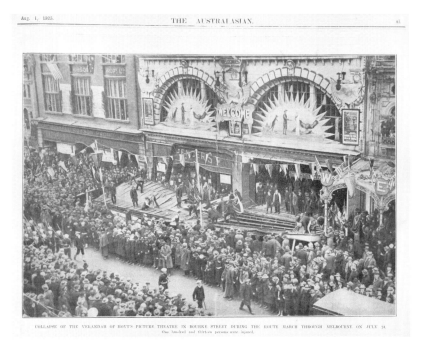

Figure 5.1 Collapse of the verandah of Hoyt's picture theatre, 24 July 1925.
Source: The Australasian (Melbourne), 1 August 1925, 77, http://nla.gov.au/nla
.news-article140717594.

The Over-Exuberant Crowd and Third Party Liability

Fifteen years later, and in a very different factual context, Isaacs J was given another opportunity to consider the limits of negligence where the immediate cause of the injury was the intervention of a third party. In 1925 the American fleet visited a number of Australian cities. It was an important public and political event and Melbourne, as the then home of the Commonwealth Parliament, received the largest contingent of forty-three ships. To celebrate the visit a large parade of visiting sailors was organised through the streets of Melbourne and crowds thronged to give their enthusiastic support. One place where crowds had gathered was on a verandah that covered Spencer's drapers and Hoyt's de Luxe Picture Theatre in Bourke Street. The exact number of people on the verandah watching the parade was a matter of dispute but at the very least there were twenty-five people on the balcony.[63] Of these most were people whom

---

[63] A contemporary report suggests that about thirty people were on the verandah (*Argus*, 25 July 1925, 30), various witnesses at the trial gave figures between twenty and seventy-five (NAA, A10074, 1927/45, *Hoyt's Proprietary Ltd v. O'Connor*, Appeal Book, Transcript of Evidence), the official report of the Full Court of the Supreme Court of Victoria decision stated that the

the defendant, Hoyt's Pty Ltd, had expressly or impliedly permitted to be present on the verandah but there were a small number – about five – who had jumped from the slightly higher adjacent Theatre Royal verandah onto the Hoyt's verandah as the procession moved up Bourke Street.[64] Shortly after these extra persons had come onto the verandah, it collapsed, first the front section and ten minutes later the section closest to the wall. A large number of people were injured – 140 in some reports – and the parade had to be halted while the injured were treated and taken to hospital.[65] One person later died, a subsequent coronial enquiry finding the death was caused by accident.[66] Questions were asked in the Victorian Parliament, and the Melbourne City Council conducted the 'fullest' investigation into the incident.[67] There is little doubt that, even allowing for journalistic licence, the description of the events as 'harrowing' and involving a 'terrible scene' accurately reflected the aftermath of the accident[68] although, remarkably, the parade continued on some forty minutes after the original collapse, the Marines resuming their formation after having been involved in assisting the police in crowd control.[69] Overall the accident was considered as an unfortunate blip on an otherwise successful event.[70]

One of the victims of the accident, Joseph O'Connor, sued the defendant Hoyt's Pty Ltd for the serious injuries he had suffered.[71] As the case unfolded, it was based on two distinct arguments. The first was that the verandah had been carelessly constructed or maintained. Most of the evidence at trial went towards this issue but there was little evidence to support the allegation and Mann J summed up to the jury very strongly against the plaintiff on this point.[72] The second argument was more difficult and related to the defendant's management of the crowd that was watching the procession when the verandah

---

plaintiff's witnesses said there were between sixty and one hundred people and that the defence admitted that there were between twenty-five and forty people (*O'Connor v. Hoyt's Proprietary Ltd* [1928] VLR 65, 67), and in the High Court Isaacs and Powers JJ noted there were at least thirty (*Hoyt's Pty Ltd v. O'Connor* (1928) 40 CLR 566, 578).

[64] Although there was some evidence that there was barbed wire between the verandahs, it seems that there was only some wire which may in fact have been electricity and other wires: A10074, above n 65.

[65] *Argus*, 25 July 1925, 30; *Age*, 25 July 1925, 15.

[66] *Age*, 17 September 1925, 13; 9 October 1925, 13; *Argus*, 9 October 1925, 9.

[67] *Age*, 27 August 1925, 14.

[68] *Age*, 25 July 1925, 15; *Argus*, 25 July 1925, 30.

[69] The officer commanding the marines was commended on his great promptitude and presence of mind in assisting in crowd control: *Age*, 25 July 1925, 15.

[70] See the reports in *Age*, 25 July 1925, 16–17, *Argus*, 25 July 1925, 31–32.

[71] It seems that O'Connor's was something of a test case with at least thirty claims made but held over awaiting the result and more to be commenced if the result was favourable. The defendant's solicitor believed that O'Connor's legal expenses were contributed to by other victims of the accident: Affidavit of James Edward Martin in support of stay of execution pending Privy Council appeal, A10074, above n 65, paras. 9–11.

[72] *Argus*, 18 June 1927, 29. It was argued, unsuccessfully, on appeal in both the Full Court of the Supreme Court and in the High Court that Mann J should have withdrawn this charge from the jury and that his failure to do so resulted is a miscarriage of justice. This issue is not relevant for present purposes and is not discussed further.

collapsed. This argument itself had two aspects. The first was that, given that the verandah was designed and built as a verandah, the defendant was careless in not making enquiries as to whether it was safe to use it for the different purpose – as a stand from which to watch events on the street below – for which the defendant knew it was being used. But what was the effect of the additional load on the verandah being caused by the 'trespassers' from the Theatre Royal?

Mann J's summing up dealt with this in two ways. First, he said that if the jury found that the verandah gave way because of the load it was expected to bear then it did not matter which part of the verandah fell first. This was in response to the defendant's submission that the verandah had given way on the side where the trespassers had jumped on it. But Mann J directed the jury that they still needed to consider whether the fall was caused by the dropping down of the men from the Theatre Royal. After a curious instruction that suggested the argument was legally irrelevant where it was improper for Hoyts to have any of their invited guests on the balcony,[73] he turned to the specific issue of the trespassers, and after painting a picture which made it almost certain that the jury would think the entry by the interlopers inevitable, left it to the jury 'whether that course of conduct on the part of the people so situated [the intruders] was not just such a course of conduct as the defendants might reasonably have anticipated'.[74] Put simply, Mann J's summing up on this point suggested that foreseeability that people might come, uninvited, onto the verandah would be sufficient to attribute responsibility. It did not separate two distinct issues – the issue of causation (whether in fact the extra weight from the trespassers caused the verandah to fall) and, in modern terms, scope of liability (whether the defendant should have been legally responsible for any damage attributable to the trespassers). And while defendant's counsel, R.G. Menzies, objected to this part of the summing up, he too focused on foreseeability and fault rather than causation.[75] It was seemingly accepted on all sides that if the interloper's actions were reasonably to be anticipated, Hoyt's could be liable if reasonable steps had not been taken against this risk. Given Mann J's strong inclination that the steps taken to keep the intruders off the verandah were inadequate and the paucity of evidence as to negligent construction, this view was undoubtedly influential in the jury of six finding for the plaintiff and awarding £1500 as damages.

The defendant unsuccessfully appealed to the Full Court of the Supreme Court of Victoria.[76] On the trespasser point, Dixon KC put the argument

---

[73] A10074, above n 65, Appeal Book, Judge's Summing Up, 85, 88–89. His reasoning seems to have been that as the presence of the Hoyt's guests created a risk, it was 'not material' whether the presence of the additional people on the verandah was the last straw. Menzies for the defendant objected to this part of the summing up and it was not restated when the judge further instructed the jury after counsel's intervention.

[74] Ibid., 85.

[75] Ibid., 88.

[76] [1928] VLR 65.

succinctly. The defendant had no duty of care, he said, to prevent the incursion of strangers onto the verandah. As he put it:

> In all cases where the act of a third person is a link in the chain you start with the first step – the negligence complained of – and it is only when the first step brings about the happening of the accident that liability ensues.[77]

The description of Dixon's argument in the report of the case is in summary form but its gist seems to be as follows. As there was no duty to prevent the incursion of strangers on the verandah, any negligence had to relate to the treatment of persons who were on the verandah with Hoyt's consent. But in Dixon's argument there was simply no evidence that the number of people who were on the verandah with consent created a risk of its collapsing. This was a difficult argument to overcome if the negligence alleged related to the number of people on the verandah so it seems plaintiff's counsel changed tack. The negligence was not simply the possibility of overloading the verandah so that it would collapse but in overloading it beyond the capacity for which it was designed. It was this argument that appealed to a unanimous Full Court. This required the defendant to make enquiry from competent experts as to the suit-ability of the structure for this new use and this they had not done; they had simply taken the risk.[78] Moreover, the addition of the trespassers and their pos-sible causative effect made no difference. Once negligence was found in admit-ting guests on to the verandah in the absence of enquiry, that negligence was at least a direct contributing cause of the accident and this was sufficient to make the defendant liable for the whole of the plaintiff's damage.[79] This too was an innovative ruling.[80] Whichever lens one views the result through, however, one thing is clear: the fact that at least some aspect of the overcrowding was attrib-utable to the deliberate, wrongful act of a third party did not prevent liability from arising. Given the line that Isaacs J and the Privy Council had taken on this issue in *Rickards*, it is no surprise that there was a further appeal from the Full Court decision to the High Court.

The High Court Splits – In Unexpected Ways

In an unusual result, the High Court split 2-2 in the appeal with the conse-quence that the plaintiff retained his verdict. As Dixon KC's Notice of Appeal explicitly attacked, among other reasons, the trial judge's direction (or lack of it) in relation to the impact of the interveners on the collapse of the verandah, it is

---

[77] Ibid., 68.
[78] Ibid., 71–72.
[79] Ibid., 73.
[80] Although English and Victorian authority was cited in support, those cases dealt with situations where each of the independent causes were considered to have caused the harm. *The Bernina* (1886) 12 PD 36; (1888) 13 App Cas 1; *Bean v. Harper & Co.* (1893) 18 VLR 388. There was no similar finding in *Hoyt's*.

no surprise that the judgments in the High Court deal directly with the issue.[81] Three very different judgments were given. Allowing the appeal and ordering a new trial, Knox CJ clinically dissected the flaws in the reasoning of the courts below. The problem with Mann J's summing up was that the questions he left to the jury dealt with the question of fault without considering causation. As he put it, the question submitted to the jury 'was whether, in expostulating with the intruders to try and stop them from coming on to the awning or in telling them they must not come on, the appellant as proprietor took all reasonable care. In my opinion, the true issue was whether the appellant had proved to the satisfaction of the jury that but for the unauthorized intrusion of these persons the awning would not have fallen'.[82] This was more than a procedural error in the summing up: it went to a key question of the limits of the defendant's responsibility:

> The appellant, having permitted the use of the awning for a purpose for which it was not intended, might properly be held responsible for the consequence of such permitted user; but, if the appellant could establish that the accident was caused by the unauthorized acts of persons who were in fact forbidden by the servants of the appellant to come on to the awning, and that it would not have happened but for the unauthorized acts of those persons, to hold the appellant still liable seems to me to put the duty of an occupier too high.[83]

Starke J reached the same conclusion. While accepting that liability could arise if the defendant's negligence together with the independent actions of the trespassers caused the damage, the defendant's case was that they were not negligent vis-a-vis their own guests and liability could only be founded on its failure to stop the trespassers entering on the verandah. Citing the leading English authority for the no liability rule in relation to damage caused by third parties,[84] Starke J could not 'assent to the view that an occupier of property is under a duty to prevent the intrusion of trespassers upon his property, or to foresee that such an intrusion was likely and would cause damage'.[85] For Starke J the no-liability rule was not based on any context-specific analysis of whether the intervention was foreseeable in fact[86] and he emphatically rejected any suggestion that because the state of the verandah might be attractive to those without permission wanting to use it some kind of implied permission through allurement was created. Paradoxically, however, Starke J was somewhat relieved that the verdict was upheld as he thought the case should have been argued as a public nuisance claim based on the very strict duty owed by the occupier of

---

[81] A10074, above n 65, Notice of Appeal.

[82] (1928) 40 CLR 566, 575.

[83] Ibid., 574–575.

[84] *Weld-Blundell v. Stephens* [1920] AC 956.

[85] (1928) 40 CLR 566, 586.

[86] '[I] cannot assent to the view that an occupier of property is under a duty to prevent the intrusion of trespassers upon his property or to foresee that such an intrusion was likely and would cause damage': ibid.

property abutting the highway to keep his property from being a danger to the public using the highway and that a retrial with a proper direction on this point would almost certainly result in a verdict for the plaintiff.

In different ways, then, Knox CJ and Starke J asserted a 'no liability for the deliberate wrongful acts of third parties' rule. The joint judgment of Isaacs and Powers JJ – almost certainly written by Isaacs J – took a very different approach. The judgment was explicit that the ground on which the verdict was upheld was not any ground related to special duties owed by the owner of property abutting a highway (the ground on which Starke J thought the decision might have been justified). Rather, the evidence justified the jury in holding 'the appellant responsible for the total overloading of the verandah, including the persons, regarded as not authorized, and for the consequent collapse of the structure'.[87] The fundamental consideration was that O'Connor's claim was not based on his being an invitee or licensee but upon his inherent and independent right as a passenger on the King's highway. The gist of the complaint was that the defendant negligently used the stand '*as between the appellant and himself*' (italics in original).[88] While it was not necessary to sheet home responsibility to the defendant that everyone on the verandah was an invitee or licensee, the defendant was only liable if the responsibility for the unauthorised people was '*in some way*' imputable to Hoyt's. The question of law, thought Isaacs J, was whether 'the doctrine of anticipated action' applied to this case and he thought it did. He did so on the basis of general principles rather than authority:

> It is true that no case exactly in point can be found; but though that circumstance should make a Court cautious, it is no reason for denying the right to redress. This is a claim rested on the common law. While it is perfectly true that new principles are not now to be invented by the Courts but must be left to the legislature, it is equally true that long established principles of the common law regulating the relations of society are not to be denied their just application to those relations merely because the circumstances attending them are novel and more complex.[89]

While English authority was cited for this very general principle,[90] none was cited in relation to the specific question the court had to answer and for that task Isaacs J went back to first principle. This was that a man exercising rights of property must have due regard to the rights of others and if by negligence another was injured 'he is responsible unless some valid answer is available'. Conscious that the decision he was about to make was controversial, he went further into the 'rationale of the matter'. Negligence was the taking of the care the law required in the circumstances but whether care was required and its

---

[87] Ibid., 577–578.
[88] Ibid., 578.
[89] Ibid.
[90] The general nature of the support is shown by his citation of *Bracton*, Book 1, ch. 2.

extent was a matter of law. In some cases – such as the relation between invitor and invitee – the necessity and extent of care was well established. However,

> In other circumstances, for instance in the present case, the question has not been expressly settled, and has given rise to considerable discussion and some difference of opinion. That is only to be expected from the multiform and changing aspects of life in a progressive society.[91]

While the task gave rise to dispute, there was no suggestion that it was something that an Australian court was incapable of doing and Isaacs J went on to hold that, on the facts of the case, Hoyt's was required to take steps to prevent overloading the verandah by permitted 'or by the advent of additional persons whose presence, though unpermitted, ought in the circumstances have been anticipated'. Whether the circumstances ought to have been anticipated was a fact which allowed local conditions and expectations to be taken into account. Similar processions to the one by the American sailors were not infrequent in Melbourne and it was a matter of 'common knowledge' that people mount on verandahs and such points of vantage. As he put it:

> Human nature being as it is, local habits being known, and previous similar processions having taken place, when the appellant created indications of space and convenience for a further number and apparent safety – because appearances were all that would naturally influence outsiders – and with but a step down to reach the verandah on the part of those persons whom everyone would expect to swarm on the neighbouring structures, what ought the appellant reasonably to have anticipated?[92]

As the jury was perfectly entitled to say that the intervention should have been anticipated – by creating in effect an allurement, or inducement, or temptation – Hoyt's was responsible for the interveners' conduct. It did not matter whether they were instrumental in creating the final or additional stress in bringing down the verandah. If the jury found that the attempts to keep them off the verandah were inadequate liability could be imposed.

One should not overstate the significance of the *Hoyt's* decision: probably because of the variety of approaches to the law represented in the split judgments it was rarely cited by contemporary cases. Moreover, Isaacs J's discussion of the 'rationale of the matter' was soon superseded by the speeches in *Donoghue v. Stevenson*.[93] Nonetheless, there are features of the decision that are worthy of note. First, implicitly in the direction of Mann J and explicitly in the joint judgment of Isaacs and Powers JJ, the idea that liability in negligence for a danger caused by the conduct of third parties was imposed on the basis that the conduct of the third parties was anticipated – reasonably foreseeable in modern parlance – was accepted. While English authority recognised

---

[91] (1928) 40 CLR 566, 580.
[92] Ibid., 582.
[93] [1932] AC 562.

circumstances where an occupier could be liable for third party interventions, they were not, as Starke J pointed out, situations where the sole basis of liability was the foreseeability of the acts of trespassers and the failure to exercise reasonable care to prevent those acts. The point was made abundantly clear by Lord Sumner in *Weld-Blundell v. Stephens*,[94] decided only eight years previous by the House of Lords. The issue in that case arose out of a third party's use of a libellous letter and Lord Sumner rejected the imposition of liability on the originally negligent party on the basis that the intervening act was foreseeable.[95] Yet this is exactly what the doctrine of anticipated action did. Perhaps the fault lay with Dixon KC who in argument accepted that unless the defendant allured the interveners there was no liability but, despite Isaacs J's vivid description of the verandah as an attractive place for interlopers to stand, one is hard-pressed to say that the verandah was an allurement any more than the valuable contents in a house were an allurement to a burglar. Moreover, Isaacs J gave another example which gave allurement a meaning which in no sense accorded with any kind of tacit encouragement by the occupier for third parties to come on to the premises. What if during a public procession, he asked, the owner of a verandah displayed some emblem calculated to arouse public indignation and resentment so that a number of persons spurred by the feelings so engendered mounted the verandah to tear down the emblem with the result that the verandah falls and hurts a passer-by? He thought liability should be imposed: even though the interlopers were trespassers, 'the consequence is what the property owner should have anticipated from his own act' and the owner's liability would not be defeated by the plea that the interveners were trespassers.[96] This is clearly inconsistent with basing liability on the authority or expectation of the owner. It is impossible to believe that Isaacs J was unaware of what Lord Sumner had said in *Weld-Blundell* and it is hard to avoid the inference that he simply ignored an authority that would prevent him from reaching what he saw as the just result in the circumstances.

Second, basing the liability on what was foreseeable allowed for local conditions to be taken into account so that notions of responsibility could legitimately vary depending on where the events took place. On this approach, what might have been expected of crowds in London was irrelevant: what was important was what was expected in Melbourne. Moreover, the discussion of Isaacs J of the process by which the law could be extended beyond existing authority – the application of existing principles to novel circumstances in his words – allowed considerable scope for judicial assessment of the law that was appropriate for Australian conditions.[97] It is striking that the justifications for

---

[94] [1920] AC 956.
[95] Ibid., 987–988.
[96] (1928) 40 CLR 566, 581.
[97] During the 1920s there are a number of other decisions of Isaacs J where he explicitly referred to notions of developing the law in accord with the needs of a progressive society: see *Cofield v. Waterloo Case Co. Ltd* (1924) 34 CLR 363, *Bourke v. Butterfield and Lewis Ltd* (1926) 38 CLR

extending responsibility mentioned by Isaacs J do not refer at all to how far English authority had extended. There was no doubt that the equities – viewed broadly – were all with the plaintiff, a quite different situation from *Weld-Blundell*. It is noteworthy that in several places Isaacs J drew a clear distinction between the owner's relationship with the passers-by as opposed to the interveners. The evidence given by the management of the Hoyt's Theatre indicated an extremely lackadaisical approach as to who was on the verandah.[98] It was not a case where the defendant had carefully controlled access to the verandah and had then been hijacked by a group of malicious interveners who had deliberately harmed third persons even if, as Starke J noted, this was how the defendants had argued the appeal. While Isaacs J's approach can be reconciled with his judgment in *Lothian v. Rickards* – the likelihood of the intervening conduct in *Lothian* was less than in *O'Connor* so that it was unforeseeable – it is tempting to see the difference in the character of the intervening conduct.[99] The high-spirited, thoughtless enthusiasm of those who jumped on the verandah was very different from 'the acts of a malicious person bent on destruction' whom Isaacs J assumed to be the intervener in *Lothian*. This is not to say that Isaacs J's approach was the best way to deal with this issue: it could be argued convincingly that allowing liability in his 'offensive emblem' example gives insufficient weight to the autonomous actions of responsible agents (and possibly has implications for freedom of speech). My point is simply that at some level value judgements are required to determine the scope of a defendant's responsibility for damage caused by third parties and that through a number of courts and judges a variety of approaches were taken to determine how those judgements should be made that did not always reflect the contemporary English position. For Isaacs J, fault and foreseeability drew that balance acceptably on the facts of Hoyt's and as applied to those facts this was hard to deny. A commercial property owner could not simply 'hope for the best' as Hoyt's had done in respect of its management of the verandah. And in the end perhaps the defendant recognised that, for whatever reason, the courts had reached a result that was

354 (breach of statutory duty) and *Wright v. Cedzich* (1930) 43 CLR 493 (loss of consortium). Sawer referred to this as a 'cryptosociological' approach: G. Sawer, 'Ejectment without cause from a place of entertainment' (1935–1938) 1 *Res Judicatae* 24.

[98] See, for example, the evidence of George Frederick Griffith, Managing Director of Hoyt's Theatres Ltd, who initially said he authorised no one to go on to the verandah at all but after admitting in cross-examination he authorised at least two people he agreed that he could 'easily' have given permission to other people he had forgotten about: A10074, above n 65, Appeal Book.

[99] Isaacs' notebooks contain an extract from a decision of Holmes J in Massachusetts that 'wrongful acts of independent third parties … are not regarded by the law as natural consequences of his wrong and he is not bound to anticipate the general probability of such acts' and the Privy Council decision in *Dominion Natural Gas* case is noted: 'Papers of Sir Isaac Isaacs, 1883–1969', NLA, MS2755, Series 3, Box 5, Items 241–360. Other extracts from the same section are from cases involving negligent intervening acts where foreseeability is the deciding factor indicating he was aware of the importance of the nature of the intervening act.

unlikely to be reversed: while a petition for leave to appeal to the Privy Council was prepared there is no record of it being presented.[100]

Conclusion: Third Party Liability Shanghaied?

There was little further discussion of liability in negligence for the acts of third parties in the period of this study. Shortly after *Hoyts*, the Full Court of the Supreme Court of Western Australia by majority held that a municipal council was not liable for injury to a pedestrian caused when he fell over a seat.[101] The seat had been installed by the council and had been moved into a dangerous position by an unknown third party. At trial McMillan CJ had seen the key question as 'Was it or was it not the duty of the council to anticipate the wrong acts of mischievous persons?' and found that that risk of the seat being moved should have been considered by the Council.[102] The majority of the Full Court disagreed but for different reasons: Northmore J thought there was no reason for the Council to anticipate the third party's conduct whilst Draper J held that the Council was not responsible because of the 'subsequent volitional and mischevious interference of unauthorised third parties'.[103] Whether foreseeability of the third party interference was enough to found liability remained unclear and it remained so at the end of this period of study. This was so despite the High Court decision in *Smith v. Leurs* in 1945. At the beginning of the school holidays in December 1943, Brian Leurs and his friends were engaged in what Latham CJ described as 'semi-hostile' play in suburban Black Forest in Adelaide when Brian Smith was hit in the eye by a shanghai fired by Leurs.[104] As it was clear that the parents could not be vicariously liable on the facts for their adopted son's actions, any liability of the parents in the law of negligence had to be rooted in notions of responsibility for damage caused by the conduct of a third party. This point was largely obscured, however, because it was accepted without discussion by all but one of the judges who heard the case that parents could be responsible in negligence for failing to control the acts of children – even the thirteen-year-old Brian Leurs[105] – and the question rested simply on

---

[100] A10074, above n 65, Affidavit of James Edward Martin in support of stay of execution pending Privy Council appeal, paras. 12–13.

[101] *Subiaco Municipal Council v. Walmsley* [1930] WAR 49.

[102] *WA*, 21 November 1929, 20; *Daily News* (Perth), 20 November 1929, 2.

[103] *Subiaco Municipal Council v. Walmsley* [1930] WAR 49, 57.

[104] The 'keystone cops' character of the interaction, where rival groups chased each other around the neighbourhood, is detailed in the press reports of the trial: *News* (Adelaide), 7 November 1944, 6; *The Advertiser* (Adelaide), 8 November 1944, 8.

[105] The trial judge, Mayo J, clearly thought that Brian Leurs' age was relevant (see [1944] SASR 213, 218, 221) but in the Full Court Reed J noted there was no evidence that boys of that age generally were likely to shoot shanghais at humans or that their son was likely to do so. This recognises a reasonable degree of autonomy in the child but in Reed J's judgment this went only to breach of duty, it being assumed that the parents were under a duty.

whether any duty imposed on the parents had been breached.[106] After the argument that a shanghai was an 'essentially' dangerous chattel was rejected, the decision turned simply on what reasonable parents could be expected to do in these circumstances. It is an example of how this kind of liability could be controlled at the breach stage: the judges almost unanimously thought that the suggested precaution – withdrawing the shanghai from the boy before he left the household – was unworkable and unreasonable. Even on this point, however, the sensitivities attached to imposing liability on parents for the torts of their children made the case unusual and quite different from the previous cases discussed in this section.[107] It is only in the judgment of Dixon J in the High Court that an attempt at a wider generalisation, beyond liability of parents for the torts of their children, is made. In a passage oft-cited in later cases, Dixon J sent out of the general duty position where third party actions were involved:

> But, apart from vicarious liability, one man may be responsible to another for the harm done to the latter by a third person; he may be responsible on the ground that the act of the third person could not have taken place but for his own fault or breach of duty. There is more than one description of duty the breach of which may produce this consequence. For instance, it may be a duty of care in reference to things involving special danger. It may even be a duty of care with reference to the control of actions or conduct of third parties. It is, however, exceptional to find in law a duty to control another's actions to prevent harm to strangers. The general rule is that one man is under no duty of controlling another man to prevent his doing damage to a third. There are, however, special relations which are the source of a duty of this nature. It appears now to be recognized that it is incumbent upon a parent who maintains control over a young child to take reasonable care so to exercise that control as to avoid conduct on his part exposing the person or property of others to unreasonable danger.[108]

On one level it is surprising that this statement should have become as influential as it has. Dixon J sets out no 'test' for determining when this exceptional duty might be owed. But the real importance of the statement lies in its failure to mention foreseeability of the acts of third parties as a factor in determining whether the special duty should be owed. Perhaps Dixon J assumed that such a requirement would be present but as the only authorities he cites – and does not discuss – deal, understandably, with the specific liability of parents for the conduct of their children no clear answer is discernable. And although Dixon J does not express it as a formal criterion for imposing a duty in this situation, the reference to 'control' is also significant. In combination with the character of the intervening conduct, the presence or absence of control, outside of

---

[106] *Smith v. Leurs* [1944] SASR 213; *Smith v. Leurs* [1945] SASR 86; *Smith v. Leurs* (1945) 70 CLR 256. This was how contemporary English cases involving guardians had dealt with the issue: *Ricketts v. Erith Borough Council* (1944) 113 LJKB 269.

[107] [1945] SASR 86, 9 (Angas Parsons J), 89 (Napier CJ) in the Full Court of the South Australian Supreme Court.

[108] (1945) 70 CLR 256, 262.

children cases, could help explain the different results in *Rickards v. Lothian* and *Hoyt's v. O'Connor*. The malicious lavatory-blocker was an unknown and hence uncontrollable figure, to be anticipated only in the abstract, but the presence of the interlopers in Hoyt's was known and there was a very real capacity to control them (even if liability would turn on whether any measures taken to control them were reasonable). This is not to say that in Australia or in England the foreseeability of the third party's intervention was jettisoned after Dixon J's judgment: the amorphous role of foreseeability in the various analytic elements of the negligence action made it impossible to excise it from discussions of a defendant's responsibility in these circumstances. But it can be claimed with some legitimacy that Dixon J's judgment, with its emphasis on the exceptional nature of the liability, required later courts to explain *why* the relationship between the parties was special so as to impose the duty.

Dixon J had foreseeability in mind (although talking about breach and not duty) when later on in his judgment he bemoaned the fact that '[a]s so often happens in the law of tort, the liability of the party is seen to depend on a vague and uncertain standard giving little guidance either to judge or litigants'.[109] Moreover, where liability was denied on the basis that the intervention was not foreseeable, there remained the problem as to whether this was a statement of fact or of law. There is a world of difference between saying that an intervening wrongful act *did not have* to be foreseen (as Starke J indicated in *Hoyt's*) and saying that it was not foreseen: the former is a normative statement not susceptible to challenge through evidence while the later – which may have been Isaacs J's approach – varies depending on the facts. The difference is illustrated by an example from a Canadian law journal in 1946: a commentator was asked whether a farmer could claim for damage to crops caused by trespassers on his land as a result of a plane crash. Citing *Rickards v. Lothian* in the Privy Council, he thought no: 'the damage was caused by the crowd committing a trespass and it is not to be contemplated that someone else will commit a tort' and later '[b]ut people are supposed to be able to reason, and it is not a probable consequence of one tort that someone else will commit another tort'.[110] These must be normative statements – a plane crash would be exactly the kind of event at which one might expect trespassers – but as discussed above it is unclear whether *Rickards* really was authority for this view.[111] But whether Dixon J's approach to responsibility is preferable to that adopted by earlier Australian judges is ultimately not to the point for present purposes. It is simply the final in a thoughtful line of indigenous judicial contributions as to the appropriate boundaries of responsibility in the tort of negligence where the immediate cause of the plaintiff's harm was the act of a third party.

---

[109] Ibid., 263.

[110] *Fortnightly Law Journal*, 1 November 1946, 11.

[111] There is little discussion of the issue in the Privy Council and after his judgment in *Hoyt's* it seems that Isaacs J's view in the High Court in *Rickards* was that the intervention was not foreseeable as a matter of fact.

6

Negligence and the Vexing Question of Shock-Induced Harm

During the first half of the twentieth century, Australian courts struggled to find coherent reasoning to deal with cases where the plaintiff's injury was not caused as a result of a physical impact. In the language of the time, the question was the extent of a defendant's liability – usually but not exclusively in negligence – for 'nervous shock'. While this study begins in 1901 and cases before that time have generally not been considered, in this instance it is impossible to understand the twentieth-century cases without some understanding of the problems – both legal and moral – that arose from the Privy Council decision in *Victoria Railway Commissioners v. Coultas*, in 1888, which limited recovery for shock-induced mental harm. From the beginning to the end of the period, Australian courts considered liability for nervous shock in the shadow of a technically binding but discredited decision. Their largely successful attempts to avoid a rigid application of the legal rules set out in that case illustrate well the practical flexibility inherent in the doctrine of precedent as it applied to Australian courts. And in at least one Australian jurisdiction – New South Wales – the arguments moved from the judicial to the political realm. The interest and political will shown in passing reform legislation showed both a willingness to alter common law rules to more accurately reflect community perceptions about when mental harm should be recoverable and a determination to set rules independently of developments in England.

Coultas: Villain or Hero?

On the evening of 8 May 1886, James Coultas, a tailor carrying on business in Collins Street, his wife Mary and Mary's brother were in a buggy on Swan Street in Richmond when they went to cross the railway line at the East Richmond crossing near Burnley station.[1] An attendant employed by the Victorian Railway Commissioners was responsible for managing the crossing. When the buggy arrived the gates of the crossing were closed but the attendant opened the gate for them and James Coultas drove the buggy on to the line and followed the light

---

[1] *Age*, 17 November 1886, 5; *Argus*, 17 November 1886, 7.

carried by the attendant across the line. At this point, the attendant noticed that a train was coming and told Coultas to go back. In fact, 'only by keeping his presence of mind and doing exactly the reverse of the thing the gatekeeper ordered, i.e., he went on instead of turning back',[2] he escaped collision but only by drawing the buggy into the small gap between the railway line and the far gate (which had not been fully opened). When the train rushed past, Mary Coultas, who was within five or six weeks of her confinement, fainted as a result of the shock of the near miss, miscarried, and suffered poor health as a result of the accident. In November 1886, Mary and James Coultas successfully sued the Railway Commissioners for the negligence of their employee (the gate attendant). An appeal to the Full Court of the Supreme Court of Victoria was rejected[3] but the Commissioners' further appeal to the Privy Council was successful.

The contemporary importance of the issue at stake in *Coultas* can be gauged by the Commissioner's decision to appeal to the Privy Council. The issue was seen as one of remoteness of damage, as it had been in the Victorian courts, because it was clear that a railway company owed a duty of care with respect to level crossing accidents.[4] It was only with an increasingly sophisticated understanding of duty of care, and a change in the law governing remoteness of damage, that it would later be argued that this question might be better seen as a duty of care question than as one of remoteness. And on this remoteness question the Privy Council found against Mrs Coultas: 'Damages arising from mere sudden terror unaccompanied by any actual physical injury, but occasioning a nervous or mental shock, cannot under such circumstances, their Lordships think, be considered a consequence which, in the ordinary course of things, would flow from the negligence of the gate-keeper.'[5] Their Lordships were more sympathetic to the policy arguments that had been raised before the Full Court. To allow recovery in this kind of case would extend liability beyond what had previously been held to be its limits and would allow anyone suffering a serious nervous shock to claim for mental injury. And there was an additional risk if liability was allowed: 'The difficulty which now often exists in case of alleged physical injuries of determining whether they were caused by the negligent act would be greatly increased, and a wide field opened for imaginary claims.'[6]

For critics of restrictive rules relating to the recovery of damages for mental or emotional harm, *Coultas* represents, if not the nadir, then at least a shared position at the bottom of the table for decisions that have hampered the development of the common law. In part, as Mendelson has pointed out, the decision was the result of the considerable contemporary uncertainty over the existence

---

[2] *Australasian*, 31 March 1888, 34.
[3] (1886) 12 VLR 895.
[4] D. Mendelson, 'The Defendants' Liability for Negligently Caused Nervous Shock in Australia – Quo Vadis?' (1992) 18 *Monash University Law Review* 16, 20 (fn 19); *The Interfaces of Medicine and Law: The History of the Liability of Negligently Caused Psychiatric Injury (Nervous Shock)* (Ashgate, 1998) 57–58.
[5] (1888) 13 App Cas 222, 225.
[6] Ibid., 226.

and physiology of nervous shock.[7] But contemporary reaction to the decision shows that views as to the recoverability of damages for shock, particularly arising out of railway accidents, was mixed. A letter from R.W. Pennefather, who appeared as a junior for the plaintiff at trial and before the Full Court, caustically set out the judgment's shortcomings: he thought the risk of imaginary claims 'quite beside the question'.[8] From a non-legal perspective, the *Melbourne Punch* was also hostile:

> If there is no mistake about the cable message, we can only say that the finding is an extraordinary one, and one not based upon justice. Shock, fright, mental injury, even death, may be caused by a narrow escape from accident as in the *Coultas* case, and the Railway Commissioners will not be liable, however great the negligence, because no actual 'impact' took place. The contention is opposed to all common sense. The English law recognises the fact that there can be assault without battery, but its Privy Council maintains that there can be no injuries without impact. Mr. W.S. Gilbert need not go further than the Privy Council for the subject of his next absurd comic opera.[9]

But there were a variety of less critical responses. *The Argus* took the view that while the decision settled the law it was also hard on the individual plaintiffs.[10] It also recognised the wider context – railway accidents – and thought the decision should alleviate the need to reduce legislatively awards against the Commissioner, a course of action that had been suggested.[11] In England the issue of personal injury compensation to victims of railway accidents, usually passengers, had been the subject of reports in 1867 and 1870.[12] There were concerns that, in a railway accident, claims were 'made up'. There is no suggestion that these concerns – reflected in the *Coultas* decision – were limited to the mother country. In a long and thoughtful comment, a commentator for *The Age*, after recognising the scepticism that attached to shock claims arising out of railway accidents, wrote:

> If a precedent were set for the recovery of damages for injuries caused by a mental shock, it would be hard to say where the range of liability could terminate. Of course wherever the line of demarcation be drawn by the courts there are sure to be instances of injustice on the one side or the other. This is inevitable in all human legislation, as well as in the administration and interpretation of

---

[7] Mendelson, above n 4, ch. 2.

[8] *Argus*, 16 March 1888, 5.

[9] *Melbourne Punch*, 9 February 1888, 1.

[10] A similar view was taken in *Australasian*, 31 March 1888, 34.

[11] *Argus*, 16 March 1888, 7. The extent of the liability in negligence of the Victorian Railway Commissioners was the subject of debate at the time of (and after) *Coultas*. The *Victorian Railway Commissioners Act 1883* (Vic) s. 74 subjected claims to a number of procedural limitations (including a six-month limitation period) and the *Railways Act 1896* (Vic) s. 21 required all actions for losses caused by sparks from railway engines to be referred to arbitration. One commentator argues that these limitations defeated 'a number of meritorious claims': P. Finn, *Law and Government in Colonial Australia* (Oxford University Press, 1987) 109.

[12] Mendelson, above n 4, 63.

the statutes. It is an extremely nice point upon which the Victorian and British judges have differed, but it is not surprising that the latter, feeling the full responsibility of their decision, have hesitated about setting a precedent which might be productive of undesirable consequences throughout the Empire.[13]

And lest it be thought that there was any kind of cultural cringe at play in justifying the Privy Council decision, the comments of *The Queenslander* on the *trial* decision are instructive. It noted 'men no better than ourselves are eating the bread of idleness on the strength of a slight jar to the nervous system in a so-called railway accident'. The decision in favour of the Coultas' was the '*reductio ad absurdum* of railway accident (?) damages'. It finished: 'We have heard of damages for very slight accidents indeed, but this is the first time we have known damages given for escaping one.'[14]

The purpose of this contextual analysis of *Coultas* is two-fold. First, there is no suggestion that *Coultas* was generally considered an unacceptable decision. There was academic criticism but there was also support for the practical considerations that underlay it. There was certainly no inevitability that the treatment of *Coultas* by Australian courts was predetermined by inherent flaws in the original judgment. Second, there was sufficient ambiguity surrounding the decision to allow considerable scope for distinguishing the decision. Even at the time, it was not absolutely clear what it decided. For example, the ratio of the decision is probably that the damages were too remote rather than that impact was necessary, as the advice itself says this. But as Pennefather pointed out in his letter to the editor, 'the decision rests upon the assumption of it, and cannot on any other grounds be supported'.[15] The problem lay in the ambiguity that surrounded the expression 'nervous shock'.[16] The early case law on nervous shock considered, not always clearly, two distinct questions. The first question was causal. Could an injury inflicted through shock – or to be more accurate not inflicted by direct impact – give rise to a claim in negligence? In theory, this causal question was independent of the type of injury that the shock caused, and whether the damage the shock caused was recoverable was a different and unrelated question. However, in determining the causal question the issue arose as to the role that the shock (or in *Coultas*, the fright) played. In the Privy Council, at least part of the advice suggested that 'actual physical injury' was a different injury from 'mental or nervous shock' but if this was correct nervous shock could not be considered simply as a causal mechanism. It was this aspect of the decision that Thomas Beven criticised and in doing so he gave content to the expressions 'nervous' and 'mental' shock.[17] Put simply, nervous shock was description of both a causal mechanism that produced some physical

[13] *Age*, 16 March 1888, 5.

[14] *The Queenslander*, 27 November 1886, 857–858.

[15] *Argus*, 16 March 1888, 5.

[16] Mendelson, above n 4, ch. 2; D. Butler, 'Identifying the compensable damage in "nervous shock" cases' (1997) 5 *TLJ*, 67–70.

[17] T. Beven, *Negligence in Law*, 2nd edn (Stevens and Haynes, 1895) 76–83.

consequence as well as the name for certain of the physical consequences that the shock produced. On the other hand, mental shock – 'mere' fright – did not produce consequences and of itself was not an injury for which damages could be awarded. The distinction had its limits – the difference between nervous and mental shock depended on the consequences they produced – but understanding this difference is important in understanding the Australian case law on 'nervous shock' during the period of this study.

Coultas: The Clayton's Case?

Whatever its merits in the politicised context of railway accidents, *Coultas* seemed much less appealing in other areas and Australian courts were keen to distinguish this binding precedent from an early date. This was first demonstrated in a case just before the period of this study, *Rea v. Balmain New Ferry Company*.[18] The plaintiff was a young woman who was injured when thrown off a gangway onto one of the defendant's ferries due to the negligence of an employee of the company in letting the ferry leave before the gangway had been withdrawn. She suffered a sprained ankle which healed but subsequently developed physical symptoms and both plaintiff and defence medical experts thought she was suffering from some kind of disease or condition. At the very best for the plaintiff the evidence was that the sprained ankle was a contributing cause of the condition, the primary cause being the shock of the accident. At trial the jury found for the plaintiff, answering positively a question on whether the sprain contributed to the disease and awarding her £500. They also awarded £5 if it was found that the sprain did not cause the disease. Leave was granted to move for a verdict for the defendant or to enter judgment for £5.

Arguing for the rule, the defendant's counsel submitted the damages were too remote: the disease was not the result of the sprain but of fright or shock and hence was not the ordinary result that flowed from the negligence. The interactions between bench and bar indicate that the judges saw the issue as one of whether shock-induced physical harm was recoverable. Darley CJ opined to counsel that he could not see why the plaintiff should not recover 'for two separate kinds of physical injury'. And when counsel submitted that *Coultas* decided that persons are not liable for the result of nervous shock, Cohen J responded: 'It seems to me that mental shock is practically equivalent to mere fright. Nervous shock, which may or may not co-exist with mental shock, is in reality a physical injury.'[19] It is not clear whether Cohen J saw nervous shock itself as an injury or whether it was a composite term that covered both the disease with which the plaintiff had been diagnosed and how it was caused. The gist though was clear: the plaintiff had suffered a physical injury and the Full Court, without bothering to call on counsel for the plaintiff, dismissed the rule.

---

[18] (1896) 17 NSWR 92.
[19] Ibid., 96.

Describing the *Coultas* case as 'a very peculiar one', Darley CJ noted that it had not met with entire approval in England, had not been followed by the Irish Court of Exchequer and that its interchangeable use of mental and nervous shock had been criticised by Beven. While the case was no doubt binding on the court, '…I do not feel inclined to extend the principle of the decision in any way…'.[20] He was able to distinguish *Coultas* as in this case there was impact and a physical injury resulting from the negligence. In his view, '[w]e cannot separate that injury entirely from the illness which immediately followed it.' While it was impossible to say how much of the illness was caused by the injury [the sprained ankle] and how much by the fright or shock, 'all we know is that the physical injury must have been one of causes which contributed to the illness.'[21] Stephen J agreed: the disease was, or may have been, the result of several causes and this was enough. It was not necessary 'to deal with such cases as those of mere fright, or fright resulting from an inadequate cause'.

Rea demonstrates there were practical ways in which the limits of *Coultas* could be avoided. Problems for the plaintiff would still arise where there was nothing that could be described as impact but where there was *Rea* suggested very little evidence was required to link the ultimate injury to the impact. It is interesting that the defendant's counsel did not argue that the disease or injury for which the plaintiff was claiming was not the natural and probable result of the impact. In hindsight this seems a worthwhile argument but the attraction of a global no-recovery rule for nervous shock where the impact was causally irrelevant was too tempting. But the failure of the argument also had its costs. A search of leading metropolitan newspapers for the expression 'nervous shock' during the period of this study reveals literally hundreds of court cases where a plaintiff, along with some kind of (presumably) impact physical injury, claimed damages for 'nervous shock'. The reports are often of lower court decisions and are usually descriptive and in the absence of further evidence it is impossible to say conclusively whether these claims were contested by defendants. Their persistence in the newspaper records, however, suggests that these claims were certainly not exceptional and that plaintiffs expected to be able to claim something for this kind of damage if the elements of a cause of action (usually negligence) were established.

An instructive example of this turn in the law can be seen in a rare case where there is more information than just the bare facts. In *Sealey v. The Commissioner for Railways*,[22] decided in October 1914, the plaintiff was a passenger on a suburban train between Brisbane and Sandgate (a bayside suburb of Brisbane) when an open door of her train was hit by a passing train, causing the glass in the door to shatter. A piece of the glass hit the plaintiff in the face, causing her minor cuts, but her own doctor diagnosed her as having

---

[20] Ibid., 98.
[21] Ibid.
[22] [1915] QWN 1.

shock, insomnia, and a recurrence of previous diabetes symptoms. In his view, '[t]he nervous effects could have been produced by alarm or fright caused by a swinging door.'[23] The Commissioner's expert said simply that any shock she had received was slight and what injury she had suffered was negligible. Moreover, in cross examination it was suggested that the plaintiff was making use of the accident to extort money from the Commissioner. Counsel for the defendant also forced an admission from the plaintiff's husband that he had previously had an action against the railway department and that in that action he had complained of insomnia, nerves, and a very bad arm. He denied that he had an enmity against the department or that he had threatened to make the department 'sit up' for the accident to his wife.[24] This was a tangible example of the kinds of concerns that had motivated the *Coultas* decision but the approach taken by Australian courts meant it had to be argued that the plaintiff had suffered no damage (in effect, had fabricated the claim). For when the trial judge summed up to the jury, Macnaughton DCJ said, distinguishing *Coultas*, that as there was an actual impact which injured the plaintiff, although very slightly, damages for the shock to her system were not too remote.[25] Not too much should be read into one jury direction but the result of such a direction was that it was difficult for defendants to challenge claims for nervous shock where there was impact. It is unclear whether, as a matter of law, impact was sufficient or whether there needed to be some evidence linking the shock to the consequences for which the plaintiff was claiming. As the evidentiary requirement could be minimal – illustrated in *Sealey* – the practical results were similar for the defendant: the only way to defend was to deny any nervous shock at all (or to deny an element of the cause of action as was done successfully in *Sealey* where the jury found no negligence).[26]

Perhaps the widest understanding of 'impact' in this early period is found in *Daly v. The Commissioner of Railways*.[27] Here the plaintiff was a passenger on a train from York to Newcastle (now Toodyay) in Western Australia when her carriage derailed after hitting a horse on an unfenced portion of track and she was thrown onto the floor of the train. She subsequently suffered continuing pain in her head and back. During the trial of the action for negligence the defendant's counsel applied for a nonsuit, one ground being that, following *Coultas*, no action lay for nervous shock[28] (the plaintiff's doctors having opined that the illnesses resulted from a shock to the system).[29] Stone CJ refused the nonsuit on this ground. He accepted he was bound by *Coultas* and the only question was whether it could be distinguished. For reasons he did not explain,

23 *Brisbane Courier*, 30 September 1914, 4.
24 Ibid.
25 [1915] QWN 1.
26 *Brisbane Courier*, 1 October 1914, 3.
27 [1906] WAR 125.
28 *WA*, 29 June 1905, 4.
29 *Daily News* (Perth), 27 June 1905, 3.

he held that the plaintiff was not injured physically but merely suffered from mental shock. This prevented him from distinguishing *Coultas* in the manner that had become commonplace in Australian courts. But *Coultas* was distinguished on another ground. Drawing on the defendant counsel's submission,[30] he held that in *Coultas* there had been no collision or impact but in *Daly* the circumstances were entirely different: the plaintiff was in a railway carriage when a horse was collided with, and she was thrown from her seat in consequence of the engine and some of the carriages being derailed.[31] It seems Stone CJ was saying that there had actually been impact here even if it had not resulted in injury and this was sufficient to distinguish *Coultas* (although technically the Privy Council made no finding on whether impact was necessary at all). Stone CJ ultimately held for the plaintiff and when the defendant appealed to the Full Court all three judges supported the late Chief Justice's conclusions but were more conservative in their reasoning on the *Coultas* point. Parker CJ did not accept that the plaintiff suffered no physical injury; the Chief Justice when he said that there was no physical injury meant no 'observable' physical injury. That some of the consequences of her involvement in the accident – adverse impact on memory, loss of power to her legs – were not injury to bone or muscle did not prevent them from being physical injuries.[32] But as the plaintiff had also suffered unconsciousness this reasoning was entirely consistent with the cases discussed above. There were some physical injuries caused by impact (unconsciousness) and some by nervous shock (memory, loss of power to legs) and *Coultas* did not prevent a claim in these circumstances. But Parker CJ went further: assuming that the injuries were only mental he thought that the claim could also succeed. Expanding on Stone CJ's reasoning, there was no contact with the engine or any part of the Commissioner's railway in *Coultas* whereas in *Daly* 'the plaintiff was a passenger on the line, and the result of the accident was to throw her off her seat, and throw her against other people, and to cause her to become insensible.' Observing for good measure that *Coultas* had been doubted in England, he found that the facts of *Daly* allowed it to be distinguished.[33] Although not spelt out directly, it seems that impact without injury would suffice. McMillan J was less adventurous: he thought there was physical injury on the facts and though a bit flummoxed by the comments of one of the doctor witnesses that there was an injury to the nervous system, 'however that may be I can see nothing in the *Coultas* case which prevents us from upholding this judgment.'[34] Burnside J simply agreed with his brethren that *Coultas* was distinguishable.[35]

[30] *WA*, 29 June 1905, 4.
[31] *WA*, 4 July 1905, 4.
[32] (1906) 8 WAR 125, 127.
[33] Ibid., 125–126.
[34] Ibid., 129.
[35] Ibid. It has been suggested that the presence of a contract between the parties was a factor in overcoming any limitation created by *Coultas* (P. Handford, 'Psychiatric injury in breach of a relationship' (2007) 27 *LS* 26). However, none of the judges expressly mentions this when

A New Legal Landscape: *Polemis* and *Hambrook*

While *Daly* was hardly a landmark decision, it represents in Parker CJ's alternative reasoning the most significant attempt to avoid the restrictions of *Coultas* undertaken in Australia during the first half of the twentieth century. But while *Coultas* remained authoritative, it had to be distinguished and there were limits on how far this could be done, especially by state courts. It was only towards the end of the period of this study that the High Court of Australia heard two cases on liability for mental harm that allowed it to confront the *Coultas* problem directly. By the time they did, however, the legal landscape surrounding *Coultas* had changed significantly. As early as 1901 an English court had gone beyond *Coultas* by allowing recovery for negligently inflicted nervous shock where the plaintiff reasonably feared for her own safety.[36] It was not until *Hambrook v. Stokes Bros Pty Ltd* in 1925 that an English court would make a new contribution to this area but to understand *Hambrook* it is necessary to consider the change made by the Court of Appeal decision in *Re Polemis, Furniss and Withy*.[37] In *Coultas* the gist of the Privy Council decision was that the shock-induced harm was not a natural and probable result of the defendant's negligence. That formulation was the remoteness test adopted in *Smith v. London and South Western Railway* in 1870.[38] But after the decision in *Polemis* this test was replaced by one of directness: once the breach of duty was established the defendant was responsible for harm caused directly to the plaintiff irrespective of whether it was the natural and probable result of the defendant's breach. As a result, the Privy Council's finding that shock-induced harm was too remote was now based on an incorrect remoteness of damage test. And while the Court of Appeal in *Hambrook v. Stokes Bros* had no need to worry about whether the English jurisprudence was consistent with *Coultas*, its decision showed the possibilities that arose under a new remoteness test.

Hambrook v. Stokes Bros[39] involved a claim by a husband for loss of dependency resulting from the death of his wife. His wife had suffered a severe shock when she feared that her children may have been injured by a lorry that had been carelessly left at the top of a hill and careered down a narrow street along which her three children were walking. At the time the lorry was careering down the street she could not see her children as the road turned slightly and

discussing *Coultas* and while there are references to the plaintiff being a passenger, in counsel's submission to Stone CJ on the nonsuit (*WA*, 29 June 1905, 4) and in Parker CJ's judgment, this was to point out how she suffered impact as a result of the accident. If the ground for decision was the plaintiff's contract with the Commissioner it would have been unnecessary to discuss the impact question (which was clearly central to the reasoning). While Burnside J does mention the existence of a contract, he does so with reference to the negligence question and not the *Coultas* point.

[36] *Dulieu v. White* [1901] 2 KB 669.
[37] [1921] 3 KB 560.
[38] (1870) 6 LR CP 14.
[39] [1925] 1 KB 141.

they were out of her sight. At the trial the jury was given the *Dulieu v. White* direction – that the action would lie only if the deceased had feared for her own safety – and as there was no evidence of this the jury found for the defendant. This is not the place for a detailed critique of the decision but it is necessary to explain why a new legal framework was adopted to deal with these types of cases. The clearest exposition was given by Atkin LJ who explained that it no longer mattered – since *Polemis* – whether the consequences of the wrong could reasonably be anticipated by the wrongdoer. If a wrong was committed, it was immaterial if the particular injury was not contemplated as long as it was direct. If there were to be any limits on the claim for shock-induced injury, they would need to be in other elements of the cause of action in negligence: duty and breach.[40] It is not easy to discern whether the judgments use duty or breach for this purpose. In an era where duty was not as sophisticated as it would become post *Donoghue v. Stevenson*, and where there was authority that a 'duty' was owed by a driver to persons on the highway (as was Mrs Hambrook), references to the 'extent' of the defendant's duty are ambiguous. But what is clear is that at the *liability* stage the judges engaged in an assessment of what the defendant ought to have foreseen or anticipated as a result of his negligence.

How this new development played out in Australia was first considered in the politically charged case of *Johnson v. The Commonwealth* in 1927.[41] The reported case was one of four actions brought by Jacob Johnson and Tom Walsh and their respective wives Amy Johnson and Adela Walsh, arising out of the arrest and attempted deportation of Messrs Johnson and Walsh who were officials with the militant Seaman's Union.[42] Johnson and Walsh challenged the legality of the 1925 amendments to the Immigration Act under which they were arrested and the High Court found that provisions under which Johnson and Walsh had been deported were beyond the powers of the Commonwealth so that their detention was unlawful.[43] Johnson and Walsh brought actions against the Prime Minister Stanley Bruce, the Superintendent of Commonwealth Police, Robert Yates, and the Commonwealth for illegal arrest and imprisonment. The cases were heard on consecutive days. Walsh was not called as a witness and Johnson was only called to verify his identity and was asked no questions. The defence called no evidence. The only issue for the jury was damages; for the three weeks' detention in Garden Island Walsh was awarded £25.[44] The Johnson jury initially found for the defendant (!) before the trial judge, Gordon J, told the foreman he did not think they had appreciated the point (i.e. that they were to assess damages) he had impressed upon them. Undeterred,

---

[40] As Mitchell points out, Atkin LJ's ratio lies in the remoteness issue as duty and breach were conceded (P. Mitchell, *A History of Tort Law* (Cambridge University Press, 2015) 98) but his obiter comments on duty were extremely influential in later cases.

[41] (1927) 27 SR (NSW) 133.

[42] G. Nicholls, *Deported: A History of Forced Departures from Australia* (UNSW Press, 2007) ch. 4.

[43] *Re Yates; Ex Parte Walsh* (1925) 37 CLR 36.

[44] *SMH*, 26 March 1927, 20.

the jury consulted and the foreman advised that they would award no damages. Gordon J told them they must award something, small or large, and after further consultation a verdict of £20 was returned.[45]

In the midst of these proceedings the Commonwealth demurred to Amy Johnson's claim. Only one of the two counts need concern us here, the other relating to a claim for loss of consortium. The first claim was based on the wrongful and malicious entering into the dwelling house occupied by the Johnsons and assaulting and forcibly removing Jacob Johnson in Amy's presence whereby she suffered a severe shock with resultant adverse physical consequences. The Commonwealth argued that no action for mental anguish or illness lay for acts done in her presence to another not causing any apprehension of danger to herself. Lamb KC submitted that *Coultas* prevented a claim for shock-induced injury but also that shock of itself was not a good cause of action. Apart from a very novel argument that there had been a breach of duty to the plaintiff through interference with the plaintiff's right to enjoy the privacy of her own home – and that, in light of *Polemis*, any direct damage resulting from the breach was recoverable – Dr H.V. Evatt and his brother Clive for the plaintiff argued that a reasonable man in the defendants' position would have anticipated the damage to the plaintiff. The case was stronger than *Hambrook* because the defendants were acting wrongfully and the effects of their acts must have been in contemplation of the defendants before committing their acts. Put simply, the argument was that if negligent conduct which foreseeably caused nervous shock was actionable, all the more so where the defendants were acting wilfully.

The Full Court of the Supreme Court of New South Wales unanimously dismissed the demurrer. Writing for the court, Ferguson J, citing *Wilkinson v. Downton*,[46] dismissed *Coultas* as not applying to any element of wilful wrong. This required him to discuss the elements of the *Wilkinson* action. He noted the 'calculated to cause harm' requirement and the application of *Wilkinson* in *Janvier v. Sweeney*.[47] He also noted that in *Janvier* Bankes LJ had cited with approval the comments of Phillimore LJ in *Dulieu v. White* that there was no reason why shock-induced injury should not be recoverable if the relevant duty was owed and breached. Somewhat elliptically, Ferguson J went on to say that 'these principles' were applied in *Hambrook*. But what principles? What was common to *Dulieu v. White* and *Wilkinson v. Downton* was that shock-induced harm was recoverable, but the causes of action which gave rise to this recovery were different. This intermingling led Davidson J to propound a novel, hybrid liability principle:

> I think the nervous shock and resulting physical illness complained of by the plaintiff might fairly and reasonably have been anticipated as a consequence of

45 *Daily Advertiser* (Wagga Wagga), 29 March 1927, 2.
46 [1897] 2 QB 57.
47 [1919] 2 KB 316.

the assault committed upon her husband in her presence and as it is admitted…
that the assault was without lawful justification, I am clearly of the opinion that
the count discloses a good cause of action.[48]

To say that this drove a coach and horses through *Coultas* is an understatement. Not only was this wider than *Wilkinson* – where some form of intention
to harm the plaintiff was required – but a cause of action was seemingly established simply by showing that shock-induced harm was a foreseeable result of
a wrong to another. Such a principle was wider that anything that could be
gleaned from *Hambrook*. Nor could it be said that the point had not been drawn
to the court's attention: in argument Lamb KC had submitted that it had never
been suggested that a wrongful act against A, and not against B, but causing
shock to B, constituted a cause of action on the part of B.[49] There first of all had
to be a wrongful act against B. If this represented Australian law, it was hardly
hamstrung by *Coultas* – it had gone further than any contemporary English
development in allowing recovery for what might be called relational nervous
shock. Perhaps the ruling was in part motivated by the high-handed manner in
which the arrest of her husband had been made: a later article in *Truth* noted,
among other indelicacies, that the arresting officers had entered the bedroom
where she was in bed to read the warrant.[50] But if there was any judicial sympathy it was not replicated by the jury who sat in the subsequent trial: although
she was awarded £60 – three times the amount her husband received for being
arrested – this was a long way short of the £5000 that was claimed.[51]

It would be nearly ten years before the limits of recovery for shock-induced
harm came before appellate courts again but dissatisfaction with the law – and
in particular the perceived strictures imposed on it by *Coultas* – were becoming
increasingly apparent. While it was possible for some Australian commentators
as late as 1928 to discuss the issue with reference to only English case law,[52]
developments in the 1930s made this increasingly anachronistic. In Victoria,
Maurice Blackburn's persistence resulted in a statutory amendment to alter the
effect of *Coultas*. Despite the support of lawyers inside and outside the House,
the attempt to bring Australian law into line with the rest of the Empire – which
was Blackburn's justification for dealing with this subject – was controversial.
His first private members' bill on the topic, introduced in 1930, was not discussed but his second, introduced in 1931, was and the clause that amended
Coultas used language that did not attract universal support.[53] It also revealed

---

[48] (1927) 27 SR (NSW) 133, 137.

[49] *Evening News* (Sydney), 15 February 1927, 9.

[50] *Truth* (Sydney), 17 April 1927, 6. In the trial of the action, her counsel commented that she
had been treated by the Commonwealth 'in a manner to bring a blush to the face of Ned
Kelly': *Evening News* (Sydney), 11 April 1927, 9.

[51] *SMH*, 13 April 1927, 14. Ada Walsh's case was settled for the same amount with an additional
twenty guineas for medical expenses.

[52] A. Stirling, 'Liability for nervous shock' (1928) 2 *ALJ* 46 where no Australian decision, not even
the recent *Johnson* case, is mentioned.

[53] Victoria, *Parliamentary Debates*, Session 1931, Vol. 186, 2551–2566.

that among some non-legal members there was support for *Coultas*. It passed the Assembly, but after one member of the Legislative Council proposed that the clause be rejected[54] and others suggested that other parts of the bill needed amendment, the bill was sent to the Statute Law Reform Committee, a joint Committee of the Parliament, for comment.[55] This Committee sent it out to the Supreme Court judges for comment[56] and their report on the bill indicated disagreement with some clauses and suggested amendment of others. That bill did not proceed but Blackburn introduced a new private members' bill in September 1932, entirely in accord with the Judges' Report including their suggested amendment to the *Coultas* clause.[57] This watered-down bill passed the Assembly[58] and the Legislative Council (where it proceeded as a government bill) without amendment.[59] Section 4 of the *Wrongs Act 1932* (Vic) stated that: 'In any action for injury to the person the plaintiff shall not be debarred from recovering damages merely because the injury complained of arose wholly or in part from mental or nervous shock.' Contemporary commentators were satisfied that this would achieve the desired result of altering the law as laid down in *Coultas* for Victoria.[60]

Other attacks were also being made on *Coultas*. A commentator in the *Australian Law Journal* argued for a system of precedent in which Australian courts should consider themselves free to depart from the case because of the inconsistent English authority.[61] This was not *Dulieu v. White* or other cases that disapproved of *Coultas* expressly but was *Re Polemis*, a decision that had already been applied by the High Court.[62] More radically, a Canadian court decided not to follow *Coultas* by arguing that Privy Council decisions were only binding on courts of the colony from where the appeal originated. Australian commentary thought the reasoning in support of this proposition doubtful[63] but recognised that 'the principle itself is an attractive one as affording an escape to all, except the unfortunate person who is either shocked in Victoria or sues in the Victorian Courts, from the effect of the *Coultas* decision.'[64] And

---

[54] Dr Harris, North-Eastern Province.

[55] Victoria, *Parliamentary Debates*, Session 1931, Vol. 186, 3605–3616.

[56] Public Records Office Victoria, VPRS 266/P0000/964, letter Attorney General to Sir Leo Cussen, 19 November 1931.

[57] Extensive searches at the Victorian Parliament and the Public Record Office of Victoria failed to locate a copy of the report.

[58] Victoria, *Parliamentary Debates*, Session 1932, Vol. 190, 2676–2677.

[59] Ibid., 2816–2817.

[60] 'Current Topics' (1933) 6 *ALJ* 357; 'Wrongs Act 1932 (Victoria)' (1933) 7 *ALJ* 228. The commentator ('A.T.F.') did note that the reference to an action for injury to the person may not extend to claims under Lord Campbell's Act provisions.

[61] W.N. Harrison, 'Precedent in Australia' (1934) 7 *ALJ* 405.

[62] *Dickson v. Commissioner of Railways* (1922) 30 CLR 579.

[63] 'Such an astonishing conclusion would never commend itself to an Australian court': N. Landau, 'The duty in cases of nervous shock' (1939–1941) 2 *Res Judicatae* 139, 140.

[64] 'The Coultas case again' (1933) 7 *ALJ* 101. As was later noted, even the reservation was unfounded since the passing of the *Wrongs Act 1932* (Victoria): 'The Coultas case yet again' (1933) 7 *ALJ* 140.

a trial judge in South Australia dismissed a *Coultas* challenge in a case where the plaintiff mother claimed in respect of a change in her nervous condition caused by being told that her recently born child had been burnt as a result of a hospital's negligence.[65] An argument that she could not recover as she was only told about the injury was rejected, seemingly on the ground that the hospital's duty on admitting the plaintiff extended to taking care to avoid anything that might prejudice her health and comfort.[66] *Coultas* was distinguished because there was evidence of physical consequences – the production of tears – and this physical disturbance was enough to ground the claim. With this kind of *de minimis* requirement for establishing physical consequence any limitation imposed by *Coultas* was apparent rather than real.

Nervous Shock in the Age of Duty of Care

The time was ripe, then, to challenge the formal orthodoxy of *Coultas* and *Bunyan v. Jordan* was a good case for testing increasingly porous boundaries. Lucy Bunyan worked for Arthur Jordan in a general store in Blacktown, a small township (then) to the west of Sydney. On 19 October 1934 she was working in the store on a late-night opening day. When she returned to the shop after dinner she went into the partitioned-off office at the back of the store. Jordan was there together with another assistant. There was a revolver on the table and he emptied some bullets in her presence to show the two women that it was loaded. She left and returned to the office sometime later and saw some poison on the table. She left again and overheard Jordan say to the other assistant in the office that he was going to shoot himself or shoot someone. Bunyan then left the store whereupon the assistant came out and repeated to Bunyan what Jordan had told her. She then heard a shot but saw Jordan five or ten minutes afterwards. And when she delivered the takings of the day to him in the office just after closing time, Jordan began to tear up the pound notes, saying he would not be there in the morning to mend them and that they would hear of a death before morning. A doctor was called and some medication was given to the intoxicated Jordan. Bunyan alleged that shortly after these events she began to feel ill. The doctor she attended three days after the incident diagnosed neurasthenia with associated physical and mental symptoms. He gave evidence that the condition could have been caused by the incidents of 19 October.[67]

---

[65] *Brown v. The Mount Barker Soldiers Hospital Incorporated* [1934] SASR 128. An unenthusiastic comment by the unsuccessful defence counsel was written for the *ALJ*: S.H. Skipper, 'Damages for shock' (1934) 8 *ALJ* 286.

[66] Hence when the defendant counsel argued that the spark flying out was no breach to the mother, Piper J responded that he was not so sure of that: *The Advertiser* (Adelaide) 7 September 1934, 13. As Atkin LJ had argued in *Hambrook v. Stokes Bros Pty Ltd*, the breach of duty to the primary victim – in this case the child – was also a breach to the secondary victim – the mother.

[67] These facts are taken from NAA, A10071, 1936/43, *Bunyan v. Jordan*, Transcript of Proceedings.

There were four counts in Bunyan's claim against Jordan: negligence causing her to fear immediate personal injury, breach of an implied promise that
the shop in which she was employed would be a fit and proper place for her to
work in, assault, and maliciously producing a revolver and putting the plaintiff
in fear of immediate personal injury with the resultant adverse consequences
for which she claimed. At the end of the plaintiff's case, the defendant's counsel
successfully applied for a nonsuit. Maxwell J found that there was no evidence
to support the second and third counts and we need not consider them further.
As regards the first and fourth counts, he found that there was nothing to justify the conclusion that the plaintiff feared for her own safety. But in an unusual
course that was criticised in the appellate court, Maxwell J allowed counsel for
Bunyan to conduct the case, even in the absence of a formal amendment of the
pleadings, on the basis the claim was for breach of a legal duty, in effect, not
to terrify the plaintiff by a wrongful action causing mental shock followed by
physical consequences. In support of this counsel for the plaintiff understandably relied on Ferguson J's extremely wide general principle in *Johnson*, noted
above. But Maxwell J limited the principle and in doing so formally introduced
one of the factors that would influence liability for negligently caused mental
harm well beyond the period of this study. When Ferguson J had set out his
general principle, he had in the preceding sentence quoted Lord Wensleydale
that the 'relationship of the parties' was an important factor in determining the
consequences to be anticipated from the defendant's conduct. There is no suggestion that Ferguson J saw this as a formal limitation but this is how Maxwell
J interpreted it: while it was not necessary to have a blood relationship (e.g.
the betrothed in *Janvier v. Sweeney*), 'I can see no case amongst those to which
I have been referred which extends the principle to which it must be extended'
if the plaintiff was to win.'[68]

Maxwell J saw the claim as relational: it depended on Bunyan's reaction to
harm to someone else. But it is not clear whether this was the gist of the claim
(and to be fair to Maxwell J counsel's argument was not clear on this point).
Unusually, the press report of Maxwell J's decision prompted a comment in the
Australian Law Journal where it was noted that there were two types of shock
claim: the first involved shock from seeing an actionable wrong committed
against another, and the second where the plaintiff suffered ill health 'through
agitation caused by a false alarm wilfully given by the defendant or by unlawful threats made by him'. While the inadvertent (from the defendant's view)
harm to a person as a result of the defendant's wrongful conduct to a third
person might require a consideration of the relationship between the plaintiff
and the third party, this was not so where the defendant's conduct was designed
to produce fear in the plaintiff. It was perceptively noted that the musings in
Hambrook v. Stokes Bros as to the types of relationship that might found a claim
were irrelevant to the second category of claim, and while the cases in that

---

[68] The judgment is not reported but is contained in Transcript of Proceedings, ibid.

category (*Wilkinson*, *Janvier*) had involved statements or threats about persons closely connected to the plaintiff, 'this does not appear to limit the application of the decisions in those cases which proceeded upon a broad principle...' If the evidence was as set out in the report, the case should have been left to the jury: Jordan's statement might well have been one that 'was made suddenly and with apparent seriousness' and which could not fail to produce grave effects 'upon any but an exceptionally indifferent person'.[69]

The distinctiveness of claims for shock-induced harm was recognised by Jordan CJ when the nonsuit was appealed to the Full Court of the Supreme Court of New South Wales.[70] In an analytically impeccable judgment, Jordan CJ considered first the *Wilkinson* claim but found that there had to be both an intention to alarm another as well as the doing of an act of a kind reasonably capable of terrifying a normal human being or was known to the defendant to be likely to terrify the individual plaintiff for reasons special to that person. He found that there was no evidence of an intention to injure – which was not quite the same thing as an intention to alarm – and hence there was no claim under this cause of action. Jordan CJ then considered liability for 'injurious fright' in negligence. In a masterly judgment he incorporated the recent observations of Lord Atkin in *Donoghue v. Stevenson* to explain how the duty concept was now central to determining liability.[71] The test was whether in the circumstances a reasonable man would realise that the person in question was likely to be exposed to the consequences of his act, and would realise also that the act was of a kind likely to cause physical injury. He saw no reason why the general principle should not apply where the sense 'through the medium of which the physical injury was communicated was that of touch, sight or hearing, and whether it is the tissues or the nerves that are affected'.[72] As for *Coultas*, Jordan CJ simply avoided express mention of it while explaining why it could not be followed: in light of *Re Polemis*, and citing *Hambrook* and *Johnson*, 'if a person acts negligently in a public street and thereby causes an accident, it is not easy to see how, upon principle, he can escape liability for illness caused to a person lawfully using the street, as a result of nervous shock which he has sustained through witnessing the accident'.[73]

However, Jordan CJ was acutely conscious that if all was to be thrown back to the duty and foreseeability, that test had to be applied carefully. Foreseeability was judged in light of the effect on 'an ordinary human being' and a person was not bound 'so as to conduct himself as to deprive persons who are prone to make a fuss about nothing at all opportunities of indulging their proclivity, nor to be tender for special susceptibilities which he has no reason to suppose exist'.[74] More generally, the standards by which the foreseeability question was

---

[69] 'Nervous shock: a moot case', Current Topics (1936) 9 *ALJ* 426.

[70] (1936) 36 SR (NSW) 350.

[71] The attempt was noted in 'Liability of builders', Recent Cases (1936) 10 *ALJ* 150.

[72] (1936) 36 SR (NSW) 350, 353.

[73] Ibid., 354.

[74] Ibid., 355.

answered changed over time: 'Spectacles which would have been viewed with equanimity by our stronger stomached ancestors of the eighteenth century, who took pleasure in viewing public executions and public floggings, would cause general horror in these softer times, at any rate in the community in which we live.'[75] But this was not the only caution to be exercised. In an era of jury trial, it was unacceptable that all forms of human behaviour should be exposed 'to the arbitrary and unfettered discretion'[76] of a jury and judges must decide whether there was any evidence on which the action could be founded before the jury had its say. Picking up on Atkin LJ's comments in *Hambrook*, he noted that where the nervous shock arose from witnessing the agony or peril of another, 'the relationship of that person to the observer'[77] may be decisive. And after this excursus into the relevant principles Jordan CJ dismissed the appeal summarily without explanation: he felt 'no difficulty' in saying that there was no evidence to go to the jury that Lucy Bunyan's harm was a foreseeable result of Jordan's conduct.[78]

The judgments given by the High Court on appeal were disappointing. Unlike in the Full Court, *Coultas* did figure in the arguments: counsel for the appellant plaintiff began by saying the case was one of deliberate injury and not a case of mere negligence and this distinguished it from *Coultas*.[79] But counsel for the respondent, after arguing there was no intention, also submitted there was no duty to the appellant to take care she did not suffer harm and that *Coultas* was still good law. In reply, Dwyer for the appellant seems in part to have abandoned his earlier submissions and argued that the cause of action was based on the ordinary duty to avoid causing harm to others and that *Coultas* should not be followed![80] Similar conceptual ambivalence is contained in the judgments. Latham CJ dismissed the *Wilkinson* claim primarily on the basis that the conduct was not calculated to cause the harm. The negligence action was dismissed because the harm was not an anticipated result of the conduct but it is unclear whether Latham CJ saw this as going to the duty of care or breach of duty.[81] Dixon J's judgment is tantalisingly short. Relying on an American article by Roscoe Pound, he dismissed the *Wilkinson* claim because Jordan did not 'intend to bring upon the plaintiff a nervous breakdown or any physical harm'. How this squared with *Wilkinson* itself – where the defendant's practical joke was not intended to cause any permanent harm – was ignored. As

---

[75] Ibid.

[76] Ibid.

[77] Ibid.

[78] Stephen J in a short judgment largely followed the approach of Jordan CJ. Davidson J found a general duty not to cause harm, including nervous shock, which could be breached by malicious, wilful or negligent conduct taking the form of acts or words as long as harm was to persons who were closely and directly affected by the act. Like Jordan CJ he too found no evidence that the harm could be anticipated.

[79] (1937) 57 CLR 1, 4–5.

[80] Ibid., 6.

[81] Ibid., 13–14. McTiernan J dismissed the appeal on similar grounds: 18.

for any claim in negligence (or action on the case as he put it), the reasonable likelihood of nervous shock resulting from the act formed an essential element of any action. This was not present on the facts.[82] Rich J's judgment spent more time discrediting the claim rather than explaining why it should fail[83] and Evatt J's short dissenting judgment says nothing about negligence and relies on his view that Jordan wilfully caused alarm to Bunyan and this on the facts was sufficient to found the *Wilkinson* tort.[84]

Whatever the limitations of the decision relating to a cause of action for intentionally inflicted mental harm, it is striking that in an action where negligence was discussed and *Coultas* argued, the case was not mentioned at all in the judgments. Jordan CJ did not mention the case either but his reasoning addressed the central tenet of the case and showed how it was inconsistent with later authority. The omission to address the status of *Coultas* left its uncertain shadow hanging over this area of law: it was one thing to think it was irrelevant and another to have High Court authority saying so. But to reach this latter position the High Court would have to address the difficult issue of disagreement with a technically binding Privy Council decision and if the desired result could be reached without doing this all the better.

Whatever the position in the High Court, the 'avoidance' strategy was continuing apace in New South Wales. In September 1936, a jury awarded Annie Lyall Hay £750 against the Commissioner for Road Transport and Tramways primarily for the severe nervous shock she suffered when, due to the negligence of an employee of the defendant, the plaintiff's mother, aged sixty-one, fell from the tram from which the plaintiff was helping her to alight and was killed.[85] Although the plaintiff suffered some minor physical injuries the case was fought on the basis that the nervous shock was the result of her witnessing her mother's fall and death. Relying, presumably, on *Coultas*,[86] counsel for the defendant submitted that the jury should be directed that the plaintiff was not entitled to damages for nervous shock in the manner in which it occurred. This was rejected by the trial judge, Bavin J, who expressly relied on Jordan CJ's judgment in *Bunyan* in support of his decision. And five months after the High Court decision in *Bunyan*, the same approach as in Hay's case was adopted in *Barnes v. The Commonwealth*.[87] The defendant demurred to the plaintiff's claim that a servant of the defendant had sent a letter to the plaintiff wrongfully advising her that her husband had been admitted to a mental hospital. Treating the case as one of negligence and involving the existence of a duty, the Full Court unanimously dismissed the demurrer. Davidson J cited Jordan CJ's judgment in

---

[82] Ibid., 16–17.
[83] Ibid., 15–16.
[84] Ibid., 17–18.
[85] *SMH*, 8 September 1936, 7; 9 September 1936, 10; 10 September 1936, 9; *Truth* (Sydney), 13 September 1936, 19.
[86] The newspaper report does not detail the grounds of the application.
[87] (1937) 37 SR (NSW) 511.

Bunyan – despite the fact that the High Court judgments, although not reported, were cited to them – in support of applying a simple test of foreseeability. The employee sending the letter must have recognised that he was communicating serious information which could affect the recipient's feelings and the subject matter of the communication was reasonably likely to cause shock to an ordinary person in the position of the wife.[88] Another member of the *Bunyan* court, Stephen J agreed: the employee must have realised the risk of passing on information that was capable of causing a shock to the recipient.[89] Again counsel for the defendant raised *Coultas*; again the judgments made no reference to it.

Chester v. Council of the Municipality of Waverley

It was in this relative state of flux that the final case in this area in the period of this study, *Chester v. Council of the Municipality of Waverley*, was decided.[90] On a Saturday afternoon in August 1937, a seven-year-old boy, Max Chester, was drowned when he fell into a trench that had been left inadequately guarded through the negligence of the defendant's employees. The plaintiff, Janet Chester, was Max's mother and had been searching for him throughout the afternoon when he did not return as expected after lunch. She was present at the trench when, at about 6.30 p.m., his body was pulled from the trench. Some witnesses suggested there was some life in the body when removed from the trench, and he was worked on by lifesavers and ambulancemen for a period after his removal,[91] but the evidence before the courts was that he was dead when removed from the trench. Of Polish extraction and Jewish faith, Janet Chester had only been in Australia for two months when the accident happened; she had come to join her husband, Hyman, who had arrived six months earlier.[92] After some changes, the final pleading alleged two counts: the first was that the defendant had negligently secured the trench and that the plaintiff had been present and witnessed the removal of Max Chester and sustained severe nervous and mental shock, and the second count was a claim to have suffered damage without the allegation of shock.

At the end of the plaintiff's case, the defendant counsel sought a nonsuit on the basis that *Coultas* prevented the claim. The application for a nonsuit was ultimately successful – but not on the *Coultas* ground! Monahan AJ recognised that while Ferguson J in *Johnson* had stated that *Coultas* was still binding on

---

88 (1937) 37 SR (NSW) 511, 515.

89 Ibid., 516–517. Even though Davidson J cited Jordan CJ in *Bunyan*, paradoxically, the third member of the court, Maxwell J, simply added that the case fell within the test laid down by Davidson J in *Bunyan*.

90 (1938) 38 SR (NSW) 603; (1939) 62 CLR 1.

91 The ambulancemen were reported to have attempted to revive the child for forty-five minutes: *Truth* (Sydney), 15 August 1937, 19.

92 NAA, A10071, 1938/73, Chester v. Council of the Municipality of Waverley, Transcript, 32.

The flooded street excavation in Allen's Parade, Waverley, in which Max Chester, aged 7, was drowned on Saturday. The boy had been missing for six hours when the police found the body.

Figure 6.1 Flooded trench in *Chester v. Council of Municipality of Waverley*. *Source*: *SMH*, 16 August 1937, 12 (http://nla.gov.au/nla.news-page1188096).

a New South Wales court, doubt was thrown on *Coultas* because of the Full Court decisions in *Bunyan* and *Barnes*, especially as in the former *Coultas* had been cited to the High Court (where as noted above it was studiously ignored). Monahan AJ confessed that he would feel 'great difficulty' if he had to decide the matter[93] but, following the long tradition discussed above, he found another ground for decision and did not have to pronounce whether *Coultas* remained authoritative. While the plaintiff relied on both the Full Court decision in *Bunyan* and the English Court of Appeal decision in *Hambrook v. Stokes Bros*, it was the latter that formed the basis of the claim. But in a detailed analysis of the case, Monahan AJ determined that *Hambrook* was only authority for situations where the shock which caused the harm was a shock occasioned by a threat and fear of contemporaneous menace to the safety of the child. Here the plaintiff's shock was a 'belated cognisance of an injury caused some appreciable time before [sic] by the negligent act' and this was not covered by the authorities.[94]

[93] Ibid., 71–72.
[94] Ibid., 73.

Only one judgment was given in the unsuccessful appeal to the Full Court. And while Jordan CJ adopted in general terms the same approach as in *Bunyan*, the duty of the defendant – here a person 'doing anything' in or in the vicinity of a public highway – was defined much more precisely than for the factual context in *Bunyan*. After detailing the various duties owed in what might be called a variety of impact accidents, he went on to describe the 'nervous shock' duty:

> If he thereby creates a horrifying spectacle which so injures the nervous system of a passer-by or bystander or other eye witness as to cause him physical injury, there is authority which suggests that he may be liable for this, if the spectacle was of a kind likely to cause such damage to an ordinary normal person; and that the duty to persons exposed to the consequences of the act may include a duty not to bring into existence, as the direct result of carelessness, scenes of accident so horrifying as to be likely to excite injurious horror in the minds of normal persons of ordinary firmness and mental stability, to an extent capable of causing them actual physical nervous disease.[95]

He was prepared to accept that similar bystander liability could apply where the bystander witnessed a non-impact injury to another (such as falling into a pit) but only where the bystander was in the vicinity of a serious accident and only if the injury was caused 'by witnessing the agony or hearing the screams' of the victim.[96]

It was not only the extent of the detail that differed from *Bunyan*. As became clear later in the judgment, the examples were not descriptive indicators of the kind of case in which recovery would be allowed. Rather, they delimited the extent of the duty. Mrs Chester was not at the scene when her son fell in the trench and while she was at the scene when his body was removed 'she was then there not in the character of a wayfarer startled by a distressing sight, but of a person looking for the body of a child then believed to be dead.'[97] The plaintiff's reliance on *Hambrook* was something of a double-edged sword: Jordan CJ now noted that the extent and limits of that case had not been decided. Jordan CJ gave a hint of what would become the 'aftermath' doctrine: if the accident had been caused in a public place and horrifying effects of the accident were still evident at the scene at which it occurred 'in the shape of mangled bodies which have not yet been removed' a passer-by who came across the scene and suffered a physical injury (through nervous shock) might have a claim but these were not the facts of *Chester*. And finally, Jordan CJ raised what seems almost a taxonomical objection. The gist of the claim was for bereavement and it was the lack of a claim for this under the New South Wales equivalent of Lord Campbell's Act that 'has prompted this attempt to extend what was decided in the case of *Hambrook v. Stokes Bros* to lengths which are unwarranted by either principle

---

[95] (1938) 38 SR (NSW) 603, 606.
[96] Ibid., 607.
[97] Ibid., 608. The resemblance to the reasoning of the majority in *Alcock v. Chief Constable of South Yorkshire* [1992] AC 310, is striking.

or authority'. This appears to be a direct response to the criticism of the law made by the plaintiff's solicitor, Abram Landa, at the earlier Coroner's enquiry that there was no remedy for pain and suffering associated with a child's death.[98] Whatever the flaws of the fatal accidents' legislation, they were not, in Jordan CJ's views, to be remedied by crafting a remedy out of nervous shock claims.

While Jordan CJ's judgment in *Bunyan* could not be said to show sympathy with this class of claim, there is a strong sense in *Chester* that these claims must be limited. Perhaps the genie should not have been allowed out of the bottle at all but if it was it needed to be strictly confined. Paradoxically, the one thing that would not contain the genie was *Coultas*. At last dealing with the issue, Jordan CJ doubted whether the case meant anything more than that damages could not be recovered for mere mental perturbation. For reasons that are not entirely clear, he thought the evidence of physical injury was meagre but would have allowed the case to go to the jury if this had been the only issue.[99]

The sentiment that this kind of claim should be limited also characterised the unsuccessful appeal to the High Court.[100] This is clearest in the judgment of Rich J who held that as the plaintiff was not using the road or was a witness to the death she could not claim. He exhibited no sympathy for the claim. Not all the consequences of an injury could be compensated, he noted, as 'the law must fix a point where its remedies stop short of complete reparation for the world at large, which might appear just to a logician who neglected all the social consequences which ought to be weighed on the other side'.[101] Attempts to extend the law had led to its present 'amorphous' condition and these 'so-called' developments seemed to consist 'in a departure from the settled standards for the purpose of giving plaintiffs causes of action unbelievable to a previous generation of lawyers. Defendants appear to have fallen entirely out of favour. In this respect perhaps judges are only following humbly in the footsteps of juries'.[102] Latham CJ and Starke J were less explicit in their dislike of the action. Both rejected the claim because the harm was not foreseeable to the defendant council. Starke J thought this was because the shock the plaintiff suffered as a result of seeing the body after the accident was not within the ordinary range of human experience; it was so remote that it did not have to be foreseen by the defendant. For Latham CJ the emphasis was more on the commonplace nature of death and the knowledge that the spectacle of death did not in most cases produce anything more than a temporary consequence. Whether this lack of foreseeability went to the existence of a duty or breach of duty is much more difficult to discern as Latham CJ's judgment wobbles between different views. One section critiqued the existence of the duty for which the plaintiff contended by reference to its analogical extensions (e.g. if the duty applied to these facts, it would

---

[98]   *SMH*, 26 August 1937, 9.
[99]   (1938) 38 SR (NSW) 603, 608.
[100]   (1939) 62 CLR 1.
[101]   Ibid., 11.
[102]   Ibid., 11–12.

also apply to other similar cases) while in a later part he stated the question was the 'definition, the scope and extent, of any duty'.[103] Further,

> Thus in the present case the circumstance that the plaintiff in fact suffered a shock does not establish the existence of any duty in the defendant or any breach of duty by the defendant. The question which must be asked in order to determine whether the defendant was negligent or not is whether the defendant should have foreseen that a mother would suffer from nervous shock amounting to illness if she saw the dead body of her child where the death of the child had been brought about by the negligence of the defendant towards the child.[104]

This suggests that there had been no breach of duty on the facts, a conclusion supported by an earlier part of Latham CJ's judgment where he cited with approval dicta from Scrutton and Warrington LJJ in *Re Polemis* that if the injurious consequences of the defendant's conduct could not be foreseen that conduct could not be a *breach* of duty. Another difficulty is the curious manner in which he distinguished the recent English Court of Appeal authority in *Owens v. Liverpool Corporation*[105] where a number of plaintiffs claimed successfully for nervous shock when a tram collided with a hearse carrying a relative's coffin and the coffin was in danger of being thrown on the road. He distinguished the case because there the duty and breach had been satisfied but the relevant breach was, apparently, a breach of the duty not to injure the plaintiffs by driving carefully. As the plaintiffs had not been injured by the tram hitting them, but by what they saw, any breach of duty must, on Latham CJ's earlier reasoning, have been based on the foreseeability of nervous shock to bystanders watching the events unfold. But unpacking the decision in this way would have made any distinction drawn between witnessing the accident (*Chester*) and seeing a coffin containing a dead body (*Owens)* difficult to maintain, so the discussion remained superficial.

There have been no shortage of critics of the majority decision in *Chester*, none stronger than the dissenting judgment of Evatt J. Like Jordan CJ in *Bunyan*, Evatt J attempted to unpack the various elements of the cause of action for negligently inflicted nervous shock and relate them to one another in a way that incorporated the change made by *Donoghue v. Stevenson*. But the judgment begins by making a powerful normative claim as to why a claim in this situation ought to succeed. As Lord Wilberforce would do nearly fifty years later in another nervous shock case, *McLoughlin v. O'Brian*,[106] Evatt J portrays the facts in graphic and human terms. In the trench 'the menace of death was very great and very near', like most mothers placed in a similar situation 'she was tortured' between the fear he had been drowned and the hope he was still alive, and her 'long agony' in the wait between the fear he had been drowned and

[103] Ibid., 8–9.
[104] Ibid., 10.
[105] [1939] 1 KB 394.
[106] [1983] 1 AC 410.

its certainty,[107] appeal to core human emotions associated with parenthood.[108] A dose of contempt for the defendants is also present: he refers to the 'courageous' decision of the defendant to call as a witness another child who saw the deceased child playing around the trench. One can only fully understand the bitterness of the comment when one sees the description in the transcript of the child giving evidence: it was obviously a traumatic experience for the child to relive the events.[109] Evatt J then engages in a scholarly analysis of the legal authorities. The judgment is too long to discuss in detail[110] but three features are noteworthy. First, Evatt J discusses a wide variety of comparative caselaw and academic literature. Rescuer cases from the United States, Winfield's text on tort (published in 1937), Stallybrass' 8th edition of Salmond from 1934, and articles from the *Harvard Law Review* (Magruder)[111] and the *Canadian Bar Review*[112] are all cited. Not only are these sources cited, they are critiqued: Evatt argues – not just states – that certain views taken by Winfield and Magruder are wrong. This kind of detailed engagement with secondary literature was extremely rare in Australian appellate courts. Second, Evatt J's rejection of the potential limitations on an action for negligently inflicted nervous shock was rigorously argued. In his view, if the duty was based on foreseeability, one could not exclude those who had a predisposition to suffer nervous shock: these were members of the community foreseeable by the defendant.[113] Nor did the shock need to relate to a precisely contemporaneous danger or injury to another: it would extend to sight or hearing of the actual or apprehended casualty, its attendant circumstances and its immediate consequences.[114] Once it was understood that two duties could arise out of the same conduct – a primary duty to the person in danger or injured and a secondary duty to the person suffering nervous shock as a result – there was no separate breach question to answer for the secondary duty for a breach of the primary duty was necessarily a breach of the secondary duty (as he illustrated by reference to the rescue cases).[115] And attempts to circumvent *Re Polemis* by requiring the damage actually suffered to have been reasonably foreseeable before a breach of duty could be found were castigated. The duty was based on foreseeability of some damage to a class of persons of which the plaintiff formed part and once this was satisfied there was no further limitation other than directness.[116] While not all of these views

---

[107] (1939) 62 CLR 1, 15, 17.

[108] B. McDonald, 'Justice Evatt and the lost child in Chester v Waverley Corporation (1939)' in A. Lynch (ed.), *Great Australian Dissents* (Cambridge University Press, 2016) 64–68.

[109] A10071, above n 92, Transcript 48–51. Plaintiff's counsel at trial, Clive Evatt (Evatt J's brother) also hinted that the child had been coached.

[110] See further McDonald, above n 108, 64–73.

[111] C. Magruder, 'Mental and emotional disturbance in the law of torts' (1936) 49 *Harv L Rev* 1033.

[112] (1933) 11 *Can Bar Rev* 516.

[113] (1939) 62 CLR 1, 24–27.

[114] Ibid., 20–22.

[115] Ibid., 44.

[116] Ibid., 29.

remain – or ever were – accepted as law, the discussion has a strikingly modern ring to it, perhaps because of the pre-eminence given to the duty of care question as determining liability in this class of case.

The final point to note about Evatt J's judgment is that, at face value, there is no evidence of developing any law for Australia as opposed to England. In fact, he begins his judgment by saying the case was of considerable general importance concerning a rule of the common law of England. Later in the judgment, in response to Jordan CJ's comments that the action was an attempt to evade the limits of Lord Campbell's Act provisions in New South Wales, English law is used to dismiss the argument. 'However that may be', he said, 'the existing legislative provision as to the measure of damages should not prevent Australian courts from applying the common law of England in accordance with the principles adopted by the courts of England; principles which are not to be rejected or evaded merely because they have introduced into the law an element of humanity and common sense alike.'[117] But Evatt was not simply following English law for its own sake: the enthusiasm for the English cases was based on their affirmation of the position Evatt already held. And when Evatt turned to consider the old chestnut of *Coultas*, English law was again his ally. He rejected the case as preventing liability where, in the absence of impact, the plaintiff had suffered nervous shock as a result of negligence. Adopting the line taken throughout many of the nervous shock cases discussed in the period of this study, nervous shock was 'an actual physical disturbance of the nervous system'. This had not been recognised at the time *Coultas* was decided. As a result of the new understanding, the decision was not applicable to these facts, a conclusion he supported by reference to English cases as well as academic opinion.[118] Old habits were dying hard but they were dying. In his comment on the case, the Australian academic G.W. Paton noted almost ritually that *Coultas* was likely to create difficulties in certain states but was happy enough with Evatt's solution, 'a convenient method of avoiding the effects of this generally discredited decision'.[119] Little wonder that, beginning the discussion of the House of Lords' decision in *Bourhill v. Young*, a commentator for the *Australian Law Journal* mused: 'Now that *Victorian Railways Commissioners v. Coultas* (13 AC 222) is dead and almost forgotten, what limitation are we to place on the liability for nervous shock caused by fright?'.[120]

In due course, Evatt's opinion was recognised in Australia as representing the correct approach to cases of negligently inflicted mental harm, at least where secondary victims were concerned, but, at least judicially, this occurred outside the period of this study. But in a sign of things to come, its importance was first

---

[117] Ibid., 46.

[118] From the Canadian Bar Review ((1933) 11 *Can Bar Rev* 516) and Winfield's textbook (*Textbook of the Law of Tort* (Sweet and Maxwell, 1937) 86). The result was described by one commentator as 'a very fair interpretation' of *Coultas*: N. Landau, above n 63, 140.

[119] G.W. Paton, 'Nervous shock' (1939) 17 *Can Bar Rev* 541, 545.

[120] (1942) 15 *ALJ* 392.

acknowledged by Lord Wright in *Bourhill v. Young* in 1942.[121] His Lordship expressly noted the existence of the *Chester* decision and commented that in determining the extent of any duty owed to susceptible plaintiffs, 'The dissenting judgment of Evatt J will demand the consideration of any judge who is called upon to consider these questions.'[122] It had taken time but the English courts were becoming interested in what Australian judges had to say about their mutual common law. Moreover, writing in *Res Judicatae*, the journal of the University of Melbourne Law School, Landau clearly preferred Evatt J's dissent. Finding Evatt's analogy with the rescue cases helpful, he noted that Lord Atkin's neighbour principle had in this context 'done good service in enabling legal precepts to be brought into closer conformity with the moral sense of the community', and it could similarly have been employed 'without any undue strain' to allow recovery for 'the terrible anxiety of waiting for the water-filled trench to reveal its secret' and then to experience 'the hideous shock' when the secret was revealed.[123] Like Evatt J, Landau was incredulous that Janet Chester's nervous shock was not foreseeable. It is no surprise that in a similarly tragic case decided shortly after *Chester*, *Richards v. Baker*,[124] Mayo J found no difficulty in giving judgment in favour of a mother who suffered from nervous shock when her four-year-old son was hit and killed by a drunk motorist whilst walking on the edge of a road.[125] The boy had been holding his mother's hand at the time he was hit. Mayo J did not distinguish *Chester* simply by saying on these facts the nervous shock was a foreseeable consequence of the defendant's conduct (which it surely was). Rather, he found that the mother was already owed a duty by the defendant as she was a fellow road user: the duty 'did not depend upon her relationship to the boy. Compare *Chester v. Waverley Municipal Council*'.[126] The judgment relied on the defendant's conduct frightening *her*, producing consequences that could be readily foreseen. The retreat to 'fear of injury to oneself' as the basis of any duty is understandable given the *Chester* decision but the failure to adopt the general approach of *Chester* and the just decided *Bourhill v. Young* meant the case was of little precedential value. And there was not even a theoretical possibility of a *Coultas* argument being run against liability: it had been legislatively reversed in South Australia in 1939.[127]

---

[121] [1943] AC 92.

[122] Ibid., 110.

[123] Landau, above n 63, 143. A similar sentiment was expressed in more measured tones by G.W. Paton (above n 119).

[124] [1943] SASR 245.

[125] The bare facts conceal an extremely sad set of circumstances. The mother was on her way home after preparing for a local school concert in a community in which the family was liked and established (*Leader* (Angaston), 10 December 1942, 1). The defendant was clearly very drunk and, after the Coroner recommended criminal proceedings (*Leader* (Angaston), 17 December 1942, 1, 4) was subsequently tried and imprisoned for six months on a charge of dangerous driving causing death (*Advertiser* (Adelaide), 10 February 1943, 6; 11 February 1943, 4; 12 February 1943, 3; 19 February 1943, 3; 4 March 1943, 4).

[126] [1943] SASR 245, 249–250.

[127] Wrongs Act Amendment Act 1939 (SA) s. 28.

New South Wales and Statutory Liability for Nervous Shock

A more general solution to the *Chester* problem was suggested by Landau. Building on a comment by Winfield, he suggested one way of avoiding unfortunate results was to give the foreseeability question, as well as the breach question, to the jury. While this was consistent with his view that 'all our common law is essentially empirical',[128] there is no suggestion that judges were keen to divest themselves of the control that maintaining the duty question as one of law gave them over juries.[129] But if community standards could not be inculcated into judgments without the consent of the judges, they could if mandated by Parliament and it is to Parliament we must turn for the final twist in the nervous shock story. The raising of the matter in Parliament was the culmination of Abram Landa's, solicitor for both Lucy Bunyan and Janet Chester, fight to change the law to relax the rules allowing recovery for negligently inflicted nervous shock. The passage of the Law Reform (Miscellaneous Provisions) Act 1944 (NSW) s. 4 owes much to Landa's perseverance and perhaps demonstrates that community standards – at least as represented through membership of the Legislative Council – were not quite as uniform as Landau had imagined.

In the run-up to the 1941 election, the leader of the Labor Party, William McKell, made it part of the party's election manifesto to reform New South Wales law so it would accord with the best legal developments.[130] One manifestation of this promise was the introduction of compulsory third party liability insurance for motor vehicles and a bill was introduced in April 1942. Landa, who was re-elected to the Legislative Assembly in the 1941 election after a period out of Parliament, moved an amendment in the Second Reading debates in April 1942 to deal with the *Chester* problem. Citing Goodhart's comment that 'in the long run Dr Evatt's opinion will prevail', Landa said the amendment to reverse the result in *Chester* was 'the logical and humane view to take'.[131] He noted he had acted for Mrs Chester and excused himself if he became emotional during the debate. He had a long experience in this type of case 'and knew the sadness that emerged from them'.[132] His amendment was certainly unusual, it being not an amendment to the substance of the Motor Vehicle (Third Party) Insurance Bill but to the Compensation to Relatives Act 1897 (NSW). The nervous shock amendment was pithy: a new clause was suggested stating that damages were recoverable for injury occasioned by nervous or mental shock caused by or arising out of the death of the deceased person.[133] The difficulty

---

[128] Landau, above n 63, 144.

[129] See, for example, the comments of Jordan CJ in *Bunyan v. Jordan* (1936) 36 SR (NSW) 350, 355.

[130] *The Australian Worker* (Sydney), 30 December 1942, 5.

[131] NSW, Hansard, Legislative Assembly, 29 April 1942, 3115.

[132] Ibid., 3114–3115.

[133] The linking of the nervous shock claim in *Chester* to a claim under the Compensation to Relatives Act 1897 (NSW) was a common theme of the debate: see pp. 131–32, 135 above and note Paton's comment that what was 'really needed' was an action by which a parent could sue for the loss of a child, for in such a case the nervous shock might be regarded as damage consequential on the death (above n 119).

with the amendment was that it linked the claim for nervous shock with the claim for loss of dependency and even Landa himself was somewhat unclear on how the two were related[134] but the amendment was accepted by the Assembly. It had a less favourable time in the Legislative Council, being criticised, among other things, for allowing recovery when the plaintiff may have been hundreds of miles away when the deceased was killed: this was 'entirely new legislation and, as the Minister knows, there is no parallel in British jurisprudence for it'.[135] While *Coultas* was raised against the amendment,[136] of greater substance was the concern that it might exclude recovery where the nervous shock was consequent upon injury rather than death.[137] The amendment was rejected by the Council and, over the strong dissent of Landa,[138] this was accepted in the Assembly.

Undeterred, the McKell government introduced amending legislation in December 1942 in what was colloquially called the 'Nervous Shock Bill' (formally the Law Reform (Torts) Bill 1942). The aim was less ambitious than in the original amendment, the bill simply mirroring the provisions of South Australian amending legislation (which itself mirrored the Victorian legislation discussed above) that lifted any limitation on recovery merely because the injury arose from mental or nervous shock.[139] But the legislation allowed opponents of nervous shock liability a platform to vent well-established objections.[140] The member for Albury, the former United Australia Party Premier Mair, might have been talking about the *Coultas* decision when he queried whether physical injury could be caused by shock and voiced fears over how extensive the liability would be, what would be the cost of the amendments (especially insurance premiums) and whether the 'condition of the person receiving a shock' should be considered.[141] Paradoxically, he also wondered if shock-induced injury was a feature of modern life, negligence should be the trigger for compensation,[142] a concern also shared by Landa,[143] although in Mair's case the issue was raised as another reason for rejecting the legislation. He was unsuccessful: the bill passed the second reading and was not amended in its Committee stage. However, before it was sent to the Council, an event occurred that forced an important re-think in the form the amendment should take.

---

134 NSW, Hansard, Legislative Assembly, 6 May 1942, 3298–3299.

135 NSW, Hansard, Legislative Council, 12 May 1942, 3389 (Bradley).

136 Ibid., 3453 (Manning).

137 NSW, Hansard, Legislative Council, 19 May 1942, 3639–3640. Another concern was that the amendment to the Compensation to Relatives Act 1897 (NSW) should not be in a bill concerned with motor vehicle insurance.

138 Who insinuated the Council's rejection was due to the influence of the insurance industry: NSW, Hansard, Legislative Assembly, 10 June 1942, 3893–3894.

139 NSW, Hansard, Legislative Assembly, 16 December 1942, 1422 (Martin, Attorney General).

140 For a comic example of the opposition see the 'poem' in 'Nervous Shock Bill' in 'Hits, skits and jingles', *Armidale Express*, 11 January 1943, 6.

141 NSW, Hansard, Legislative Assembly, 16 December 1942, 1424 (Mair).

142 Ibid., 17 December 1942, 1497 (Mair).

143 Ibid., 1499–1500 (Landa).

There were two broad themes that underlay the first two attempts to amend the law. The first was that the *Chester* decision was unsatisfactory and the law needed to be amended so that Evatt J's approach would apply to future cases.[144] The second was that the way to do this was to modernise the law to bring it into line with English developments. In introducing his initial amendment, Landa said, 'We should bring our law into line with the law of England, having in mind *Coultas* and *Chester*'; in fact he thought his amendment did not go as far as English law.[145] Similar sentiments were expressed by Attorney General Martin, in introducing the Nervous Shock Bill: at varying times he stated the aim of the legislation was to 'bring the law in New South Wales into line with that prevailing in England and elsewhere…', that the bill removed 'the hand of yesterday, and allows cases of nervous shock to be adjudicated upon in New South Wales in the light of English decisions', and that Evatt J 'made certain very strong references to the need for altering the law, and bringing it in line with the law in England'.[146] This was understandable as Evatt J's dissent was founded in part on the English cases of *Hambrook v. Stokes Bros* and *Owens v. Liverpool Corporation*. It was also an easier 'sell': if *Coultas* was not good enough for England and the courts were powerless to intervene, it was for the legislature to bring New South Wales law into line.

The decision of the House of Lords in *Bourhill v. Young*, which became known in Australia at the end of 1942, caused a fundamental rethink in the proponents of the reform.[147] Its immediate effect was that the Law Reform (Torts) Bill 1942 was withdrawn. Almost a year later, the Law Reform (Miscellaneous Provisions) Bill 1943 was introduced, in November 1943. Speaking on the First Reading of the bill, the Premier, McKell, stated that the previous bill was withdrawn because of the House of Lords' decision and because in light of that decision the previous bill would have had to have been amended to achieve its desired purpose.[148] English law, which had once been the light on the hill, was now an obstacle to be overcome. In McKell's words, '*Hay v Young* put an end to all hopes that the liberal English trend might be followed and further developed by our courts by declaring the trend to be ill-founded.'[149] In his view, with the liberal trend checked, even if the [Nervous Shock Bill] had become law, the plaintiff would still have failed.[150] In hindsight, it is interesting that the decision in *Bourhill* was thought to end all hope for liability in the *Chester* scenario. The facts of *Bourhill* were so markedly different from those of *Chester* that it was far from certain that their Lordships would have reached the same

---

[144] McKell, 'A long overdue reform', *The Australian Worker* (Sydney), 30 December 1942, 5.
[145] NSW, Hansard, Legislative Assembly, 29 April 1942, 3115; 6 May 1942, 3299 (Landa).
[146] Ibid., 16 December 1942, 1422; 17 December 1942, 1495, 1496 (Martin).
[147] M. Lunney, 'Unseen networks: the legal professions' involvement in the *Law Reform (Miscellaneous Provisions) Act 1944* (NSW)', *ALJ*, forthcoming.
[148] NSW, Hansard, Legislative Assembly, 18 November 1943, 880 (McKell).
[149] Ibid., 1 March 1944, 1430 (McKell). *Hay v. Young* is the same case as *Bourhill v. Young*.
[150] Ibid.

conclusion. It is also striking that none of the suggested legislative reforms in New South Wales were directed towards allowing people in the position of the pursuer in *Bourhill* to recover hence the criticism could not have been directed to the actual result reached in the case. But it is certainly true that some of their Lordships seemed doubtful about the case law developments on which Evatt J had based his *Chester* judgment and it was this perception that seems to have forced the amendment to the law to be rethought.[151]

The result was that, in addition to the amendment suggested in the Nervous Shock Bill, a new clause was added in the Law Reform (Miscellaneous Provisions) Bill 1943:

> 4(1) The liability of any person in respect of injury caused by an act, neglect or default by which any other person is killed, injured or put in peril, shall extend to include liability for injury arising wholly or in part from mental or nervous shock sustained by any member of the family of the person so killed, injured or put in peril.[152]

There was little debate on the nervous shock clauses in the Assembly but there was serious opposition in the Council. In the Second Reading debate, Captain Bradley argued that the class of plaintiffs who could sue was both too narrow (by ignoring the extent of the suffering as an eligibility criterion) and too wide (because of uncertainties surrounding the meaning of 'put in peril').[153] More persuasively, he queried whether there was any spatial or temporal limits on when recovery could be allowed.[154] Replying for the government, Downing thought the legislation would not allow the claim where the shock was suffered as a result of reading of the death of a relative in a newspaper,[155] but when Bradley asked whether a family would not be entitled to claim where the man was working hundreds of miles away, Dowling retreated, saying 'it may be preferable were I to pursue this discussion privately'.[156] The issue had not been solved when the bill reached the Committee stage in the Council, as Manning for the Opposition proposed a number of amendments, the most important of which inserted the words 'within the sight or hearing of a member of his family' as a condition for the claim. The pragmatic reason for the amendment was clear. 'Suppose "thirty or forty" people hear of the accident, and they all bring actions for negligence to recover damages for shock. What is to be the effect on the community? Is

---

[151] See Lunney, above n 147. Some commentary on *Bourhill* certainly suggested a conservative approach. In Australia, for example, the author of 'From an Englishman's Notebook' who, in summarising Goodhart's article on *Bourhill* ('Bourhill v Young' [1944] *CLJ* 265), wondered whether the development of knowledge on sound conditions of mental health 'may lead us back to the reasoning of the Privy Council's decision [in *Coultas*]': (1944) 18 *ALJ* 198.

[152] Clause 4(2) provided wide definitions of 'member of the family', 'parent' and 'child'.

[153] NSW, Hansard, Legislative Council, 15 March 1944, 1695, 1703–1704 (Bradley).

[154] Ibid., 1703 (Bradley).

[155] Ibid., 1707 (Dowling).

[156] Ibid.

that a proper load to place on the community?'[157] But Manning also based his argument on doctrine: no duty was owed to people who were nowhere in the vicinity, and if clause 4 was not amended, 'it involves a complete remodeling of the law of negligence based on the complete absence of the fundamental idea of the whole law of negligence, namely the existence of a duty.'[158] Manning was no legal amateur: he was a distinguished lawyer[159] and although he had close links with the insurance industry,[160] his formulation of the problem as one relating to duty demonstrates how pervasive that analysis had become (albeit it is far from clear why he thought no duty would be owed). And, paradoxically, the response of Downing for the government was that the necessary limits could be applied through the law relating to causation and remoteness of damage![161] It is somewhat surreal that the justification for the legislation was in part overcoming the limits of *Coultas* while at the same time suggesting remoteness limits on recovery of damages for nervous shock.

In truth, as an opponent of the clause had argued, *Coultas* was in effect disregarded in New South Wales.[162] The real need for the bill was to overcome the result in *Chester*, and Downing argued that the amendment would not achieve that aim.[163] Despite his suggestion that the amendments 'made it [the bill] conform to the insurance companies' desires,'[164] the amendment was passed. It received a predictably hostile reception when it returned to the Assembly. *Chester* was again the benchmark: the Council's amendment would preclude recovery in that situation. Both McKell and Landa highlighted the influence of the insurance lobby on the Council[165] but when the bill returned to the Council it refused to budge. Responding to suggestions that the amendment would reduce the scope of liability by preventing liability in a case like *Hambrook*, Manning pointed out that the legislation expressly said that the amendment was an extension of the law.[166] *Hambrook* situations therefore would not be affected. The temperature of the debate was rising: with respect to the failure to impose temporal or spatial limits he referred to the 'absurdity' of the provision and that 'the thing is too ludicrous, I think, to waste time on.'[167] The Council

---

[157] NSW, Hansard, Legislative Council, 22 March 1944, 1859 (Manning).

[158] Ibid.

[159] Manning was a barrister, held the ranks of KC and KBE, and had been Attorney General for nearly nine years in the previous conservative government.

[160] He was Chairman of the board of directors of the Mutual Life and Citizens Assurance Company Limited from 1945 until 1961, and was a director of the Sydney board of the Commercial Union Assurance Company.

[161] NSW, Hansard, Legislative Council, 22 March 1944, 1860 (Downing).

[162] Ibid., 15 March 1944, 1692 (Bradley).

[163] Ibid., 22 March 1944, 1860 (Downing).

[164] Ibid., 1861.

[165] NSW, Hansard, Legislative Assembly, 30 March 1944, 2253 (McKell), 2255 (Landa).

[166] NSW, Hansard, Legislative Council, 4 April 1944, 2304 (Manning).

[167] Ibid., 2305.

held to its amendments and the bill was abandoned, McKell stating later that it was dealt with in the Council in a manner unacceptable to the Assembly.[168]

In late May 1944, a state election was held in New South Wales. McKell made express, if limited, reference to the nervous shock issue in his policy statement on 10 May: he stated that the government sought a mandate for the Law Reform Bill which was withdrawn because of amendments insisted upon by the Upper House.[169] McKell's Labor Party won the election and he made it clear that his election promise was to be kept. Battle lines were drawn early: prior to the introduction of any legislation, a spokesman for the insurance companies called the bill 'a lawyer's feast'[170] while McKell replied that the nervous shock provisions were designed to remove 'barbaric provisions from the law'. The cases showed that the persons chiefly concerned were expectant mothers and for these '...of course, it would be too much to expect the insurance companies to have sympathy'.[171]

The bill was reintroduced, in the same form, on 11 October 1944 and during the First Reading debate there was little give on either side: McKell claimed a mandate for the bill which was rejected by opponents,[172] and issue was again joined over the number of potential plaintiffs the bill created. Landa went to the nub of the issue: 'If by some chance relatively undeserving persons do get compensation, such legislation is still worthwhile if it safeguards the rights of plaintiffs in genuine cases like that of Mrs Chester.'[173] Little new emerged in the Second Reading debates and the bill proceeded to the Council where a slightly more conciliatory approach was taken.[174] For the government, Downing dismissed fears that newspapers could be liable under the legislation and restated the position that any concerns over the scope of liability could be dealt with under remoteness rules.[175] This was a hard position to defend: apart from the incongruity with *Coultas*, the position of remoteness under the general law (which Downing suggested would take care of the issue) was governed by *Re Polemis*, the case that was largely responsible for driving any limitations on recovery for nervous shock into the duty of care issue. Manning too reiterated

---

[168] NSW, Hansard, Legislative Assembly, 11 October 1944, 399 (McKell). Writing the day after the Council vote in the Labor newspaper, McKell was more animated: 'I unhesitatingly state that seldom in the history of this Parliament has there been such a sacrifice of personal rights on the altar of Mammon as that perpetrated by the Legislative Council in dealing with this particular measure' (*The Australian Worker* (Sydney) 5 April 1944, 9).

[169] It was thought a serious enough issue for Manning to defend the actions of the Council: *Northern Star*, 15 May 1944, 5.

[170] *SMH*, 26 August 1944, 5.

[171] *SMH*, 28 August 1944, 4.

[172] NSW, Hansard, Legislative Assembly, 11 October 1944, 399–404 (various members).

[173] Ibid., 403.

[174] After the bill passed the Assembly, McKell wrote a forceful piece for *The Australian Worker* as to why the Council should now pass the bill: 'All we seek to do is to rectify an anomaly which has been far too long in existence': *The Australian Worker* (Sydney), 1 November 1944, 6.

[175] NSW, Hansard, Legislative Council, 8 November 1944, 830–831 (Dowling).

his concerns over indeterminacy. His concern was not with the liability of newspapers but with how the transmission of news or information could spread the
liability too wide.[176] Unlike Landa, he thought the House should not 'ruthlessly
and in a wanton fashion inflict this potential responsibility on the whole community for the purpose of doing justice in a possible similar case to Chester...'[177]
But if a new provision that dealt with the hardship of *Chester* without 'saddling
the community with unlimited and unascertained liability' was presented he
would be in favour of it.[178] In the end, Downing and Manning conferred privately and, at last, Manning introduced amendments to overcome the difficulties. It was agreed that parents and spouses would not need to prove sight and
hearing to claim but that this would be necessary for other family members.
Downing explained the government's compromise, stating that even with the
amendment the bill was a considerable advance on the existing law and would
be of material assistance where injury was suffered by close relatives.[179] The
amendments were accepted by both Council and the Assembly when returned
to it and royal assent was granted on 8 December 1944.

It had taken four attempts but a version of the reform that Landa had inspired,
the 'first of its kind adopted in Australia' as he said of his original attempt,[180]
was now in force.[181] But the justification for the amendment had changed dramatically over these four attempts. The initial attempts to explain the change as
bringing New South Wales law into line with the law in England gave way to
an attempt simply to ensure that New South Wales law complied with the best
modern legal developments. This had always been the stated aim of law reform
in the McKell administration.[182] If that better law originated in England, so be
it, but if the liberal trend in the English cases had ceased with *Bourhill v. Young*,
that was a matter for them. In the end, the better law was based on the lead
given by an Australian judge, Evatt J.[183] By the end of the period of this study,

---

[176]   Ibid., 836–837 (Manning).

[177]   Ibid., 837.

[178]   Ibid., 836.

[179]   NSW, Hansard, Legislative Council, 5 December 1944, 1491 (Downing).

[180]   NSW, Hansard, Legislative Assembly, 6 May 1942, 3296 (Landa).

[181]   The editor of the *ALJ* Bernard Sugerman, a long time law lecturer in torts at the University
of Sydney, described the legislation as 'not ambitious in its scope': (1945) 18 *ALJ* 241. As is
evident from the discussion above, this uncharitable comment ignores both the political
controversy and the legal innovation surrounding the nervous shock provisions and reflects
his involvement with Evatt's suggestions for reform which had been broader: Lunney,
above n 147.

[182]   McKell, 'A long overdue legal reform', *The Australian Worker* (Sydney), 30 December 1942, 5.

[183]   As noted above (n 131), Landa had quoted Arthur Goodhart, writing in the *Weekly Notes*, who
had suggested that it would not be surprising to find that 'in the long run Dr Evatt's opinion
will prevail.' While Goodhart was ambivalent at best as to the *Bourhill* decision, he nonetheless
ignored *Chester* in a contemporary article on the case: A.L. Goodhart, 'Bourhill v Young'
[1944] *CLJ* 265.

there was no sense of impropriety in an Australian legislature preferring the views of an Australian judge as to how the common law should develop.[184]

A Gendered Law?

One final feature of the nervous shock case law in the period of this study worthy of comment, evident in both England and Australia, is the presence of female plaintiffs. In all the cases discussed in this chapter, the plaintiffs were women. At least at the commencement of the period of this study, this may have been due to the belief that women were more prone to this kind of illness[185] although as time progressed it became clear that men too could suffer from some kinds of nervous shock.[186] Once foreseeability became important in determining liability, however, it is difficult to avoid the conclusion that largely male stereotypes were used in determining whether mental harm was foreseeable, a phenomenon also apparent in England.[187] The brief finding that nervous shock was not a foreseeable consequence of the defendant's conduct in both *Bunyan* and *Chester* is testament to a world in which male stoicism prevailed over female sensibilities. This was rarely made explicit but in an exception Rich J commented in *Bunyan*: 'But perhaps a female clerk could not be expected to discover the incongruities of the respondent's behaviour, and to discredit the theatrical threats of a man who produced first poison and then a revolver and after the fullest advertisement of his suicidal purposes retreated with the revolver to the public thoroughfare.'[188] Combined with the feeling, expressed by both Davidson J in the Supreme Court and hinted at by Rich J in the High Court, that the claim was really only as a punishment for not getting her job back, Lucy Bunyan was unlikely to be found to be a foreseeable plaintiff. In *Chester* the influence was more subtle but equally present: by abstracting the facts to witnessing the dead body of the child, Latham CJ was able to note that 'it was not a common experience of *mankind* [my italics] that the spectacle, even of the sudden and distressing death of a child, produces any consequence of more than a temporary nature in the case of bystanders or even of close

---

[184] For Evatt's involvement with the legislation see Lunney, above n 147. Evatt was in the audience for McKell's policy speech in May 1944 where McKell made the Law Reform Bill an election issue: *SMH*, 11 May 1944, 3.

[185] See *Rea* v. *The Balmain New Ferry Company Limited* [1896] NSWR 923 where, unusually, the medical evidence given at the trial is reported in detail.

[186] E.g. shell-shock in the First World War. See further R. Lindstrom, 'The Australian experience of psychological casualties in war 1915–1939', PhD thesis, Victoria University of Technology (1997) chs. 5 and 6. In the debates surrounding the Law Reform (Torts) Bill 1942, three members made reference to shell shock as an example of a shock-induced injury which afflicted men: NSW, Hansard, Legislative Assembly, 16 December 1942, 1426 (Vincent); 17 December 1942, 1495 (Drummond and Martin).

[187] Mitchell, above n 40, 93–100.

[188] (1937) 57 CLR 1, 15.

relatives who see the body after death has taken place'.[189] One feature of Evatt J's judgment that made it so powerful was its dismantling of this reasoning, by showing, both from Janet Chester's evidence and from a more granular approach to the facts, that the plaintiff's injury was a natural response to the circumstances. Moreover, the response was to expected from parents, both male and female: 'plaintiff's condition of mind and nerve can be completely understood only by parents who have been placed in a similar agony of hope and fear with hope gradually decreasing'.[190] As Isaacs J had commented ten years previously, modern marriage was a partnership and raising children was one of the things that the partnership undertook.[191] Whether, when push came to shove, injury to a father would have been foreseeable, or if so, whether this would make the father a specially susceptible plaintiff did not have to be considered but it is interesting that when McKell tried to simplify and justify the statutory reform he did so on the basis that most plaintiffs were 'expectant mothers'.[192] Even when the law was to be expanded rather than limited, the use of a female stereotype remained prevalent.

Conclusion: Nervous Shock in Retrospect

The history of nervous shock liability in Australia is a particularly interesting example of the relationship between English and Australian law. The difference between English law and the law as laid down by the Privy Council allowed Australian courts to be extremely innovative, and somewhat daring, in their reluctance of follow the *Coultas* decision. Understandably, Australian courts were keen to find direct support from English authorities and (in particular) *Hambrook v. Stokes Bros* allowed liability to be incrementally expanded whilst ignoring the strictures of *Coultas*. But this minimalist approach downplays the intellectual effort of Australian practitioners and judges in teasing out the limits of liability for nervous shock. In particular, the judgments of Jordan CJ in *Bunyan* and *Chester*, and Evatt J in *Chester*, provided an analytical framework for the action for negligently-caused nervous shock that moved the question from remoteness to duty of care more clearly than any previous English case had done. Moreover, the issue in Australia moved from the courts to the Parliament, initially to formally end any restrictions imposed by *Coultas* but then, in the 1944 legislation in New South Wales, to expand liability beyond the new limits of *Bunyan* and *Chester*. That liability for nervous shock obtained the level of political interest that it did (at least in New South Wales) is another difference from England where the issue remained firmly in the judicial realm.

---

[189] (1939) 62 CLR 1, 10.
[190] Ibid., 17. Evatt J (25) also states that the argument rested on *parents* not suffering shock and illness from the ordeal gone through by Janet Chester. See further McDonald, above n 108, 72–73.
[191] *Wright v. Cedzich* (1930) 43 CLR 493.
[192] *SMH*, 28 August 1944, 4.

The fact that that New South Wales model was only adopted, after the period of this study, by Australian Capital Territory in 1955[193] and the Northern Territory in 1956[194] merely shows that the appropriate limits of this kind of liability were contested. That New South Wales went beyond its fellow states and territories was due in no small part to the remarkable efforts of Abram Landa, who championed reform both in the courts and in Parliament and who was arguably the leading player in giving one part of Australia a truly distinct law in this area.

[193] Law Reform (Miscellaneous Provisions) Ordinance 1955 (ACT) Part VII.
[194] Law Reform (Miscellaneous Provisions) Ordinance 1956 (NT) Part VII.

7

Negligence and the Boundaries of Liability: Government and Quasi-Government Liability

The previous chapter has considered how Australian courts dealt with liability in negligence where the unusual feature of the case was the presence of shock-induced injury. In this chapter, we consider another non-paradigm situation: where the defendant was not a private individual or entity but was a government or quasi-governmental body. In fact, the nature of economic development in Australia, with much infrastructure being financed and built by the state, meant that the potential for tortious (and other) liability was greater than in England where much of this development was carried out by the private sector. Apart from prompting legislative amendment of the Crown immunity rule, it also forced Australian courts to consider what, if any, allowances should be made to the usual rules imposing tortious liability where the defendant was a governmental body. This chapter will consider two different scenarios where these issues were raised: liability in respect of roads and rail. It is not intended to discuss every case decided during the period of this study in these situations but to take a snapshot of particular problems at particular times to provide examples of the kinds of concerns that animated the decisions of the courts.

Road Building and the Liability of the Government

As Finn has detailed, the means by which Crown immunity was abrogated in Australia were complicated and it is not intended to discuss them in any detail in this chapter.[1] The result of these changes was that by the beginning of the period of this study, in broad terms, where activities were conducted by government or quasi-governmental bodies that had a private analogy, such as building roads and railways, Crown immunity in practice did not apply.[2] While the precise mechanisms varied, there was no blanket immunity for government and the questions turned to whether, in the particular fact situation, the status of the defendant should be a relevant factor.

---

[1] P. Finn, *Law and Government in Colonial Australia* (Oxford University Press, 1987) (discussing Queensland, NSW and Victoria).

[2] The detail is complex and not required for present purposes: see further S. Kneebone, *Tort Liability of Public Authorities* (LBC Information Services, 1998) ch. 7.

One area that was controversial throughout the period of this study was liability for accidents on or around roads caused by the state of the road. As time progressed, the defendants in these actions were largely local authorities on whom responsibility for roads had been devolved by legislation but the slow pace of creating municipal authorities meant that, at the start of the period, actions relating to accidents could be brought directly against the relevant state government which had arranged for the work to be carried out. This was the situation in the first 'highway' case to reach the High Court, *Miller v. McKeon*,[3] in 1905. In 1900, the plaintiff McKeon, a local grazier, was being driven in a horse and carriage from Carroll, a small town near Gunnedah in New South Wales, towards Gunnendene. To reach their destination, they needed to cross the Namoi River at Gunnendene Crossing. The road had initially veered off to the left down to a natural ford to cross the river but sometime in the late 1870s/early 1880s a cutting had been made in the river bank to allow traffic to proceed more directly. It was accepted that 'the Government' was responsible for mak-ing this change to the road.[4] The road from Carroll to the river bank was fenced, but as the cutting was not as wide as the original road, there was a gap between the cutting and the fenced road. The accident occurred on a starlight evening when the driver stopped the horses and the plaintiff alighted from the buggy to search for the cutting. In fact, the buggy had been driven into the gap between the fence and the cutting, and as the plaintiff moved away from the buggy he fell down what he described as a quite precipitous part of the cutting.[5] He suf-fered a serious injury to his right leg which left him with a permanent disability.

At the trial at the Tamworth Circuit Court in October 1904,[6] counts in nui-sance and negligence were pleaded but the primary case related to negligence in failing to adequately warn of or prevent unknown access to the cutting. At the close of the plaintiff's case, counsel for the defendant sought a nonsuit on the basis there was no evidence to support the claims. There was no authority that failing to fence a cutting or embankment was negligent or that the cutting was a nuisance. The first of the 'public policy' arguments was also raised. For the plaintiff to win his case, counsel argued, McKeon had to prove that the Government must fence every portion of a road to prevent people from fall-ing over: 'If there was a fence at any place and it did not prove substantial, an accident thus occurring, then the Government would be liable.' The trial judge, Pring J, also seemed unimpressed by the plaintiff counsel's suggestion that white guide rails should be placed at the cutting: taking the colony as a whole this was not done 'one in a thousand times'. In granting the nonsuit, Pring J thought the litigation was not only novel but was 'an experiment'. In neither England

---

[3] (1905) 3 CLR 50.
[4] *Manilla Express*, 19 October 1904, 2. At the time the work was carried out there was no municipal authority in the area.
[5] NAA, A10071, 1905/2, *Miller v. McKeon*, Appeal Book, Judges Notes.
[6] All references in this paragraph are to the report of the trial in the *Manilla Express*, 19 October 1904, 2.

nor Australia had a successful case of this type been brought and if the plaintiff succeeded he 'did not know where the liability of the Government would cease'. McKeon appealed successfully against the nonsuit to the Full Court of the Supreme Court of New South Wales. The same public policy argument that had appealed to Pring J was given short shrift by Darley CJ: when counsel for the Government said if the case was sent back 'the court will lay down a duty on the Government to fence hundreds of miles of roads', he replied: 'No; each case must depend on its own circumstances, and it is for the jury to say whether a culvert should be fenced.'[7]

Perhaps the government was not willing to leave their fate to jury verdicts, but for whatever reason it appealed to the High Court. There was certainly some support for the view the Full Court's decision might spread liability too wide. When the case was being argued before the High Court, a contemporaneous comment put the concern pithily: 'The Government might construct a road in the interior to a log leading over a creek. The log might be dangerous to cross, but it was the best the Government could do.'[8] It was this line of thinking that informed the unanimous decision of the High Court to allow the appeal. In particular, Griffith CJ was at pains to point out that Australia was a new country and was different from England. This was not merely rhetorical flourish. After identifying the alleged negligent construction of the cutting as the cause of action, he commented on the use of English authorities in this context:

> Reference was made during argument to a great number of cases dealing with the law relating to highways in England and the doctrines that were to be applied to them. There is certainly an identity in name between highways in England and highways in this country, but the similarity is to a great extent in name only and when we come to the question of highways on their first dedication the similarity becomes even more shadowy.[9]

This justified jettisoning rules that applied in England where dedication of a highway usually involved a transfer from a private owner; in Australia it was the government that initiated the dedication. The 'Australian' rule (my phrase) imposed no higher duty than that of reasonable care in the care and management of a road, and rules from England about interfering with dedicated highways were not applicable. Rather:

> The Government of a new country forming for the first time a practicable road upon which land has been technically dedicated as a highway, but is impassable for wheeled traffic, is not bound by the rules which govern persons (other than the highway authority) who interfere with the surface of an ancient highway, as that term is understood in England. If the Government improve the so-called highway, and render it more useful to the public than it previously was, they

---

[7] *McKeon v. Miller* (1905) 5 SR (NSW) 128, 129.
[8] *Wyalong Advocate and Mining, Agricultural and Pastoral Gazette*, 20 September 1905, 4.
[9] (1905) 3 CLR 50, 58.

are not guilty of a misfeasance merely on the ground they have interfered with a highway.[10]

Moreover, any duty related only to the construction of the road, not to the failure to make changes to the road when conditions changed over time.[11] In deciding this question the Australian context was dominant. When Griffith CJ determined whether the cutting had been constructed with care, he argued: 'Every one who knows anything about the circumstances and conditions of life in Australia, must know that in hundreds and thousands of cases the Government are obliged, when first making a road, to leave it in a condition that for a crowded street would be dangerous.'[12] Road users too knew of this limitation and were expected to take care when using unfamiliar roads, including seeking advice about the state of the road before using it. This had little to do with the facts of the case – where the existence of the cutting was known – but much to do with setting boundaries between state and citizen in the new country of Australia. O'Connor J made similar points. The government's power to make roads was simply part of its executive power to carry out works for the benefit of the community. If in the course of this work – including creating the cutting – there was negligence, the government was liable 'on the same footing as their responsibility in carrying out any other public work.'[13] That such a statement could be made as routinely as it was shows just how far Australian law on Crown immunity had diverged from England. Like Griffith CJ, he saw the government's relationship with road users as correlative: those using the road had to take care in doing so. And like Griffith CJ he too referred to the 'knowledge of ordinary facts of life and conditions of travelling in Australia', to the fact that the place 'was in no way different from thousands of places in different parts of Australia which are driven on without accident, day after day, year after year'.[14] There is a real sense that road users as much as government had a responsibility to make the best of the difficulties thrust on government to establish workable infrastructure for the benefit of the community.

Despite the grandiloquence of Griffith CJ, *Miller v. McKeon* lay effectively dormant for one hundred years. Shortly after it was decided, the Full Court of the Supreme Court of Western Australia held the Commissioner for Railways liable for failing to fence a section of railway line to prevent livestock getting into a cutting on the line. Before the High Court decision, the trial judge in finding liability had said that his decision did not require that the Commissioner should fence all lines.[15] But in the Full Court, to which a summary of the recently-decided *Miller* was cited,[16] much less sensitivity to the predicament

---

[10] Ibid., 59–60.
[11] *Municipal Council of Sydney v. Bourke* [1895] AC 433.
[12] (1905) 3 CLR 50, 61–62.
[13] Ibid., 63.
[14] Ibid., 64.
[15] *WA*, 4 July 1905, 4 (Stone CJ).
[16] 'Digest of cases of federal interest' (1906) 3 *Commonwealth Law Review* 33.

of government was shown and this was not solely because the duty of the Commissioner was contractual, the plaintiff being a passenger on the train.[17] In New South Wales' cases decided shortly after *Miller*, municipal authorities responsible for roads did not always successfully defend claims against them for negligent construction of roads:[18] it was a question of fact in each case. And in the last case where *Miller* was actually used as the basis of a denial of liability, *Wenbam v. Council of the Municipality of Lane Cove*,[19] the nation-building rhetoric that had appealed when discussing country roads was held inapplicable to old suburbs in Sydney and was only just able to be defended by Cullen CJ when describing the new suburb of Artarmon:

> It is a matter of common knowledge that in many suburban areas there are new neighbourhoods which have been covered with bush until recent years, or in which the spaces marked out as highways offer obstructions in the shape of rocks and uneven ground, when settlement begins to take place. There may be very few residents in some of these outlying localities, and the degree of thoroughness that would be expected of a public body in supplying such a neighbourhood with roads within its power to construct them would be necessarily judged upon different principles from those applied in a populous city where there is constant traffic every day in the streets.[20]

Griffith CJ's reference in *Miller* to considering the 'moneys available to the Government' in determining the breach question was also criticised. In *Wenbam* evidence was led as to the amount of money collected annually for rates in the ward in which Helen-street – the site of accident – was located compared to the amount of money collected annually for rates in the municipality. Cullen CJ thought the evidence would be inadmissible if it was presented to 'distract the minds of the jury from the real issues' by which he seems to have meant only that it could not, of itself, determine the breach question. Ferguson J was more blunt: absent *Miller* he thought the evidence 'quite irrelevant' and wondered how the resources question could be left to a jury: 'I do not suppose that the jury is to be asked to consider what amount the Legislature has appropriated in any year for road making, and then to judge of the propriety of the action of the Government in allotting so much of it to this particular work.'[21] Here, too, the high-minded rationale that led Griffith CJ to include resources as a factor to be considered proved more difficult to apply in the grounded environment of early suburban-sprawl road building.

---

[17] *Daly v. The Commissioner of Railways* [1906] WAR 125.

[18] *Moody v. Municipality of Woollahra* (1912) 12 SR (NSW) 597 (in which *Miller* was not cited), on appeal (1913) 16 CLR 353; *Flukes v. Paddington Municipal Council* (1915) 15 SR (NSW) 408. In this latter case Street J held that the same rules as expressed in *Miller* applied to a municipal authority making an alteration to the existing condition of a road.

[19] (1918) 18 SR (NSW) 90.

[20] Ibid., 97–98.

[21] Ibid., 101.

Despite its limitations, *Miller v. McKeon* is important because of Griffith CJ
and O'Connor J's willingness to depart from aspects of the English law of highways. Rules developed from a fundamentally different history made no sense in
Australian conditions where anything that would unduly limit nation-building
would be unattractive to a bench that had all contributed to creating the Australian
federation. It was this aspect of *Miller* that was commented upon almost one hundred years later by another High Court considering the liability in negligence of
a road authority. In *Brodie v. Singleton Shire Council*,[22] a case concerned with the
rule that a highway authority was not liable for nonfeasance, the joint judgment of
Gaudron, McHugh and Gummow JJ suggested that the decision in *Miller* was the
start of a line of cases which developed the common law in Australia on the liability of road authorities, an initiative which was killed off in later cases.[23] Kirby J was
of the same view: when discussing the history of the nonfeasance rule, he noted
that early authority of the High Court – referring to *Miller* – might, left to itself,
have developed a suitable local rule (i.e. one that did not include the nonfeasance
rule). The implication was that an unsuitable local rule was adopted 'by a kind of
time-warp', the common law developments in the tort of negligence and the statutory regime for highways in Australia being ignored.[24] But, as Hayne J pointed
out in *Brodie*, *Miller v. McKeon* in fact said nothing to suggest that the nonfeasance
immunity did not, or should not, represent the law.[25] Griffith CJ made express
reference to the nonfeasance rule. It was no passing reference either. After quot-
ing from *Municipal Council of Sydney v. Bourke*, the Privy Council decision that
affirmed the rule for Australia, he made his position clear: 'In my opinion there
is no duty cast upon the Government except that in doing the work they must
take reasonable precautions not to cause injury to people who are invited to make
use of the work when completed.'[26] There is not the slightest hint that he thought
the rule inappropriate for Australian conditions – quite the contrary – and it is
remarkable that a case the result of which was inspired by the desire to protect
governmental bodies was resurrected as a protean base from which to argue that
an indigenous Australian law, unburdened of any English trimmings, would have
had a more expansive liability rule.

Apart from Griffith CJ's comments, contemporary statutory developments in
New South Wales show just how controversial any abolition of the nonfeasance
rule would have been. Section 73 of the Local Government Act 1906 (NSW)
stated that a municipal authority 'may within its area exercise the following
powers and shall perform the following duties', one of which included 'the care,
control, construction, formation, fencing, maintenance, and management of

---

[22] (2001) 206 CLR 512.
[23] Ibid., 562.
[24] Ibid., 589; see also his comments at 600.
[25] Ibid., 614.
[26] (1905) 3 CLR 50, 61.

all public places' (which included roads under their control).[27] Shortly after the legislation was in force, an action was brought in the District Court against the Municipality of Redfern by a woman who fell on an uneven footpath which had been constructed by the municipality.[28] Despite the formal pleading relating to only negligent construction of the footpath, counsel for the plaintiff's argument was more radical. He argued that, since the amendment to the law made by the 1906 Act, the 'Court was asked practically to decide whether municipal councils under the *Local Government Act* were responsible not only for the construction and formation of roads and footways, but also for their proper maintenance under all circumstances.'[29] In summing up to the jury, Rogers J said that under the new legislation a council was bound to maintain its footpaths in a reasonable state of repair, the answer to this question being left to the jury.[30] In fact, the jury found that the council had not been careless in its maintenance but the judge's direction caused disquiet in local authorities. Almost immediately after the decision, Redfern Council resolved to write to all the municipalities in New South Wales to advise them of the decision and its implications, and to seek co-ordinated action to 'have the municipalities' liability clearly defined and brought within reasonable limits' by the legislature.[31] At the same time, an editorial in the *Wagga Wagga Advertiser* took a very different line: it supported the increase in the liability of Councils and thought their opposition to the extra obligation unreasonable.[32] In December 1907, the *Evening News*, in an extended article, set out the basic problem. Municipalities had foisted on them responsibility for roads they did not build (formerly government roads, such as Parramatta Road) and this added to the already difficult financial position of many councils. But the article recognised that the no liability rule was a one-sided law. In a considered view, which canvassed the position in England and the United States and noted recent academic suggestions for a compromise position,[33] it ultimately came down against the old rule: 'In any case the day has passed in which any municipality can afford to lay the flattering unction to its soul that whether man or beast break their legs or necks in the ruts of a neglected highway it is no business of theirs.'[34]

Throughout 1908 the debate continued. Reviewing the effect of the 1906 amendments, the *Mudgee Guardian* thought the task of ensuring roads were in a suitable state of repair 'stupendous' and that any lack of action might be due

---

[27] Cf. s. 75 of the same legislation which gave them the 'control and management' of all public roads in their area.

[28] *Evans v. Municipality of Redfern*, District Court, *SMH*, 16 October 1907, 6.

[29] Ibid.

[30] *SMH*, 17 October 1907, 4.

[31] *Clarence and Richmond Examiner*, 22 October 1907, 5.

[32] *Wagga Wagga Advertiser*, 26 October 1907, 2. See *SMH*, 21 November 1907, 8.

[33] The suggestion of the Chief Justice of the New Zealand Supreme Court, Robert Stout, that a distinction should be drawn between formed and unformed roads: 'Local bodies' statutory liabilities' (1907) 4 *Commonwealth Law Review* 145 and 193, 201.

[34] *Evening News* (Sydney), 23 December 1907, 4.

to lack of funds for which the Council was not responsible. Nor was it keen on leaving it to the good sense of the jury to decide liability in these cases: reliance on a jury verdict was a 'frail reed from which to hold'.[35] In July the *Sydney Morning Herald* reported that the Local Government Association had recommended the legislation be amended by removing the requirement to maintain, a course of which the paper approved as part of an overall delineation by Parliament of what were powers and duties. Left to judicial decision to clarify the law, it thought that there was only one result possible: that an extended obligation would be placed on councils with respect to repair. If this was intended well and good but 'it was probably an oversight rather than the result of deliberation, and the obligations of the councils are heavy enough already'.[36] The cries for action were heeded only in part. When the government introduced amendments to the 1906 Act in November 1908, it was proposed that a council could only be liable for a failure to repair where the council had constructed the work or its care, control or management had been vested in the council. In all other cases council would only be liable where work under its direction had been negligently carried out. This was not a return to the pre-1906 position; it was rather a return to the law as stated in a Privy Council decision from 1879, *Borough of Bathurst v. Macpherson*,[37] that had itself been limited by the *Bourke* decision of the Privy Council in 1895. Understandably it was thought an unsatisfactory compromise by supporters of councils.[38] But events were to intervene before serious debate on the amendment could take place.

At the same time as statutory amendment was being discussed, the appeal in *Rohan v. Municipality of St Peters* was being heard. The plaintiff had suffered injury when thrown from his bicycle when it hit an unmarked depression in the road.[39] The defendant council argued that it had no duty in respect of nonfeasance but at trial the same Judge Evans previously mentioned directed the jury that the council was liable for any injury caused through a lack of maintenance. A more sympathetic jury found for the plaintiff.[40] This time the case was appealed to the Full Court of the Supreme Court where counsel for the plaintiff submitted that old case law on immunities had been 'got rid of' under the existing law.[41] When Cohen J asked, 'You mean that there is an absolute and imperative duty to repair?', plaintiff's counsel responded that he went to that length.[42] Predictably defendant's counsel responded by saying that whatever new local government structures had been created by the 1906 Act they could not justify the imposition of liability in favour of an individual for breach of any positive

---

[35] *Mudgee Guardian and North Western Representative*, 2 April 1908, 3.
[36] *SMH*, 16 July 1908, 5.
[37] *SMH*, 12 November 1908, 5. See also *The Farmer and Settler* (Sydney), 13 November 1908, 5.
[38] *SMH*, 20 November 1908, 11.
[39] *SMH*, 15 September 1908, 5.
[40] *SMH*, 16 September 1908, 7.
[41] *SMH*, 17 November 1908, 5.
[42] *SMH*, 18 November 1908, 7.

duty to repair. A unanimous Full Court refused to countenance any liability in favour of an individual for nonfeasance.[43] In a judgment in which the other members of the court agreed, Darley CJ found against the plaintiff's arguments on every count (doubting even whether the duty of 'maintenance' included 'repair'). His primary argument was that, even if a duty of repair was imposed by statute, there was no evidence that the legislature intended a breach of such a duty to be actionable by an individual adversely affected by the breach. While this conclusion was supported by a mix of English and Privy Council decisions, there was no hint in the judgment of any sense that these might not be appropriate for Australia. Counsel for the defendant had pointed out local councils might have 'hundreds of miles of roads under their control' and it would be 'impossible to insure that every portion would be in proper repair'.[44] The same theme was taken up in Darley CJ's judgment:

> This liability is so far reaching in a country such as this, that it is very necessary to be very certain that the statute has imposed a liability which really amounts to this that the shire or municipality within its own area becomes an insurer to each member of the public against accidents arising from the non-repair of the road. A public road may run through a shire for some 50 miles, and if every portion of that road is to be kept in such a state of repair as will insure against accidents occurring from the non-repair, no amount of rates which a shire can raise (the amount is limited) would suffice.[45]

He later supported the argument with a distinctly Australian example involving 'black soil country' over which a road passed. Assuming a duty to maintain the road, Darley CJ thought defence counsel's argument would mean that a shire or municipality would be liable to the owner of a heavy dray for delay if the road, from a want of metal, became foundrous and a dray passing along it sunk up to its axles. 'If this be so', he said, 'then indeed the liability to such an action is a very serious matter for the ratepayers both in shires and municipalities.'[46] The point is not whether Darley CJ was correct but that the invocation of a no liability rule was seen as apt for Australian conditions. Not everyone agreed with this view: as before the case, commentary about the desirability of the no-liability rule showed a range of opinions. The *Daily Telegraph*, for example, in an article on the case thought, viewed literally, that it laid down a principle that looked dangerous from the public point of view, and that even if local authorities had the law on their side they would not 'unduly strain it'.[47] But the *Sydney Morning Herald* was broadly supportive, pointing out Darley CJ's wide experience of the law of local government and of the peculiar conditions existing in the remote

---

[43] (1908) 8 SR (NSW) 649.

[44] *SMH*, 18 November 1908, 7 (submission of Cullen KC).

[45] (1908) 8 SR (NSW) 649, 652.

[46] Ibid., 654.

[47] *Clarence and Richmond Examiner*, 16 January 1909, 3, referring to an article in the *Daily Telegraph*. If the law was strained, the article suggested, 'they will provoke somebody who may succeed in bringing a hornet's nest about their ears.'

districts of the State,[48] and the rural *Molong Argus* thought the imposition of liability for nonfeasance 'monstrous' and that the Full Court's decision 'is in accordance with common sense'.[49] But perhaps more importantly, those in a position to review the decision singularly failed to do so. Leave to appeal to the High Court was refused, Griffith CJ stating simply, and somewhat cryptically, that in doing so the court expressed no opinion on the sections in question,[50] but the refusal to hear an appeal suggests no great dissatisfaction with the result. And the proposed amendment to the Local Government Act to clarify the responsibility of local councils also fell away after the decision: the Minister 'at once' withdrew the clause.[51] At least among decision-makers, the nonfeasance rule appeared to win the day.

So what does this history mean for assessing how innovative the decision in *Miller v. McKeon* really was? It is unfortunate that several members of the *Brodie* court used *Miller* as an example of a nascent Australian law of liability for highway authorities that might have encompassed, if left to its own developments, a liability for nonfeasance. There is simply no suggestion in the case itself or in the surrounding New South Wales controversy, that such a step was contemplated. More insidiously, any attempt to capture *Miller* for a 'progressive' anti-English law movement masks the genuine importance of the case. Both Griffith CJ and O'Connor J were perfectly prepared to accept that geographical and historical differences meant that not all of the English law of highways should be adopted in Australia, albeit not the immunity for nonfeasance. As importantly, these differences would lead to the liability of local authorities for roads being *restricted* in Australian conditions. That the scope of some of these limitations was contested is not surprising but the default position, as expressed in *Miller*, was that they were justified in Australia. Little is gained, and much lost, if genuinely Australian legal development is only recognised as a counterpoint to less progressive English rules.

State Railways and Their Fires: The Problem of Who Should Pay

As for roads, the history of railways in Australia was very different from England. The development of railways in Australia was largely a government enterprise but the risks created by those railways mirrored those in private hands. By the beginning of the period of this study, the operation and management of railways was vested in a government official or officials together with an associated government administration.[52] In most jurisdictions these were

---

[48] *SMH*, 24 December 1908, 5, where it was also noted that the nonfeasance rule applied in England, Canada and New Zealand, and that municipal men 'would heave a sigh of relief' in unison with ratepayers. Darley CJ had complained about the difficult travelling conditions when on circuit in regional NSW: see J. Bennett, *Sir Frederick Darley* (Federation Press, 2016) 149–151.

[49] *Molong Argus*, 11 December 1908, 4.

[50] *SMH*, 10 December 1908, 7.

[51] *SMH*, 10 December 1908, 5.

[52] Finn, above n 1, 67–69, 103, 129.

the Commissioner(s) for Railways and they remained a notable defendant to tort claims both during and after the period of this study. As Crown immunity had been abolished,[53] they were exposed to the ordinary rules of tort law unless courts could be convinced that they deserved special treatment. Arguments along these lines were generally unsuccessful unless there was explicit statutory authority justifying this different treatment. To give an illustration of these trends a small subset of cases (damage caused by fires coming from sparks from railway engines) from a particular period (the first ten years of the twentieth century) are considered below. They demonstrate that while the general principles to be applied were those of the common law, there was room for particular Australian contexts to influence court decisions.

The first reported case in the subset of cases being considered was *Dennis v. Victorian Railway Commissioners* which concerned the disastrous fire near the small Victorian town of Birregurra in early February 1901. It was reported that shortly after the express train had passed through the area in the late morning a grass fire began that spread over the course of the day. It was reported that thousands of acres of grass, miles of fencing and five homesteads were destroyed.[54] Three twelve-year-old boys were killed in the fire and three other men died later in hospital. Other firefighters suffered physical injury. There was enormous press coverage, the tone of which can be gleaned from the *Geelong Advertiser*'s headline of 16 February 1901: 'The Birregurra Horror – Overtaken by the Flames – a Harrowing Scene – Another Death'.[55] Almost immediately the finger of blame was pointed at the railway commissioners. A letter to *The Argus* from the Presbyterian manse of Birregurra, after setting out the heroics of the women of Birregurra who had fought the fire and saved the town, commented:

> It is well the Government should come to the assistance of those who have been burnt out, and who have lost their all, 'but prevention is better than cure'. There are some who assert positively that this fire was caused by sparks from the express, which passed through here at 11 o clock that morning. What actual steps have been taken to minimise the danger arising from the sparks of locomotives? Has the matter of spark-arresters ever received the serious consideration it demands? Commissions of inquiry have been appointed, and what has resulted? The devastation of property is so widespread, and the loss of life so heartrending, that our legislators cannot but be roused up to a sense of responsibility – a responsibility that necessitates action.[56]

Dennis, whose property was adjacent to the railway line and suffered damage from the fire, commenced proceedings against the Victorian Railway

---

[53] In Victoria, where Crown immunity was abrogated only in respect of claims on contract, the Commissioners were not within the scope of Crown immunity for the purposes of tort claims: ibid., 100, 108.

[54] *Bendigo Advertiser*, 11 February 1901, 4. Greater detail is provided in the *Colac Herald*, 12 February 1901, 2.

[55] *Geelong Advertiser*, 9 February 1901, 2.

[56] *Argus*, 16 February 1901, 11.

Commissioners alleging negligence in the construction and maintenance of the trains, the failure to act carefully to minimise or eliminate sparks coming from the train, and in permitting the grass in the land corridor in which the line ran to become too long. After initial proceedings were halted to allow the Full Court of Supreme Court of Victoria to decide the correct forum for the case, the whole case was sent to an arbitrator[57] who found in favour of Dennis and awarded him damages of £40. Although there was legal argument – one report described a day's proceedings as having 'a very somnolent character' as counsel combated each other's points[58] – most of the reported evidence related to technical aspects of engine design.[59] But however it was achieved, the arbitrator, Judge Chomley, was convinced as to the legal basis of the Commissioner's obligations. It had been laid down, he said, that a duty was imposed on those who had the management of a railway on which locomotive engines were used to keep land at the edge of their line, and in their occupation, in such a condition so as to minimise the risk of a fire starting or spreading from sparks or ashes falling from locomotives.[60] As burning off dead grass next to the track was a known and widely practised method of reducing this risk, the Commissioner's employees had been careless in not undertaking this work. Taking a robust approach to breach of duty, Judge Chomley gave little weight to the (in modern parlance) 'rock and a hard place' argument:

> The railway employees do not seem to me to have realised that even if it was in some degree dangerous to burn off when the most suitable time of the day could be chosen, all necessary precautions taken and immediate assistance available, it was incalculably more dangerous to leave alone dry grass liable to be ignited by the sparks from any passing train at any hour of the day, and with no one near to check the fire if it occurred.[61]

An appeal, by consent, to the Full Court of the Supreme Court by way of case stated was taken.[62] The question asked whether, assuming all the facts as established in the award were correct, the award was bad in law because the failure to burn off or render safe the grass from ignition 'cannot constitute actionable negligence'. There is some ambiguity in the case stated: did it mean that the Commissioner was under no obligation with respect to the grass at all (a modern 'duty of care' point) or was the question simply whether the failure to burn the grass could constitute a breach of that duty? Counsel for the defendants, at least in part, argued the duty point. There was no authority in either England or Victoria where a railway company was liable where the allegation

---

[57] (1901) 27 VLR 323.
[58] *Geelong Advertiser*, 14 May 1902, 1.
[59] See the reports in the *Geelong Advertiser*, 13 May 1902, 1; 14 May 1902, 1; 15 May 1902, 1; 15 July 1902, 1; 30 August 1902, 1; 1 September 1902, 4; 16 September 1902, 4; *Argus*, 16 September 1902, 8.
[60] *Geelong Advertiser*, 16 September 1902, 4.
[61] Ibid.
[62] (1903) 28 VLR 576.

against it was that it had failed to alter the natural state of the land. The public nature of the Commissioner's function was also relevant. The Railways Act 1890 (Vic) empowered the running of engines 'but enjoins no duties or obligations towards adjoining landowners, and the Commissioner, as distinct, from a private company, is not liable for an omission to do something which others might conceive to be a reasonable thing to do.'[63] The argument drew on, if not expressly relied on, statutory authority: if nothing was done beyond what was authorised and it was done in a proper manner, no action would lie even if 'special injury to a particular individual' was caused.

Ominously for the defendant, plaintiff's counsel was not called on beyond reading the case stated and the judgment that followed was entirely in the plaintiff's favour. The Court needed little convincing on the breach point. The defendant owned the land, knew that the engines no matter how well constructed or what precautions were taken would emit sparks and that at certain times of year, 'especially in this country', the probable consequence would be to set fire to the dry grass on that land.[64] As it was 'impossible to shut our eyes' to the common practice, both in Victoria and other parts of Australia, to burn off grass to reduce the risk of its catching fire, the award should stand.[65]

In between arguments relating to breach there is an important passage that seems to relate to duty. After highlighting the foreseeability, and probably knowledge, of the risk, the court rejected an argument that there was no obligation on the Commissioner:

> We think that under such circumstances, and especially in this country, where the climatic conditions are so different to those of a country like England, there is an obligation on the part of the defendant to use reasonable care to prevent ignition of the dry grass and herbage on its property through the agency of sparks which escape from the engines.[66]

That this was an extension of the law is clear from the following paragraphs of the judgment. Earlier Victorian case law had imposed liability on a public body for water damage caused by the careless design or construction of a railway embankment[67] and there was English authority that imposed liability for increasing the risk of fire by cutting grass and leaving it in heaps next to the railway tracks over which the defendant's trains ran.[68] As counsel for the defendant had pointed out, however, the latter case did not involve leaving the land untouched. But what seems to have been decisive here was the Australian context. Fire was such an obvious hazard that resulted from the defendant's activity

---

[63] Ibid., 577–578.

[64] (1903) 28 VLR 576, 579.

[65] Ibid., 580.

[66] Ibid., 579.

[67] *The Victorian Woollen and Cloth Manufacturing Co Ltd v. Board of Land and Works* (1881) 7 VLR 461.

[68] *Smith v. London and SW Railway Co.* (1870) LR 6 CP 14.

that some obligation to prevent its occurrence was required, and that view was reinforced by the actual practice of railway authorities. It is clear from the evidence given at the arbitration that the length of the grass was in the thoughts of both the adjoining landowners and the Commissioner's employees. There was statutory authority to burn off and areas surrounding the place where the grass caught fire had in fact been burnt earlier in the summer.[69] The relevant English authority was accordingly wide enough to cover a situation where Australian practice suggested an obligation ought to be owed.[70] This was so even though it was known that *Dennis* was a test case and that, while his claim was small, the total amount involved was around £6,000.[71]

Four years later the High Court had the opportunity to comment on the *Dennis* decision. In January 1905 a bushfire on the railway between Burrumbeet and Trawalla, near Ballarat in Victoria, broke out after burning matter emitted by an engine set fire to grass alongside the track and spread over a number of properties, one of which was owned by Campbell. He sued the Commissioners on the same basis as *Dennis*, the case was referred to arbitration and the arbitrator, Judge Chomley, awarded him over £600.[72] An appeal by way of case stated was lodged, the question for the Full Court being whether the presence of a licence granted by the Commissioners to a third party of the land adjacent to the rails eliminated any responsibility the Commissioners had for the state of the grass. The lease required the licensee[73] to take every precaution to prevent the spreading of fire and expressly allowed the Commissioner to enter the land and burn off grass should they consider it necessary. Unsurprisingly, both the Full Court of the Supreme Court of Victoria and the High Court (the latter without calling on counsel for the plaintiff) found that the licence made no difference.[74] Griffith CJ expressed his 'entire concurrence' with the *Dennis* decision. The Commissioners' obligation arose from the activity of

---

[69] *Geelong Advertiser*, 16 September 1902, 4.

[70] Ibid., 18 April 1903, 1, commented that pastoralists would learn 'with satisfaction' of the Full Court decision.

[71] Initially the government did not treat it as a test case, the Minister for Railways saying the claims were extortionate and would be fought (*Bairnsdale Advertiser and Tambo and Omeo Chronicle*, 23 April 1903, 3). A personal injury action against the Commissioner after *Dennis* was initially contested although I have not traced the final outcome after proceedings were adjourned and transferred to Melbourne (*Colac Herald*, 26 June 1903, 2; 30 June 1903, 4). An attempt to seek leave to appeal to the Privy Council was rejected by Hood J: the amount in issue in *Dennis* did not meet the statutory minimum and he rejected the Commissioners' request to calculate the amount in issue from all the outstanding claims (*Colac Herald*, 12 May 1903, 4). The Commissioners did not pursue an application for leave from the Privy Council itself (*Argus*, 30 September 1903, 8).

[72] *Geelong Advertiser*, 26 February 1907, 4. It was seen as a test case and leave to proceed against the Commissioners was sought once the High Court decision went in favour of the landowner (*Geelong Advertiser*, 19 September 1907, 3).

[73] The document is also referred to as a lease but it was, as Griffith CJ noted, 'a document of a singular character' and I have used licence as it seems to more accurately represent the arrangements between the parties.

[74] (1907) 4 CLR 1446. The Full Court decision was not reported.

running locomotives that emitted sparks and although the Commissioners had taken the necessary precautions to prevent sparks being omitted, 'in a country like Australia a further danger arises if there is long grass growing within the railway fences, for it is likely to catch fire and the fire is likely to spread to the adjoining land.'[75] Hence the Full Court in *Dennis* had decided that the Commissioner's obligation extended to taking precautions against this risk. The reservation in the licence allowing the Commissioners access to cut the grass meant that they retained the obligation recognised in *Dennis* and Griffith CJ was uncertain whether it was even lawful for the Commissioners to divest control of their land so that the duty to cut the grass could not be carried out.[76] In a case said to be of considerable interest to country residents,[77] the *Dennis* principle – that Australian conditions required the Commissioners' obligations to extend to acting positively to cut the grass – was affirmed.[78] This was so despite the Commissioners plea that, as the total mileage of railways in Victoria in January 1905 was about 3,381 miles, 'if on certain small portions of the land vested in the Defendants there was grass in an inflammable condition close to the railway line' this would not be evidence of negligence.[79] At no point does the scale of the obligations undertaken by the Commissioner seem to have been a factor considered in determining liability.

Four months later the High Court in *Sermon v. Commissioner of Railways* was asked to consider the liability of the Western Australia Commissioner resulting from sparks being emitted by a locomotive in a different context. In December 1904 a fire in Burges Siding, near York, caused extensive damage to grassland and infrastructure on surrounding properties. The plaintiff, one of the owners of property next to the railway lines where the fire was alleged to have started, sued the Western Australian Commissioner for Railways, alleging that the fire was the result of sparks emitted by one of the defendant's engines. There were striking similarities with the earlier cases. The action was a test case and it was clear other actions awaited its result.[80] As in *Dennis* and *Campbell*, liability depended on showing that the Commissioner had been negligent in some way in running the trains and this meant that considerable expert evidence was led as to the methods used to eliminate or reduce sparks from the train.[81]

---

[75] Ibid., 1450–1451.

[76] Ibid., 1452.

[77] *Bendigo Advertiser*, 28 June 1907, 2.

[78] Barton J agreed with Griffith CJ. Isaacs J noted that the appellant's argument started by admitting the correctness of *Dennis* and sought to distinguish the facts in *Campbell* and decided the case on the ground that there was no relevant distinction. Higgins J, in a one line judgment, noted simply that the Commissioners could not keep control of the land and escape the consequences of that control.

[79] NAA, A10074, 1907/17, *Victorian Railway Commissioners v. Campbell*, Defence, para. 10.

[80] *Daily News* (Perth), 17 October 1906, 3.

[81] See the reports of the defendant's evidence presented at trial: *WA*, 19 October 1906, 2; *Daily News* (Perth), 18 October, 1907, 4.

As in those cases, it was held ultimately that the Commissioner had not been negligent in adopting the spark-retarding procedures that had been used on the engines.[82] But in *Sermon* there was no allegation that the grass adjacent to the lines had not been cut.[83] Rather, the plaintiff alleged that the Commissioner had used a local coal ("Collie coal") and that, as this coal produced more sparks than other coal that could have been procured, its use was careless. There was little doubt on the evidence that Collie coal did produce more sparks than 'Newcastle coal' (from the east coast Australian town).[84] The problem for the plaintiff was the presence of a statutory provision that allowed the Commissioner to use 'on any railway locomotive engines consuming any kind of fuel'.[85] All of the judge (in a judge-only trial),[86] the Full Court of Supreme Court of Western Australia,[87] and the High Court[88] found for the Commissioner. All courts accepted that the statutory provision gave the Commissioner an unfettered choice as to what coal to use at what time without exposing him to the risk of his choice being categorised as negligence. The trial judge drew an analogy with the recent English decision in *London County Council v. Great Eastern Railway Company*[89] where the Divisional Court had refused to interpret a statute so as practically to require the railway company to purchase more expensive coal. Similarly, the 'Commissioner was authorised generally to use coal, and he was no more bound than was the Great Eastern Railway to use coal which was the best looking at it from the point of view of causing the least danger to the adjoining lands.'[90] In the Full Court, Macmillan J was prepared to assume that in the absence of the clause the use of Collie coal in the circumstances would be negligent but the aim of the clause was to allow the Commissioner to use 'with impunity that which it would have been *intra vires* to use even in the absence of the words'.[91] In effect, this was to find that there was statutory authority for the decision of the Commissioner and it was not for the courts to introduce limitations on the clear words of Parliament.

---

[82] *WA*, 20 October 1906, 4 (judgment of Parker CJ at trial). No appeal was taken on this point.

[83] NAA, A10078, 1907/5, *Sermon v. Commissioner of Railways* (incorrectly catalogued as Sernib), Statement of Claim, para. 6. The catch-all allegation 'failing to take reasonable precautions to prevent damage by fire caused by sparks emitted or dropped by his engine' was not, apparently, linked to any failure to burn grass. The reason may have been some doubt as to where the fire started: see the different evidence of Jas Robertson and George Lukin, *Daily News* (Perth), 17 October, 1906, 3.

[84] A10078, above n 83, Transcript of Evidence, Evidence of Edward Hume, Chief Mechanical Engineer, Government Railways, 71.

[85] The Government Railways Act 1904 (WA) s. 20.

[86] The case is not formally reported but a full report is contained in A10078, above n 83, Appeal Book, 89–93.

[87] The appeal is not formally reported but for details see *Daily News* (Perth), 2 July 1907, 2; *WA*, 12 June 1907, 4; 13 June 1907, 4; 3 July 1907, 3.

[88] (1907) 5 CLR 239.

[89] [1906] 2 KB 312.

[90] *WA*, 20 October 1906, 4.

[91] *WA*, 3 July 1907, 3.

Similar views were expressed in the High Court. An important factor for Griffith CJ was that Collie coal was the only coal yet found in Western Australia and 'to read the words "any kind of fuel" as not including the only coal found within a distance of some thousands of miles is, I think, to do violence to all the probabilities',[92] especially as he had earlier noted that Newcastle coal was 'imported by sea from the other side of the continent of Australia'. While McMillan J in the Full Court had noted that the type of clause in issue in *Sermon* was not found in similar English Acts, Griffith CJ filled out the context: it was unreasonable to require Western Australia to pay the additional costs of east coast coal. Perhaps Griffith CJ was conscious of Federation sensibilities, but the general point was made more fully by Isaacs J. While he was forced with 'considerable reluctance' to conclude that the defendant must succeed, the legislature had made its call:

> Parliament has invested him as an expert with the control and management of the great public department, and in view apparently of the nature and situation of the country, and taking into consideration its finances, resources, and development, has reposed in the Commissioner the right and duty of selecting fuel necessary or desirable to work the railways, and accordingly has left him free to choose.[93]

This is not to suggest that the decision was dictated or even significantly influenced by domestic concerns but simply to highlight the importance of the Australian context. As the evidence at the trial showed, the risk from using Collie coal was known and members of the Legislative Assembly at the time had lobbied to have its use restricted in the eastern agricultural areas in summer. The political controversy surrounding the use of Collie coal was demonstrated when, immediately after the fire, an urgency motion on fires in agricultural districts was brought before Parliament. During an animated debate, the Premier gave an undertaking that the use of Collie coal would be immediately suspended, and this does seem to have happened,[94] but various members went further, indicating that the Government had previously paid out damages for fires caused by sparks from Collie coal.[95] Whatever the truth of these political accusations,[96] however, there was no suggestion that liability would be accepted in this case, especially in light of the evidence at trial that no definite undertakings to reduce the use of Collie coal were given by either the Minister or the Commissioner. More importantly, the question was now to be determined by reference to the statutory protection introduced by the

---

[92] (1907) 5 CLR 239, 248.

[93] Ibid., 255.

[94] *WA*, 17 October 1906, 3; 19 October 1906, 2; A10078, above n 83, Transcript of Evidence, Evidence of Edward Hume, Chief Mechanical Engineer, Government Railways, 71–72; Plaintiff's Exhibits C3–C8.

[95] *WA*, Hansard, Legislative Assembly, 22 December 1904, 2172–2193.

[96] I have found no evidence of any case that was reported where the Government paid damages in respect of Collie coal fires although there are certainly suggestions that the Government would be so liable: *Daily News* (Perth), 2 March 1900, 2.

1904 Act. As McMillan J noted in the Full Court, the Railway Acts 'showed an intention by the Legislature to interfere with private rights, which intention was not to be found in Acts of permissive nature and other Acts of similar character, such as those which authorised the use of locomotives on highways'.[97] The legal reasoning was impeccable and provided a ground for distinguishing *Dennis* and *Campbell*. The result affirmed that Western Australia could choose who should bear certain of the costs associated with the use of railways.[98] More broadly, the result also reflected the different railway environments of Victoria and Western Australia: while cutting grass might have been a useful and reasonable precaution for the Commissioners to take against fire from engine sparks in both jurisdictions, when the temperature was 105 degrees Fahrenheit in the shade and a hot wind was blowing across the line in the direction of the plaintiff's property, it 'seemed a difficult thing for any engine burning any coal to pass through country of this kind, and under such circumstances, without there being the greatest risk of fire being caused, unless some precautions were taken by the adjoining landowners'.[99] The relative responsibilities of the parties were accordingly different in an environment where there were limits on the Commissioner's power to avoid the risk while undertaking the activity. But the judicial limits on this immunity were strictly enforced. Three years later, when another fire resulted from sparks from a locomotive using Collie coal and caused damage, the allegation was not that the Commissioner had been careless in using Collie coal but in failing to fit the most effective spark-arrester to the locomotive.[100] The problem arose because it was the Commissioner's practice to use Newcastle coal from trains operating out of Geraldton but when a strike limited the availability of Newcastle coal, the Commissioner argued that his paramount duty was to keep the trains running and this, in effect, outweighed any risk involved in running trains using Collie coal which were not fitted with the most effective spark-arrester. The argument convinced the local magistrate[101] if not the local paper which found the result 'hard', 'sympathised' with the settlers, and thought it 'rather strange' that the best spark-arrester had not been used.[102] In modern doctrine, the Commissioner's argument was that the social utility of the conduct (running trains) justified the risks of fire caused

[97] *WA*, 3 July 1907, 3. The result was that the unconvincing evidence of the Chief Mechanical Engineer for Government Railways as to the incidents of fire from sparks ('the risk has been minimised to such an extent that it ceases to exist') was rendered irrelevant: A10078, above n 83, Transcript of Evidence, 73–74.

[98] See also *Midland Railway Company v. Connolly* [1919] WAR 1 where statutory authority to run a railway was held to provide a defence to any action for damage resulting from a fire caused by sparks from a locomotive, there being no evidence of negligence (Newcastle coal was being used!). Cf. the evidence at the Sermon trial of Lionel White that the company that ran the Upper Darling Range Railway used Collie coal on its engines and on two occasions paid compensation for fires caused by engine sparks (A10078, above n 83, Transcript of Evidence, 56). It is unclear under what authority this railway was operated.

[99] *WA*, 3 July 1907, 3 (Full Court of WA Supreme Court).

[100] *Anderson v. Commissioner of Railways* [1910] WAR 10.

[101] *Geraldton Guardian*, 18 August 1910, 2; 20 August 1910, 3.

[102] Ibid., 20 August 1910, 2.

by that conduct.[103] This was given short shrift in the Full Court: it was readily foreseeable by the Commissioner that Collie coal would need to be used and he had failed to timeously arrange for the new spark-arresters to be fitted. The failure to do so was careless even though 'it would have put the Commissioner to considerable expense and to a certain amount of trouble'.[104] Parker CJ (the trial judge in *Sermon*) went even further:

> … I think that whether he had ample time to affix the finer mesh spark arrester or not, when he found he was compelled to use Collie coal, he had either to stop his engines working for a day or so, so as to affix the necessary and proper spark arrester, or else, if he decided to work those engines, he took the risk of being compelled to pay any persons who were injured by sparks which fell from those engines when using Collie coal without a proper spark arrester.[105]

As these cases show, the legislative and judicial judgments about where to impose the risk of fire associated with the presence of an essential public facility like railways could vary between jurisdictions within Australia. There was no history of an immunity from nonfeasance as in the case of roads and in the cases considered the courts were happy enough to impose responsibilities on state railway operators to minimise the risks associated with the Australian pestilence of fire. But where the legislature had determined the limits on what burdens could be imposed on these state enterprises, courts were equally willing to apply them without demur. In all of these decisions the experience of private railways in England's green and pleasant land gave only limited assistance.

Conclusion

The aim of this chapter has not been to provide a compendium of tortious actions against government or quasi-government bodies during the period of this study. Rather, the focus has been on a number of areas where the interaction between English authority and Australian application of that authority involved required Australian courts to decide, explicitly or implicitly, on how these would be integrated into an Australian system that was quite different from that in England. Government in Australian jurisdictions played the major role in providing key infrastructure, including roads and rail. One theme of this chapter has been that it is too simplistic to see Australian judges as just adopting the English rules relating to these areas without question. As in England, the immunity for nonfeasance for road repair was controversial in Australia, but one reason for its retention was the view among some that it was especially appropriate for Australian conditions. Conversely, unless restrained by statute, courts could modify the liability of state rail entities to deal with the requirement imposed by the risks thrown up by the Australian environment.

---

[103] See counsel's argument before the Full Court: *WA*, 19 October 1910, 3.
[104] *Anderson v. Commissioner of Railways* [1910] WAR 10, 13.
[105] Ibid., 12–13.

8

In Defence of King and Country

The previous chapter considered responses to attempts to make governments liable in tort for injuries arising out of road and railways, matters of everyday concern. But in rare situations Australian courts had to consider the extent to which the state might be liable in tort in the exercise of arguably its most important responsibility: the defence of the realm. This chapter deals with the most vexing question of whether the state could be liable for injury caused to another in the conduct of a war and most of the chapter is devoted to the contribution of the leviathan *Shaw Savill and Albion Co. Ltd v. Commonwealth* litigation to that question. But nearly forty years earlier the issue of governmental liability for defence activities was raised in the much less dramatic context of a rifle range in Randwick in Sydney.

Errant Bullets in Suburban Sydney

Other than *Shaw Savill and Albion Co. Ltd v. Commonwealth*, there is only one other authority that dealt with tort liability to third parties in relation to defence activities in the period of this study. In *Evans and Wife v. Finn*,[1] the plaintiffs were owners of a property that adjoined a rifle range. The range had been part of New South Wales' military facilities before being transferred to the Commonwealth upon federation. The defendant, General Finn, was a nominal defendant under the Claims Against the Commonwealth Act 1902 (Cth), the temporary legislation in force before the Judiciary Act 1903 (Cth) was passed. The gist of the plaintiffs' complaint was that bullets fired at the rifle range did not always remain there but entered their property and caused both minor property damage and, more importantly, made the house uninhabitable (the plaintiffs had left the property by the date of the trial).

Both at trial and in the Full Court of the Supreme Court of New South Wales the argument that different liability rules in private nuisance[2] should apply because of the nature of the defendant's activity was rejected. The range was

---

[1] (1904) 4 SR (NSW) 297.
[2] Counts in trespass to land and some kind of public nuisance were rejected at trial: *SMH*, 17 September 1903, 4.

conducted under an exercise of prerogative power, and while it was accepted that fault would be required to make the government liable if the activity was authorised by statute – the general common law rule – in the absence of legislation the government was in the same position as an ordinary citizen. Propositions to the contrary were emphatically rejected. At trial Stephen ACJ thought the Crown had no more right than a private individual to do that which placed individuals not only in terror of their lives, but actually endangered life. The Attorney-General's proposition 'was a startling one, and he could find no authority for it'.[3] While in the Full Court Darley CJ also thought there were steps that could have been taken to ensure that the range was safe for those in adjoining areas,[4] the kernel of his judgment too was that the Crown, in the absence of legislative authority, had no special privilege to interfere with the rights of property of private citizens.[5] Pring J dissented. In his view, one of the highest duties of the Sovereign was to defend the realm and while no court of law could compel the King to perform it, 'on the other hand, I think the Courts should be very slow to interfere with the King in his performance of it. Such an interference might result in the greatest danger to the empire.'[6] Starting from this mindset, it is no surprise he saw 'no difference' between an act authorised by statute and one which was performed by the Crown in the exercise of one of the high duties which it owed to the subjects, such as that of ensuring the efficient protection of the realm against enemies.[7]

The result in *Evans v. Finn* was complicated by other matters that are not relevant to the present discussion[8] but even on the prerogative point other judgments of the Full Court are difficult to reconcile with the case. In *Davidson v. Walker*,[9] both at trial and in the Full Court it was held the court had no power to review decisions around the siting and construction of a police lock-up even though it was constructed in the exercise of the prerogative. This authority, which also involved an action in nuisance, was cited by Pring J but ignored by Darley CJ,[10] prompting a Melbourne law school lecturer teaching the liability of the Crown in 1911 to note the cases were 'difficult to reconcile.'[11] Perhaps Darley CJ was concerned that the Crown attempted to approximate its position

---

[3] Ibid.
[4] *SMH*, 9 March 1904, 6; (1904) 4 SR (NSW) 297, 307–308.
[5] (1904) 4 SR (NSW) 297, 305–306.
[6] Ibid., 312.
[7] Ibid., 313.
[8] There were also issues on appeal as to the plaintiff wife's standing to sue and also over the amount of damages awarded by the jury.
[9] (1901) 1 SR (NSW) 196.
[10] It was also ignored by Owen J, who agreed with Darley CJ, even though he had reached a contrary conclusion as trial judge in *Davidson*.
[11] Sir Keith Officer, 'Lectures on Administrative Law 1911, notes written by F. Keith Officer', Melbourne University Law Library (rare books collection), 340 032, 85. Two differences are apparent *ex post* – the allegation in *Davidson* related to construction and maintenance of the lock-up, not the activity within them, and the interference in *Davidson* was amenity damage (noise) rather than a threat to physical safety. Cf. *Gordon v. Young* (1900) 21 NSWR 7.

to that of acting under legislative authority without that authority having to go through a legislative process[12] having seen the Parkes government of the 1880s ignore his decisions on Chinese immigration and detain people on executive fiat.[13] At the very least the decision in *Evans v. Finn* indicated that at least in some circumstances the exercise of prerogative powers relating to defence would not exempt the Crown from the application of ordinary rules of tort law.[14]

From Rifle Range to Active Service: *Shaw Savill and Albion Co. Ltd v. Commonwealth*

It was one thing to muse about the limits of the Crown prerogative relating to defence and to proclaim the equality of state and citizen before the law of tort in peacetime. Almost forty years later, the High Court of Australia had to answer these questions during a war. While some of the issues had been raised in earlier English cases, the analysis in *Shaw Savill* was the first comprehensive attempt to explain the limits, both substantive and procedural, in this particular context.

The case arose out of a collision at sea, in September 1940, between the *MV Coptic*, owned by the plaintiff company (although at the time of the collision in the service of the British Minister of Shipping under a charterparty)[15] and *HMAS Adelaide*, off the coast of New South Wales. The *Coptic* was steaming southbound between Brisbane and Sydney while the *Adelaide* was on its way to Brisbane to refuel. From the beginning of the war, the movement of shipping was rigidly controlled, among other reasons, to minimise the risk of collision when ships were sailing without illumination at night, a statutory requirement imposed in both England and Australia. At the time of the accident, all that was known was that the *Coptic* had been sailing on a course that had been given to her by the naval authorities in Brisbane. Just before 1.00 a.m. on 3 September the *Coptic* and the *Adelaide* collided and the plaintiff alleged the collision had been caused, broadly, either by negligence in the naval authority's procedures for organising the passage of merchant shipping

---

[12] Cf. *Hawley v. Steele* (1877) 6 Ch D 521 where on similar facts the rifle range was conducted under statutory authority and Jessel MR dismissed the claim.

[13] See J.M. Bennett, *Colonial Law Lords* (Federation Press, 2006) 27–40. The cases Darley CJ cited suggest he saw the case as raising high questions of constitutional law: (1904) 4 SR (NSW) 297, 305–306.

[14] A less kind contemporary commentator exclaimed: 'To such a shadow is the once flourishing doctrine of prerogative reduced!': (1905) 6 *J Soc Comp Legis* 180.

[15] Who retained an interest in the case because the terms of the charterparty required (in effect) that they pay for any time the ship was out of commission due to war risks but not otherwise. After Dixon J's 1947 judgment, the British government sought an assurance, which was ultimately given, that the *Coptic*'s claim for loss of hire payments would not be contested: NAA, MP691/1, 4804/74/4 – *Shaw Savill and Albion Ltd v. versus Commonwealth Australia* – High Court action for damages arising from collision between MV 'Coptic' and HMAS 'Adelaide', letter Deputy Director of Finance (UK) to High Commissioner of Australia, 9 March 1948; letter Secretary Department of Navy to Deputy Crown Solicitor, 10 February 1950.

and the associated transmission of information, or in the actual handling of the ship itself, either in the speed it was travelling or in the failure to maintain a proper lookout for other ships. Unlike in England, where the strictures of Crown immunity required the servant of the Crown to be sued individually (albeit the Crown usually stood behind the litigant and was responsible for any damages awarded), the provisions of the Constitution and the Judiciary Act 1903 (Cth) allowed the Commonwealth to be sued directly and be responsible for torts of servants of the Crown.[16]

Given the subsequent history of the litigation, it is somewhat ironic that the initial proceedings were commenced with some urgency, a necessity borne of the fact that the ship would not be long in Australian waters. After the collision, the *Coptic* was able to return to Newcastle for repairs, but almost immediately after the accident Shaw Savill and Albion indicated they would bring a claim[17] and the writ of summons against the Commonwealth, in the Admiralty jurisdiction of the High Court, was issued on 2 October 1940, less than a month after the collision. The parties agreed that the plaintiff's witnesses who were members of the *Coptic*'s crew could give evidence before a judge before they left the jurisdiction[18] but when these proceedings commenced two days later Ham KC for the Commonwealth made an application that the matter was not justiciable.[19] He had raised this at a meeting between counsel and naval representatives the previous day, basing the argument on the fact it was a time of war, that the ships were steaming without lights, and that the *Adelaide* was steaming on a selected route for naval operational reasons.[20] Ham KC thought this strategy, which had the approval of both the Solicitor General and the Attorney General,[21] would require the support of an affidavit of a Senior Naval Officer.[22] On the formal instruction of the Crown Solicitor, H.F.E. Whitlam, the First Naval Member of the Naval Board, Sir Ragnar Musgrave Colvin made a curious affidavit, stating not only 'facts' but also the conclusion that the claim was not justiciable. Two substantive grounds were raised in support of this conclusion. The first was that at the time of the collision the *Adelaide*

---

[16] (1940) 66 CLR 344, 352-352 (Starke J), 357–358 (Dixon J).

[17] NAA, MP1049/5, 2026/3/495, HMAS 'Adelaide' and MV 'Coptic' collision at sea and resultant court case Shaw Savill & Albion Limited against the Commonwealth of Australia, letter Australian manager Shaw Savill & Albion to Commodore in Charge, HMA Naval Establishments, 7 September 1940 (Figure 8.1).

[18] Ibid., letter Deputy Crown Solicitor to Secretary Department of Navy, 4 December 1940. The *Coptic* made it to Newcastle by the morning of 3 September, had emergency repairs, and then travelled to Sydney on 5 September where major repairs were undertaken. She left on 15 October 1940 (MP691/1, above n 15, Affidavit of W.P. Clifton-Hogg, 29 September 1949) hence the urgency in taking the evidence from her crew.

[19] Ibid.

[20] Ibid., handwritten note of meeting, 9 October 1940 (Figure 8.2).

[21] Ibid., letter Deputy Crown Solicitor to Secretary Department of Navy, 4 December 1940.

[22] This was to avoid any argument that the person making the declaration had no authority to do so on behalf of the Commonwealth: *Joseph v. Colonial Treasurer (NSW)* (1918) 25 CLR 32, cited by Ham KC before Dixon J and the Full Court.

was engaged in active naval operations against the enemy in the present state of war which operations were being carried out by the Government of the Commonwealth for the benefit of the nation as a whole and under the prerogative right of His Majesty and which operations were urgently required and necessary for the safety of the realm.[23]

While this was a broad public policy defence, the second ground was more operational: the voyage, the extinguishment of lights and the speed of the ship were necessary for the proper carrying out of the naval operations, but, to avoid any doubt, these were also said to be necessary for 'the public safety and the defence of the realm, and the national emergency called for the taking of the measures adopted' by the *Adelaide*.[24] Dixon J heard the evidence of the *Coptic*'s witnesses but at the end of the hearing the next day, on 10 October, he discussed with counsel the best way of proceed in what was already becoming a complicated case.[25] In light of these discussions, a conditional appearance was entered by the Commonwealth on 10 October 1940 and a formal motion to set aside the service of the writ or, in the alternative, to stay the proceedings, was made but a week later Dixon J issued a consent order that conditional pleading, including demurrers and counterclaims, could be lodged.[26] Clearly recognising the importance of the case, it was agreed by consent that the various preliminary matters (including demurrers which both sides had lodged as part of their pleadings) would be determined by the Full Court, which heard it on 30 and 31 October 1940.[27]

When the case reached the Full Court, although there were three questions to be answered the primary issue was the plaintiff's demurrer to part of the defendant's defence. Two of the paragraphs to which it took exception were the same as the ones in Colvin's affidavit mentioned above; the third simply restated the gist of these paragraphs by saying that the supposed cause of action 'consists solely in acts, matters and things done or occurring in the course of active naval operations against the King's enemies by the armed forces of the Commonwealth'.[28] It is important to remember that the High Court was not deciding the question of liability: these were preliminary points of law. Such proceedings could only end the matter in the defendant's favour (by upholding the defendant's motion to stay the proceedings or the demurrer to the plaintiff's statement of claim). Even if the plaintiff was successful in its demurrer a trial

---

[23] NAA, A10593, 1940/26 Part 1, *Shaw, Savill & Albion Co. Ltd v. The Commonwealth of Australia*, Affidavit of Ragnar Musgrave Colvin KBE, CB, 10 October 1940, para. 5.

[24] Ibid., para. 6.

[25] MP1049/5, above n 17.

[26] NAA, A472, W2022, *Shaw Savill & Albion Co. Ltd v. The Commonwealth* – Collision between *MV Coptic* and *HMAS Adelaide*, letter Deputy Crown Solicitor to Crown Solicitor, 23 October 1940.

[27] MP1049/5, above n 17 (all the procedural information is in A10593, above n 23).

[28] A10593, above n 23, Defence and Counter Claim, 25 October 1940, para. 23.

would be needed so that the plaintiff could formally establish the elements of its cause of action.

At the hearing before the Full Court the question was whether the paragraphs in the defence relating to the cause of action arising out of 'active naval operations' amounted to a defence in law. Arguing for the plaintiff, Windeyer KC submitted boldly that the duty to take care was 'not altered by the fact a state of war exists'.[29] But this was not a submission that war did not matter at all; rather, his criticism was that the grand statements in the defence were too broad to respond to the detail of the plaintiff's claim (i.e. a collision at a particular time and place). The response from Ham KC was equally bold. 'Once the position is established that there is an urgent necessity for the operations which resulted in injury to a citizen', he said, 'then it follows that because of the urgent national emergency the King has the prerogative right to wage war and to destroy property of a citizen; no duty to the citizen arises at all'.[30] The same rule applied to damage caused negligently as well as intentionally.

Three judgments were given in the Full Court in *Shaw Savill* but as Rich and McTiernan JJ agreed with Dixon J, his judgment represents the ratio of the court. In his judgment, Dixon J accepted neither view submitted by counsel. While a naval officer navigating a King's ship clearly owed a duty to merchant ships outside a theatre of war, the position was different in a war situation:

> It could hardly be maintained that during an actual engagement with the enemy or a pursuit of any of his ships the navigating officer of a King's ship of war was under a common-law duty of care to avoid harm to such non-combatant ships as might appear in the theatre of operations. It cannot be enough to say that the conflict or pursuit is a circumstance affecting the reasonableness of the officer's conduct as a discharge of the duty of care, though the duty itself persists. To adopt such a view would mean that whether the combat be by sea, land or air our men go into action accompanied by the law of civil negligence, warning them to be mindful of the person and property of civilians. It would mean that the Courts could be called upon to say whether the soldier on the field of battle or the sailor fighting on his ship might reasonably have been more careful to avoid causing civil loss or damage. No-one can imagine a court undertaking the trial of such an issue, either during or after a war. To concede that any civil liability can rest upon a member of the armed forces for supposedly negligent acts or omissions in the course of an actual engagement with the enemy is opposed alike to reason and to policy.[31]

Moreover, Dixon J saw a wide geographic scope for this immunity. In modern warfare (e.g. the bomber, the submarine and the floating mine) to limit it to the presence of the enemy or to occasions when there was contact with the enemy would be 'quite absurd'.[32] The principle 'must extend to all active operations

[29] (1940) 66 CLR 344, 349.
[30] Ibid., 350.
[31] Ibid., 361.
[32] Ibid.

against the enemy. It must cover attack and resistance, advance and retreat, pursuit and avoidance, reconnaissance and engagement.'[33] Although the immunity was broad, however, not all activities of a warship in wartime were covered. In his view, a warship proceeding to 'anchorage or manœuvring among other ships in a harbour, or acting as a patrol or even as a convoy' must navigate with the care reasonable under the circumstances with due regard to the safety of other shipping.[34] Dixon J recognised that it would not always be easy to decide on which side of the line a case fell but:

> ... if it is made to appear to the court that the matters complained of formed part of, or an incident in, active naval or military operations against the enemy, then in my opinion the action must fail on the ground that, while in the course of actually operating against the enemy, the forces of the Crown are under no duty of care to avoid causing loss or damage to private individuals.[35]

For a tort lawyer, at the heart of Dixon J's distinction is the difference between a finding of no duty and no breach of duty. In active combat situations, it was not sufficient protection to say that this circumstance would be taken into account in determining if the combatant had been careless. The scope of the obligation to take care not to negligently harm another's interest had to be balanced against the costs such a duty would impose on the efficacy of the operation itself. But this did not mean that penumbral war activities were subject to peacetime standards: the war environment might be an important circumstance in a particular case in deciding whether there was any breach of duty.

A similar result was reached by Starke J but for quite different reasons. In typically robust fashion, he rejected any defence based on *Adelaide*'s conduct being done under the prerogative of the Crown, for the benefit of the nation as a whole, or as necessary for the safety of the realm in a national emergency. In his view, this was little more than justification by way of executive fiat, the argument that was rejected almost two hundred years earlier in *Entick v. Carrington*.[36] But as far as the plea alleged that the matters complained of consisted solely in acts matters or things done or occurring in the course of naval operations against the King's enemies by the armed forces of the Commonwealth, it was a good plea. In Starke J's judgment, there was 'no doubt that the Executive Government and its officers must conduct operations of war, whether naval, military, or in the air, without the control or interference of the courts of law. Acts done in the course of such operations are not justiciable and the courts of law cannot take cognizance of them'.[37]

Whereas Dixon J had rested his judgment on the lack of any duty of care (hence the claim failed for lack of an element of the cause of action), Starke

---

[33] Ibid., 361–362.
[34] Ibid., 362.
[35] Ibid.
[36] Ibid., 355.
[37] Ibid., 355–356.

J referred to justiciability (the refusal to hear the case at all). The reference to justiciability also makes it more difficult to understand what Starke J's references to 'durante bello' mean. It is tempting to see the reference as purely procedural: acts done in the course of active operations are not justiciable when the conflict is ongoing but become so when hostilities have ceased. But there is a difference between justiciability and liability. Starke J is simply making the point that, once the immunity has ceased to apply, courts may have 'jurisdiction to inquire and determine whether matters done or occurring during its continuance affecting the rights or properties of the King's subjects were justifiable'.[38] In the cases Starke J cites in support of this proposition, the question was the legality of deliberate conduct, a quite different proposition from potential liability in negligence in a combat situation.[39] In other words, it would have been perfectly consistent with his judgment to find that negligently caused harm inflicted during the course of active operations was justifiable (i.e. did not give rise to a cause of action). But once he held that, on the facts pleaded, the matters took place in the course of naval operations, that was the end of all he had to decide, hence his comment that it was a good plea '*durante bello* at least'[40] to the complaint of the plaintiff. He did not need to decide whether the same plea might have prevented a liability if it was justiciable.

The final member of the court, Williams J, delivered potentially the most pro-plaintiff of the three judgments. Like Dixon and Starke JJ, he was prepared to accept that if 'actual hostilities' were in progress at the time of the collision the claim would not be justiciable.[41] The Commonwealth had pleaded that the action 'consists solely in acts matters and things done or occurring in the course of active naval operations against the King's enemies by the armed forces of the Commonwealth'. In his view, 'solely' meant that the particular conduct alleged to be negligent needed to be something that fell within the meaning of active naval operations. This would not be the case, for example, for a failure to keep a proper lookout.[42] But there is an ambiguity at the heart of his judgment: was it possible to dissect the causes of the accident even when there were actual hostilities, or was Williams J drawing a distinction between cases of actual hostilities – where an action was simply not justiciable – and cases of active naval operations short of actual hostilities – where justiciability somehow depended on the connection between the alleged breach of duty and the active naval operations?

In fact, it is suggested that Williams J was drawing an unhelpful analogy with a long series of cases from England, cited by Ham KC for the Commonwealth

---

[38] Ibid., 357.
[39] Ibid. Apart from academic authority, he cited *R v. Allen* (1921) 2 IR 241; *R (Ronayne and Mulcahy) v. Strickland* (1921) 2 IR 333; *Higgins v. Willis* (1921) 2 IR 386), all cases arising out of the struggle for Irish independence.
[40] Ibid.
[41] Ibid., 366.
[42] Ibid., 367.

and referred to in his judgment, arising out of naval accidents during the First World War. The issue in these cases was whether the circumstances of the accident brought it within the scope of 'war risks' (or similarly worded expressions) for the purposes of determining whether the incident was a risk covered by a policy of insurance (or, where the ship had been requisitioned by the Admiralty, whether it was a risk the Admiralty agreed to cover).[43] In these cases, as Lord Sumner noted in *Britain Steamship Company Limited v. The King*, there were two questions to answer: first, was the collision or stranding caused by any act or consequence of hostilities or by any warlike operations or consequence thereof, and, if so what?; and second, was it proximately so caused?[44] Whether the ship was engaged in warlike operations was not the only enquiry, and in a number of cases this issue was conceded and the issue for decision was whether the warlike operation was a proximate cause.[45] The reason the enquiry took this form was to do with rules peculiar to insurance law but it should be noted that the purpose of the enquiry was completely different from a case like *Shaw Savill*: it determined insurance coverage, not third party liability. There are parts of Williams J's judgment where it seems the criteria for the insurance question found their way into the liability question. At the end of his judgment, Williams J stated: 'If the plaintiff could prove that the *Adelaide* was not keeping a proper look-out it would be open to the Court to find it was this breach of duty on the part of the *Adelaide*, and not the acts she was performing in the course of active naval operations which was responsible for the collision.'[46] This was precisely the kind of reasoning that is present in the insurance cases: although the ship was involved in hostilities or warlike activities this was not the proximate cause of the loss. But it was extremely difficult to import this reasoning into questions of liability: if the ship fell within the immunity, the manner in which the loss was caused was irrelevant. As Dixon J noted, the obligation to exercise care for others disappeared completely, not partially, in combat situations.[47] The result is that while Williams J did recognise that there was a place for a combat immunity from suit, his views on the scope of that immunity are much less convincing than those of Starke J and Dixon J.

There are at least two common threads between the judgments. The first is that there are some activities in time of war carried out by the armed forces that cannot give rise to a claim for negligence by anyone injured by their negligent performance. For the majority, this was because no duty of care was owed in these circumstances; for Starke J and Williams J this was because these claims were not justiciable. The extent of the differences between the judgments depends on the consequences of a non-justiciable finding: for Williams J it seems the finding was permanent hence functionally the same result would be

---

[43] Ibid., 365–366.
[44] [1921] 1 AC 99, 127.
[45] *Attorney General v. Adelaide Steamship Company Limited* [1923] AC 292.
[46] (1940) 66 CLR 344, 367.
[47] Ibid., 361.

reached as for denying a duty of care while for Starke J justiciability and liability were potentially two different things and he said nothing about the latter.

There was much greater agreement in the second common thread. The Commonwealth had argued that its motion to have the action dismissed or stayed should have been granted because the affidavit of Sir Ragnar Colvin provided the necessary evidence to establish the immunity defence and that this evidence could not be challenged. This was unanimously rejected. While happy to accept as decisive evidence as to the need for speed and the extinguishment of lights, Dixon J thought whether the *Adelaide* was on active operations against the enemy was a question 'a court may decide for itself, and perhaps, from one point of view, it may be said ought to decide.'[48] For Starke J too 'it is the right and duty of the courts of law to determine whether the matters complained of were done or omitted in the conduct of an operation or act of war. It is not enough to say that the matters complained of were done in time of war or were operations of a warlike character connected with the carrying on of war.'[49] Williams J said simply that the evidence was not sufficient to set aside the writ. But there is also some ambiguity here as well. As Dixon J recognised, the question was whether Colvin's statement should be treated as conclusive of the point in question. For him, it was clear that Colvin's affidavit was insufficient because the Executive could not dictate the result to the court: 'I think it is a matter of fact and not of opinion and is not one which the Executive is authorized to decide.'[50] It is less clear whether this was the same view taken by other members of the court or whether they thought the problem was that the content of the evidence was insufficient to allow the court to answer the correct question; in other words, the problem was with what Colvin said, not that it was him saying it. One should not downplay the significance of this finding – on either interpretation the judgments are an important affirmation of the separation of powers – but the former view is more bullish than the latter.

The final point to note is the extent to which the decision in *Shaw Savill* represented innovation in the common law. As the members of the court noted, there were other precedents where those in charge of a naval ship had been found liable in Admiralty jurisdictions for carelessly causing harm to other ships. All three judgments referred to the case of the *HMS Hydra*,[51] two to *HMS Drake*,[52] and Starke J to the *Warilda*. These were all cases where the question of the fault of a naval ship involved in a collision with a merchant vessel was in question. Apart from the factual similarity, it is impossible to see the genesis of the *Shaw Savill* judgments in any of these cases. As Dixon J noted, the hearing in *HMS Hydra* was held in-camera so it is impossible to know exactly what arguments were raised before Hill J but the short judgment makes no reference to any question

---

48 Ibid., 364.
49 Ibid., 356.
50 Ibid., 364.
51 [1918] P 78.
52 [1919] P 362.

of possible immunity due to the war situation (it was a collision between a war-ship and a merchant ship in the English Channel). The judgments in *HMS Drake* were longer but the English Court of Appeal spent most of its time in technical discussion of the meaning of the 'not under command' signal of *HMS Drake*. The fact that *HMS Drake* was in this position as a result of being torpedoed went only, at best, to determining the reasonableness of her conduct in signalling as she did. As for the *Warilda*, she was found negligent in colliding with a merchant ship in the English Channel. Only the House of Lords judgment in the negli-gence suit is reported[53] but the contrast with the insurance judgment in the same court is striking. The negligence suit takes up only one paragraph, and is largely influenced, as in the other cases mentioned above, by the views of the expert assessors (including the mysteriously named Elder Brethren)[54] on whether there was negligence in the actions of the parties once the ships had sighted each other. Conversely, the insurance case takes up seventeen pages of the authorised reports. It is possible that any combat immunity point in the English cases was hidden in the procedural mechanisms by which these cases were brought to avoid Crown immunity but, even if this is so, the fact remains that there was no judicial discussion of a combat immunity from suit in English cases. While there were numerous cases on the meaning of hostile, warlike, or active operations, they dealt with a different question, and the weakest of the judgments in *Shaw Savill*, Williams J, fell into error by trying to use them as authority for an entirely different question. Nor does there seem to be any discussion in contemporary tort texts: none are cited in the judgments, nor do the judgments cite, in this context, support from texts from other areas.

The truth was, as Dixon J noted, that there was no authority dealing with civil liability for negligence on the part of the King's forces when in action.[55] Dixon J himself was forced to analogise with broad notions of defence of the realm and necessity[56] while Starke J and Williams J used the very different circumstances of the *Marais*[57] decision, concerning the detention of a person under martial law in Cape Colony during the Second Boer War, to support their view of the existence of the immunity.[58] Whether these are good analogies or not is not relevant here; the point is that the recognition of a sphere where general fault-based liability rules did not apply involved considerable amounts of judicial ability and creativity.

---

[53] (1920) 2 Ll L Rep 187.

[54] One class of expert assessors allowed in the Admiralty jurisdiction were senior members (the Elder Brethren) of Trinity House, a historic entity responsible for lighthouses and other navigational aids in parts of the United Kingdom.

[55] (1940) 66 CLR 344, 362.

[56] Ibid.

[57] *Ex Parte Marais* [1902] AC 115. Ham KC had relied on similar cases on the legality of intentional exercises of the prerogative (*The Zamora* [1916] 2 AC 77; *Crown of Leon (Owners) v. Admiralty Commissioners* [1921] 1 KB 595; *Attorney General v. De Keyser's Royal Hotel* [1920] AC 508) in arguing that negligent exercises were not justiciable.

[58] (1940) 66 CLR 344, 356 (Starke J), 366 (Williams J).

And Now for Something Completely Different!

Enough has been said of the *Shaw Savill* decision to demonstrate its novelty. It has also proved influential, albeit after seventy years, in England where it was discussed in detail in the Supreme Court decision in *Smith v. Ministry of Defence*.[59] In this sense the discussion of the 1940 decision in this chapter reaffirms rather than rediscovers its importance. Yet the significance of the *Shaw Savill* litigation goes well beyond what the High Court decided in 1940. There is a relatively unknown history that comes after that decision and shows how difficult in practice the boundaries drawn in 1940 were to enforce. But this history also shows a remarkable commitment, particularly by Dixon J, to the notion that it was largely for the judiciary to decide the matters in controversy in *Shaw Savill*.

The result of the 1940 hearing was that both demurrers, and the Commonwealth's motion, were rejected. This allowed the plaintiff to continue the claim albeit with the possibility that the defendant might establish that the collision took place in circumstances where the claim was not justiciable (or where the Commonwealth through its servants owed no duty of care). In April 1941, the solicitor for the plaintiff, 'desirous not to interrupt more officers in the performance of their duties at the present time than is necessary', wrote to the Commonwealth Crown Solicitor requesting details of the officers who could give 'the necessary information as to the system prevailing for securing safe lanes for traffic along the coast for that period, and any system of consequential advice to merchant ships or warships.'[60] But events now took a decidedly worse turn for the plaintiff. Ragnar Colvin's initial affidavit had contained another string to its bow: that the proceedings in the action would involve enquiries into matters which in the interests of public safety and the safety of the Commonwealth in the presently existing state of war in which the Commonwealth is engaged it is necessary should be kept secret.[61] In Colvin's affidavit, this concern led to a request, in effect, that the proceedings be held in-camera.[62] The argument was clearly raised in the High Court as Starke J and Dixon J both refer to it. For Starke J, if there was an issue of secrecy the Commonwealth could bring a motion to stay proceedings until the secrecy issue had passed or to seek a hearing in-camera.[63] Dixon J took the same view, adding that if it was thought neither of these was possible (insufficient security for in-camera hearing, evidence might be lost if hearing postponed) 'then the matter might in the end rest upon burden of proof and presumptive inferences.'[64] But when the plaintiff's solicitor decided the best way to get evidence as to the organisation of

---

[59] [2014] AC 52.
[60] A10593, above n 23, Letter G.A. Yuill to Commonwealth Crown Solicitor, 29 April 1941.
[61] Ibid., Affidavit of Ragnar Musgrave Colvin KBE, CB, 10 October 1940, para. 4.
[62] Ibid.
[63] (1940) 66 CLR 344, 357.
[64] Ibid., 364.

shipping movements was to subpoena the naval officers involved,[65] concerns over secrecy took a more concrete form. On 30 April, in a letter to the plaintiff's solicitor it was stated that a memorandum from the Minister of the Navy, W.M. Hughes, of the same date to various naval officers, including the captain of the *Adelaide*, Captain Showers, had been received, stating:

> I hereby authorise you to object to answering any questions relating to any information as to the system prevailing for securing safe lines for traffic along the coast, and as to any system of consequential advice to merchant ships or warships, and I further authorise you to instruct all officers of the Royal Australian Navy and others to object to answering said questions… In my opinion, the answering of such questions would involve matters which in the interests of public safety of the Commonwealth in the presently existing state of war in which the Commonwealth is engaged it is necessary should be kept secret, and the disclosure of the information as to such matters would be prejudicial to the safety of the Commonwealth and the efficient prosecution of the war.[66]

This was not all: when on the morning of the first day of the trial before Dixon J, Windeyer KC tried to question the first subpoenaed witness on a related topic, but one not technically covered by the certificate, this too was objected to on the basis that if it was known that this line of questioning was proposed it would have been the subject of a claim of privilege.[67] Two wider certificates were hurriedly prepared and signed by the Minister and were presented in court the next day and given effect to by Dixon J. The exhortation to naval staff that any decision on whether the certificates were required 'should not be influenced by the probable or possible effect on the action but that the matter should be considered from the point of national security and public safety'[68] must be treated with a grain of salt given what was then known about the case but the certificates were forensically a masterstroke on behalf of the Commonwealth's lawyers. If national security concerns would not found a general immunity from suit, they could starve the plaintiff of the necessary evidence to prove at least one of the allegations of negligence. In modern parlance, the Commonwealth claimed a form of public interest or state immunity for the evidence relating to the organisation and management of east coast shipping during the war. If Shaw Savill was going to win on this argument, it would, as Dixon J foreshadowed, have to rely on presumptive inferences (as the plaintiff the burden of proof would not assist it) although the Commonwealth did allow naval personnel on the *Adelaide* to testify with respect to the collision itself.

---

65 MP1049/5, above n 17, letter Norton Smith to Crown Solicitor, 29 April 1941.
66 A10593, above n 23, Affidavit of Gerard Charles Muirhead-Gould, DSC, RN, of HMA Naval Establishments at Sydney, advising of receipt of memorandum from the Minister of the Navy (W.M. Hughes).
67 Ibid., letter Deputy Crown Solicitor to Secretary, Department of Navy, 2 May 1941.
68 Ibid.

The result was that the in-camera trial dealt with only two substantive arguments: whether there was any duty of care in light of proved facts about the *Adelaide*'s mission, and whether there was any negligence associated with the collision itself. On 25 August 1941, Dixon J gave a most unusual judgment in favour of the Commonwealth. In his summary of the facts it was now revealed, probably from evidence given by Ragnar Colvin,[69] that the *Adelaide* was on a special mission at the time of the collision. The Australian War Cabinet had decided that the *Adelaide* should be sent immediately to Noumea for the purposes of installing a Free French government and to provide support for this regime against a display of force from naval forces sent to the island by or on behalf of the Vichy Government.[70] Orders were only given to Captain Showers en route. The only reason the *Adelaide* did not proceed directly to Noumea was because 'the endurance of the ship was not sufficient to make it wise to send her direct from Sydney to Noumea' without calling at Brisbane to refuel.[71] Dixon J then referred to the facts previously noted in the preliminary hearing: that the *Coptic* was sailing in accordance with routing instructions issued by the naval authorities in Brisbane and that, because both ships were sailing unilluminated, they only sighted each other with very little time to act to avoid a collision. Both ships were able to continue after the collision but Dixon J described the damage to the *Coptic* as 'considerable' while 'much less' damage was suffered by the *Adelaide*.

Dixon J then turned to the first legal issue: had the Commonwealth proved the necessary facts that the Full Court had required for any immunity to be brought into play? His answer was unequivocal: 'the Commonwealth has completely failed to do so.'[72] While recognising that the trip to Noumea involved an actual or possible naval operation, both active and warlike, and that it was possible a German raider or submarine might appear on the trip between Brisbane and Sydney, it was

> out of the question to maintain that upon the voyage to refuel at Brisbane the Commander, officers and crew of the 'Adelaide' were so engaged in operations against the enemy that they were relieved from the ordinary obligation of care for the safety of civilian life and property in the navigation of the ship. Still less is it possible to maintain that the facts place the cause of action outside the category of justiciable claims.[73]

Equally robust was his defence of the judicial role in determining this issue. The Commonwealth again argued the cases in support of its submission that

---

[69] No record of his evidence exists but the evidence he planned to give is set out in a letter to the Deputy Crown Solicitor in December 1940 and covers the matters Dixon J refers to in his judgment: MP1049/5, above n 17.

[70] For further detail on the Adelaide's role see V. Cassels, *The Capital Ships: Their Battles and Badges* (Kangaroo Press, 2000).

[71] A10593, above n 23, Judgment of Dixon J, 25 August 1941, 2.

[72] Ibid., 4.

[73] Ibid.

Colvin's evidence was sufficient to preclude the claim and, as in the Full Court decision, Dixon J was unconvinced that they applied here: 'I can see no ground for the contention that on the question of what the ship was doing, the question whether active hostilities were in progress, the Court cannot itself enquire into the true facts.'[74]

With no immunity in place, the next question was whether the collision had been caused by any negligence. Dixon J divided the allegations into two groups. The first was that the naval authorities, having assigned the *Coptic* a route, should have taken steps to ensure that the *Adelaide* was not on the same route. That this occurred suggested Captain Showers was not informed or, if informed, that he followed a route which might be expected to meet her (the *Coptic*), in the dark without lights. The second group of allegations related to the conduct of the officer of the watch when the *Coptic* was first sighted, Lieutenant Morley, in taking the wrong or insufficient evasive action to avoid a collision.

It was in dealing with the first group of allegations that the effect of the Minister's certificates became clear. The plaintiff's case required it to make out certain facts about the routing of shipping but '[u]fortunately for the plaintiffs they found themselves with an objection on the part of the Minister of the Navy to the disclosure of the information…' As Dixon J put it later, the Minister claimed State privilege and 'This claim I felt bound to respect.'[75] The limits of judicial scrutiny of executive conduct had been reached. As Captain Showers was not called as a witness – no doubt because he would have been subject to the constraints of the certificates – there was insufficient evidence on which negligence could be proved. Within the confines of propriety, however, it is clear, that Dixon J was unimpressed by the claim of state privilege:

> It is unfortunate for the plaintiffs that the facts cannot be proved and it is perhaps permissible to doubt whether the Minister's certificate or claim was not unnecessarily sweeping, particularly having regard to the fact that the hearing took place in camera.[76]

Dixon J gives no authority for his view that the claim for state immunity could not be challenged but the question had recently (in March 1941) been considered by the English Court of Appeal in similar circumstances. In *Duncan v. Cammell Laird & Co. Ltd*, a claim by the wife of one of those killed when the submarine Thetis sank during testing in June 1939, the Court of Appeal upheld a claim for state privilege by the First Lord of the Admiralty.[77] It was accepted

---

[74] Ibid., 5.

[75] Ibid., 9.

[76] Ibid., 11.

[77] The claim was made in respect of documents held by Cammell Laird but as two of the co-defendants were serving naval personnel for whom the Admiralty would accept responsibility the Admiralty was a party for all practical purposes (cf. M. Spencer, 'Bureaucracy, national security and access to justice: new light on *Duncan v. Cammell Laird*' (2004) 5 *NILQ* 277, 282, who points out not standing behind the personnel was contemplated).

that while there might be a limited possibility for a judge to view the documents themselves and decide the question, this power should be exercised very sparingly.[78] In fact, the claim for state privilege in *Duncan* was much more opaque, the certificate of the First Lord of the Admiralty stating that disclosure of the documents would be injurious to the public interest. Dixon J's views are more in sympathy with plaintiff counsel's argument in *Duncan* – that there would be a denial of justice if the certificate was accepted uncritically[79] – albeit he did not feel able to go beyond criticism of the certificate's scope.

But Dixon J was able to make a number of important substantive findings. Building on brief comments he made in the Full Court decision,[80] he held that no duty was owed by naval staff exercising powers for the safeguarding of merchant shipping against attack by the enemy or damage from mines. However prudent administratively it might be to warn or advise officers in command of naval ships of the routing and practices relating to merchant shipping, these powers involved duties of a public nature only and a failure to advise would not be an actionable wrong for which they or the Commonwealth would be liable.[81] There are shades here of the reasoning in some of the early highway immunity nonfeasance cases, reasoning which Dixon J had explained in his recent judgment in *Buckle*.[82] This conclusion framed the legal issues on this aspect of the case: if the negligence was in Captain Shower's response to any information received rather than the system by which shipping was routed and information provided, the Commonwealth could be liable for his negligence. That this remained an important issue was due to Dixon J finding that there was no negligence in either the *Adelaide* or the *Coptic* once the ships had been sighted, a conclusion made possible because Lieutenant Morley was allowed to give evidence.[83] Given the impasse reached on the other allegation of negligence due to the claim of state immunity, this meant the plaintiff lost the action. In terse language Dixon J expressed his unhappiness with this result:

> But I think it unfortunate for the plaintiffs that it was necessary during the war to bring the suit, and still more unfortunate for them that it appeared proper to the Minister, notwithstanding that the suit was heard in camera, to give a certificate

---

[78] [1941] 1 KB 640. Although Mackinnon LJ had distinguished an earlier Privy Council case where the documents had been reviewed (*Robinson v. State of South Australia* [1931] AC 704) on the ground that the State was the defendant (as in *Shaw Savill*), the case involved the 'ordinary and trading activities' of the defendant. Cf. Du Parcq LJ who thought where the State was the plaintiff, and then sought to claim state privilege to avoid handing over documents, this might be a situation where courts could scrutinise the documents.

[79] (1941) 69 Ll L Rep 84, 85.

[80] (1940) 66 CLR 344, 363.

[81] A10593, above n 23, Judgment of Dixon J, 25 August 1941, 12. Note that Dixon J had at this time an important role in domestic shipping as Chair of the Australian Coastal Shipping Control Board: see P. Ayres, *Owen Dixon* (Miegunyah Press, 2003) 128–129.

[82] (1936) 57 CLR 259, 281–282. See also his judgment in *Aiken v. Kingborough Corporation* (1939) 62 CLR 179.

[83] Apart from the references in Dixon J's judgment, there is no record of his evidence as no transcript is contained in the High Court file.

under which the Court was in effect bound to exclude from its consideration the facts material to the more important parts of the plaintiffs's [sic] case. The suit was unnecessarily burdened with the motion on the part of the Commonwealth to stay the suit or strike out the writ, a motion based on grounds which I do not think the true facts support.[84]

Dixon J's concern was given practical content in the order he made. He decreed that the suit should be dismissed without prejudice to the plaintiffs' cause of action, and without prejudice to any further proceedings which the plaintiffs may be advised to take against the Commonwealth in respect of the damage suffered in the collision. He noted that after the war, and perhaps even before the war was over, the reasons for the secrecy may have disappeared and there would be no reason why the facts surrounding the routing instructions, and the knowledge of the *Adelaide*'s command, could not be investigated.[85]

After more delay,[86] both parties appealed to the Full Court. No documentation of the appeal has survived in the High Court file except the unusual order. On 28 April 1942, the Court decreed that the suit should be stayed with liberty to either party to restore it to the list for further hearing 'upon the conclusion of hostilities or such earlier date as the evidence for which the respondent has claimed privilege can be given without prejudice to the safety of the realm'.[87] If either party wanted to call further evidence, the case was to proceed in the original jurisdiction of the court before any justice, the evidence given in the earlier hearing to be presumed and treated as evidence in the further hearing. If neither party wanted to call further evidence, the appeal before the Full Court would proceed on the evidence in the first trial. While the Full Court did not agree to the suggestion of the plaintiff's counsel that they have two bites at the cherry – by having the Full Court hear the appeal on the existing evidence and only grant an adjournment if he lost – Ham KC's objections as to the wide discretion granted to the plaintiff in the order were also ignored.[88] The Full Court required Windeyer KC to elect whether to appeal on the existing evidence or seek an adjournment. When he elected for an adjournment the gist of Dixon J's decree was upheld: as it was impossible to proceed to a (fair) final judgment in the absence of the privileged evidence the Full Court would allow the plaintiff to 'tread water'.

Irrepressibly, the plaintiff pushed on. As foreshadowed in the Full Court hearing, in July 1942, the plaintiff's solicitor wrote to the Commonwealth Crown

---

84 A10593, above n 23, Judgment of Dixon J, 25 August 1941, 17. See also 13, where Dixon J comments that the failure to prove the first part of the plaintiff's case 'arises from the claim for privilege which, under the exigencies of war, the Minister for the Navy thought it right to make'.
85 Ibid., 17–18. An unusual costs order was also crafted: 18–19.
86 Various extensions of time were applied for and granted to both parties, and in February 1942 Dixon J needed to amend a previous order to ensure confidentiality in the preparation of the Appeal Book.
87 A10593, above n 23, Order of Full Court, 28 April 1942.
88 MP1049/5, above n 17, letter Deputy Crown Solicitor to Crown Solicitor, 1 May 1942.

Solicitor with another unusual suggestion.[89] Given the indefinite nature of the stay, he pointed out that the evidence which would then be available in a court might be difficult if not impossible to obtain. The solution suggested was that a record or note of the evidence should be taken 'but that this should be kept in secret in the custody either of the Commonwealth Crown Solicitor or of the naval authorities until the case can be safely re-opened'. A series of questions (interrogatories in effect) were attached dealing with the part of the case covered by the privilege and it was suggested answers could be placed on affidavit and kept as previously suggested. While the letter said that the evidence might 'with advantage' be obtained in the manner suggested, the Commonwealth saw no such advantage. Apart from doubting the legal status of such answers,[90] the advice from its counsel was that the need to respond at all to the request depended on the Commonwealth's view as to the continuing need to claim privilege.[91] The handwritten notation on a Department of the Navy minute paper said it all: 'To modify the previous ruling is the thin edge of the wedge towards abandoning the ruling. This would cause endless trouble in any future case of a similar nature… Propose N.B [Naval Board] stands firm.'[92] In October 1942, the plaintiff was notified that full effect was to be given to the certificates of May 1941 as the same need for secrecy still existed. The plaintiff's solicitor made one final attempt to take matters forward. On 2 November 1942, he took out a summons, returnable before Starke J on 6 November, seeking permission to deliver interrogatories.

The Commonwealth crushed this attempt to outflank its defence. On 5 November, a Legal Officer at the Sydney Office of the Crown Solicitor sent a telegram to the Minister for the Navy in the Curtin Government, John Makin, asking him to continue Hughes's previous certificates for any interrogatories that might be issued. Makin responded affirmatively the following day.[93] At the hearing on 6 November, Starke J indicated that the telegram from Makin was not a sufficient claim for privilege but he stood the matter over to allow an adequate certificate to be prepared, advising Windeyer KC that he would allow him to be heard only if he considered the certificate inadequate.[94] The following day, Sir Guy Charles Cecil Royle, the current First Naval Member of the Naval Board, deposed that answering the interrogatories would be against the public interest and national defence[95] and this obviously satisfied Starke J as the application was not renewed.

---

[89] A10593, above n 23, Affidavit in Support of Summons, 2 November 1942.
[90] MP1049/5, above n 17, letter Deputy Crown Solicitor to Crown Solicitor, 27 July 1942.
[91] Ibid., Advice (Henchman), 24 August 1942; Opinion (Ham KC), 6 September 1942.
[92] Ibid., Department of Navy Minute paper, 3 October 1942 (Figure 8.3).
[93] A10593, above n 23, Affidavit of Ronald John Withnall, Legal Officer of Sydney Office of Crown Solicitor, 6 November 1942.
[94] A472, above n 26, letter Deputy Crown Solicitor to Crown Solicitor, 23 November 1942.
[95] A10593, above n 23, Affidavit of James Bernard Foley, Paymaster Captain of the Royal Australian Navy, 7 November 1942.

But a battle only had been lost and the war remained to be won. Two and a half years later, on 29 June 1945, the plaintiffs' solicitor wrote to the Crown Solicitor requesting that the privilege be waived. There was considerable reluctance in navy circles to waive the privilege, it being feared (among other concerns) that the information disclosed might be useful to the enemy in future wars.[96] One officer even hoped that it would be possible to claim an 'all time' privilege on the basis of national security.[97] In the end, it was the British Admiralty's advice that there seemed to be no objection to the formerly privileged evidence now being given that was decisive[98] and on 2 November 1945 the Commonwealth agreed that the privilege was to be waived and an order to that effect was made by McTiernan J.[99] The expedition that had marked the initial hearing in 1940 was markedly absent in the post-war phase and it took a series of summonses and orders setting down a trial date before the second hearing commenced in October 1947. The trial judge was again Dixon J[100] and during the course of proceedings he expressed exasperation over the confused nature of this new hearing. Dixon J's concerns related to what he should do with his findings in the original trial and whether the parties agreed to accept them or not. There was some discussion between bench and bar over whether there had been any agreement as to how to treat the earlier trial given the Full Court's order in 1942 but, despite Dixon J's concern that he was being kept in the dark and that this would lead to a 'muddled affair',[101] the case in fact proceeded only with new evidence relating to the first allegations of negligence (the routing and information allegations) in the vein of a trial that had been adjourned.

Shorn of the protection of privilege, and with the benefit of evidence from the only three witnesses called – Captain Showers, Thomas Hawkins, the Secretary of the Commonwealth Naval Board and Secretary for the Navy Department, and Francis Taunton, Yeoman Signals on the *Adelaide* – the true facts of the case were revealed in a light most unfavourable to the Commonwealth. It became clear that the naval arrangements for traffic between Brisbane and Sydney involved the separation of traffic by the creation of two corridors, a north and south corridor, about 24 miles apart. When the collision took place, the *Coptic* was in its lane (the westerly of the two); it was the *Adelaide* that had departed

---

[96] MP1049/5, above n 17, Department of Navy Minute Paper, 3 August 1945; Department of Navy Minute Paper (Director of Naval Intelligence) 4 September 1945; Department of Navy Minute Paper, 14 September 1945.

[97] Ibid., Department of Navy Minute Paper, 14 September 1945.

[98] Ibid., NLO Draft Signal; telegram NLO London to ACNB 496, 28 September 1945.

[99] A10593, above n 23, Affidavit in Support of Summons to Deliver Interrogatories, 1 February 1946, paras. 16–20.

[100] He expressed his concern at this appointment, saying 'I thought a new Judge really ought to have done this. I feel that it is very unsatisfactory for me to do it.': NAA, A10593, 1940/26 Part 2, *Shaw Savill & Albion Co. Ltd v. The Commonwealth of Australia*, Transcript of Proceedings, 108.

[101] Ibid., 110, 112. Dixon J's concern was whether the parties wanted him to re-hear the matter or not and what impact that might have on any subsequent appeal to the Full Court: see 107–112.

from its course.[102] As Dixon J put it in his judgment, the substance of the matter 'is that for a considerable length of time Adelaide kept to a route closely approximating to the route prescribed for south-bound merchant ships.'[103] On the evidence, this was not done in ignorance. The question, as Dixon J noted, was whether it was reasonable for the *Adelaide* to do so. One possible argument in its favour was that the Noumea mission was of great urgency but the evidence at the trial revealed that Captain Showers only knew the precise nature of the mission after the collision.[104] Another possibility for exculpation was the use of an identification system that allowed naval vessels to be aware of other ships in particular ocean areas. This generated a VAI number (vessels in area indicated). The system, however, was cumbersome and owing to these limitations and to the low priority VAI messages received compared to other service messages, Dixon J found the VAIs 'were in 1940 irregular and sometimes much delayed': it seems the VAI for *Coptic* was not received at all by radio reception on the *Adelaide* but was delivered by hand when the ship docked in Brisbane![105] In light of this history, Dixon J held that no-one on the *Adelaide* should have placed any reliance on the absence of a VAI as indicating there were no ships in the area and found that this was in fact the case. Nor was Dixon J impressed by the other justifications put forward. While there was an operational need to reach Brisbane by a certain time in the afternoon the suggestions that sailing further east would have exposed the *Adelaide* to adverse currents or would generally have taken longer were rejected; the time savings were minimal in light of the countervailing risks. And even if he did not expressly refer to it, Dixon J was conscious of his 1940 view that the war context could be relevant to both breach and duty:

> I wish to throw no doubt of any kind upon the proposition that the reasonableness of the course taken must be judged according to the exigencies of an active operation in time of war, and I think, moreover, that it is important in deciding the question at this date to guard against the tendency to lose the sense of urgency and of the paramountcy of any consideration affecting naval or military operations which, during the war, rightly governed our outlook upon such matters.[106]

Even judged by this standard, it is hard not to agree with the result reached by Dixon J. The *Adelaide* had deliberately strayed from the northbound lane on its trip to Brisbane, even adopting a converging (with the southbound lane) rather than diverging course when her true position west of the northbound lane was ascertained.[107] It had no guarantee that there would be no other ships in the

---

[102] Figure 8.4, MP1049/5, above n 17.
[103] A10593, above n 100, Judgment of Dixon J, 13 November 1947, 4–5.
[104] Ibid., 6.
[105] Ibid., 8–9.
[106] Ibid., 10–11.
[107] Ibid., 14–15.

southbound lane and if there were the lack of illumination made a collision a real possibility. Any possible benefits in such a course were 'an insufficient justification'[108] and 'certainly not such as to make it reasonable for a ship of war' to take the risk at the expense of other ships in the area.[109] While one can sympathise with Captain Showers – and it must be said his career did not suffer[110] – it seems the adrenalin of the 'secret' mission overcame the requirement of fairly obvious prudence in navigation.[111]

Remarkably, the Commonwealth threatened to take the litigation even further, lodging an appeal in December 1947 against Dixon J's finding of fact, including whether the *Adelaide* was engaged in active naval operations at the time of the collision.[112] Time allowed for a more considered review of the evidence[113] and in July 1948 the plaintiff had a final victory, successfully petitioning that the appeal be dismissed for want of prosecution.[114] Even in defeat the Commonwealth proved recalcitrant. Although the matter was referred to the Principal Registrar of the High Court to assess final damages, there was no formal reference to the Registrar but there were protracted negotiations before an interim payment of £20,000 was made in September 1950 and a final payment of £4,263.7.7d was made in October 1951.[115] But the parties could not agree on the date from which interest was payable on damages in Admiralty cases in the High Court, and the case came yet again before Dixon J in May 1953 where he ruled in favour of the plaintiff.[116] The final act was the order for taxation of costs, in July 1954, where the plaintiff recovered the sum of £2147.19.2d, a seemingly modest amount given the fourteen years it had taken to finish the litigation.[117]

Viewed from seventy years hindsight, how should we view the 'package' that was the *Shaw Savill* litigation? Apart from the merits of the 1940 decision, when one looks to the subsequent case history there are important differences from

---

[108] Ibid., 10–11.

[109] Ibid., 14.

[110] He retired as a Rear Admiral in 1955. His entry on the Navy Website states, with masterful if accurate understatement, that his time in Adelaide was 'slightly marred' by the collision: www .navy.gov.au/biography/rear-admiral-henry-arthur-showers.

[111] Showers handled the difficult Noumean operation with considerable skill, the Chief of the Naval Staff advising the War Cabinet that he had rendered excellent service in a situation requiring considerable discretion and sound judgement: NAA, A2676, 574 Attachment 1, War Cabinet Minute No. 574 – Report of Commanding Officer of HMAS 'Adelaide' on mission to New Caledonia, Extract of War Cabinet Minute, 23 October 1940.

[112] A10593, above n 100, Notice of Appeal, 3 December 1947, paras. 12–13.

[113] A472, above n 26, letter Assistant Crown Solicitor to Crown Solicitor, 29 January 1948; letters Deputy Crown Solicitor to Crown Solicitor, 7 April 1948, 5 May 1948.

[114] A10593, above n 100, Order under Rule 3 Section 5 of Appeal Rules.

[115] MP691/1, above n 15, a file concerned solely with the machinations surrounding the assessment of damages.

[116] (1953) 88 CLR 164.

[117] This was the final judicial order, albeit that the parties did not agree interest on the taxed costs until November 1954: MP691/1, above n 15, letter Deputy Crown Solicitor to Secretary Department of Navy, 16 November 1954.

the approach in England in *Duncan v. Cammell Laird*. The Court of Appeal decision in that case was noted above; this was upheld by the House of Lords in 1942, with the result that the public interest privilege rested solely on Executive assertion.[118] While the 1940 *Shaw Savill* decision also showed deference to Executive judgements,[119] the assertion that there were some things that the judiciary 'can and perhaps ought to decide' strikes a quite different tone. The later history of the litigation showed this was not just rhetoric. Dixon J found that there was no evidence for the Commonwealth's assertion about the nature of *Adelaide*'s activity when the collision happened, and while in the 1941 trial he accepted the state privilege for evidence claimed by the Commonwealth he both expressed his displeasure at its scope and, more importantly, crafted an order which placed a temporal limit on its operation.[120] The Full Court order of 1942 did the same thing. In contrast, there was no suggestion that the public interest certificate in *Duncan* v. *Cammell Laird* was limited: in fact, one of the reasons it was linked to 'public interest' rather than 'national security' was precisely because it would be available beyond the war.[121] This was so even though some of the documents had been available, and had been referred to, in a public enquiry into the disaster in the second half of 1939.[122] Paradoxically, that litigation also proceeded in spite of the issue of the certificate and with some of the very documents for which privilege had been claimed. As Spencer points out, however, this was only because of a change of heart in the Treasury Solicitor's department[123] as one of the *defendants* now wanted to use a document covered by the order[124] with the result that proceedings commenced before the war was over.[125] This should not hide the fact that while in both cases there were attempts by Government legal departments to wear down the plaintiffs, it was the executive (in *Duncan*) rather than the judiciary (as in *Shaw Savill*) that dictated the scope of the order so that disclosure was not a matter of Executive favour. Nor can any differences in approach be explained by some subliminal sympathy for the plaintiffs' claims: *Duncan* involved Lord Campbell's Act

---

[118] [1942] AC 624.

[119] For example, the decision not to illuminate ships at night.

[120] For criticism of the *Duncan* decision see the summary, together with C.A. Wright's comments' in the *Canadian Bar Review* (1943) 59 *LQR* 102–103; and note an earlier Australian comment on the Court of Appeal decision that in measured tones suggested a judicial right of inspection should be recognised: B.H. Rowan, 'The Crown and the production of documents: *Duncan v. Cammell Laird & Co. Ltd*' (1939–41) 2 *Res Judicatae* 239.

[121] Spencer, above n 77, 292.

[122] The 'Bucknill' enquiry; see further ibid.

[123] The Treasury Solicitor's Department provided advice for many other parts of government.

[124] Spencer, above n 77, 293–297. The defendant's need for the documents also scuppered the Admiralty's prior request for an in-camera trial.

[125] [1943] 2 All ER 621 (Wrottesley J) although not without delays: the Australian *Army News*, 21 June 1943, 3, reported that the plaintiffs 'appealed' to 'chief Justice' Lord Caldecote in July 1942 where he expressed the view that the case could not be heard during the war. Spencer (ibid) notes that there were constant delays in getting the case listed so this is perhaps another example of the hurdles the plaintiffs had to overcome.

claims in circumstances of great public sympathy for the victims[126] while *Shaw Savill* concerned damage to a commercial ship. Taking all this into account, the result is that, in this context at least, the *Shaw Savill* litigation demonstrated the High Court's commitment to rule of law values at a time of extreme pressure in a way that stands in marked contrast to the approach of the House of Lords.[127]

Moreover, the value of judicial scrutiny of executive claims to immunity is illustrated when one realises that there was never any doubt that the Commonwealth recognised that someone for whom they were responsible had been at fault for the collision. Later on the day of the accident, an enquiry held by Showers found that the cause of the accident was the negligent lookout of the officer of the watch.[128] This was one of the documents on which the Commonwealth claimed privilege when the case first went to trial in 1941. Nine days after the accident, Rear Admiral Crace suggested to the Naval Board that any Court-Martial arising out of Shower's report of 3 September should be postponed until the finding of the civil proceedings 'in order that the finding of the former may not prejudice the latter'.[129] The Deputy Crown Solicitor in his letter to the Crown Solicitor of 23 October 1940 noted that the facts so far as *Adelaide* was concerned 'indicated that the "Adelaide" proceeded north from Sydney to Brisbane at a speed of 20 knots on a course which had been allotted to merchant vessels proceeding south from Brisbane to Sydney…'.[130] After the hearing of the first trial, but before judgment, the first member of the Naval Board minuted that:

> I am of the opinion that Captain Showers cannot be absolved from blame in connection with this collision. I consider that, having decided to set a course to the northward on what he knew was the route for southbound merchant shipping, he neglected to take adequate precautions for the safety of his ship… It had been my intention when judgment was given in the Civil Proceedings which have taken place, to propose that Captain Showers should receive the displeasure of the Naval Board for his negligence.[131]

A draft communication to that effect was prepared at the end of August 1941,[132] but when Dixon J's judgment came out at almost the same time, one advisor quickly realised the risks of pressing ahead with any kind of action against Showers. It was a reasonable inference, he said, that if the evidence as

---

[126] Although the fact that a large charity fund for victims had been established was thought by the Treasury Solicitor to be a factor that might take away public sympathy for tort actions and encourage the victims to settle.

[127] The plaintiffs were ultimately unsuccessful in their claims in *Duncan*: *Woods v. Duncan* [1944] 2 All ER 156 (CA); [1946] AC 401 (HL).

[128] MP1049/5, above n 17, letter Captain Showers to Secretary, Naval Board, 3 September 1940.

[129] Ibid., memo Rear Admiral Commanding HM Australian Squadron to Secretary, Naval Board, 11 September 1940.

[130] A472, above n 26.

[131] MP1049/5, above n 17, minute 1st Naval Member re Captain HA Showers RAN, 4 July 1941 (Figure 8.5).

[132] Ibid., minute Head of 'N' branch to Secretary, First Naval Member, 28 August 1941.

to Shower's knowledge of the *Coptic*'s route had been available to the court, the finding would have been against the Commonwealth. As it seemed certain the owners of the *Coptic* would take the matter further, action should be deferred until it was known how Shaw Savill intended to respond to the judgment.[133] This was agreed, and when the same advisor a month later reported, he had knowledge of the recommendation of September 1940 that proceedings be deferred and was able to say confidently that 'any prospect of a court martial must be dropped as more than a year has already elapsed and any such court may prejudice later civil proceedings.'[134] Hence from very early after the accident the Commonwealth was aware that it was very likely caused by someone for whose negligence they were responsible. Moreover, the Commonwealth played a canny forensic game. Its counterclaim against Shaw Savill for negligence in relation to the collision seems to have been largely strategic. Before judgment in the first trial it was agreed that if the Commonwealth was not found liable it would not pursue the counterclaim[135] but when it became clear Shaw Savill would appeal, the Deputy Crown Solicitor thought 'in view of the importance of the matter and of the fact the plaintiff was appealed, I think it is essential that defendant should also appeal…'.[136] Even publication of the 1940 Full Court hearing – which was not heard in-camera – was delayed.[137]

It is striking that the interests of the likely innocent defendant were completely absent from any of these discussions. Although Dixon J had expressed his view in the initial stages of the litigation, in early October 1940, that the better procedure might be not to 'press ahead with proceedings in a case such as this arising out of damages whilst vessels were engaged on purposes in connection with the War but to endeavour to arrive at some settlement, e.g. by payment of compensation as an act of grace for damages', this was not accepted by the Naval Board, probably because counsel for the Commonwealth thought their defence sound.[138] Yet the Commonwealth persisted in this view even though the legal argument on justiciability was lost in every hearing and even though it knew its own servants were at fault. Viewed with hindsight, the claim to both an immunity in negligence and state privilege in evidence seems more about the individuals involved convincing themselves that the national interest required them to obstruct the claim. This conclusion is reinforced both by

---

[133] Ibid., handwritten note (author unidentifiable), undated (Figure 8.6).

[134] Ibid., handwritten note (author unidentifiable), 21 October 1941. While the suggestion that the conveying of the displeasure of the Naval Board to Showers should be deferred until after the civil proceedings were complete was rejected, it is unclear from the file whether the recommendation that he be admonished at the time took place because this was conditional on showing that he was aware of the *Coptic*'s movement: handwritten note (author unidentifiable), notation of 22 October 1941 to note of 21 October 1941 (Figure 8.7).

[135] A472, above n 26, letter Deputy Crown Solicitor to Crown Solicitor, 4 June 1941.

[136] Ibid., letter Deputy Crown Solicitor to Crown Solicitor, 25 November 1941.

[137] Ibid., letter Deputy Crown Solicitor to Crown Solicitor, 19 May 1942, noting that Starke J had caused an enquiry to be made as to why no report had been published.

[138] Ibid., letter Deputy Crown Solicitor to Crown Solicitor, 23 October, 1940.

the Naval Board's remarkable ability to approbate and reprobate when it came to Shower's conduct in relation to the Noumea operation[139] and the continuing censorship, first requested by the Censorship Liaison Officer (Navy) in October 1940, of any reference to the collision in any outward communications.[140] The two different questions of whether the action could be defended on public interest grounds, and whether the public interest grounds could be used as a forensic strategy in litigation, were blurred from the outset of the litigation with the result that what became most important was not to lose the litigation rather than the applicability of any substantive defence. A more balanced view of the situation may have seen the accident for what it was – a naval cock-up with consequences for which the common law of Australia required the Commonwealth to pay – and in retrospect both the formal defence and the litigation strategy looks like a well-intentioned but deliberate cover-up. The 'true' facts of *Shaw Savill* only reinforce the good sense of the High Court judges who refused to accept uncritically executive assertions that would limit the scope of negligence liability and the rules of evidence in the national interest.

Conclusion

The law of tort rarely interacted with the Commonwealth's defence obligations during the period of this study but when it did judges were confronted with issues of high constitutional importance. The two cases discussed in this chapter seem worlds apart in terms of their contemporary importance but there are important commonalities between the two. In both cases, Australian courts had no difficulty in accepting that there were situations in which the state could not be made liable for injuries arising out of its defence activities, either because the common law recognised an immunity or because of some form of statutory authority. But equally important was the recognition that executive authority of itself could not justify an infringement of private rights. Where the common law had to decide the boundary was blurred and messy as the *Shaw Savill* marathon demonstrated. Yet the history of this extended litigation is testament

---

[139] For approbation see above n 111. See also letter Secretary of the Naval Board to Rear Admiral Commanding HM Australian Squadron, 20 October 1940 recommending the Naval Board's approbation be conveyed to Showers over his handling of the Noumea operation, and the First Naval Member's handwritten comments on Shower's report that he had carried out a 'difficult and dangerous task with excellent judgement and success' (Figure 8.8). He also recommended the report be conveyed to the Department of External Affairs whose Secretary upon seeing it remarked that he was struck with the evidence of 'initiative, clear thinking and decision' of the Commanding Officer in 'most difficult and confusing circumstances': letter Secretary Department of External Affairs to Secretary Department of Navy, 23 October 1940 (all in NAA, MP1049/5, 1877/11/115 – Report on Commanding Officer of HMAS "Adelaide" On mission to New Caledonia).

[140] NAA, MP150/1, 521/201/239 – Legal Action taken in collision between *HMAS Adelaide* and *SS Coptic*, letter Controller of Post and Telegraph Censorship to Censorship Liaison Officer, 23 January 1941, seeking permission to forward the High Court judgment to plaintiff's solicitors in London.

to the good sense of requiring some justification for claims that the national interest prevented an action to have some scrutiny. This is not to claim that all Australian judges in all situations felt compelled to uphold traditional rule of law values in the face of executive attempts to remove judicial oversight but when they did they ought at least to be given credit for a commitment to the rule of law that compares favourably to contemporary developments in England.

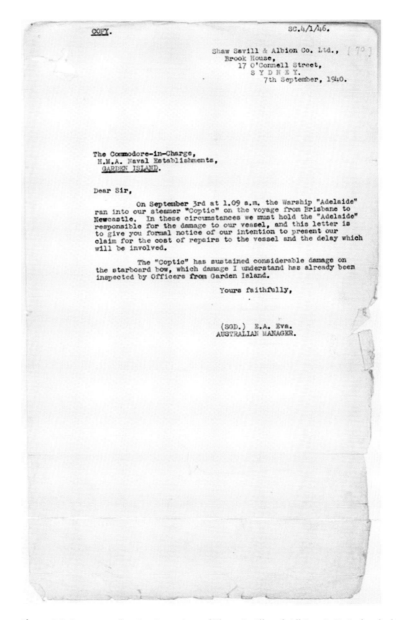

Figure 8.1 Letter confirming intention of Shaw Savill and Albion & Co Ltd to hold Commonwealth responsible for damage to MV *Coptic*.

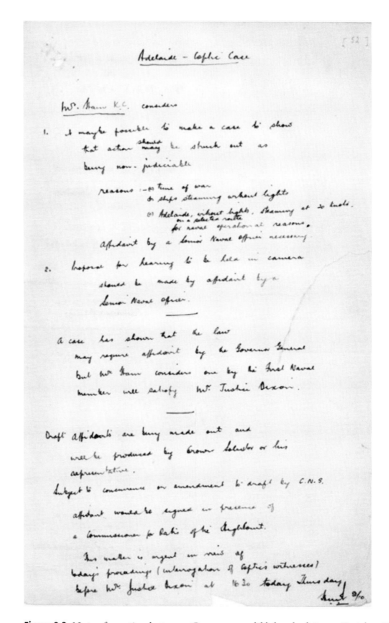

Figure 8.2 Note of meeting between Commonwealth's legal advisors, October 1940.

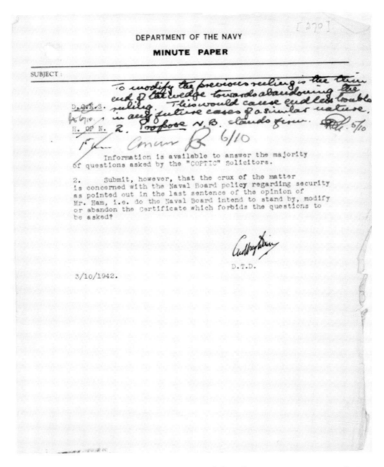

Figure 8.3 Department of Navy Minute with handwritten annotation refusing to waive privilege.

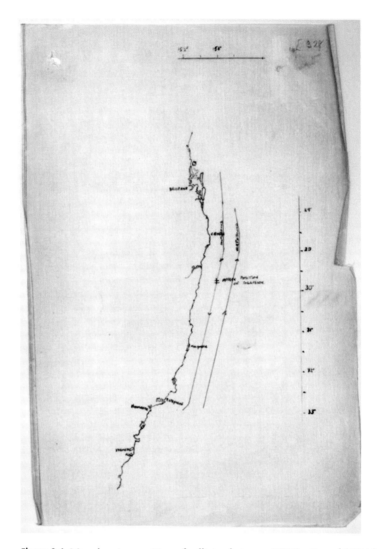

Figure 8.4 Map showing position of collision between *MV Coptic* and *HMAS Adelaide.*

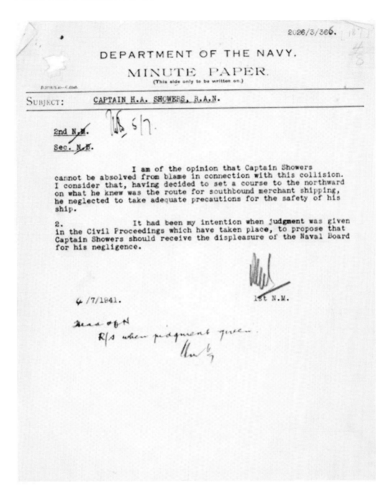

Figure 8.5 Minute of First Naval Member criticising Shower's conduct in relation to the collision.

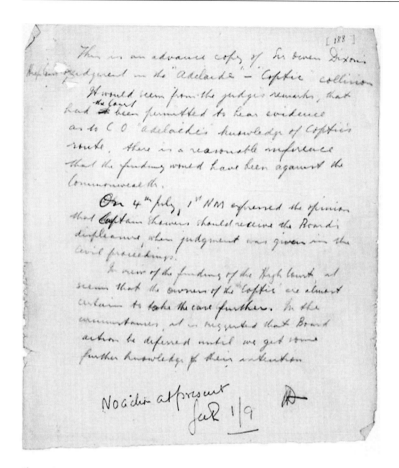

Figure 8.6 Department of Navy staff member note on effect of court martial on civil trial.

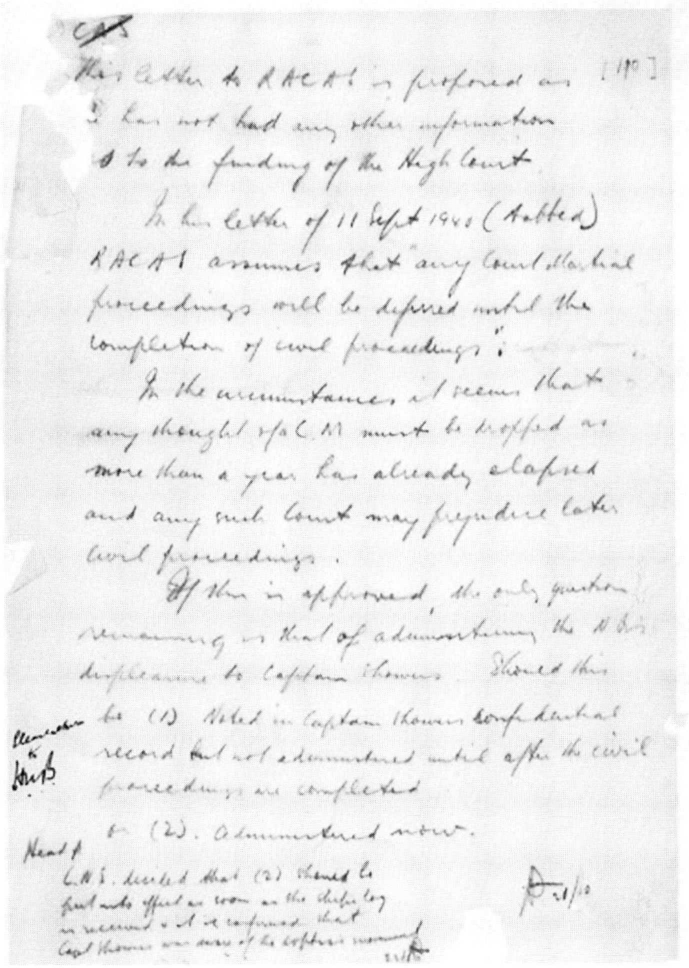

Figure 8.7 Department of Navy staff member note on effect of court martial on civil trial.

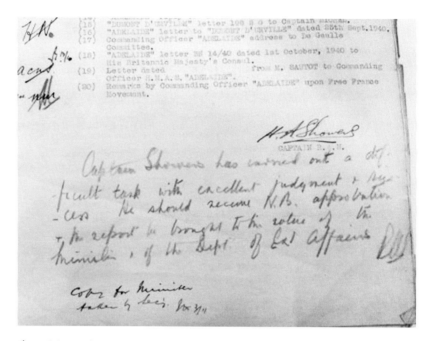

Figure 8.8 Handwritten comments of First Naval Member on Captain Showers'
Noumea Mission.

9

Environment and Australian Tort Law: The Problem of Fire and Weeds

This chapter considers the factor that was most different between England and Australia: the physical environment. Most of the chapter is devoted to one factor in that environment – fire – because the climatic conditions in Australia allowed fire to cause harm in a way that could not be replicated in England.[1] Cases involving fire were brought at all levels of court in Australia and Australian courts had to apply and adapt English rules established in very different circumstances. The chapter also considers, briefly, other challenges presented by attempts to 'acclimatise' Australia by the introduction of non-native flora. Both the law and its application in this context were far from certain, and while Australian courts had 'no little difficulty'[2] in working out when and whether to adopt rules of strict liability, their attempts to do so created a distinctively Australian gloss on the law in this area.

A Hot, Dry Country

Liability for damage caused by the spread of fire had been the subject of discussion in English cases for nearly five hundred years before white settlement in Australia. This might suggest that the legal rules were well settled but even by the beginning of the period of this study important, fundamental questions about the basis of liability for fire remained authoritatively unanswered.[3] Three

---

[1] English cases involved urban, domestic or commercial settings: see *Musgrove v. Pandelis* [1919] 1 KB 314; *Job Edwards Ltd v. Birmingham Navigation Co Proprietors* [1924] 1 KB 341; *Collingwood v. Home and Colonial Stores Ltd* [1936] 3 All ER 200; *Mulholland and Tedd Ltd v. Baker* [1939] 3 All ER 253.

[2] I. Lewis, 'Liability for the escape of fire' (1935) 8 *ALJ* 399, 402.

[3] For a contemporary commentary see P. Winfield, 'The myth of absolute liability' (1926) 42 *LQR* 37, 46–50. See also F. Newark, 'The Accidental Fires Act (Northern Ireland) 1944' (1944–46) 6 *NILQ* 134; A. Ogus, 'Vagaries in the liability for the escape of fire' [1969] *CLJ* 104; J. Foote, 'Liability for fire before 1880' (1969) 20 *NILQ* 141. For the differing views of textbook writers compare J. Salmond, *Law of Torts* (Stevens and Haynes, 1907) 210–215; F. Pollock, *The Law of Torts*, 7th edn (Stevens and Sons, 1904) 489–492; J. Clerk and W. Lindsell, *The Law of Torts*, 2nd edn (Sweet and Maxwell, 1896) 372–375; 370–374; H. Smith, *Addison on Torts*, 6th edn (Stevens and Sons, 1887) 370–374.

inter-related but separate questions played out in the Australian case law. First, was liability for the spread of fire strict or fault-based? Second, if liability was strict, what, if any, relationship did this strict liability for damage caused by the spread of fire bear to the more general strict liability recognised in *Rylands v. Fletcher*?[4] Third, if liability was fault-based, what were its limits? Would it extend to negligent failures to control fires? Other subsidiary questions arose within all of these major issues: to what extent was an occupier vicariously (used in its widest sense) liable for fires lit by servants, licensees or even strangers? And even if liability was fault-based to what extent could the very different local conditions in Australia be taken into account in determining what amounted to fault?

The discussion proceeds in a largely chronological manner.[5] The first section considers the case law from the beginning of the period of this study to 1914, the date of the seminal *Whinfield* decision of the High Court of Australia. The second section deals with *Whinfield* and the third considers the case law in the fifteen years after *Whinfield* to assess the impact of the decision in practice. The final section considers the cases from the early 1930s until the end of the period of this study when, at least in theory, the legal rules applying to fire were settled.

Duties on Private Landowners with Respect to Fire

Between 1901 and 1914, liability for damage caused by the spread of an existing fire, whether deliberately lit or not, was debated. There was no consensus but the generally accepted view was that liability for a fire lit by an occupier was strict. Conversely, there was authority that there was no liability for failing to stop a fire that a person knew was on his land but had not lit except, perhaps, if that person had intervened and made the situation worse.

Two cases from South Australia in this early period demonstrate different notions of responsibility attaching to damage by fire where the defendant was a private landowner. In *Havelberg v. Brown*,[6] a number of Port Lincoln farmers sued the defendant, a neighbouring farmer, for the destruction of their crops and fencing when a fire spread to their properties. The fire had started in a log on the defendant's property, and, although the defendant did not light it, he and his employee took steps to put the fire out and then to reduce the risk of it

---

[4] (1868) LR 3 HL 330.

[5] A detailed list of cases involving damage caused by fire, before and during the period of this study, was compiled by the Bushfire Co-operative Research Council: www.bushfirecrc.com/sites/default/files/managed/litigation-table/australian_bushfire_cases-01.htm. Not all of these cases involve questions of liability.

[6] [1905] SALR 1.

spreading. These were unsuccessful and when the wind later picked up the fire spread to the plaintiff's property causing the damage.

The primary case for the plaintiffs was that the defendant had been careless in failing to prevent the spread of fire.[7] At the Local Court in Port Lincoln the magistrate directed the jury that the defendant could be liable even if he had not lighted the fire if he had not taken all reasonable precautions to stop it from spreading and the jury returned a verdict in favour of the plaintiffs. On appeal to the Full Court of the Supreme Court of South Australia, the arguments traversed the nature of liability for damage caused by fire and demonstrated the uncertainty that surrounded that liability. Although there was considerable discussion over whether liability for fire was strict, in the end only one strand of the cases on fire was taken up. Whatever special liability attached to a person for *his* fire, it did not extend to fires caused by a stranger or started by accident. Counsel was asking the court to extend the English common law and hold that a person could be responsible for a fire on his premises howsoever caused. In Way CJ's view this was impermissible: 'I do not think judicial authority extends to legislating to create new liabilities in that manner.'[8] But the reasoning in support of this conclusion did not rest simply on how far the English cases had gone: he turned to consider the practical implications of imposing such a duty. Should a legal duty apply in all cases, irrespective of age or sex? Should it be made applicable in spite of the absence or illness of the owner, or in the case of a fire out of his sight or without his knowledge? Was it to apply to a man who is weak and unskilful?[9] In analytical terms, Way CJ's argument was that the difficulties created by imposing a duty could not be mediated through a flexible approach to breach, an argument that has been used in modern contexts to deny a duty of care.[10] But Way CJ's reasoning went further. While it might 'appear startling' that no duty was owed, this was an example of an imperfect obligation: a moral rather than a legal duty.[11] But in the local Australian context this was not problematic:

> The slightest reflection must shew any one how difficult it would be to frame a law that would be applicable to all cases, and any one who has seen, as most of us have, the frequent bush fires in the hills adjacent to Adelaide, will understand that there really is no necessity for any such law. People not only extinguish

---

[7]   There was a formal count that the plaintiff brought the fire on the land but this does not seem to have been argued at trial (*The Advertiser* (Adelaide), 31 March 1906, 5) and, as Way CJ noted, there was no evidence that he did light the fire ([1905] SALR 1, 7–8).

[8]   [1905] SALR 1, 11.

[9]   Ibid.

[10]   The early cases on illegality in tort provide an example: *Smith v. Jenkins* (1970) 119 CLR 397; *Pitts v. Hunt* [1991] 1 QB 24.

[11]   A similar argument was made by Gordon J: [1905] SALR 1, 16.

dangerous fires from self-interest, and for the preservation of themselves and their families, but in the summer we see every week the whole countryside turning out and using the utmost endeavours to prevent danger to life and injury to the property of others.[12]

The immunity recognised, however, was only for nonfeasance. As the defendant had acted (by taking steps to put out the fire and stop it spreading), he could be liable if this made things worse and while the Full Court seemed confident there had been no breach of duty a nonsuit (as opposed to a directed verdict) was entered to allow the plaintiff to lead new evidence.[13] While a somewhat romanticised ideal of community underpins the no duty reasoning in the written judgment, Way CJ was not always as confident in his fellow citizens: in argument he said he would be sorry to lay down from the bench a principle which would indicate that if a man saw a lighted match thrown on his grass he was not under an obligation to put it out.[14] The pragmatic arguments against the view that no duty was owed were put powerfully by plaintiff's counsel: 'Settlers [in the Port Lincoln area] might have drought and rabbits to contend against, and they were prepared to face these difficulties… but, they could not protect themselves against those who would in the summer months, light fire, or who would nurse a large tree burning for their own purposes, or a fire lit by someone else, with ripe crops around.'[15] The plaintiffs had apparently moved to the region after a seven-year drought forced them from the north and 'in a moment the earnings from the 500 acres they had cleared were swept away through the carelessness of the defendant.'[16] An editorial was deferentially critical of the decision. While recognising that the Full Court's ruling was clearly in accord with the law and that the reasoning of Chief Justice properly exposed the difficulties of extending the law as the plaintiff suggested, closer analysis reveals considerable disquiet with the result. Allowing that the law as laid down was in accord with common sense, 'it is, to say the least, startling to learn in a country that at certain seasons may be largely denuded of its wealth by devastating conflagrations that a man's safest legal course when confronted with the fire fiend may be to do nothing.' While agreeing with the Chief Justice that community fighting of bushfires was common, that was not the point:

> Probably no one is more sorry than himself that he, unwittingly, gave the flames a chance to spread and cause so much injury; but that does not help the unfortunate

---

[12] [1905] SALR 1, 11. Way CJ had some idea of rural conditions, owning a large merino sheep property near Minto: J. Emerson, *First Among Equals: Chief Justices of South Australia Since Federation* (University of Adelaide Press, 2006) 31.

[13] It was reported that instructions to commence new proceedings (*The Register* (Adelaide), 29 July 1905, 6) were given but no further trace appears in newspaper records.

[14] *The Advertiser* (Adelaide), 14 July 1905, 3.

[15] Ibid.

[16] Ibid.

plaintiffs, who lost their crop without having a fair chance – as Brown had – of protecting it. From this point of view the verdict of the Local Court is justified by reason and morality, and the jury are entitled to commendation for innocently crediting the law with requiring that a man should be as rigorously careful to protect his neighbour against the spread of an accidental fire as he is now expected to be to save him from the possibility of becoming the victim of smallpox or other infectious disease.[17]

For present purposes, what is important is not so much the result of the case – which was overruled nearly sixty years later when similar facts took place in Western Australia[18] – but the tenor of the argument. Both on and off the bench, there was a struggle as to how to apply fairly abstract English authority to the very different conditions that applied in early twentieth-century South Australia. The risk of fire was so great in this environment that there was a strong case – moral and legal – for a duty to act. No doubt the dominion of property had its place but in a sparsely populated and dry country fire was a community risk and there was a strong argument, as the writer of the editorial commented, that it would be 'regrettable if the judgment should tend to weaken the sense of obligation in reference to the care of other people's property'.[19]

At common law, the situation where some form of strict liability for damage caused by fire was best established was where the defendant lit a fire. Two cases from this first period illustrate that Australian courts recognised that liability was in these circumstances strict. This was by reference both to old English case law – some of which dated to the fifteenth century – and to the general strict liability principle of *Rylands v. Fletcher* into which the old cases were held to have been incorporated. In early 1906, the Full Court of the Supreme Court of Queensland in *Kellett v. Cowan*[20] allowed an appeal in favour of a lodger in a hotel whose property was damaged when the plaintiff's attempt to fumigate hotel rooms resulted in a fire that spread to other parts of the hotel. The liability found by the Full Court was ostensibly fault-based. Viewed more closely, however, the liability recognised was more strict than the ordinary fault requirement. Cooper CJ thought the principle from the English case of *Turberville v. Stamp*[21] was that the respondent was liable for all damage caused by the spreading of a fire lit

---

[17] *The Register* (Adelaide), 19 July 1905, 4.

[18] *Hargrave v. Goldman* (1963) 110 CLR 40. See further M. Lunney, 'Goldman v. Hargrave' in C. Mitchell and P. Mitchell (eds.), *Landmark Cases in the Law of Tort* (Hart Publishing, 2010) ch. 8.

[19] *The Register* (Adelaide), 19 July 1905, 4. The short comment in *The Advertiser* (Adelaide) (19 July 1905, 4) was more circumspect, noting that the judgment would be of distinct value to people living in districts where fires are easily started and difficult to extinguish.

[20] [1906] St R Qd 116.

[21] (1697) 12 Mod 152; 88 ER 1228. The case is reported numerous times in the nominate reports of the period.

by him unless he used every effort to subdue and control the fire and those efforts were frustrated by some non-preventable force. If these conditions were not satisfied, the fire was due to the negligence of the person light-ing it.[22] Real J showed greater awareness of the special nature of this fault-based liability: as there was no force or event that prevented the *Turberville v. Stamp* rule applying, there was negligence *within the rule of law applicable to fire* [my italics].[23] And Chubb J thought the 'duty to use extreme care' was expressed by Blackburn J's famous statement in *Rylands v. Fletcher*.[24] The precise nature of liability for the fire that one lit as revealed in the judg-ments was thus elusive.[25]

Several months later a different approach was taken by the Full Court of the Supreme Court of Western Australia. In *Craig v. Parker*,[26] the defen-dant, a property owner near York in the eastern farming districts of Western Australia, had lit a fire which spread to the plaintiff's land and caused damage. The trial judge, Burnside J, held that the case was decided by the application of *Rylands v. Fletcher*, a well-known principle which had been 'acted upon in every part of the world where the English common law receives any respect. It is the law in England, America, and throughout Australia and New Zealand'.[27] The authority to support the application of this universal principle to fire was not English but from New Zealand,[28] Victoria[29] and South Australia,[30] and Thomas Beven's citation of Turton J's judgment in *Turberville v. Stamp* as authority that the rule may not apply to fires in the field was rejected as not reflecting the majority view.[31] The legal analysis was backed up by the contex-tual: 'If in a country like England the lighting of a fire is considered dangerous, such an action in a climate like ours must be still more dangerous.'[32] Burnside J did not see this liability as based in negligence; after concluding that *Rylands v. Fletcher* applied to impose liability he noted that it was not necessary to hold that the defendant was guilty of negligence. The Full Court agreed, McMillan J noting that *Rylands* was based on the old rule that a man was bound to use his land in such a way as not to injure his neighbour. There was, accordingly,

---

[22] [1906] St R Qd 116, 122–123.

[23] Ibid., 124.

[24] Ibid.

[25] See also *Mitchellmore v. Salmon* (1905) 1 Tas LR 109 where Clark J's short judgment seems to base liability on negligence and on *Rylands v. Fletcher*.

[26] [1906] WAR 161.

[27] The judgment is not reported but it is reproduced in *Eastern Districts Chronicle*, 12 August 1905, 3.

[28] *Dougherty v. Smith* (incorrectly spelt 'Doherty') in the report. The only reference I have located is in *New Zealand Times*, 29 July 1887, 3 (an ex-tempore decision of Prendergast CJ delivered in the Supreme Court in Banco).

[29] *Sheehan* v. *Park* (1882) 8 VLR 25.

[30] Probably *Cottrell v. Allen* (1882) 16 SALR 122.

[31] *Eastern Districts Chronicle*, 12 August 1905, 3.

[32] Ibid.

no need to consider whether the defendant was guilty of any negligence, but McMillan J did so, and his discussion suggests that *Rylands* could not be seen as an example of an onerous duty to exercise care. Such a duty would still fall within negligence and its discharge required express recognition 'of the differences between local conditions and those existing in England where some of the cases relating to fire have been considered'. A much greater degree of care would be required of a person in a country 'of this kind' from that which would be expected from one bringing fire upon land in a cooler and wetter climate and breach would depend on whether there was 'a departure from that high degree of care such as is necessary here by persons responsible for making a fire in these sun-dried localities'.[33] Thus even if strict liability under *Rylands v. Fletcher* could not be imposed, McMillan J made it clear that the negligence standard, as adapted to apply in the eastern farming districts of Western Australia, was at the least more stringent than anything that might have been suggested in English cases.

The most comprehensive analysis of the liability for fire in the pre-*Whinfield* era was *Young v. Tilley*, a decision of the Full Court of the Supreme Court of South Australia. A number of nineteenth-century cases in South Australia had held that liability for the spread of fire was different from ordinary negligence but precisely how was less clear. In *McDonald v. Dickson* in 1868,[34] Gwynne J took the view that the only evidence of negligence that needed to go to the jury where the fire was deliberately lit was that the fire was lit outdoors. Although the Fires Metropolis Act 1774 (UK) s. 86 had taken away liability for accidental fires, once lit deliberately 'he was liable without any special negligence being proved.'[35] A number of different views were given in *Cottrell v. Allen* in 1882. Andrews J saw the liability as based on a kind of imputed negligence[36] while Way CJ and Boucalt J thought the liability for fire fell within *Rylands v. Fletcher*.[37] Although there were different shades of reasoning, there was no doubt that there was something different about liability for damage caused by fire.

The large fires in the Adelaide Hills in the late summer of 1911–12 provided the opportunity for the South Australian Supreme Court to revisit the issue. In *Young v. Tilley*[38] the parties were neighbours and on a hot February day the defendant's wife lit a fire in an iron tank to boil a billy. Sparks from the fire caused surrounding dry grass to catch fire, and the fire spread to the plaintiff's land, causing damage to feed and fencing.[39] At the Local Court the presiding magistrate would have found for the defendant but for the authorities

---

[33] [1906] 8 WAR 161, 163–164.
[34] (1868) 2 SALR 32.
[35] Ibid., 33.
[36] (1882) 16 SALR 122, 125.
[37] Ibid.
[38] [1913] SALR 87.
[39] *The Register* (Adelaide), 2 May 1912, 5; 3 May 1912, 9.

mentioned above and his offer to reserve a point of law for the Full Court was accepted by the defendant.[40] Before that court the nature of liability for fire was extensively canvassed. In an impressive display of learning from counsel for the plaintiff, authorities from not only England and Australia but also the United States, Canada and New Zealand, as well as the views of a large number of textbook writers, were canvassed. The leading judgment was given by Buchanan TJ who in a tour de force found that liability for fire deliberately lit was not based on negligence. The common law, via a custom of the realm, imposed liability for damage caused by fire on the person responsible for that fire. Inconsistency in old texts was interpreted in favour of a form of strict liability, and he held that any allegation of negligence in the declaration was formal and non-traversable. Following the English case of *Filliter v. Phippard*,[41] a judgment concerned with the statutory defence in the Fires (Metropolis) Act 1774 s. 86, the application of that section in South Australia was given a limited application, its effect being to 'do away with the presumption that the fire was kindled by the occupier of the premises'[42] and allowing a defence for fires of accidental in origin. In light of this discussion, he turned to consider the earlier South Australian cases discussed above and thought that these authorities were conclusive in favour of the plaintiffs.

The structure of the judgment is suggestive of how Australian courts approached English judgments in this period. Buchanan TJ does not ignore the earlier South Australian cases but he assessed their authority against the earlier English case law. In this respect, the most interesting part of the judgment is his view that the custom was based on the 'like good sense' as the doctrine in *Rylands v. Fletcher*.[43] Though it is not entirely clear, it seems he saw liability for fire as a specific example of the wider *Rylands* principle, as did his fellow judges Murray J[44] and Way CJ.[45] There was little English authority on this point, and while Buchanan TJ and Murray J cited *Jones v. Festiniog Railway Co.*[46] that case involved a fire caused by sparks from locomotives setting fire to adjoining property rather than a deliberately lit fire. Conveniently, there was found to be no inconsistency between the results in the South Australian cases and the English authorities but it is inaccurate to see this conclusion as based on some kind of mechanical procedure. And while the law that was analysed was clearly English, its application had a distinctly Australian flavour. Section 86 of the 1774 Act prevented strict liability for accidental fires but whether the fire began accidentally, Buchanan TJ said, depended on the particular circumstances. *Vis major* or Act of God – the exceptions to liability set out by Blackburn J in

---

[40] Ibid., 4 May 1912, 14.
[41] (1847) 11 QB 347; 116 ER 506.
[42] [1913] SALR 87, 100.
[43] Ibid., 97.
[44] Ibid., 101–192.
[45] Ibid., 103.
[46] (1868) LR 3 QB 733.

Rylands – meant in the present case the presence of 'some elemental force of an extraordinary character, and such as could not reasonably have been foreseen' was required and in answering this question, '[T]ime, place and all the circumstances needed to be considered.'[47] They were very different from England:

> In England a whirlwind being, as I believe, an almost unknown phenomenon might well be regarded as *vis major*, but… an ordinary whirlwind could not be regarded in the same light in South Australia, where whirlwinds are at certain seasons of the year a common occurrence. In the present case no fact is found suggesting anything extraordinary or incapable of being anticipated. We have a spark flying from a fire – one of the most ordinary ways by which a fire spreads – and igniting the grass upon which it falls on a day in January in the middle of a South Australian summer. It would have been extraordinary if the grass had not been ignited…[48]

The result was that strict liability for the spread of fire deliberately lit was for a short time enshrined in South Australian law together with an acceptance that the Australian natural environment was unpredictable and may not be an excuse for a fire that spread.[49]

The Retreat: *Whinfield's* Case

At the time that *Young v. Tilley* was decided a Victorian case was wending its way through the system that would change the approach to liability for fire in Australia. In *Whinfield v. Lands Purchase Management Board of Victoria and State Rivers and Water Supply Commission of Victoria*, the plaintiff was in the familiar position of being the owner of land that was damaged in December 1911 when a fire lit by one McTavish for domestic cooking purposes spread in the hot windy conditions. The land on which McTavish was camping was owned and occupied by the Lands Purchase Management Board ('the Board') on behalf of the Crown. McTavish was camping on the land as he was using it as a base from which to carry out his employment with the State Rivers and Water Supply Commission ('the Commission'). There was evidence that McTavish had been careless in his management of the fire.[50]

At first glance, the case had little to do with strict liability for fire because there had been negligence associated with the spread of the fire. The primary question was whether any vicarious liability could attach to McTavish's negligence. This may explain why the initial action was commenced only against the Commission and most of the evidence went to the content of the relationship

---

[47] [1913] SALR 87, 102.

[48] Ibid.

[49] In *Havelberg v. Brown* [1905] SALR 1, Way CJ stated, obiter, that the authorities suggested that liability for fire required negligence but he recanted in *Young*, noting that he disagreed with Salmond's view that negligence was required.

[50] He was convicted of a summary offence in relation to the fire: NAA, A10074, 1913/32, *Whinfield v. Lands Management Board*, Appeal Book, 20.

between the Commission and its employees.[51] As the trial judge, Hodges J, was giving judgment the plaintiff applied successfully to discontinue the action, presumably because it was realised there may be an alternative defendant.[52] Several months later, a new action was brought with both the Commission and Board as defendants.[53] At the close of the plaintiff's case, A'Beckett J stated he would enter judgment for the Board while at the close of evidence he directed the jury to enter judgment for the plaintiff against the Commission.

Both parties appealed to the Full Court of the Supreme Court of Victoria which unanimously allowed the Commission's appeal and rejected the plaintiff's cross-appeal.[54] In neither defendant's case was the nature of liability for fire really in issue. The action against the Commission failed because the workers (including McTavish) were not acting in the course of employment when camped on the land. The Board also had no responsibility because, in effect, the workers were trespassers on the land and the Board had no knowledge of their conduct. While the community split over the merits of the decision – with one landowner saying that if the Full Court was correct 'landowners will have to take the law into their own hands'[55] – none of these concerns relate to the question of liability for fire generally. This is clear from a contemporary legal comment which saw the case as primarily about when a landowner could be vicariously liable for a fire lit by someone else on his property.[56]

The case took quite a different turn when it reached the High Court. Counsel for the plaintiff argued that the occupier of the land was liable for damage caused by fire lit by anyone on the land with the owner's permission independently of any negligence, either because of special rules attaching to fire or because it fell within the rule in *Rylands v. Fletcher*. Without seeking the assistance of the respondents' counsel, both Griffith CJ and Isaacs J, who gave the substantive judgments, emphatically rejected the view that strict liability for fire, if it existed, applied to these facts. The discussion in Griffith CJ's judgment seems to merge the two basis of potential strict liability for fire. The first part appears to deal with the specific common law rule applying to fire. He rejected a wide reading of *Filliter v. Phippard*:[57] that case interpreted the meaning of an 'accidental' fire and he thought it was limited to its own facts. More broadly, he thought it was obvious that a fire may be accidental in the ordinary acceptation of that word if it arose from a fire intentionally lit being unintentionally and unexpectedly communicated to some inflammatory material near it just

---

[51] *Bendigo Advertiser*, 28 February 1912, 4; 10 June 1912, 7; 11 June 1912, 5.

[52] This explanation was given in the introductory report of the new trial: *Bendigo Advertiser*, 6 December 1912, 4.

[53] *Bendigo Advertiser*, 6 December 1912, 4. I have found no report beyond the first day of the trial but the result was noted in *The Australasian*, 14 December 1912, 13.

[54] *Bendigo Advertiser*, 19 June 1913, 4.

[55] *Bacchus Marsh Express*, 5 July 1913, 2.

[56] *The Australasian* (Melbourne), 28 June 1913, 53.

[57] (1847) 11 QB 347; 116 ER 506.

as much as if it arose from a flash of lightning. But irrespective of any changes made by the 1774 Act, liability for damage by fire was always based on negligence 'although in some cases the evidence required to prove negligence was very slight, and the duty to prevent a fire on a man's own land from spreading was regarded very stringently.'[58] Griffith CJ accepted that in the case of fires lit to clear ground the duty to keep it from spreading 'was practically treated as unqualified' and amounted to 'such care as will prevent injury to others, unless excused by the Act of God or *vis major*'.[59] All this is about the common law 'special' fire action and there was nothing especially radical about Griffith CJ's treatment of the issue (except, perhaps, his failure to mention *Young v. Tilley*, a leading, recent state case on the issue). But then Griffith CJ introduced a further limitation: in no case had this special liability 'been applied to the case of a fire lawfully lighted for domestic purposes or other ordinary purposes of occupation of land and accidentally spreading without negligence'.[60] Although not explicit, this must be a reference to the non-natural use requirement in *Rylands*. Implicitly, this brought the special fire liability within *Rylands* and the strictness of the liability imposed through *Rylands* for the spread of fire was constrained where the fire was for domestic purposes. It is hard to see that any of this was consistent with *Young v. Tilley* which is, perhaps, why it was ignored.[61]

While the link between any special rule for fire and *Rylands* liability was a matter of inference in Griffith CJ's judgment, it was explicit in the judgment of Isaacs J. Counsel had argued that the Board was liable on the *Rylands* principle, and the proposition urged – 'one of great general importance' – was that as fire was always dangerous unless confined, a person who introduces it upon his own land was liable subject to the defences of inevitable accident or act of a third party. Isaacs J was concerned to correct this view, taken at trial and implicitly accepted in the Full Court, which supposed that negligence was immaterial to liability for the spread of fire. All had changed since the recent decision of the Privy Council in *Rickards v. Lothian*[62] and with one exception he left out 'all consideration of previous cases'. In a scholarly analysis of *Rylands v. Fletcher*, Isaacs J emphasised the non-natural use element highlighted in *Rickards*. Viewed in this light, considering liability for 'fire' was too broad:

> Now it seems to me to follow that where the question is as to a domestic fire, a fire lit for the purpose of cooking food or supplying bodily warmth, the position of the person lighting it is inherently stronger, because its essentiality as a feature of life is based on the common requirement of humanity. No one can assert that

---

[58] (1914) 18 CLR 606, 615.

[59] Ibid.

[60] Ibid.

[61] A forlorn attempt in the 1930s to argue its virtue was made in response to an article on liability for fire that omitted discussion of it. While regretting its omission, in reply the author of the article (correctly) concluded that it was not consistent with *Whinfield*: 'Correspondence' (1935) 8 *ALJ* 453.

[62] [1913] AC 263.

the presence of such a fire is 'an increased danger', that is, increased beyond that occasioned by the ordinary use of the land, or, phrasing the notion differently, that the use of the land for such a purpose is a 'special use'. On the contrary, fire for the maintenance or ordinary comfort of life, is a necessary adjunct of civilised existence, and an elemental purpose of the use of land by the human race.[63]

Why did Griffiths CJ and Isaacs J decide to enter into the wider question of the nature of liability for damage by fire? It was not required to decide the case: as neither defendant was responsible for McTavish lighting the fire, this was in effect the act of a trespasser, a likely exception to any special liability rule for fire whether sui generis or as part of *Rylands*.[64] To do that, however, was to avoid the problem of how to deal with liability in a related and fairly common scenario. As Griffith CJ noted, it was necessary in the sparsely settled regions of Australia for camps to be set up and fires to be used: this 'may be taken to be the ordinary actual mode of use in Australia (and I suppose elsewhere) of the land on which such camps are pitched'. To impose liability on those who occupied the land for fires lit by those camping there, even with consent, would be to interfere adversely with a practice that served an important social and economic function. In Griffith CJ's words:

> It would be a shocking thing to lay down as a rule of law that in a country like Australia, where probably hundreds, if not thousands, of men travelling on foot in sparsely settled districts ask every day for permission to camp for the night on private property, the owner by granting such poor hospitality becomes responsible for the lighting of a fire by the wayfarer to boil his 'billy' or keep himself warm.[65]

This passage reveals an important difference between *Whinfield* and some of the earlier cases. It was one thing to hold an occupier to a strict or at least highly onerous duty for a fire for which they were individually responsible – as in *Young v. Tilley* – but quite another to impose a vicarious liability for a fire lit by another when that other was not even an employee. More broadly, the problem with *Whinfield* was that while it clarified the general basis on which liability for fire was imposed, it did so in a particular context: the responsibility of a landowner for a fire lit by another. There was no reason why the general principle articulated in *Whinfield* would not apply across the board but while the prosaic reasoning of Griffith CJ might resonate for the innocent landowners the equities between the parties were much closer when the fire was lit by the defendant. As the next section demonstrates, the role of *Rylands* in determining liability for fire remained uncertain despite the decision in *Whinfield*.

---

[63] (1914) 18 CLR 606, 619.

[64] Hence Rich J found it unnecessary to discuss whether *Rylands v. Fletcher* was applicable: ibid., 622.

[65] Ibid., 616.

Unravelling the Mystery: Liability for Fire after *Whinfield*

The initial cases after *Whinfield* involving liability for fire reveal a number of different interpretations of the case. In *Bugge v. Brown*,[66] the High Court considered the liability of an employer for the negligently lit fire of his employee which spread and caused damage to the plaintiff's property. While the primary issue was the employer's vicarious liability, counsel for the plaintiff had also argued the old strict liability rule that the owner of land was liable for a fire kindled or kept by his servant irrespective of negligence and irrespective of whether this was in the course of employment. This argument was dealt with peremptorily: Isaacs J noted that the court ruled against this in argument and that whatever 'may have been anciently considered the true rule of the common law, the rigorous proposition so contended for cannot now be maintained'.[67] The following year, in another appeal concerning liability for the carelessly lit fire of an employee, the only basis of liability canvassed before the High Court was vicarious liability.[68] *Whinfield* is not referred to in either High Court judgment. Conversely, in *Watego v. Byron Shire Council*,[69] one of the defendant's arguments was based on *Whinfield*. Through its employees it had 'promiscuously' lit a fire for the purpose of clearing land to make a road. Relying on *Whinfield* it argued that this road building was not a non-natural use of land in a young county.[70] The trial judge was inclined to think that negligence was necessary but as plaintiff's counsel did not argue the point and there was evidence of negligence on which liability could be based no definitive ruling was given.

A different approach was taken in two Western Australian cases in the early 1920s. In *Prout v. Stacey*[71] a contractor on the defendant's land lit a fire that spread to the plaintiff's adjoining land. The magistrate's finding in favour of the plaintiff was upheld. McMillan CJ held, simply, that once it was proved that the fire escaped from the defendant's land, 'it is not necessary to consider whether there is any negligence or not, because once this is established the doctrine of *Rylands* v. *Fletcher* applies'.[72] As this statement could not have been consistent with *Whinfield*, it comes as no surprise to find that *Whinfield* was not cited at all. Two years later, in *Baker v. Durack* in 1924,[73] McMillan CJ was again confronted with a claim by a farmer when the deliberately lit fire of his neighbour spread and caused damage to his land. McMillan CJ found no negligence against the defendant but held that the outcome was governed

---

[66] (1919) 26 CLR 110.

[67] (1919) 26 CLR 110, 115. This view was also adopted by Higgins J (at 130).

[68] *Whitfield v. Turner* (1920) 28 CLR 97. This was also the only issue before the Full Court of the Supreme Court of New South Wales: *Turner* v. *Whitfield* (1919) 19 SR (NSW) 345.

[69] (1920) 5 LGR 82.

[70] Ibid., 84.

[71] [1922] WAR 20.

[72] Ibid., 21.

[73] [1924] WAR 32.

by *Craig v. Parker*, a case discussed above (and which he knew having been part of the Full Court that heard the appeal) that pre-dated *Whinfield* where the principle of *Rylands v. Fletcher* was applied. *Whinfield* was not cited but defendant's counsel argued something that at first glance looks similar: *Rylands* did not apply because 'burning off is necessary in this country for the purpose of bringing land under cultivation'.[74] McMillan CJ interpreted this as a reference to Turton J's dissenting judgment in *Tuberville v. Stamp* rather than an argument about giving substantive content to the non-natural use requirement in *Rylands* and was, accordingly, able to dismiss it as a minority view. As the strong wind blowing on the day of the fire was a 'wind of a kind with which we are familiar', there was no defence of Act of God and the plaintiff succeeded. Even though the judgment failed to recognise that *Whinfield* had any impact at all, the defendant's appeal to a High Court consisting of Isaacs J was dismissed. Despite the fact that argument canvassed the results of 'similar suits in various countries',[75] in an unreported judgment Isaacs J for the court (he and Starke J) determined that it was unnecessary to decide whether the defendant was liable in the absence of negligence because there was 'abundant' evidence of negligence.[76] Whatever the merits of this course of action, it was unfortunate that the opportunity of reasserting the *Whinfield* position was not taken.

It was left to the Supreme Court of Victoria, and to the rarefied atmosphere of Toorak (a well-to-do Melbourne suburb then as now) to provide some order to an increasingly splintered law. In *Pett v. Sims Paving and Road Construction Co. Pty Ltd*[77] the defendant was responsible for paving a drive on the residence of the Lord Mayor of Melbourne, Sir Stephen Morell, when sparks caused a fire in the plaintiff's next door garden and residence.[78] Irvine CJ left two questions for the jury: was the fire caused by sparks from the defendant's plant? (to which the jury answered yes) and was there any negligence by the defendants or their servants? (to which the jury answered no).[79] On these findings both parties moved for judgment. Counsel for the plaintiff felt confident enough to argue a special rule of strict liability for the owner of land for any fire lit with his consent but this was rejected. In Irvine CJ's view, this arbitrary rule for fire was difficult to fit with modern ideas of legal principle, was rejected by some modern writers (Salmond) and, most importantly, had been rejected by Isaacs J in *Bugge v. Brown*.[80] But he recognised that this did not deal with the wider argument that 'anyone who uses fire in any place and in any circumstances becomes an insurer of all persons who may be affected by its escape'. In Irvine CJ's view, there was no such general rule but there were two classes of case where this kind

---

[74] Ibid., 33.
[75] *Daily News* (Perth), 10 September 1924, 10.
[76] WA, 11 September 1924, 6.
[77] [1928] VLR 247.
[78] *Argus*, 18 April 1928, 19.
[79] *Argus*, 21 April 1928, 34.
[80] [1928] VLR 247, 251–252.

of liability might be imposed: cases falling with the rule in *Rylands v. Fletcher* and cases where the conduct amounted to a nuisance at common law.[81] In an impressive analysis, Irvine CJ explained the limits of both of these areas of liability. As far as *Rylands* was concerned, he analysed English cases which might be authority for (in modern terms) a general rule of strict liability for dangerous things and rejected them.[82] He broadly accepted Salmond's analysis that the cases were really examples of nuisance[83] but in one of the cases – a 1918 decision of the Court of Appeal not considered by Salmond – he politely but firmly held that it should not be taken as extending the rule in *Rylands v. Fletcher*. There were two reasons for this:

> [F]irst, to extend that principle beyond a liability attaching to the ownership of land or occupancy of land, to which it is in express terms limited, would open such an extensive field for the principle of insurance, including everything which is likely to cause mischief if it escapes out of any person's control – at all events, in a highway – without any negligence on his part that I feel justified in thinking that any such general rule was not really contemplated or intended by the learned Judges who sat in the Court of Appeal in that case. The other consideration relates to the principle of *Rickards* v. *Lothian*, adopted by the High Court in *Whinfield* v. *Lands Purchase Board*. It is difficult to see how the rule can be extended to an area in which this specific exception or limitation had no application. It might be more correct to say that, instead of the natural use of land being an exception to the rule itself, the non-natural use of land is a necessary element of the rule itself, the proof of such non-natural user falling on the party desiring to bring his opponent within the absolute liability of insurance.[84]

With this analysis, Irvine CJ limited *Rylands* to operations carried out on the defendant's own land or at the most on the highway. He did not think that the defendant – a contractor paid by the owner to install a road – was an occupier – but even if it was there was no evidence that the tar-paving of a road – 'not an unusual mode of access' – was not a non-natural use of land hence the plaintiff's claim failed on this ground. Even though not argued, he then considered whether the activity amounted to a nuisance and held it did not. If the escape of fire causing damage was a nuisance, there was no need for the rule in *Rylands*; moreover, the non-natural use limitation would be ineffective as natural use of land was no defence to a nuisance action. Accordingly, any nuisance action would lie not because the thing the defendant created or maintained was likely to do mischief if it escaped but *itself* was likely to escape. Although the jury made no express finding on this point the best inference that could be drawn was that the jury did not regard the paving operations as

---

[81] Ibid., 252.
[82] *Jones v. Festiniog Railway Co.* (1868) LR 3 QB 733; *Powell v. Fall* (1880) 5 QBD 597; *Gunter v. James* (1908) 24 TLR 868; *Mansel v. Webb* (1918) 88 LJKB 323.
[83] J. Salmond, *The Law of Torts*, 6th edn (Stevens and Sons, 1924) 286.
[84] [1928] VLR 247, 254–255.

unsafe in the circumstances.[85] The analysis had already gone beyond what was strictly necessary to determine the case but Irvine CJ went one step further. On the established facts he thought the case fell under a different rule: any person taking in hand an operation known to be dangerous or hazardous unless every care which was reasonably practicable was taken was liable if damage resulted to others and such care was not taken: 'in other words, that the amount of care required is greatest when the danger is greatest'.[86] The undesirable practical consequences of a strict liability rule in Australian conditions were again raised: 'It would, too, be a serious bar on the natural use of grazing lands in Australia if landowners could not burn fire-breaks on their land without becoming liable as insurers to all other owners should the fire spread, though every practical precaution had been taken against it so spreading...'[87] While he thought the spread of the fire may be good evidence of negligence itself, the liability remained fault-based and not strict.

Irvine CJ deserves enormous credit for drawing together the disparate theoretical threads underpinning liability for fire into a coherent whole. His recognition that there were cases where nuisance and *Rylands* could overlap and that *Rylands* 'may merely amount to a definition of one kind of nuisance'[88] presages Lord Goff's analysis in *Cambridge Water Co Ltd v. Eastern Counties Leather plc*[89] nearly seventy years later even if the High Court of Australia chose a different rationalisation of *Rylands* at about the same time.[90] Equally noteworthy is his treatment of the English case law. Certainly he was fortified by Salmond's views but he engaged with the existing English and Australian decisions, teasing out the implications for an explanation of the law that encompassed all heads of liability. And as was often the case the ultimate conclusion was reinforced by consequentialist reasoning unique to the Australian environment.

Fault – Whose Fault?

While *Pett* was infrequently cited in later cases, it seems to have largely[91] marked the end of the road for any special strict liability rule that applied only to fire. The change can be seen in Western Australia where the old rule had hung on longest. In *Mattinson v. Coote*[92] in late 1929, an owner of land sued a contractor for negligently using a motor truck on the land which starting a fire that spread caused damage. At trial Draper J determined liability solely on the basis of negligence. In his view the defendants were not occupiers, a conclusion he found

---

[85] Ibid., 257.
[86] Ibid., 258.
[87] Ibid.
[88] Ibid., 253.
[89] [1994] 2 AC 264.
[90] *Burnie Port Authority v. General Jones Pty Ltd* (1994) 179 CLR 520.
[91] Although not completely: see discussion below.
[92] [1931] WAR 18. See also *WA*, 16 November 1929, 9.

confirmed by *Whinfield*. He also rejected an argument that liability could be imposed in the absence of negligence largely on the basis of the *Pett* reasoning. He had earlier held that the use of motor trucks in farming operations was 'in these days' an ordinary method of farming. The appeal to the Full Court considered only the negligence issue.[93]

While the demise of a special strict liability rule for landowners for fires eradicated one form of strict liability, attention turned to alternate ways in which a landowner might be made strictly liable for the negligence of their employees and independent contractors. In *Bugge v. Brown*, the defendant landowner was sued for damage caused by a fire which had been negligently lit by his employee. The key issue was whether the employer's instructions had limited the scope of the employee's duties so as to make the employee's actions outside the course of employment. This description of the legal problem rather formalises what in reality was a brief conversation between a farmer and his labourers before the latter left to do their work. During the course of preparing for thistle cutting, the employee, the elderly Winter, was given some food for lunch which he was expected to cook. Winter initially said that he had agreed with Brown that he should cook the food in or near an old chimney and it was on this version of the facts that he was convicted before the magistrates of careless use of fire.[94] But a month later he had a change of heart and declared Brown had told him to cook the food at an old homestead, and when he gave this contradictory evidence at the trial leave was given to plaintiff's counsel to treat him as a hostile witness![95] Contrary to the musings of the magistrates, Irvine CJ had no difficulty in finding the act of Winter negligent given the high temperature, brisk wind, and proximity of dry grass to the chimney, but thought the vicarious liability point more difficult.[96] He took the view that the prohibition limited the scope of employment: cooking was no part of Winter's job and the handing of the food to him was linked to a condition as to where to cook the food.[97] A contemporary comment on the case noted that as the usual practice of the defendant was to provide his employees with cooked meat, the 'necessity for cooking was unique' and it was difficult to argue it fell within a general authority to cook as there was no such authority.[98] A majority of the High Court allowed the appeal, including Isaacs J who summarised the law into eleven principles and minutely analysed the facts to show that the employer's responsibility was to provide

---

[93] Ibid., 24–26; *WA*, 28 June 1930, 8. See also *Crowe v. Albany Road Board*, a decision of a local magistrate imposing liability for damage caused by a fire lit to burn scrub as part of road work under *Rylands* and negligence: *Albany Advertiser*, 22 October 1931, 3.

[94] *Donald Times* (Vic), 15 January 1918, 3; *St Arnaud Mercury*, 12 January 1918, 2.

[95] NAA, A10074, 1918/23, *Bugge v. Brown*, Transcript, 5, 11–12, Exhibit F. There was also evidence from a disgruntled ex-employee who backed up Winter's original story and said that Brown had asked him to persuade Winter to say he had been instructed to go to the homestead to cook the food: Transcript, 7.

[96] [1918] VLR 413, 416.

[97] Ibid., 417.

[98] *The Australasian* (Melbourne), 17 August 1918, 39.

food to the employee hence the actions of the employee fell within that general obligation.[99]

Whatever the merits of this approach generally, there was considerable contemporary disquiet because fire was involved. The majority decisions were condemned by elements of the rural landowning (and hiring) class.[100] The case also prompted an attempt at the Victorian Farmers' Union at its annual meeting in September 1919 to pass a resolution favouring legislative delineation of a landowners' responsibilities in the event of fires caused by their employees but it was opposed and ultimately hived off to the executive of the union.[101] But the most powerful critic was Brown himself, who put his case in a letter to *The Argus* shortly after the High Court decision:

> The verdict in the case has caused consternation amongst those people in this immediate district who employ labour in the summer time. No one's financial position is secure if he should employ men of a certain type, yet we employers in the country, in order to get our work done, are forced at certain times of the year to avail ourselves of any men who offer their services… This judgment has very far-reaching effects, and I trust should I be permitted leave to appeal to the Privy Council, that employers both in the country and in the cities, will once again find ourselves placed on a sure footing.[102]

But although it was reported in January 1920 that Brown had obtained leave to appeal to the Privy Council[103] this must have been only a preliminary matter as six months later it was reported in *The Australasian*, somewhat regretfully, that leave had in fact been refused. Determined that this would not be seen as acquiescence, the paper noted that there were many reasons other than the merits why the Privy Council might refuse leave and that 'the danger to pastoralists and other landowners from the existence of such a decision is obvious'. The enthusiasm for the cause detracted somewhat from the legal analysis – the example of a spiteful employee wilfully lighting a fire upon a station which would extend to adjoining stations, and cause incalculable damage and perhaps ruin the employer, was clearly a situation where the employee was acting outside the course of employment – but the sympathy expressed for Brown no doubt represented the view of many landowners in rural areas.[104] Despite the furore, however, there is little evidence that the reasoning in *Bugge v. Brown* was ever seriously challenged. There are no reported cases where it is discussed throughout the remainder of the period, and while odd lower courts found in favour of employers where agricultural workers had deviated from their set work, these were rare.[105]

---

[99] (1919) 26 CLR 110, 116–129.

[100] *Sydney Stock and Station Journal*, 25 April 1919, 16; *Argus*, 1 July 1919, 3; *The Australasian* (Melbourne), 5 April 1919, 31.

[101] *Argus*, 29 September 1919, 8.

[102] *Argus*, 9 April 1919, 10.

[103] *Sydney Stock and Station Journal*, 9 January 1920, 5.

[104] *The Australasian* (Melbourne), 24 July 1920, 8.

[105] *Bennett v. Porter, Benalla Standard*, 6 July 1923, 5. Cf. the magistrate's decision in the case reported in the *Warwick Daily News*, 3 August 1935, 7.

A broader analysis of the scope of an employer's liability for fire was undertaken by Napier J in the Supreme Court of South Australia in *Wardle v. McInnes*,[106] argued in the second half of 1930. Here the plaintiff sued for damage to his land when the defendant employed an independent contractor to fumigate for rabbits which he did by burning off some bracken. This resulted in a fire which eventually spread to the plaintiff's land. Napier J's judgment is important because it explicitly separates two questions that had sometimes been determined together in previous cases: what was the basis of liability for damage caused by the spread of fire, and for whose acts could the owner/occupier be liable irrespective of the basis of liability. On the former question Napier J thought liability was based on the maxim *sic utere tuo ut alienas non laedas* but he interpreted this in accord with *Whinfield* and *Bugge*. The use of fire in the ordinary way for domestic purposes was a natural use of land and involved the 'ordinary duty of care' to prevent injury to one's neighbours. However, an owner was not responsible for the acts of his licensees for *merely* allowing fire to be used on his land (emphasis in original).[107] Conversely, if the use amounted to a nuisance, 'as it must when fire is used for extraordinary purposes involving an unreasonable threat to one's neighbours', the use was at his peril: 'he takes upon himself the absolute duty to prevent it escaping and it is unnecessary to prove negligence.'[108] Between these cases – and presumably here is meant the ordinary domestic use of fire (attracting ordinary care) and the extraordinary use (attracting strict liability) – were 'many other uses involving duties of care appropriate to the circumstances' where fault was the basis of liability.

The second issue, and the one most in issue in *Wardle*, was vicarious liability. Drawing not on any fire cases but on the non-delegable duty of care cases dealing with building work on land, Napier J held the owner liable for the contractor's conduct. The owner was to be taken to have authorised the use of fire given the nature of the task entrusted to the contractor: lighting the fire was not a casual or collateral act vis-a-vis the task the contractor was employed to do.[109] In effect, the authorisation was deemed to have occurred because the defendant should at least have known that fire might be used by the contractor and that might result in damage. Although the contractor had been negligent in lighting the fire, this was not necessarily the reason the owner was liable. The fire was also unlawful as it was contrary to the applicable fire legislation and this non-compliance might make the liability for the fire fall either under *Rylands v. Fletcher* or nuisance which in Napier J's view were not separate grounds of liability: they were both 'an injury in the nature of nuisance'. This would result in the defendant owner being liable: he had the 'duty of taking care that he did not bring McLay upon his land to do this mischief to his neighbours, and

---

[106] [1930] SASR 450.
[107] Ibid., 452.
[108] Ibid. The language suggests this is *Rylands* v. *Fletcher* liability and that this was a form of nuisance.
[109] [1930] SASR 450, 456.

he neglected that duty'.[110] The non-delegable duty rationale is subject to the criticism that it can conflate fault and strict liability – where the contractor was strictly liable under *Rylands* the owner was in breach of a duty to be careful by the contractor's conduct that itself was not careless – but one should not be too hard on Napier J; attempts to explain non-delegable duty remain elusive even today. Suffice to say that the removal of the ownership or occupation of land per se as the basis for imposing strict vicarious liability for fires lit on that land required a further elaboration of when the owner was liable for a fire lit by others and Napier J attempted to do this. But whatever the reasoning he was happy the result reached was just:

> If any landholder is obliged, or desires, to have this work done at a time when it is unlawful or dangerous to burn, I think that it is a fair thing – as between neighbours – that he should employ servants or agents for whom he is responsible, rather than escape liability by employing a contractor, who has the inducement offered by a lump sum contract, to do the work in the easiest way, irrespective of the risk to other people.[111]

Perhaps this sentiment appealed to the High Court, whose members found no difficulty in dismissing the appeal.[112] There was no need for a broad excursus into the law relating to fires: the question was treated as one of non-delegable duty and once it was accepted that the owner knew or ought to have known that fire would be used, liability was imposed. Whether this vicarious liability rested on the contractor's fault was not determined. Evatt J's short judgment suggested fault was required. Relying on Privy Council authority – *Black v. Christchurch Finance Co.*[113] – he stated that once the use of fire was authorised by the owner there was a duty to 'neighbouring landowners to see that reasonable care is exercised to prevent the fire from spreading… The occupier himself must see to it that due care is taken by the independent contractor and his servants'.[114] But while reaching the same result Dixon J took a slightly different path. In a similar vein to Napier J, he held that to burn vegetation at that time 'must be considered as introducing an exceptional danger and not as an incident natural or proper in the use of land in an ordinary manner'.[115] The duty of the occupier to take care that the land was used and operations carried out so that 'his neighbours are not exposed to injury by exceptional dangers' was 'not confined to dangers arising from acts of himself or his servants'.[116] The earlier reference to natural use of land suggests that Dixon J saw the owner's liability as rooted in the strict liability for the spread of fire within the rule in *Rylands v. Fletcher*. The

---

[110] Ibid., 457.
[111] Ibid.
[112] (1931) 45 CLR 548.
[113] [1894] AC 48.
[114] (1931) 45 CLR 548, 552.
[115] Ibid., 551.
[116] Ibid., 552.

other judges in the High Court relied simply on the *Black* decision as author-ity for a non-delegable obligation arising in these circumstances. But Napier J had also pointed out that in *Black* Lord Shaw 'seems to hesitate between the view of an absolute or a qualified duty, with respect to preventing the escape of fire, lighted for the purpose of burning off, in the course of clearing virgin country.'[117] In a country where vast amounts of agricultural work were done through employees and contractors, this was a point of considerable practical importance if anyone was alert enough to take it.[118]

Refinements – The Meaning of Non-natural Use

By the beginning of the 1930s, the legal basis on which liability for fire was imposed had been largely settled. While the precise limits on the vicarious (in its broad sense) liability of an owner for fires lit on his land with his permission were uncertain, there was no doubt that the liability to which this attached was based on either negligence or on *Rylands v. Fletcher*. But in this later action considerable uncertainty remained around the concept of non-natural use and it was to this issue that the leading cases in the final period of this study turned. An early unsatisfactory example (because of the findings of fact) is the deci-sion of the Queensland Supreme Court in *Thompson v. Gosney*.[119] The plaintiff claimed a fire from the defendant's adjoining sugarcane farm had spread and caused damage to his property. The claim at first instance was based on neg-ligence[120] but in the Full Court the plaintiff argued, unsuccessfully, *Rylands* as well as negligence. Of the majority only Webb J considered *Rylands* and stated it was inapplicable without giving reasons[121] but Brennan J, dissenting, thought that there was an unnatural user of land 'inasmuch as the defendant, being a cane farmer who was burning trash and knew there was long grass about, should have taken precaution to get the fire well in hand'.[122] There is a sugges-tion here that non-natural use is a very fact specific concept: it was the circum-stances in which the burning of cane 'trash' took place, rather than burning cane trash considered more abstractly, that determined unnatural use of land. But the more individualised the enquiry the more difficult it was to separate non-natural use from the negligence question, as appears to have happened in Brennan J's judgment.

The meaning of non-natural use in the fire context came up in the last signifi-cant case in this area during the period of this study, *Webber v. Hazelwood*. The events took place in the Urangeline district, south of Lockhart, in the Riverina

---

[117] [1930] SASR 450, 453.

[118] Cf. Lewis, above n 2, 404, where *Black* was rationalised as involving an occupier's liability for the acts of an independent contractor under *Rylands*.

[119] [1933] Qd R 190.

[120] *Daily Mercury* (Mackay), 1 November 1932, 3; 10 November 1932, 2; 24 November 1932, 6.

[121] [1933] Qd R 190, 196.

[122] Ibid., 197.

area of New South Wales. The defendant, a well-known farmer and a member of the local pasture protection board and Lockhart Council, was sued when sparks from a tree stump burnt in a clearing fire several days earlier on his property ignited dry grass causing a fire that spread and damaged the plaintiff's property.[123] The cause of action seems to have been negligence and the evidence and the summing up of the trial judge were addressed to this issue.[124] In response to specific questions the jury found that there was no negligence on the part of the defendant or his agent[125] but also that the fire was not an Act of God. After the verdict counsel for the plaintiff argued that, as Act of God had been negatived, 'it threw on defendant the duty of insurance; He contended that the burning of stubble, was not a natural use of the land, and on the admitted facts it was the duty of defendant to keep the fire in.'[126] This was rejected by the trial judge; the onus was on the plaintiff to establish non-natural use and he refused to direct the jury that burning off at the time of year in question was not a natural and proper use of land.[127] This was no doubt prompted by evidence from both plaintiff and defendant witnesses that it was usual to burn stubble in February in this area even if in breach of the relevant fire legislation.[128]

The appeal to the Full Court of the Supreme Court of New South Wales turned solely on the non-natural use question.[129] Counsel for the plaintiff appellant had some trouble with his argument. Burning stubble might be husbandry, he argued, but it was not a natural use of land to bring a dangerous substance onto it. *Whinfield* was cited in support as well as *Musgrove v. Pandelis*, a difficult case from the English Court of Appeal where the fire had not been lit deliberately.[130] His best argument was that this fire was lit with the purpose that it spread (it was admitted that the aim was to burn out 100 acres of land) and hence was not a domestic or natural user.[131] Counsel for the defendant relied on the trial judge's reasoning: a large majority of farmers in fact burnt off in February and the test was 'for what use and in what way do farmers carry on their operations?'[132] Jordan CJ delivered the only judgment. After reciting the

---

[123] For background see *Albury Banner and Wodonga Express*, 3 March 1933, 41.

[124] *The Lockhart Review and Oakland Advertiser*, 10 October 1933, 2; 17 October 1933, 1, 4; *Daily Advertiser* (Wagga), 11 October, 1933, 3; 12 October 1933, 3.

[125] The fire was lit by the defendant's son but it was accepted that the defendant was liable if lighting that fire attracted liability.

[126] *The Lockhart Review and Oakland Advertiser*, 17 October 1933, 4.

[127] NAA, A10071, 1934/25, *Hazelwood v. Webber*, Transcript Record of Proceedings, 141–143.

[128] There was some ambiguity as to whether the rules had been recently changed to allow burning in February at the time the fire in question was lit but on the plaintiff's own evidence it was clear that 70 per cent of farmers in the region had burnt stubble in February at a time when it would have been unlawful: *The Lockhart Review and Oakland Advertiser*, 10 October 1933, 2.

[129] (1934) 34 SR (NSW) 155.

[130] The case was tactfully dealt with by Jordan CJ by noting it as an authority that any special rule for fire had now been subsumed within *Rylands v. Fletcher*.

[131] (1934) 34 SR (NSW) 155, 156.

[132] Ibid., 157.

now conventional view that any strict liability for fire fell with *Rylands*, he ana-lysed the primary English cases as well as *Whinfield*. In his view, one could not determine the non-natural use question in respect of things present on land by reference to the thing itself. Whether a thing was dangerous or not depended on the quantities and circumstances in which it was present. No use could be regarded as natural or normal if it involved the deliberate bringing upon or into existence something of a kind inherently dangerous to neighbouring land unless introduced 'in such quantities and under such conditions that there is no substantial risk of its escape in such a way as to cause damage in the absence of negligence'.[133] The risk Jordan CJ is referring to here is not the risk that the sub-stance will escape as such but the risk whether it will escape *and cause damage*. It was this second element that made the circumstances all important.

Turning to concrete rural settings, Jordan CJ thought that some things such as sheep, cattle or poultry were regarded as so inherently dangerous to crops that there was always absolute liability for their escape.[134] Although he does not expressly say so, Jordan CJ here brings the old action for cattle trespass within the wider *Rylands* principle. He cites no authority and the attempt is unconvincing. As he pointed out in the next sentence, fire was not treated so drastically and it is hard to see why chickens should be treated as more danger-ous than any kind of fire. But the kernel of the judgment lies in its treatment of fires for agricultural purposes. Any lighting of a fire for ordinary purposes of agriculture or industry 'where the fire is of such magnitude and is used for such purposes that there is no substantial risk of its getting out of hand in such a way as to cause damage in the absence of negligence' came within the principle of *Whinfield*'s case. This applied to fires for domestic purposes, to fires lit to burn out particular (tree) stumps and to fires to burn dead animals or to destroy piles of rubbish. But it did not apply to the fire in this case: it had been lit to spread over a large area of land and this went beyond 'anything which could be said to be the natural ordinary or normal user of the land'.[135] Consistent with an earlier part of his judgment where he said that the usual meaning of the adjectives 'natural', 'ordinary' or 'normal' did not of themselves determine the liability under *Rylands*,[136] it did not matter that it was common in the district to make fires for the purpose of burning off stubble. In doing so he implicitly rejected an argument by the defendant's counsel that natural use of land was a question of fact.[137] Finally, after relying primarily on the English cases for deter-mining the principle, the result was supported by two Australian and two New

---

[133] Ibid., 163.
[134] Ibid.
[135] Ibid., 164.
[136] Ibid., 159.
[137] Cf. Lewis, above n 2, 403, who argued that *Hazelwood* supported the view that this was a question of fact. While recognising the High Court affirmed the decision, he did not appreciate its rejection of this view.

Zealand cases.[138] Given the vastly different geographic and climatic conditions in England it could hardly have been otherwise.

Similar sentiments were expressed by the High Court when the case reached there on appeal.[139] In the joint judgment of Gavin Duffy CJ, Dixon, Rich and McTiernan JJ, the conventional position was restated: the special responsibility arising from the use of fire had come to be regarded as no more than an application of a wider general rule governing the liability of occupiers 'who introduce an agency from which harm may reasonably be expected unless an effective control of it is maintained'.[140] The exception for natural use of land seems to have been seen as a defence; it was a ground of excuse or exception.[141] While it was recognised that allowing an owner to use land was not possible without introducing some risk to neighbours, absolute liability was only imposed where the owner introduced on his land a potential source of harm that required 'continual and effective control to prevent mischief'. Even here, there were limits: when the use of the element or thing which the law regarded as a potential source of mischief was an accepted incident of some ordinary purpose to which the land was reasonably applied, the prima facie rule of absolute liability for the consequences of the escape gave way.[142] But how would this apply in an agricultural context? In an important passage the joint judgment claimed the issue for the courts and found for the plaintiff:

> Now in applying this doctrine to the use of fire in the course of agriculture, the benefit obtained by the farmer who succeeds in using it with safety to himself and the frequency of its use by other farmers are not the only considerations. The degree of hazard to others involved in its use, the extensiveness of the damage it is likely to do and the difficulty of actually controlling it are even more important factors. These depend upon climate, the character of the country and the natural conditions. The question is not one to be decided by a jury on each occasion as a question of fact. The experience, conceptions and standards of the community enter into the question of what is a natural or special use of land, and of what acts should be considered so fraught with risk to others as not to be reasonably incident to its proper enjoyment. In Australia and New Zealand, burning vegetation in the open in midsummer has never been held a natural use of land.[143]

Starke J delivered a separate judgment which, while concurring, expressly recognised the contingent nature of the 'natural use' enquiry. 'The law relating to legitimate enjoyment of lands must necessarily develop as conditions alter and methods improve', he said, and '[w]hat may be regarded as a dangerous and

---

[138] *Sheehan v. Park* (1882) 8 VLR 25; *Piper v. Geary* (1898) 17 NZLR 357; *Kelly v. Hayes* (1903) 22 NZLR 429; *Council of the City of Newcastle v. Australian Agricultural Company Ltd* (1929) 29 SR (NSW) 212.

[139] (1934) 52 CLR 268.

[140] Ibid., 275.

[141] Cf. Irvine CJ's views in in *Pett*, above n 84.

[142] (1934) 52 CLR 268, 277.

[143] Ibid., 278.

extraordinary use of lands in one generation may well, in another, become but an ordinary and legitimate enjoyment of those lands'.[144] This change might well be a question of fact but he agreed with the joint judgment both that the burning off in this case was not a reasonable or natural use of land, irrespective of the evidence as to the prevalence of this use, and that the question was one for the judge and not the jury.

While the separation of fault-based liability and strict liability under *Rylands* for damage resulting from the spread of fire underpins the judgments – both in the Full Court and the High Court – in *Hazelwood*, there was considerable scope for the two bases of liability to be merged as a result of the focus on context in the non-natural use enquiry. This is evident in two South Australian decisions that followed *Hazelwood*. In *McCarty v. Leeming*[145] two members of the Supreme Court of South Australia in obiter, and one as his ratio, held that the burning off of domestic rubbish in a residential backyard occupied by the defendants could be a non-natural use of land. Unlike *Hazelwood*, where time, place and circumstance were considered at a fairly generic level (e.g. burning off stubble in midsummer), the 'circumstance' considered here was in relation to the actual fire that caused the damage (five feet from a boundary fence). If non-natural use was to be decided at this level of granularity, it would become difficult in practice for it to extend liability beyond what would be imposed in negligence and it is no surprise that Cleland J also found 'if relevant' that the lighting of the fire 'in the circumstances' amounted to negligence.[146]

The same issue arose six years later in *Tolmer v. Darling*.[147] The case involved liability for damage associated with a fire that started when the car one of the defendants was driving passed over a drain, causing the charcoal used as part of a gas-producing unit in the motor vehicle to spill out and set fire to adjoining herbage. While Richards J decided the case on the basis of negligence, the arguments at trial had primarily canvassed strict liability as the defendant's defence was that the driver neither knew of nor ought to have known what had happened to the gas unit. While obiter, Richards J's discussion of non-natural use is nonetheless instructive. The specific gas-producer was not dangerous; if care was used in installing and using it, it was not a source of danger. More generally, by the experience, conceptions and standards of the community – the language of *Hazelwood* – the use of gas-producers 'for obtaining the motive power of vehicles on the public roads had become a natural or ordinary use of the roads'.[148] In other words, considered as a class, the use of gas-producers viewed generally was a natural use. This was the level of abstraction required by *Hazelwood*. But immediately after, Richards J said that this did not necessarily dispose of the question of absolute liability 'when applied to the particular

---

[144] Ibid., 281.
[145] [1937] SASR 432.
[146] Ibid.
[147] [1943] SASR 81.
[148] Ibid., 85.

producer which was attached to the defendant's car on the occasion in question or when applied to the use which was being made of it on that occasion'.[149] As in *McCarty*, this individualised enquiry into the precise use of the producer made it almost impossible to separate the factors that would make such use negligent from those that determined the non-natural use requirement.[150]

The final cases on fire in the period of this study demonstrate two related points. The first is that, even though throughout the period there were increasingly certain judicial pronouncements as to the basis of the liability, plaintiffs' counsel periodically continued to argue for varying forms of 'stricter' liability. Hence in *Collins v. Commonwealth of Australia*[151] the plaintiff demurred to a plea that the fire that spread and caused damage had been lit in a confined enclosure for the purposes of cooking a meal and there was no negligence in it escaping. Jordan CJ in the Full Court of the Supreme Court of New South Wales had little difficulty in finding the plea not demurrable: a fire lit for domestic purposes of warming a room or cooking did not attract liability in the absence of negligence.[152] He might have added that this had been the law for the previous thirty years.

The second point was that, by the end of the period, the non-natural use component of the *Rylands* action was increasingly a limiting factor in applying strict liability and this may have encouraged recourse to the almost mythical 'ancient' liability rule for fire. Both of these issues can be seen in the final case for the period, *The Commissioner of Railways v. Wise Bros Pty Limited*,[153] in 1946. The defendant ran a flour mill from where a fire had started and spread to the plaintiff's adjoining property, damaging buildings, plant and rolling stock. The plaintiff's rather curious pleading alleged three causes of action: negligence, non-natural use and negligence and non-natural use. While most of the argument at trial, and before the Full Court of the Supreme Court of New South Wales and the High Court, considered whether the defendant had been guilty of negligence in the precautions they had taken to prevent the spread of fire, the trial judge had held that the use of the land as a flour mill was 'not unnatural'[154] and this provided the opportunity for the strict liability question to be resurrected on appeal. And while the 'having two bob each way' pleadings might be explicable forensically, they were also rooted in a belief that the law as to special rules for fire remained uncertain. Both Jordan CJ and Davidson J seemed to agree: the former described the law as involving 'considerable obscurity'[155]

---

[149] Ibid.

[150] On the general point see D. Williams, 'Non-natural use of land' [1973] *CLJ* 310 although none of the cases discussed here are mentioned. It was assumed without argument that *Rylands* would apply on the facts.

[151] (1945) 62 WN (NSW) 245.

[152] Ibid.

[153] (1947) 47 SR (NSW) 233.

[154] *Jerilderie Herald and Uran Advertiser*, 17 October 1946, 3.

[155] (1947) 47 SR (NSW) 233, 238.

while the latter said the case 'involved another of the troublesome problems' arising from damage resulting from the spread of the fire.[156]

Jordan CJ's comment is somewhat puzzling. Twelve years earlier, in *Webber v. Hazelwood*, he had succinctly described the law for fires brought into existence deliberately or negligently as falling within *Rylands* in the modern law. The problem in *Wise* seems to have been that while the defendant did bring a fire onto the land deliberately – part of its production process involved using a boiler and fire box – there was no evidence linking that fire with the fire that actually started on the defendant's premises. In what must be thought of as something of a long shot, plaintiff's counsel tried to reinvigorate the supposed old common law rule for strict liability for accidental fires on land even though it was clear that this rule no longer applied for fires deliberately or negligently started by the owner, a situation where the justification for applying the rule would seem to be stronger. Unsurprisingly, any notion of strict liability for accidental fires was rejected on appeal to the Full Court of the Supreme Court of New South Wales, Jordan CJ holding that the special rule for fire required both that the fire was brought into existence by the owner or by someone for whom he was responsible, and that this was in the course of a use which was not natural, ordinary or normal.[157] But if accidental fires were not covered by any strict liability rule, did they subject the occupier to any liability rule? Foreshadowing *Hargrave v. Goldman*[158] – and without reference to the contrary ruling in *Havelberg v. Brown*[159] – Jordan CJ held, relying on *Sedleigh Denfield v. O'Callaghan*,[160] that an occupier of land who found a fire on the land caused by accident or by a third party came under a duty to use reasonable means to extinguish or prevent it from spreading.[161] In this way accidental fires were brought within the usual fault-based liability of occupiers for damage caused by fires started on their land.

The plaintiff appealed to the High Court where the main issue – and undoubtedly the cause of the appeal – related to evidence of negligence but plaintiff's counsel also submitted that *Hazelwood v. Webber* did not prevent the plaintiff from succeeding on the strict liability argument.[162] The *Hazelwood* court did not consider the propositions before this court; while it afforded the defendant another means of defence, 'it does not affect the plaintiff's right to have his case determined on the basis of absolute liability'.[163] This argument rested in part

---

[156] Ibid., 241.
[157] Ibid., 239.
[158] (1963) 110 CLR 40.
[159] [1905] SALR 1.
[160] [1940] AC 880.
[161] (1947) 47 SR (NSW) 233, 239. The slightly earlier New Zealand Supreme Court decision reaching the same conclusion (departing from its earlier no liability rule) in *Boatswain* v. *Crawford* [1943] NZLR 109 (noted in 'New Zealand Letter' (1943) 17 *ALJ* 90) was not cited.
[162] (1947) 75 CLR 59.
[163] Ibid., 64.

on the ruling in the High Court in *Hazelwood* that the Fires (Metropolis) Act 1774 s. 86 was not in force in New South Wales but it received little discussion in the High Court. Most substantively, Latham CJ held that the common law relating to fire was authoritatively stated in *Hazelwood* and as the finding that the use of land was not non-natural was unimpeachable there could be no strict liability. He also noted that there was no evidence that the fire that had been brought on to the land was the fire that caused the damage; on this ground too the case did not fall within the strict liability rule.[164] Starke, McTiernan and Williams JJ held simply that the use was not non-natural. All members of the court except Rich J – who did not consider the issue – were fortified in their views by the very recent decision of the House of Lords in *Read v. J Lyons & Co. Ltd*,[165] a case in which the non-natural use requirement was emphasised and which, according to Williams J, was in accord with the view of non-natural use taken in *Hazelwood v. Webber*. This was true only at a formal level and the obiter finding in *Read v. Lyons* – that the manufacture of munitions in a time of war was a natural use of land – was a long way from the fire in issue in *Hazelwood* but it illustrated the malleability of the non-natural use concept. But more importantly, *Read v. Lyons* stressed the exceptional nature of the liability under *Rylands* and the importance of non-natural use to this action. The same point had been made explicitly nearly twenty years earlier by Irvine CJ in *Pett*. This increased reluctance to find a use non-natural combined with the increasing specificity with which the non-natural use enquiry was made effectively emasculated strict liability for fire on any grounds in Australia.[166]

'Smoke gets in your eyes' – Concluding Reflections

It is easy to see the history of litigation surrounding damage caused by fire as a simple progression from older ideas of strict liability to the more modern paradigm of fault-based liability. Viewed from a suitable altitude this is a largely correct synopsis. What the analysis of the Australian case law shows is that looking at the start and end points can sometimes obscure the path by which that end point was reached. There was no linear progression from strict to fault-based liability nor was there a consistent view that fault-based liability for damage caused by the escape of fire was the most equitable way to allocate losses caused in this way. The machinations of the state courts as well as the High Court reveal a composite array of factors at play: the precedential value of general principles of English law, the differentness of the Australian environment, and the continuing need to reconcile the Australian factors with changes

---

[164] Ibid., 68.

[165] [1947] AC 156.

[166] See, for example, *Eastern Asia Navigation Co. Ltd v. Freemantle Harbour Trust Commissioners* (1951) 83 CLR 353 where Latham CJ and Kitto J held that the use of dieseline by ships in Freemantle Harbour was a natural use of land.

to the English principles which were universally accepted as forming the cornerstone of the law. Within this matrix, however, there are three features that merit special comment.

The first, noted earlier, was the tenacity with which notions of a special strict liability for damage caused by the escape of fire retained currency in Australia. Accepting that not too much should be read into decisions by counsel to make arguments in the instrumental desire to win cases, it nonetheless remains the fact that right up to the end of the period, in the *Wise* case, it was still thought that strict liability was worth raising as a potential ground of liability. This was in part due to the necessary deference paid to the somewhat inscrutable English law that surrounded special liability rules for fire and its uneven application in Australian jurisdictions but its longevity also suggests that the idea itself was not inconsistent with community standards of fairness. In a contemporary comment on *Hazelwood* it was noted that Canadian courts had been anxious to relax the effects of the rule in *Rylands* and that where fire was started for the purpose of agricultural husbandry negligence was required to establish liability. The reason was entirely pragmatic: in a new country, not closely settled, the application of the doctrine of absolute liability was likely to discourage the desired and essential economic development.[167] That such arguments did not prevail in Australia (or New Zealand) suggest that the retention of a form of strict liability was based on a conscious choice to protect innocent farmers from, in Australian conditions, a highly dangerous if at times beneficial farming practice. The reluctance to see non-natural use as a question of fact reinforces the notion that this was a judgment not to be watered down by sympathetic local juries. This is reinforced in the cases from the earlier part of this study. The helplessness of victims is a common theme in counsel's arguments in the cases: in rural communities there was no defence against a fire that went out of control and if one farmer attempted to benefit himself by using an agent known to have this dangerous propensity there was nothing logically or intuitively appealing about preferring that person's interest over those of his neighbour. This philosophy underpins much of the case law on the responsibility of those who lit fires throughout this period, and even when it was authoritatively recognised that strict liability was based on *Rylands*, the interpretation of the non-natural use requirement in *Hazelwood* was careful to respect this tradition. And even if the non-natural user limitation was to effectively end one kind of strict liability, the imposition of the non-delegable duty of care recognised in *Wardle v. McInnes* imposed another.

The reasons for the somewhat Janus-faced view in relation to liability for fire can be seen in the ambiguous relationship fire had to the Australian environment. As Stephen Pyne points out, fire was central to the 'Europeanising' of the

---

[167] J. Shatin, 'Burning off' (1935–38) 1 *Res Judicatae* 68.

Australian landscape and to the opening up of land for white settlement.[168] Its use, however, involved something of a Faustian bargain: while fire was necessary to make the country suitable for settlement it also threatened those very settlements when it escaped into an uncontrollable bushfire. Moreover, as basic settlement gave way to more established land uses – which even at the beginning of this study was the predominant model – any community of interest in the use of fire rapidly dissipated into a series of incompatible self-interested practices. As Pyne argues:

> Even among the Europeans there were incompatibilities. The fire practices of the grazier did not synchronise with those of the farmer, and both challenged the fire expectation of the forester. The miner burned everyone's land indiscriminately. The urbanite understood only the terror of the bushfire. Each of these groups so evolved, moreover, that practices suitable for one time and place were unacceptable at a later time. The 'white blackfellow' hunting kangaroo and loosely herding semiwild ponies – a vanguard of early settlement – became anathema as farming matured and as forestry claimed jurisdiction over the wooded bush. The pastoralist burning his snow lease became anachronistic in an age of pasture improvement with 'sub and super'. The selector waiting for a blistering northerly before lighting up his few acres of new slash amid a forest thick with ring-barked tinder menaced the wheat fields and paddocks of more established farmers.[169]

In light of these competing visions for the appropriate use of fire, it is no surprise that there was no consensus – at law or elsewhere – on the appropriate liability standard for fire. Even when forestry became more important after the First World War, professional foresters could not agree on the role, if any, for fire in the management and protection of forests. But there was one constant throughout the period of this study: the periodic large-scale conflagrations that consumed large areas of (particularly) Victoria, South Australia and New South Wales caused by too carefree an attitude to the risks caused by fire.[170] As Collins notes in relation to the devastating 'Black Friday' fires of 1939, the evidence presented to the subsequent Royal Commission revealed that 'Australia was a nation of fire lighters who constantly, deliberately and often carelessly lit fires everywhere and in all seasons, including the height of summer.'[171] While it is tempting to see the confining of strict liability for fire damage within the *Rylands* exception and then the emasculation of that exception as Whiggish progression, it should be remembered that in *Hazelwood v. Webber* non-natural

---

[168] S. Pyne, *Burning Bush: A Fire History of Australia* (Allen and Unwin, 1991) 244. For a rustic literary example see S. Rudd, 'Starting the Selection' and 'The Night We Watched for Wallabies' in *Dad and Dave* (Angus and Robertson, 1964 reprint, first published in 1903 in *On Our Selection*). Pyne himself cites the more cerebral example of Patrick White's *The Tree of Man* (Penguin, 1961, first published 1956).

[169] Pyne, above n 168, 185.

[170] For example, see Pyne's description of the causes of the 'Black Sunday' fires of 1926: Ibid., 270,

[171] P. Collins, *Burn* (Allen and Unwin, 2009, first published 2006) 60.

use was interpreted so as to *impose* strict liability. The facts of that case are illustrative of the kinds of conflict between fire users noted by Pyne and the emphatic emphasis that non-natural use was a question of law suggests a reluctance to jettison strict liability as a loss allocation tool where fire escaped and caused damage. And if by the end of the period of this study strict liability for the spread of fire had effectively been curtailed, this was not simply the result of the importation of English authority. As Pyne comments:

> Australia could not abolish bushfires any more than they could abolish the bush but they had to engage both constructively… How Australians used and reacted to fire thus encapsulated how they lived and related to Australia. Reforms in fire practices demanded a reformed bush, as it would help create, a reformed bushman; a new Australia necessitated a new Australian.[172]

The flexibility of fault-based liability, in particular the ability to impose a very high standard of care, was well able to take account of the new Australian's different kind of engagement with fire.

The second point worth noting is the virtually non-existent relationship between the legislative framework surrounding fire and civil claims for damage caused by fire. Legislation regulating the use of fire was amongst the earliest legislation introduced by the self-governing colonies.[173] The detail of this legislation is beyond the scope of this book but in general it became increasingly detailed and prescriptive during the course of the twentieth century. Yet it is surprising how little of this legislation featured in civil litigation associated with damage caused by fire.[174] The primary discussion of the legislative framework arose in relation to negligence and the use of statutory standards to prove breach of duty. While Australian courts never bought into 'statutory' negligence, the legislative standards acting only as a guide,[175] there was something slightly incongruous about the relatively detailed statutory regulation on the one hand and its lack of influence in setting standards when injury resulted from the very risk the regulation was intended to alleviate. This issue was not unique to fire regulation but fire legislation was primarily concerned with risk rather than with other regulatory functions as was the case with traffic legislation (for example). More generally, the legislative framework within which the use of fire was regulated was largely ineffective. Collins notes that evidence to

---

[172] Pyne, above n 168, 317.

[173] See for example An Act to restrain the careless use of Fire 1854 (Vic); Ordinance to Diminish the Dangers resulting from Bush Fires 1847 (WA); An Act for regulating Buildings and for preventing Mischiefs by Fire in the Town of Launceston 1853 (Tas); Careless Use of Fire Prevention Act 1866 (NSW); Bush Fires Act 1854 (SA); Careless Use of Fires Prevention Act 1865 (Qld).

[174] The standard clause provided only that nothing in the legislation, or criminal proceedings for breach, affected a civil claim for damage although the precise wording differed among jurisdictions: compare Rural Fires Act (Qld) 1927 ss. 11, 27; Careless Use of Fires Act 1912 (NSW) s. 9; Bush Fires Act 1913 (SA) s. 25, and *Hazelwood v. Webber* (1934) 52 CLR 268, 275.

[175] As the trial judge directed in *Hazelwood*: *The Lockhart Review and Oaklands Advertiser*, 17 October 1933, 4.

the Royal Commission after the Black Friday fires of 1939 was that hardly anyone was ever charged so that 'rural fire lighting continued unabated despite the
law'.[176] The ambiguity that surrounded the content of such legislation and the
ambivalence that characterised attitudes to compliance with it is demonstrated
by the evidence of the protagonists in *Hazelwood v. Webber*. The defendant,
a member of the Orana Shire Council, did not profess any knowledge of the
requirements imposed on burns by the Careless Use of Fires Act 1912 while the
plaintiff also admitted to failing to comply with the legislation and that he knew
of only one farmer on one occasion who had ever complied with the requirement for a fire-break of a certain size![177] This impotence no doubt contributed
to its invisibility but it nonetheless remains surprising that counsel did not
attempt to argue by analogy with the legislative standards more than they did.

The development of the liability rules for fire within Australia reveals one
further subtlety. When reading all but McHugh J's judgment in *Burnie Port
Authority v. General Jones Pty Ltd*,[178] there is a sense that strict liability was
seen, and perhaps was always seen, as anomalous in Australian conditions.
Hence in the joint judgment, the '*ignus suus*' (strict liability for fire) rule was
said to be formulated as 'appropriate to urban circumstances in medieval
England' and that 'though fire is an exceptional hazard in Australia, contemporary conditions in this country have no real similarity to urban conditions
in medieval England where the escape of domestic fire rivalled plague and war
as a cause of general catastrophe'.[179] Similarly, Brennan J thought it arguable
that the 'natural and social conditions of this wide brown continent' made
absolute liability rules for the escape of fire an intolerable burden.[180] While
it is tempting to see the rejection of strict liability by the end of the period of
this study, whether under a special liability rule or under *Rylands*, as a fairly
explicit rejection of English rules that were inapplicable in Australia, the problem is that a detailed analysis of the cases shows that the rejection of special
rules for fire was not a foregone conclusion. There is no suggestion in the pre-
Whinfield cases that strict liability for fire was an inappropriate English rule
being forced onto reluctant Australian judges. Rather, what is striking is the
willingness with which strict liability was upheld. This was not – or not just –
because there was a line of English cases based on mediaeval policy concerns
that had to be applied. Strict liability was not the only response to damage
caused by fire but neither was it so out of touch with perceptions about fair
loss distribution that it was frowned upon as inherently un-Australian. This
was especially so when the fire was deliberately lit by the defendant or someone for whom he was responsible rather than by mere licencees (and even here

---

[176] Collins, above n 171, 55.
[177] A10071, above n 127, Transcript Record of Proceedings, 7–8, 117.
[178] (1994) 179 CLR 520.
[179] Ibid., 534.
[180] Ibid., 565–566.

the liability of the landowner was stricter than usual because of the vicarious liability for the negligence of independent contractors). All of this might lead us to be slightly sceptical about suggestions that the rejection of any special liability rules for fire was because of an inherent unsuitability for Australian conditions. To the contrary, the evidence is that Australians and Australian courts were at the very least open to alternatives to fault-based liability in this area. To focus overly on the form of the legal rule risks missing the important contemporary social dynamics that recognised the Jeckyll and Hyde nature of fire use in Australian contexts and supported the application of legal rules long after they became largely obsolete in England. In fact, liability for fire was a rare example of where it was thought *colonial* courts set out the contemporary law which might be followed in England.[181]

Other Noxious Elements

While fire was the most pervasive of risks of (certainly) rural Australia, it was not the only one. At the start of the period of this study, 'prickly pear' was an endemic problem in Queensland and New South Wales, resulting in a variety of legislative attempts to eradicate the plant.[182] In 1907, in *Osborne v. Sparke*, a Muswellbrook farmer attempted to impose liability on a neighbour whom he alleged had failed to control the prickly pear on his property. The plaintiff argued that the spread of the plant had caused holes in the dingo-proof fence that separated his property from the defendant's with the result that dingos had entered and killed many sheep. Even a cursory glance at the pleadings indicate that the action would have its difficulties: for example, exactly how causation would be proved was an immediately obvious problem.[183] But the defendant was unwilling to surrender his fate to a jury verdict and demurred to the statement of claim.

There was good reason for the defendant's course of action. The claim was based in trespass and nuisance but it did not allege that the prickly pear was brought on to the land by the defendant or that the defendant had been careless in his management or control of the land. Nor was *Rylands v. Fletcher* pleaded. As Griffith CJ put it in the High Court, the case 'rested entirely upon the presence of the prickly pear on the defendant's land extending up to and injuring

---

[181] (1915) 59 *Sol J* 785, discussing the Full Court of Supreme Court of South Australia's decision in *Young* v. *Tilley* [1913] SALR 87 which by the time of the article had, paradoxically, been sidelined by *Whinfield*.

[182] See, for example, Prickly-pear Destruction Act 1901 (NSW); Prickly Pear Selections Act 1901 (Qld), Prickly-Pear Destruction Act 1912 (Qld).

[183] The defendant pleaded that the fence was defectively constructed and in poor repair so that dingoes could enter the property irrespective of any damage caused by prickly pear and that 'all the country round the plaintiff's station swarms with dingoes and that station itself has never been free of them': NAA, A10071, 1907/35, Sparke v. Osborne, Transcript Record of Proceedings, Amended Statement of Defence.

the fence'.[184] In more general terms, the question was whether an occupier of land could be liable in nuisance (trespass was not argued) where the nuisance consisted merely of something that was naturally present on the land which caused an interference with a neighbour's use and enjoyment of land. English case law had imposed liability in nuisance where an occupier's trees had spread but it was, at the most favourable for the plaintiff, uncertain as to whether the liability was limited to where the trees had been planted or otherwise used by the occupier.[185] This was important because in *Giles v. Walker* the English Court of Appeal had rejected a claim by an occupier for damage caused by the spread of wild thistle from his neighbour's property.[186] Almost as succinctly as the Court of Appeal had rejected the action in *Giles v. Walker*, Simpson CJ in Equity rejected the defendant's demurrer. Citing no cases, he held that if a man allowed trees to overhang his neighbour's land and cause damage, this was a nuisance which the neighbour could abate or for which he could bring an action for damages. The source of the tree made no difference:

> [I]t makes no difference in principle whether trees have been planted by the defendant or his predecessors or whether they are of natural growth, nor whether they are valuable property or merely noxious weeds; in each case if they have been *allowed* to overhang and do damage the above remedies are available.[187]

The italicisation of 'allowed' (in the original) suggests that Simpson CJ was basing liability on something more than the mere presence of the prickly pear. The defendant had argued that any liability was based on the maxim *sic utero tuo ut alienum non laedas* and that there was in fact no use of the land. Perhaps Simpson CJ thought that by emphasising that the defendant had allowed the prickly pear to exist this difficulty could be overcome.

Given the practical significance of the decision to landowners, it is no surprise it was appealed directly to the High Court. To force a landowner to take steps to eradicate prickly pear in his neighbour's interest had serious implications: as counsel for the appellant defendant argued, the first instance decision 'would render the defendant liable for every kind of noxious thing that came from his land to the plaintiff's land'.[188] In response, plaintiff's counsel was forced into making a controversial and difficult submission. Aware of *Giles v. Walker*, he accepted that there was no liability for the spread of weeds where the spread was caused by seeds germinating as these were independent plants but 'if the plant which causes the damage remains part of the parent stem' the owner was liable. More dramatically, he argued that every owner of land was under a duty

---

[184] *Sparke v. Osborne* (1908) 7 CLR 51, 56.
[185] *Crowhurst v. Amersham Burial Board* (1878) 4 Ex D 5; *Lemmon v. Webb* [1894] 3 Ch 1; *Smith v. Giddy* [1904] 2 KB 448.
[186] (1890) 24 QBD 656.
[187] *Osborne v. Sparke* (1907) 7 SR (NSW) 842, 845.
[188] *Sparke v. Osborne* (1908) 7 CLR 51, 54.

to prevent things growing on his land from injuring his neighbours and that in England no distinction between cultivated trees and wild growths had been made. Griffith CJ retorted: 'There is no analogy between the conditions in this country and those in England', an observation only reinforced by counsel's response that the only difference was that 'there are more wild growths here than there'.[189]

The High Court unanimously allowed the appeal. Griffith CJ's judgment intertwined analysis of English authority with an application of the law that was sensitive to Australian conditions. If there was no liability for allowing thistles to spread to a neighbour's land, there was no liability for the spread of prickly pear. If there was any difference between the plants it was 'that a person who is afflicted by having prickly pear on his land is perhaps more deserving of sympathy than the man who has only thistles'.[190] Neither was he impressed with the 'stem' argument: if this was the rule it was 'founded on some strange caprice such as one certainly would not expect to find in the common law'.[191] But equally important was the consequentialist reasoning in support of his conclusion: 'Anyone who has seen prickly pear growing as it grows in some parts of Queensland, for instance, knows that it would cast an intolerable burden upon the owner of land if he were compelled to warrant all his neighbours from its spreading into their land.'[192] O'Connor J too was influenced by the nature of the plant, variously described by him as a pest and noxious weed, in support of his decision. If the first instance decision was correct, he said, a 'very heavy burden' was placed on all landowners on whose land prickly pear was growing.[193] By way of contrast, Isaacs J studiously avoided any reference to prickly pear, his judgment considering the liability for the damage caused by the natural spread of plants 'of any kind'.

Sparke v. Osborne had little lasting effect on the law although its contemporary importance should not be disregarded.[194] Apart from a brief supportive reference in a case involving swine fever in New South Wales in 1920,[195] it figures little in Australian case law before it was effectively reversed in *Hargrave v. Goldman* in 1963.[196] It was powerfully criticised by the English academic A.L. Goodhart in 1930 in the course of arguing for an opposite conclusion,[197] most

[189] Ibid., 55.
[190] Ibid., 59.
[191] Ibid.
[192] Ibid.
[193] Ibid., 67.
[194] The High Court decision was noted in a wide variety of newspapers of regional NSW (Maitland, Scone, Lismore, Wagga Wagga, Wellington, Albury) and Queensland (Townsville, Charters Towers, Darling Downs, Rockhampton) as well as daily papers in Sydney, Adelaide, Launceston and Perth.
[195] *Ruhan v. The Water Conservation and Irrigation Commission* (1920) 20 SR (NSW) 439, 444.
[196] (1963) 110 CLR 40.
[197] A.L. Goodhart, 'Liability for things naturally on land' [1930] *CLJ* 13, 28–29.

of which was unjustified,[198] but was more influential in the United States where it was said to have influenced the First Restatement's view that the occupier had no liability for damage caused by natural conditions.[199]

From a broader perspective, however, the decision is consistent with the approach increasingly taken in the fire cases throughout the period of this study. While agreeing with the result, O'Connor J refused to hold that there could never be any circumstances where overhanging trees or growth were actionable. It could be a nuisance but 'there must have been some act done by the landowner in the use of his land which rendered the wild growth more likely to injure, or there must have been some use or adoption of it by the land-owner which put him in the same position as the growth brought by him upon his land.'[200] A deliberately planted hedge, like a deliberately lit fire, might be sufficient to impose liability, although it was unclear whether the liability in nuisance for the hedge matched the strict liability for fire, whether under its own rule or under *Rylands v. Fletcher*. While there was no explicit link made between these two areas of liability for the escape of things on the land, the idea is the same. It was one thing to impose stricter forms of liability for things brought onto the land: by the time of this study the damage caused by attempts to 'acclimatise' Australia by introducing non-native flora and fauna, of which prickly pear and rabbits were the best known examples, was self-evident, and if one wanted the potential benefits of this course of conduct one took the risks as well. But it was quite another thing to foist a common law obligation to do something to eradicate natural dangers for which the occupier was not responsible. Even if the inspiration was English, the 'no liability for nonfeasance' rule fitted with Australian perceptions about what was suitable for their land. It also fitted well with the doctrinal basis for imposing liability: one must not *use* his land to the detriment of his neighbour. The problem with this impeccable legal logic, recognised by Way CJ in argument in *Havelberg v. Brown*, was that it produced socially undesirable outcomes when the imbalance between the burden to avoid the risk and the damage caused if the risk materialised was very great.[201] It would take a later Austral-Britain, Sir Victor Windeyer, to articulate

---

[198] Goodhart had two main criticisms. The first was that Griffith CJ was confused between liability associated with non-natural use of land and liability for things naturally on land. This was true but it was not until Stallybrass' article the previous year ([1929] *CLJ* 376) that the importance of the distinction was highlighted. The second was that Griffith CJ based his decision on the fact that the landowner's obligation would be intolerable if liability was imposed yet recognised that legislation imposed a similar duty: apparently, argued Goodhart, 'the burden was not so intolerable when imposed by legislation'. But Goodhart omits the next sentence in the judgment where Griffith CJ dealt explicitly with this point: 'But that is always done by the legislature, and special precautions are taken to endeavour to ensure the common benefit without causing special injustice to the individual' (at 60). Griffith CJ's point was that the less regulated burden of the common law was quite different from the legislative burden.

[199] See D.W. Noel, 'Nuisances from land in its natural condition' (1943) 56 *Harv L Rev* 772, 777–778; G.W. Paton, 'Liability for nuisance' (1942) 37 *Illinois Law Review* 1, 18.

[200] *Sparke v. Osborne* (1908) 7 CLR 51, 70–71.

[201] See above n 14.

a middle course – a duty *to* act to prevent harm to neighbours from the natural condition of the land, but only one of reasonable care – which reconciled the competing demands of legal logic and socially acceptable outcomes.[202]

Conclusion

This chapter has discussed the importance of environment in Australian tort law in the period of this study. The predominance of the fire cases reflects the importance that fire had in Australia in reality and rhetoric. Especially in non-urban environments, Australian courts were confronted with an agent that was both necessary for development but incapable of absolute control. In doing so they discussed liability rules in contexts that were markedly different from the rare excurses into the subject of contemporary English cases. But pestilence came from many sources in Australia and the blight of prickly pear provides another example where Australian courts had to balance the competing interests of landowners to arrive at compromises thought suitable for the British people in the Great Southern Land in a physical environment very different from that of Britain.

[202] See above n 18.

10

Sport and Recreation: Tort Law and the National Pastime 1901–1945

For modern Australians, sport and recreation are at the heart of what it means to be an Australian. The historian Richard Cashman puts it well: 'Our culture of sport – the character of play, the behavior of players and spectators, language, architecture, club identity – has become recognisably Australian, and its importance is generally agreed: most Australians would be surprised by any suggestion that sport was not a cornerstone of Australian life.'[1] During the period of this study, many Australian participated in and/or watched sport and related recreational activities even though, as historians of sport have pointed out, the opportunities for women and marginalised ethnic groups to be involved were limited.[2] This interest in sport can be traced to the origins of white Australia: British colonisation brought British sport and recreational activity to Australia where in the context of vastly different physical and cultural settings sport was a tangible link to the mother country. But while these differences gave sport an important role in defining the national character, they also operated centrifugally to encourage divergence. These changes were subtle rather than radical: while new sports – such as Australian rules football, and surf lifesaving – were rare, conventional sports such as cricket were organised in ways different from England to suit peculiarly Australian environments. By the end of the nineteenth century, '… there was a growing self-confidence within Australia about sport and other issues and Australian participants no longer simply followed a lead set by Britain.'[3] As Stuart Macintyre puts it, the games inherited by the settler societies of England were invested with distinctive local qualities: 'The early blurring of distinctions between the genteel amateur and the plebian professional, better standards of nutrition and health, and the generous provision of facilities made for high standards of performance.'[4]

---

[1] R. Cashman, *Paradise of Sport: The Rise of Organised Sport in Australia* (Oxford University Press, 1995) 205.

[2] Ibid., ch. 5.

[3] W. Vamplew, 'Australians and sport', in W. Vamplew and B. Stoddart (eds.), *Sport in Australia: A Social History* (Cambridge University Press, 1994) 7.

[4] S. Macintyre, 'Prologue', ibid., 6.

This chapter considers the role of tort law in the sporting culture of Australia at the beginning of the twentieth century and its relationship to similar issues in Britain. At the outset, it should be admitted that tort law played a very limited role in sport in both Britain and Australia. The reasons for this are complicated and beyond the scope of this study. No doubt in some sports the 'amateur' concept was influential: amateur sport was valued for its role in character-building[5] and recourse to law might be seen as adversely affecting the purity of the sport. The perceived public benefit of the activity militated against the bringing of private law actions for damages where injury was caused to participants, spectators, or even bystanders. But this can only be a partial explanation because amateur sport existed alongside professional sport and recreational activities where commercial interests provided an incentive to bring claims yet even here actions were rare.[6]

While there are very few reported actions, it is also inaccurate to portray the sporting past as a 'liability-free' zone. Australian courts were asked to make decisions on liability in a wide variety of sporting and recreational contexts and, while the chances of success were very low, the fact that the claims were made at all indicates an acceptance that law had its role in setting the boundaries of what was acceptable 'play' for Australians at leisure.

Three types of actions will be considered in this chapter. The first series of actions considers some early cases where it was established that engagement in a recreational activity was not a ground for limiting the rights of a plaintiff who suffered damage and also considers cases where a participant attempted to sue a fellow participant for injuries resulting from the conduct of that participant. The rare examples from this period suggest that notions of consent or voluntary assumption of the risk operated to prevent most claims, at least in the minds of those who engaged in the activity. The second considers the more common action where a competitor, spectator, other participant or bystander sued the persons or body responsible for organising the activity during the course of which the injury occurred. While cases are also rare in this area as well, there is an interesting divergence between the various types of recreational activity. For example, although examples of actual litigation were rare, contemporary comment on cases from England involving golf and cricket suggests a keen awareness of the possibility that legal actions were just around the corner. The final actions considered concern Australians suing in respect of injuries and losses caused as a result of horse racing, including some (in retrospect) novel claims for pure economic loss both for and against race clubs. The greater frequency of cases reflects the greater commercial underpinnings of horse racing compared

---

[5] R. Cashman, above n 1, ch. 4.

[6] Especially outside horse racing: for a rare exception see *Hill v. Smith*, an action by an Australian Rules footballer, against a masseur (*The Daily News* (Perth), 13 September 1938, 9).

to other sport and recreational activities[7] and evidences a widespread belief that horse racing was the national sport.

Fellow Competitors: No-Go Areas?

From early on in the period of this study it was established that those engaged in recreational activities were generally entitled to the same protection of the law of negligence as those who were not. For example, participants in recreational sailing races successfully sued fellow sailors not engaged in the races for damage caused to their boats resulting from negligent navigation.[8] The law of negligence also came to the aid the Torrens Rowing Club when its eight-oar rowing boat was broken in half by the wash due to the negligent handling of a commercial tug on the Port Adelaide River. Finding for the club in the Port Adelaide Local Court, Sinclair SM affirmed that the racing boat 'had as much right to the river, so long as she observed the rules of navigation, as the larger boat'.[9]

Examples of actions against fellow competitors are much harder to find. There are rare examples of trespass to the person actions being brought but they did not involve incidents that occurred as part of the playing of the game.[10] There was no difficulty in bringing a claim where the parties were jointly engaged in an activity but were not competitors: hence a person who was assisting a cyclist to start a race recovered against the starter of the race when the starter discharged his gun with the result that pellets struck and injured him.[11] But examples where the alleged negligence was that of a fellow competitors are much rarer. In 1910 an action in the District Court of New South Wales involving the owner of a horse against the jockey of another horse that had collided with the owner's horse and caused damage in the course of an exercise gallop was dismissed seemingly on the ground that the defendant jockey was not careless: the press report of the case is thin on detail but there are suggestions that the jockey was not under an obligation to exercise care.[12] A similar case, but this time in race conditions, was commenced in 1927. As a result of an accident during the running of the Richmond Thousand Trotting race in Melbourne

---

[7] Stoddart argues that horse racing should be considered as an industry, a business more than a sport, and placed in a different category: B. Stoddart, 'Reflections past and present' in Vamplew and Stoddart, above n 3, 278. This is reflected in the structure of the chapter.

[8] *SMH*, 13 December 1905, 7; *Evening News* (Sydney), 12 December 1905, 4; *SMH*, 15 December 1905, 4; *Age*, 28 September 1910, 12, 29 September 1910, 5; *Argus*, 29 September 1910, 11.

[9] *The Register* (Adelaide), 14 May 1912, 7.

[10] Often assault cases involving participants in cricket matches, usually involving some form of provocation occurring during the match which resulted in assaults either on the field or after the game had ended: see for example *Argus*, 12 April 1933, 5; *Windsor and Richmond Gazette*, 5 April 1935, 9; *The Telegraph* (Brisbane), 8 January 1930, 2. See also an unusual case involving false imprisonment brought by a gatekeeper at the Sydney Cricket Ground against the Secretary of the NSW Cricket Association: *SMH*, 19 April 1939, 20; 21 April 1939, 13.

[11] *Parisi v. Gallogly*, *The Telegraph* (Brisbane), 2 December 1929, 20.

[12] *Evening News* (Sydney), 15 October 1910, 16.

(during which twelve of the twenty-two starters fell),[13] the driver of the horse that was responsible for the falls, John James, was sued by the owner of one the horses that fell for the loss of the sulky and for the 'loss of the services' of the horse in the Richmond Thousand and further races.[14] The novelty of the claim was indicated by the *Sydney Sportsman*: its headline read 'Driver Toomey Makes Racing History' and it was noted that:

> The lawyers will have no precedent to quote should Toomey's writ come on for hearing, for it may be said without fear of contradiction that it will be the first case of the sort that has ever occupied the attention of a judge, and jury.[15]

The judge and jury never had their say on the race, the action being discontinued six months later and judgment entered for the defendant.[16]

A rare example of a successful action by one competitor against another is *Beyer v. Drews* in 1937.[17] Both plaintiff and defendant were riding in a cycling road race organised by the Bundaberg Wheelers Club. Beyer alleged that during the course of the race Drews elbowed him, causing him to fall onto the road and suffer injuries which kept him off work for three weeks. The defence was not *volenti* – that this was a risk accepted by participants in a race – but contributory negligence through Beyer swaying into Drews. Magistrate A.E. Aitkin found the defendant guilty of negligent riding and awarded damages to Beyer. The novelty of the case is indicated not only by the heading in the press reports[18] but also in the interstate reporting of the decision of a regional magistrate. The Queensland representative of the *Referee* in Sydney thought that the decision (from Bundaberg in North (!) Queensland) 'will have an important bearing on the future control of amateur cycling in Queensland' and that 'in more than 25 years' experience, the writer has never known a similar happening'.[19] Melbourne's *Sporting Globe* commented that the decision would make riders 'more careful' when competing in events.[20]

The only other example of competitor liability found in the period of this study occurred in 1939.[21] Eileen Singer was knocked unconscious while putting on the 9th green on the Brighton municipal links course in Melbourne. She had been hit by a shot played by the defendant, Otho Edgar, who did not think that he could hit his three wood that far but, unexpectedly, played a 'phenomenally good shot', his subsequent shout of 'fore' being ineffective to warn Singer. The

---

[13] *SMH*, 1 November 1927, 14.

[14] Different reports have James suspended by trotting stewards for six or twelve months for his ride: *Sydney Sportsmen*, 15 November 1927, 7; 29 May 1928, 7.

[15] *Sydney Sportsmen*, 15 November 1927, 7.

[16] *Argus*, 18 May 1928, 13; *Age*, 18 May 1928, 12.

[17] *The Courier-Mail* (Brisbane), 27 May, 1937, 17.

[18] E.g. 'Unusual case for damages': *Maryborough Chronicle, Wide Bay and Burnett Advertiser*, 29 May 1937, 8.

[19] *Referee* (Sydney), 3 June 1937, 21.

[20] *Sporting Globe* (Melbourne), 2 June 1937, 10.

[21] *Argus*, 1 November 1939, 2; 2 November 1939, 7; *Age*, 1 November 1939, 13; 2 November 1939, 4.

trial judge in the Second County Court, Book J, accepted expert evidence that a reasonably safe distance between the players for the shot in question was 200 yards and held that the defendant was within that distance when the shot was played. The fact that shots were in practice often taken inside the 'safe' distance was irrelevant: 'It is quite plain that that sort of risk is frequently taken... My view is that if a man does it within that distance he takes the risk of having to compensate anyone he may injure.'[22] As a later comment noted, the case was a warning to future golfers, especially on municipal courses which were generally more crowded and populated with less experienced golfers.[23] There may have been a class bias in this comment: municipal courses were more egalitarian than the exclusive private courses where membership reflected social status rather than ability.[24] But while the case was in one sense a robust affirmation that common practice, even on a golf course, did not determine questions of breach of duty, in another sense the only surprise is that such a case had not succeeded earlier.

The absence until late in the period of this study of a case on golfer liability did not stop contemporary press comment on cases from England and elsewhere where the liability of golfers had been considered.[25] In 1933, a decision of a New York court finding a golfer liable to someone injured off the course when the ball was sliced badly by the defendant was noted[26] and prompted considerable discussion, the *Evening News* in Rockhampton commenting that there was 'always a risk' that negligence could be proved but that a golfer's general insurance would usually cover this kind of risk.[27] As early as December 1933 it was noted that England was well behind Australia in providing insurance for golfers: clubs generally insured their members against hitting and injuring persons outside the course and for injuring caddies[28] and other employees of the club. Golfers were not covered when they hit another member with a ball when a round was being played as clubs 'believe that no member would sue another in such circumstances'. That this belief was by this time unrealistic is evident when the article in the next sentence noted that a member could still be liable if it was shown he was negligent and provided overseas examples of where this had happened.[29]

[22] *Argus*, 2 November 1939, 7.
[23] *Argus*, 3 November 1939, 4.
[24] B. Stoddart, 'Golf', in Vamplew and Stoddart, above n 3, 80–82.
[25] For comment on an early New Zealand case see *The Advertiser* (Adelaide), 15 March 1910, 10; 16 March 1910, 8. (for details see *Manawatu Standard*, 15 March 1910, 6; *Wairarapa Age*, 16 March 1910, 5). More generally see *The Australasian* (Melbourne), 22 July 1922, 59; *Evening News* (Sydney), 19 April 1924 4; 20 November 1936, 4 (repeated from the English *Solicitors' Journal*), *Sydney Sportsman*, 19 April 1927, 6.
[26] *Referee* (Sydney), 24 August 1933, 13.
[27] *Evening News* (Rockhampton), 1 November 1933, 16.
[28] On liability for injury to a caddy see *Examiner* (Launceston), 29 September 1936, 6 (noting an American case and its critical commentary).
[29] *Referee* (Sydney), 7 December 1933, 18.

Perhaps the most interesting 'hypothetical' discussion of competitor liability took place in the context of cricket rather than golf. At the height of the controversy arising out the 1932–3 Ashes series (Bodyline), a barrister mused that, at least for the first time the tactic was used, an action by an injured batsman against the bowler might lie as any implied consent of the batsman would not extend to the risks created by this form of bowling. But once the batsman 'knew what to expect', it would be difficult to recover as by entering the game they would be deemed to accept the risk of injury from the bowling.[30]

During the period of this study, however, all these views were largely expressions of what the future might hold. The Beyer and Singer cases were very rare examples of successful actions against fellow participants, and even where this type of action existed in a slightly variegated form, such as actions by owners against jockeys, no liability was found. But competitor liability was only one context in which litigation could arise out of sporting and recreational activities. Those involved in organising the activity, either though providing the ground or equipment, or managing the conduct of the activity itself, were also exposed to action. In this context, even if Australians could not be described as serial litigators, they showed themselves, at least in some contexts, more willing to sue organisers than competitors.

Golf, Cricket, Rugby – Testing the Water

Actions against organisers of sport and recreational activities have a long history in Australia. One of the earliest cases, from 1915, was a successful action against the starter of a rowing race, it being found by the trial judge in a judge-only trial that he was careless in not delaying the start of a later race with the result that the rowers in two separate races crossed paths and the plaintiff was hit in the head by an oar from another rower. This 'novel' lawsuit was subjected to mildly discontented comment in the Sydney *Referee*[31] and before the Full Court of the Supreme Court of New South Wales, the eminent Sydney barrister H.R. Curlewis 'could find no case which even remotely resembles this' and argued both that the starter was under no duty and, if he was, there was no breach.[32] The judges in the Full Court too seemed to find the plaintiff's case hard to grasp. It was accepted that there were some duties imposed on a judge – such a starting the race on time – but there was no evidence of other duties and the court was reluctant to impose any ad-hoc duties created by the circumstances. It was always 'very easy to be wise after the event', noted Pring J, but it was going too far to say that an earlier storm put a duty of enquiry on the starter

---

[30] *Townsville Daily Bulletin*, 27 February 1933, 3. Criminal liability was a different matter as evidenced by the Law School at the University of Sydney setting a question for students in the criminal law examination based on bodyline bowling and asking about the potential criminal liability of the bowler if a batsman died: *The Evening News* (Rockhampton), 21 February 1933, 12.

[31] *Referee* (Sydney), 17 February 1915, 11.

[32] *Goodsell* v. *Moore* (1915) 15 SR (NSW) 228.

to check whether earlier races had been delayed.[33] There is no sense here of the welfare of the rowers being within any duty assumed by the starter.

Despite this early case, actions against organisers were rare, even in sports like golf, cricket and rugby where the scope for injuries to both spectators and bystanders was greater because of the popularity of the sport and the nature of the game. It is clear, however, that the general expectation was that someone injured would inevitably test the law by bringing an action. This is evident in the commentary surrounding reports of cases from other jurisdictions, mainly English, where actions had been brought. Cricket and golf again were the main targets[34] and the concerns were expressed not only by organisers but also by local councils that allowed sport to be played on their grounds.[35] The matter was sufficiently serious for an article in May 1932 in Local Government section of the *SMH* to be published allaying the fears of local councils.[36] Noting that 'it seems to be a quality of the Australian people that as soon as the first shock of injury is over there comes the feeling that somebody ought to be made to pay', it was argued that the risk of accident from a misdirected golf ball 'was actually very slight'. While recognising that there had been cases from abroad, 'the risks are so small that those councils which are worrying over the matter can set them aside'. A later article inspired by the Bodyline controversy reassured local councils that liability to participants and spectators – which could only be based on occupiers' liability – would be exceptional.[37] But whatever the merits of denying the batsman or spectator a claim, the reasoning could not apply where balls were hit outside the ground with the result that a passer-by was injured. While the article had largely dismissed that risk for local councils, later comment reminded readers that liability turned on a finding on negligence. While the English case which prompted the note – a case against the club by a person hit when a ball was hit out of the club's ground – found against the plaintiff, it was recognised that this was simply a finding on negligence which could vary depending on the facts.

Despite the lingering concerns over liability, only one case was found where liability was imposed on a golf club for injuries to a person hit by a golf ball outside of the course. In the New South Wales District Court, Erna Watson sued a representative of the Northcote Golf Links when a golfer on the course sliced a shot that hit the windscreen of the car she was in and she suffered a facial injury from the splintered glass. Liability, however, was not contested, it being accepted by the defendant that on English authority[38] the defendant was responsible for a nuisance.[39] Four years later, when liability was not conceded,

---

[33] Ibid., 231–232.

[34] *The Express and Telegraph* (Adelaide), 19 September 1918, 4 (bystander injured by cricket ball hit out of the ground).

[35] *Maryborough Chronicle, Wide Bay and Burnett Advertiser*, 3 May 1927, 4.

[36] *SMH*, 26 May 1932, 7.

[37] *SMH*, 19 January 1933, 6.

[38] *Castle v. St Augustine Links* (1922) 38 TLR 615.

[39] *SMH*, 9 December 1936, 23; *Truth* (Sydney), 13 December 1936, 13.

the plaintiff had less success.[40] In September 1939 Cyril Thomson alleged he was a passenger on a tram on Pittwater Road, Manly, when a golf ball from the Manly-Warringah Public Golf Course hit a stanchion of the tram and ricocheted into his nose, breaking it. From the press report the action was based on negligence, and despite the paucity of precautions – it seems there was only a two-strand wire fence five yards from the tee from where the ball was driven – the jury found for the defendant. But the defendant had been refused a non-suit, and the defendant's defence was not just that it exercised reasonable care ('It was impossible to prevent players hitting balls out of the course even if a fence 100ft high were erected') but also that the plaintiff had sued the wrong person: it was the player and not the club that should have been sued. As a decision on carelessness the Thomson decision set no precedent but coming as it did at the end of a long period where even unsuccessful cases were rare, it could be seen as belonging to an earlier era. By the end of the 1930s, as they had done previously, commentators relied on overseas precedents, especially British, to evaluate liability. Those precedents were increasingly suggesting that organisers/occupiers could be liable.[41] In a case where an Irish golfer sued a player and a club, and was awarded damages against the club for injury caused by a golf ball whilst playing on the course, the *Sydney Mail* recognised the decision was a surprise but strongly advocated the result:

> Not only will clubs need to exercise greater care in laying out their courses, but players will also have to avoid the possibility of injuring players by making their shots carefully. On too many occasions there is a lack of the ordinary rules of common-sense.[42]

Cricket and even rugby were coming under the spotlight. The decision in an English case, where a schoolboy had successfully recovered damages against a school when playing in a game of school cricket, was commented upon. The boy was fielding at silly mid-on less than ten yards from the bat, and several cricketers gave evidence that this was a dangerous position.[43] The report's thumbnail sketch of liability rules relating to sport included the statement that persons who were neither players or spectators 'will always have an action for damages', citing cases of injury to people passing by on roads near golf courses. This was incorrect but the sentiment was clear. And even in rugby liability was canvassed. Several newspapers reported the comments of Hilbery J in an

---

[40] *SMH*, 18 April 1940, 11.
[41] See, for example, the discussion of the cases in 'The Errant Cricket Ball', published in the English *Law Journal* in December 1936 and republished verbatim in the *LIJ* of Victoria: (1937) 11 *LIJ* 23.
[42] *Sydney Mail*, 28 December 1938, 29. The Irish decision was overturned on appeal, a result that attracted little press interest but was noted in the *ALJ* as interesting in its facts and useful in application 'although laying down no essentially new law': (1939) 13 *ALJ* 282. For a more prosaic view of the precautions a golfer should take to avoid liability see *The Telegraph* (Brisbane), 3 June 1938, 15.
[43] *Evening News* (Rockhampton), 19 December 1939, 7.

English case that schoolmasters had to realise how 'grievously dangerous' their position was and that he was 'looking forward to an action alleging negligence of a schoolmaster in allowing boarders to – or perhaps even making boarders – play Rugby. It is a highly dangerous game in the eyes of many.'[44]

Speedway

One area in which Australian courts were at the forefront of determining liability was in the new sport of 'Speedway'. The second half of the 1920s saw the introduction in both Australia and England of regular commercial motorcycle racing on small tracks to which the public paid a fee to view. By the end of 1930, Australian courts had given three decisions on cases involving injures caused at Speedway events, two involving spectators and one involving a participant. There was no English authority directly on point; the Court of Appeal did not give its decision in *Hall v. Brooklands Auto Racing Club*, which considered similar issues in the context of motor racing, until the middle of 1932.

The first of two cases in Queensland that arose out of accidents at Davies Park in South Brisbane took place in December 1927. In August of that year the plaintiff, a minor, was injured when a motorcycle crashed into the protective fence surrounding the track and caused a paling to fly out and hit the plaintiff (who was watching from the spectator area). He alleged negligence against Olympia Motor Speedway (Brisbane) Ltd, the organisers, in not taking adequate protection for members of the public watching the event. The case is not reported and the detail of the evidence in newspaper reports is sketchy[45] but it seems the defendant argued that by reference to contemporary Australian tracks the precautions taken were adequate.[46] Another strand of the defendant's argument seems to have been that the accident itself was unforeseeable, counsel submitting to the magistrate that it could not be foreseen that a motor cycle would take on the characterisation of a 'buck jumper'.[47] The magistrate found for the defendant: the defendant had exercised reasonable care and the safety fence provided adequate protection (despite improvements being made post-accident).

Five months after the first accident, Edward Chatwood was attending the Davies Park speedway for the first time and was injured when a motorcycle, after being involved in a collision with another bike, cleared the protective fence and hit him. He sued the defendant, National Speedways Ltd, one of

---

[44] *Longreach Leader*, 22 May 1937, 2. When counsel suggested that it was the mother of a boy of eleven and twelve who says what is safe, Hilbery J replied: 'Then they ought to play Rugby as mothers would have it played.'

[45] *The Telegraph* (Brisbane), 16 December 1927, 2; 17 December 1927, 2; 31 January 1928, 5; *Brisbane Courier*, 16 December 1927, 8; *Daily Standard* (Brisbane), 16 December 1927, 7; 1 February 1928, 5.

[46] *Truth* (Brisbane), 18 December 1927, 16.

[47] *The Telegraph* (Brisbane), 17 December 1927, 2.

Figure 10.1 Charlie Spinks, Billy Lamont, Dick Smythe and Vic Huxley on the Davies Park Circuit in Brisbane. In the *Chatwood* case, Spinks and Smythe were in a collision, which resulted in Spinks' motorcycle going over the fence.
Source: Photograph from speedwayandroadracehistory: www.speedwayandroadrace history.com/brisbane---davies-park-speedway.html.

the myriad of companies founded by A.J. Hunting, the leading promoter of speedway racing in Australia, and while this was a different corporate entity, in essence the management of the venue was in the same hands as it had been for the earlier accident.[48] This time the plaintiff was able to attack not the structure of the fence but its height. There was an interlocking mesh fence, described variously in evidence as between two feet nine inches and three feet six inches high, with a picket fence of similar height one foot next to the fence. At the time of the accident, some parts of the fence had been extended to a height of up to six feet but this had not been done at the place where the accident occurred. There was also evidence that one other motorcycle had gone over the fence. Moreover, while there was a warning sign near where the plaintiff was sitting, it only warned against leaning on the fence. As in the previous case, evidence was given on behalf of the defendant company that 'the fence at Davies Park compared more than favorably with other tracks'.[49] The suggested precaution of an automatic cut out – which would stop the motorcycle once the rider's hands left the handles – was also rejected: it had been tried and rejected because 'if it were enforced it would kill speedway racing'.[50] The gist of the defendant's argument was that it was impossible to protect spectators from every eventuality

[48] *Daily Standard* (Brisbane), 13 June 1928, 9; 19 June 1928, 7; 23 June 1928, 8; *Telegraph* (Brisbane), 12 June 1928, 3; 23 June 1928, 5; *Brisbane Courier*, 19 June 1928, 8.
[49] *Brisbane Courier*, 19 June 1928, 8.
[50] Ibid.

but this did not convince the magistrate that the condition of taking reasonable precautions was met and he found, without providing reasons, for the plaintiff.

The defendant appealed to the Full Court of the Supreme Court of Queensland where the appeal was unanimously rejected.[51] In that court, the defence crystallised into three parts: the only duty owed to the plaintiff was that owed to an invitee and as that only required action in respect of hidden dangers – which the risk of a motorcycle going over the fence was not – there was no breach; that even if a duty of reasonable care was owed it too was not breached, and that the defence of assumption of risk (*volenti*) applied. Each was robustly rejected. The plaintiff's uncontradicted evidence was that he thought he was safe where he was sitting; this ruled out the *volenti* defence. As the plaintiff was a contractual entrant, the duty owed was not that owed to an invitee but a duty to see that reasonable care was taken in providing adequate safety to patrons and on the facts the Full Court agreed with the decision of the magistrate that this had been breached. The reported decision, however, does not give a flavour of the robustness with which all three judges challenged appellant counsel's arguments. To the submission that there was no hidden danger, Webb J commented that persons unaccustomed to the place would not know of any hidden danger and that the majority of people could not say if the fence was safe; rather, the company held out that there was a proper safety fence for the protection of the public.[52] When counsel submitted that the defendant held out nothing more than that it would protect anybody 'to the extent of three feet', Brennan J mused that when the bicycle skidded 'people had to get down below the 3 feet fence'![53] Nor was the court impressed by suggestions that to impose liability here was to subject the defendant to an impossible standard. If the fence had to be high enough to prevent bicycles getting into the crowd and injuring people, as the court indicated, defence counsel responded: 'Then if a bicycle jumps 20ft, as has been stated, there must be a safety fence 20ft high. That would be absurd.' But the quasi-strict nature of the liability was reiterated by Brennan J: 'It would not pay the Speedway to do that, but they take the risk.'[54] And to the admittedly extreme argument that even if there was no protective fence at all there would be no action as the *volenti* defence would apply, Macnaughton J, after noting that if proprietors had no or small fences 'so much the worse for the proprietors if accidents happened', opined that the presence of a fence, together with the warning sign, would lead the spectator to think it was there for his protection. He went on: 'I think that many people go expecting to see accidents to the riders but they do not expect to have accidents themselves. It is like the gladiatorial games.'[55]

[51] [1929] St R Qd 29.

[52] *Daily Standard* (Brisbane), 24 July 1928, 5; *Telegraph* (Brisbane), 24 July 1928, 5.

[53] Ibid.

[54] Ibid.

[55] *Telegraph* (Brisbane), 24 July 1928, 5; *Brisbane Courier*, 24 July 1928, 14. In a more literary vein, the comment on the case in the *ALJ* began: 'The Englishman admittedly takes his pleasures sadly but is entitled to take them safely': (1928) 2 *ALJ* 166.

Four years later, the English Court of Appeal took a different view of what protection spectators were entitled to expect when watching the gladiators. In *Hall v. Brooklands Auto Racing Club*,[56] the plaintiff was a paying spectator at the Brooklands racing circuit when he was badly injured after a collision between two cars resulted in one of the cars flying (in the air) off the track and into the crowd watching from the side of the track. Several people were killed and many (including the plaintiff) were injured. Much of the legal discussion turned on the possible difference between the duties owed to the plaintiff by the defendant club under the contract by which he entered and the duty owed to him as an invitee but for present purposes this can be simplified by saying that liability turned on the reasonableness of the precautions taken by the defendant in light of the risks and dangers that the defendant could assume spectators took by coming to the event. A key factor for all three judges in allowing an appeal against a jury verdict in the plaintiff's favour was that the accident was held to be unforeseeable: there was no evidence that any car had broken through the limited barrier separating the pedestrian concourse from the track since the track was opened in 1907.[57] Both Scrutton and Greer LLJ, however, saw the case as being relevant to the wider question of the duty owed by an occupier/ organiser to spectators in sports and activities where risk of injury to spectators was clearly foreseeable but remote. The ambit of any duty to exercise care to the spectator was limited by the spectator's realisation of the 'danger incident to the entertainment',[58] hence the spectator at Lords 'does not expect any struc-ture which will prevent any ball from reaching the spectators'.[59] Unsurprisingly given the attitude to colonial authority, *Chatwood* was not cited, and although the cases could be distinguished – a motorcycle had previously gone over the fence – the application of broadly the same law was quite different. As in *Chatwood*, the plaintiff in *Hall* testified that he felt completely safe where he was standing; there was no sense he felt he was engaging in any risky behaviour. The imbalance between the knowledge of the parties as to the spectators' safety was at the heart of criticism of the *Hall* decision by A.L. Goodhart in the *Law Quarterly Review*.[60] He thought the analogies with cricket and golf were not in point because in those cases 'the spectator is as capable as foreseeing the risk as is the promoter'.[61] Goodhart doubted whether the Court of Appeal had in mind that 'a distinction could be drawn between the level of knowledge of risks of the spectator and an expert promoter' and if it had a different conclusion

---

[56] [1933] 1 KB 205.

[57] Cf. A.L. Goodhart's criticism as to the relevance of this fact: 'Apparently, as a dog is permitted one bite before his owner can be held liable, so a motor car is to be allowed one accident before it is necessary to guard against danger': (1933) 49 *LQR* 156, 157.

[58] [1933] 1 KB 205, 217 (Scrutton LJ).

[59] Ibid., 214 (Scrutton LJ).

[60] (1933) 49 *LQR* 156.

[61] See also an earlier Australian critic who disliked the analogy because the 'usual protections' that could be expected to be taken for spectators' safety in the different sports were so divergent that 'it was confusing to illustrate the one case by the analogy of another': (1932) 6 *ALJ* 226.

CLAIMED DAMAGES

Len Jones, the Lithgow (N.S.W.) dirt track rider, whose claim against the South Australian Motor Sporting Club for damages was dismissed (see story on this page).

Figure 10.2 Len Jones.
Source: *Referee* (Sydney), 22 October 1930, 21, http://nla.gov.au/nla
.news-article131159389.

might have been reached. This, of course, was the thrust of the Full Court's reasoning in *Chatwood*: it was unacceptable for the defendant to say that the risks were reciprocally perceived and hence must be accepted by the spectator. And if *Chatwood* went too far in solving the knowledge imbalance by imposing quasi-warranty protection for the spectator's safety, its depiction of the ill-informed spectator needing protection from the risks of a new sport reflected, perhaps, a more egalitarian view of the attendee at popular sporting events than the Englishmen who attended Lords or went to the Derby.[62]

Any thought that *Chatwood* might usher in a wider responsibility of organisers to all who participated in the sport was quickly corrected in the third of the trilogy of speedway cases which demonstrated that the gladiators themselves might have a much more difficult time in recovering than spectators. The leading South Australian venue for speedway was the Speedway Royale at

---

[62] Examples of spectators given by Greer LJ: [1933] 1 KB 205, 224. Greer LJ's attendee at Epsom may well have been an inaccurate construct: see M. Huggins, 'Second-class citizens? English middle-class culture and sport 1850–1910' (2000) 17 *The International Journal of the History of Sport*, 1, 25–26.

Wayville. In January 1928, the plaintiff, a professional rider contracted to ride for the defendant, was injured at that venue. He alleged that as he drove the bike so as to avoid a collision with another competitor's bike, he was forced into a safety fence, and was thrown against a post through what he considered was the defective condition of the fence and track established by the defendant.[63] The defence was simply that the fault was not that of the fence or track but of the plaintiff in driving negligently so that he lost control of the bike. Angas Parsons J, sitting as a judge of the Civil Court, found for the defendant. The evidence showed that the plaintiff had ridden his motorcycle 'so fast and so close to the fence' that he failed to avoid the offside handlebar of his bike becoming entangled and he was thrown from his machine and run over by another competitor. On this view of the facts it was impossible to say that the fence was not as safe for the purpose of this dangerous sport as reasonable care and skill could make it, or that it was improper in any way in design, construction, or condition.[64]

While there were clearly good grounds for distinguishing between competitors and spectators, in retrospect it is interesting that the possibility that competitors in an admittedly dangerous sport might in the course of competing make errors of judgement in the heat of the moment does not seem to have influenced the decision. The aim of the sport was to drive fast and it was clearly foreseeable that errors might be made in determining a 'safe' speed in the context of a dangerous sport. Although it is not expressly stated in evidence, the fact that the handlebar was entangled suggests the use of a wire mesh safety fence which would clearly entail the risk of catching handlebars too close to it. But as the racing cases considered in this chapter indicate, competitors had only mixed success when arguing that allowances should be made by organisers for competitors making spur of the moment decisions. Here the *volenti* defence, in spirit if not in strict law, governed; as the Sydney *Referee* summed up the result of the case in its headline, 'Rider's Own Fault'.[65]

The Special Position of Horse Racing

The greatest number of cases involving tort and sport in the period of this study came from the various forms of horse racing although the numbers are no more than a handful of cases. There was potential for more actions in this setting because they were not confined to physical injuries in racing accidents but also encompassed actions for injuries to horses and associated economic losses. The variety of isolated examples, however, must not mask the fact that there remain very few actions even in this area. Here, too, there seems to have

---

[63] *News* (Adelaide), 23 September 1930, 9; *The Register News-Pictorial* (Adelaide), 24 September 1930, 17; *Advertiser* (Adelaide), 25 September 1930, 28. There was also an equivalent claim in contract for breach of an implied term.

[64] *The Register News-Pictorial* (Adelaide), 17 October 1930, 11; *News* (Adelaide), 16 October 1930, 9; *Advertiser* (Adelaide), 17 October 1930, 17.

[65] *Referee* (Sydney), 22 October 1930, 21.

Figure 10.3 Rufe Naylor.
Source: *Truth* (Sydney), 13 January 1935, 2, http://nla.gov.au/nla.gov.au/nla
.news-article169346063.

been little recourse to the law to deal with injuries associated with the conduct
of the sport. But the commercial nature of horse racing also threw up another
challenge for tort law involving not negligence but trespass and this section
begins by considering these cases.

Rufe Naylor was a well-known racing figure in Sydney in the 1920s and
1930s.[66] Throughout 1934, he was involved in a dispute with the Australian
Jockey Club ('AJC'), the main non-proprietary[67] racing club in New South Wales.
In March, the AJC had disqualified him 'during the pleasure of the committee'
for giving false and misleading evidence before a committee of enquiry of the
club.[68] Naylor sought injunctions against the club preventing it from excluding
him from Randwick racecourse because the disqualification was made without
jurisdiction and the club had no power under its byelaws to keep him off the

[66] J. O'Hara, 'Rufus Naylor', *Australian Dictionary of Biography*, Vol. 10 (Melbourne University
Press, 1986).
[67] Meaning the club did not own the land on which the racecourse was located.
[68] *SMH*, 30 March 1934, 7.

course upon his paying the admission charge. His arguments were reluctantly upheld by a majority of the Full Court in December 1934.[69] On 12 January 1935, Naylor attended a race meeting at another racecourse in Sydney, Canterbury Park. The club that ran Canterbury had previously written to Naylor saying his presence at the course was 'not required', and warning turnstile operators that he should not be admitted, but Naylor found his way on to the track. When he was discovered, he was told his presence was not required and he was escorted off the course.[70] He subsequently sued the Canterbury Park Racecourse Company Ltd for assault. The defence was that Naylor was a trespasser and reasonable force could be used to evict him but in reply Naylor pleaded that he had been granted a licence to enter the course when he paid his admission fee and that this licence could not be revoked in breach of contract until after the purpose for which it had been granted (viewing the races) had expired. The defendant company demurred and the case went before the Full Court. The legal issue was one that had a long history: whether a contractual licence could be unilaterally revoked by the licensor, even in breach of contract, so as to make the licensee a trespasser if he did not leave within a reasonable time after the revocation. The pre-Judicature Act English decision of *Wood v. Leadbitter*[71] had decided that this was indeed the law, a decision influenced very much by the same concern to exclude undesirable characters from racetracks that underlay the racing clubs' treatment of Naylor.[72] Like James Wood, Rufe Naylor was no stranger to the turf.[73] During the 1930s, worries over SP (starting price) off-course betting and the associated drop off in crowds at race meetings it produced had prompted race clubs to attempt to limit betting information from leaving the course.[74] As part of this process the telegraph offices at a number of Sydney race tracks were closed at the end of 1934.[75] Naylor was involved in an attempt to circumvent these restrictions. In April 1935 – the period between issuing his writ and the Full Court hearing – he was charged alongside four others with offences against the Commonwealth Wireless Telegraphy Act 1905–1919 for transmitting betting information via Morse code from inside Rosehill racecourse in what experts said was 'the first occasion in racing history that such an intricate and successful method had been evolved by which information from the betting ring could be sent to people outside the ground'.[76] The conviction was delayed until January

---

[69] *SMH*, 21 December 1934, 8. Davidson J thought the claim was 'practically devoid of merit on the facts'. The AJC successfully appealed to the Privy Council: for the protracted history see *SMH*, 7 March 1935, 11; 26 May 1936, 12; 27 February 1937, 17; *Truth* (Sydney), 13 June 1937, 13.

[70] *Truth* (Sydney), 13 January 1935, 2.

[71] (1845) 13 M&W 837.

[72] P. Polden, 'A Day at the races: *Wood* v. *Leadbitter* in context' (1993) 14 *JLH* 28.

[73] And to betting more generally; he had, ultimately unsuccessfully, sought to establish his own lottery: *SMH*, 28 October 1931, 15; 1 December 1931, 7; 5 March 1932, 10; 17 March 1932, 9; 28 October 1932, 9, and more generally J. O'Hara, *A Mug's Game: A History of Gaming and Betting in Australia* (UNSW Press, 1988) 174–175.

[74] The sophisticated means, and scale, of these activities are described in O'Hara, ibid., 191–192.

[75] *Daily Advertiser* (Wagga Wagga), 8 April 1935, 6.

[76] *SMH*, 8 April 1935, 9.

1936 only because of some doubts over the validity of the Commonwealth legislation; he was fined £5 plus costs.[77] He was not a first offender: he had been warned not to transmit betting information in code in 1931 and had in 1930 given up bookmaking after being questioned by the AJC about alleged co-ownership of racehorses with a large punter, Fred Angles.[78]

But while there was little sympathy with removing without cause a character like Naylor, the legal principle applied to a much wider range of public entertainments where the equity of arbitrary removal was much harder to discern. In 1915, the English Court of Appeal in *Hurst v. Picture Theatres Limited*[79] had distinguished *Wood v. Leadbitter* in a case where a patron had been removed, found ultimately to be without cause, from a picture theatre before the end of the performance. The reasoning of the majority had two strands. The first was that the licence granted to *Hurst* was a licence coupled with a grant (some kind of property interest) and it was well established that such licences were irrevocable without cause until the grant had expired. The second was that *Wood v. Leadbitter* was decided before the Judicature Acts had merged the dispensation of law and equity but since those Acts the ejected person could plead (to the defence that he was a trespasser) that in equity the licence was irrevocable as it would have been specifically enforced. The issue for the Full Court in *Naylor* was whether it would follow the Court of Appeal in *Hurst* in distinguishing *Wood v. Leadbitter* but, despite the eminence of its source, the Full Court showed no inclination to do so.[80] Jordan CJ rejected the notion that a licence given for value could not be revoked unless justified as a breach of contract; 'startling consequences would follow where the licence has relation to what would otherwise be a trespass to the person'.[81] He thought the result in *Wood v. Leadbitter* would add to the preservation of order in places of entertainment and that the alternative view would increase the risk of disturbance and breach of the peace.[82] He was nonplussed by the decision in *Hurst*: it was 'not easy' to see exactly upon what basis the majority reached their decision. The suggestion that the plaintiff had an interest through the right to look at the performance so as to make the licence irrevocable 'seems to have no support in authority', and the Court of Appeal had misinterpreted authority to hold that equity would have specifically enforced the licence.[83] In the end, Jordan CJ consoled himself by querying whether the Judicature Acts really made any difference in this class of case but noted that, as those Acts had not been introduced in New South

---

[77] *SMH*, 21 January 1936, 11.
[78] O'Hara, above n 73. On Fred Angles see *The Sun-Herald* (Sydney), 14 May 1961, 45, 68. Fred Angles brother was Cyril Angles, the race broadcaster, who was given his start at 2KY by Naylor and was a co-defendant in *Victoria Park Racing v. Taylor*, discussed below: B. Griffin-Foley, *Changing Stations: The Story of Australian Commercial Radio* (UNSW Press, 2009) 291, 293.
[79] [1915] 1 KB 1.
[80] (1935) 35 SR (NSW) 281.
[81] Ibid., 285.
[82] Ibid., 286–287.
[83] Ibid., 287–288.

MR. A. B. COWELL.

Figure 10.4 A.B. Cowell.
Source: *Truth* (Sydney), 25 April 1937, 23, http://nla.gov.au/nla.news-article169600293.

Wales, *Hurst*'s case was inapplicable.[84] In reaching this conclusion, Jordan CJ also ignored Bernard Sugerman's argument for Naylor that what was sought to be restrained was the pleading of 'inequitable defences' rather than a technical question of when equity would enforce a licence.[85] This argument in favour of the result in *Hurst* was raised by Professor Geldart in 1915[86] and was cited favourably, if only in obiter, by Evatt J in *JC Williamson Ltd v. Lukey* in 1931,[87] but did not even merit a mention in Jordan CJ's judgment.[88]

Shortly after *Naylor* was decided, another case came before the Full Court of the Supreme Court of New South Wales where the same issue was raised. A.B. 'Bossie' Cowell was a Sydney trainer who in July 1934 had been disqualified for twelve months by stewards but on appeal had the disqualification removed but lost his training licence.[89] This may have been the reason why at a subsequent meeting at Rosehill racecourse he paid for admission but when his presence was discovered his licence was terminated and he was removed from the course

---

[84] Ibid., 288.
[85] Ibid., 283.
[86] (1915) 31 *LQR* 217, 219.
[87] (1931) 45 CLR 282, 306.
[88] Hence the guarded language of the note on the case in the *ALJ* that *Naylor* 'appears' to reject this reasoning: (1935) 9 *ALJ* 196, 197.
[89] *SMH*, 21 July 1934, 18; 28 July 1934, 20.

by employees of the defendant. It was clear that his only chance of success in an action against the club was in the High Court as *Naylor*'s case had just been decided, and in accordance with plaintiff counsel's wishes the Full Court expedited the appeal by entering judgment for the defendant without argument or reasons.[90]

By a majority of 4-1 the High Court upheld the decision in *Naylor* and refused to follow *Hurst*.[91] All members of the High Court found that *Hurst*'s reasoning based on an 'interest' in seeing the picture was flawed. Latham CJ thought the majority in *Hurst* ignored the distinction between a proprietary right and a contractual right, Starke J that the reasoning was based on a fallacy, and, most powerfully, Dixon J who said that Buckley LJ's reasoning 'entirely misconceives what is meant by a licence coupled with a grant'.[92] Dixon J was equally forceful in rejecting the assertion that an equity arose in favour of the licensee: to so decide the majority in *Hurst* demonstrated 'a very remarkable confusion of principle'.[93] The reason behind Jordan CJ's silence over the existence of a broad equity against pleading inequitable defences found voice in Latham CJ: the idea that a general equitable principle might be invoked to prevent the defendant pleading that the licence had been revoked was without authority and rested on a 'vague assumption' that equity would prevent the defendant gaining an 'unconscientous' advantage by his conduct.[94] Even pragmatic arguments in *Hurst*'s favour were rejected: Latham CJ thought there were arguments from convenience on both sides and that 'the denial of the principle will create more difficulties than are thought to be involved in its continued assertion' while Dixon J said there was 'much to be said against the result in point of policy and, except that it may establish an otherwise unknown head of equity, I see nothing liberalising in it'.[95] While the presence of English academic criticism of *Hurst* was important for three of the majority judges, Dixon J also relied on American case law to show that the argument in favour of the ticketholder's equity 'does not seem to have occurred to anyone in America'.[96] It is striking that Evatt J, dissenting, makes no reference to the position in the United States as he not infrequently referred to United States case law and academic literature in his judgments (as he did several months later in the *Victoria Park Racing* case, discussed below). Rather, a more conservative Evatt J argued for the maintenance of consistency with English law as represented by *Hurst* to preserve the general

---

[90] *SMH*, 25 October 1935, 6.

[91] *Cowell v. The Rosehill Racecourse Co. Limited* (1937) 56 CLR 605. Apart from the substantive question as to the correctness of *Hurst*, there were also procedural questions relating to the pleading of equitable defences in common law courts in NSW. These are not relevant for present purposes and are not discussed further.

[92] (1937) 56 CLR 605, 616 (Latham CJ), 627 (Starke J), 632 (Dixon J).

[93] Ibid., 636.

[94] Ibid., 620.

[95] Ibid., 621–622 (Latham CJ), 636 (Dixon J).

[96] Ibid., 638.

principles of common law and equity throughout the Empire[97] although there is little doubt he also saw the *Hurst* position as more appropriate to modern conditions (and cited Canadian case law and academic writing to support this). Geoffrey Sawer agreed that *Hurst* was more suitable for contemporary society but disagreed with Evatt J that on the authorities *Naylor* was wrong and *Hurst* right. Rather, he suggested that a 'frankly cryptosociological' approach would reject the view expressed in *Naylor* that the decision was a good thing from a social point of view. In language redolent of both youth and the times, he wrote of that view:

> It is submitted that this is a reversion to feudalism or a landslide to fascism. The police are capable of dealing with public disorder; there is no reason why the property owner should be endowed with their powers, whatever may have been the case in mediaeval England when the law of property came into being or whatever may be case in Germany under the notorious 'Leader Law' of Hitlerism.[98]

Contemporary press reports were more grounded in the racing context but equally conscious of the power the decision gave to racing clubs.[99] Cowell began an appeal to the Privy Council 'in defence of what he believes to be the rights of every British citizen' in which he was expected to be assisted by his many friends[100] but their largesse apparently ran out: leave to appeal was granted by the Privy Council in December 1937[101] but there is no record of the appeal being prosecuted. The case which 'to a certain extent, will define the liberties and rights of the people'[102] was thus decided against the people, although it was not long before the House of Lords tentatively supported the result in *Hurst's* case[103] and, later, that Dixon J's suggestion that the solution might lie in liberalising the rules relating to awards of damages for non-pecuniary loss for breach of contract[104] were taken up. Yet the potential (and obvious) unfairness to innocent spectators did not sway the majority in *Cowell*, in part because of the equally obvious risk and unfairness to race clubs trying to rid the course of unwanted visitors. Perhaps the scales were more finely balanced for Naylor and Cowell than for the unloveable James Wood: the race clubs' interest in acting was as much economic as altruistic. But there remained a sense of irony when, in responding to the submission of Cowell's counsel that all Cowell would get

---

[97] Ibid., 643. Keith Aicken (later a Justice of the High Court) commented that none of the other judges shared 'the compunction so keenly felt by Evatt J in refusing to follow a decision of the Court of Appeal': 'Revocability of licences' (1935–38) 1 *Res Judicatae* 240, 242.

[98] G. Sawer, 'Ejectment without cause from a place of entertainment' (1935–1938) 1 *Res Judicatae* 24, 26.

[99] *Truth* (Sydney), 25 April 1937, 23; *Referee* (Sydney), 29 April 1937, 4.

[100] *Truth* (Sydney), 20 June 1937, 19.

[101] *SMH*, 16 December 1937, 11. The compelling submission was that the correctness of *Hurst* needed to be determined by the Privy Council.

[102] *Truth* (Sydney), 15 November 1936, 12.

[103] *Winter Garden Theatre (London) Ltd v. Millennium Productions* [1948] AC 173.

[104] (1937) 56 CLR 605, 632; 'Hurst v. Picture Theatres not followed' (1937) 11 *ALJ* 4.

for breach of contract was the admission charge of four shillings, Latham CJ retorted: 'So he preferred to go for £5000!'[105] If the legal inadequacy of the *Hurst* reasoning allowed scope for discussion, it was the Australian context that suggested a contrary view had its merits.[106]

Accidents and Liability

While accidents to spectators were fortunately rare, when they did occur there was very little chance the unlucky victim would recover. In November 1929, after Henry Cooke was injured by a runaway riderless horse that had been competing in a hurdle race and broke through or jumped over a fence to enter the South Hill Reserve (where horses were not meant to enter), he sued Arthur Hiskens (on behalf of the Moonee Valley racing club).[107] Cooke, who had paid to enter the course, alleged that the defendant club was negligent in failing to employ a system for regaining control of riderless horses. As there is no further record of proceedings it is impossible to know if the case was dropped or settled. And when in March 1935 the broker Hugh O'Connor was kicked and injured by a horse which was spooked by a train whistle while walking between two rows of horse stalls at Rosehill Racecourse, his later claim was the subject of a successful non-suit application.[108] This was so even though the defendant had placed a guard rail ten feet before the front row of stalls but had done nothing for the back row where O'Connor had been when he was kicked.[109] The justification for the result was no doubt the same as that of Reed J in the New Zealand Supreme Court where a similar claim earlier in the same year was dismissed by applying the *Hall v. Brooklands Auto Racing Club* reasoning. The risk of a horse kicking was one the ordinary spectator appreciated as much as the racing club so there could be no breach in omitting to take steps to warn of or eradicate it.[110] It took an unfortunate accident to a greyhound trainer – he was hit by the mechanical hare in the bull pen, the place where the dogs are collected post-race – for recovery to be allowed[111] but this bore no real similarity to the previous cases: a mechanical hare was no horse, and the problem could be perceived as relating to the premises, rather than the activity conducted on the premises, an area where judges and juries were happier imposing liability even in recreational contexts.[112]

---

[105] *SMH*, 18 November 1936, 16; *Truth* (Sydney), 22 November 1936, 12.

[106] Jordan CJ's judgment in *Naylor* was alive to the possibility that a licence might be enforced in equity but not one that related to entering premises to view a spectacle: W.M.C. Gummow, 'Equity: the equity of Sir Frederick Jordan' (1991) 13 *Syd LR* 263, 276.

[107] *Argus*, 4 November 1929, 9.

[108] *Truth* (Sydney), 8 December 1935, 15; *SMH*, 4 December 1935, 8; 5 December 1935, 6.

[109] Perhaps he was closer to the horses than his evidence suggests as he did admit he went to the back stalls to inspect a horse in which he was interested: *SMH*, 4 December 1935, 8.

[110] For Australian comment see (1935) 9 *ALJ* 307–308.

[111] *Maitland Daily Mercury*, 28 February 1938, 7.

[112] A commonly cited example was *Francis v. Cockrell* (1870) LR 5 QB 501 where the plaintiff was injured when a grandstand on a racecourse collapsed.

Owners of horses who sued racing clubs over defects in the track or organisation of racing had mixed success. In an early case from 1922, Emilie Plant, the
owner of Carabost, sued successfully the Wagga Licensed Victuallers' Racing
Club at the Wagga Quarter Sessions for the injury to and reduction in value
of her horse after it struck a fence post. The alleged negligence was leaving an
open space in a fence surrounding the racecourse, and forming the boundary of the racing track, with the result that Carabost, after racing 200 yards
past the post of a race it had won, swerved towards the opening, hitting the
post. Judge Bevan instructed the jury that, as the horse was on the premises at
the invitation of the club, adequate protection was required for its safety and
if reasonable care had not been exercised to achieve this the verdict must be
for the plaintiff. The jury awarded Plant £30 of the £100 sought.[113] A different
result was reached when in November 1924 the plaintiff's horse, Rosecar, was
running second in the Jumpers Flat Race at Elwick in Hobart when a horse that
had escaped from a club official ran onto the track and collided with it.[114] In a
very balanced summing up, Ewing J told the jury to decide whether the horse
breaking away was pure accident or the result of negligence and whether the
failure to have an attendant on the gate was careless.[115] The inscrutable jury
verdict in favour of the club makes it difficult to discern possible reasons for
the different results between the Carabost and Rosecar cases but one possibility
suggests itself: in Carabost's case there was a problem with the infrastructure of
the course itself while in Rosecar, at least for the escape of the horse, this was
the result of the idiosyncratic nature of the horse itself. This was a risk that all
owners had to understand and accept; there were limits as to the protection that
could be provided for horses acting as horses.

Throughout the 1930s there continued to be isolated actions by owners
against organisers of racing for injuries to their animals. These were unsuccessful, demonstrating that the Carabost case was extremely unusual.[116] While
most cases were decided on granular negligence enquiries, occasionally the
wider public interest of recreational activities was tacitly acknowledged. When
a starter commenced a trotting race despite an out-of-control horse being on
the track, the resulting collision killed both horses. The subsequent action in

[113] *Daily Advertiser* (Wagga Wagga), 10 November 1922, 3; 11 November 1922, 4; *SMH*, 14
November 1922, 9.

[114] *Best v. Tasmanian Amateur Jockey Club*, *The Mercury* (Hobart), 31 July 1925, 3; 1 August 1925,
7. The observable injury was very slight and the main loss alleged was the loss of the chance of
the horse winning later races in the season: *The Mercury* (Hobart), 31 July 1925, 3. Whether
this was consequential or pure economic loss was not a matter raised in argument.

[115] *The Mercury* (Hobart), 1 August 1925, 7. Although Ewing J reserved a question of law on
whether the claim was barred by a provision of the rules by which the plaintiff was bound, a
verdict was taken on whether the club had exercised reasonable care.

[116] See, for example, *Carroll v. Nelson Park Pty Ltd*, where an action for damages for the death of
a greyhound resulting from an alleged misalignment of a fence post at a Geelong greyhound
track was dismissed by a jury: *Gippsland Times*, 11 September 1941, 3; *Argus*, 6 September
1941, 3; 9 September 1941, 8.

negligence failed: although the trial judge decided the case on the ground the track was clear when the trotting race was started, the fact that the race was being run as part of an exhibition organised by a provincial show society was also important. It was a common practice, not only at country shows, but at the Sydney Royal Show, for at least two and sometimes three events to be in progress in the ring at the same time and as long as reasonable safeguards were taken to see that horses were not roaming about the ring unattended, the judge saw no reason why that practice should not be continued.[117] The reasoning is premised on the social utility of the activity (provincial shows) justifying the risks associated with multiple events; as the judge put it, the burden would be too great of any society 'to demand that they should, before starting a trotting race or a hunting contest, remove every other animal from the ring'.[118]

Despite being the participants most obviously at risk from the careless organisation of racing, jockeys rarely sued for personal injury resulting from racing accidents and in the few cases they tried they were unsuccessful. In a reported case, *Watson v. South Australian Trotting Inc*,[119] the plaintiff jockey was injured when he alleged his horse tripped over a detachable rail which had been knocked off by another horse during the course of a race. In fact, in what was described as a 'remarkable fluke',[120] the driver of the horse in front of the plaintiff's horse had suddenly found a dislodged rail through the footrest of his gig.[121] Holding the reins with one hand, he threaded the rail through the footrest after checking there were no horses behind him but it seems the plaintiff's horse shied at the rail and fell. After finding the plaintiff was an invitee, Murray CJ found that the course was reasonably safe for the purposes of racing and that there was no unusual danger, the risk of a fallen rail being self-evident to anyone who inspected the track (which the plaintiff did not do).[122] But there was also another ground for rejecting the claim: the circumstances of the accident – rail falling, being thrown to the ground by another jockey, horse shying and then collapsing – could not have been anticipated by a reasonable man.[123] If risks had to be foreseen at that level of detail before there was any obligation imposed on the race club, either under occupiers' liability or general negligence law, it is no surprise that there were few successful actions. Arguments of this nature may explain the different tack taken by the plaintiff jockey in an early case from 1922. The jockey was injured in the pre-race canter at Tenterfield races in New South Wales when one rein broke and his mount fell under a

---

[117] Esery v. North Coast National A and I Society, *Northern Star* (Lismore), 15 December 1938, 12.

[118] *Newcastle Morning Herald and Miners' Advocate*, 15 December 1938, 2.

[119] [1938] SASR 94.

[120] *News* (Adelaide), 10 November 1937, 7.

[121] The plaintiff was not in a gig; the horse was ridden 'in the saddle': *The Mail* (Adelaide), 8 June 1935, 1. At the time, trotting races could take place with horses mounted by jockeys or driven in a sulky.

[122] [1938] SASR 94, 102–103.

[123] Ibid., 102.

fence.[124] He alleged both that the bridle was defective and, more controversially, that the horse was of a fractious and vicious disposition, difficult to manage, and addicted to bolting, and that he should have been warned about its nature. The claim against the defendant, the person who supplied the bridle,[125] was dismissed, the judge finding that there was no evidence for either count of negligence and that the case was a most unfortunate one though 'clearly' the defendant could not be held responsible for the accident.[126] As is evident from all the cases involving racing, there is a strong sentiment that those who dealt with horses knew the risks of doing so and could not be heard to complain if horses behaved as horses. It should be noted, however, that this strong strain of individual responsibility was mitigated by the presence of Distressed Jockeys' Funds in many Australian race clubs which ameliorated some of the losses caused by injury and may also be an explanation for why so few jockeys sought legal redress for accidents.

Hit in the Hip Pocket: Negligence and Claims for Pure Economic Loss

Towards the end of the period of this study, two cases from Queensland involved courts in deciding claims in negligence against racing organisers where the claims were not for physical injury but for purely economic losses. In both cases, the negligence claims were enmeshed with detailed consideration of the rules of racing that governed the clubs and individuals who made the decisions that were later called into question. While discussion of the interaction between the rules governing racing and private law actions was muted, both cases required an Australian court to determine the scope of potential liability for negligence in this highly regulated environment and, more broadly, illustrate the recourse to law to solve economic disputes arising out of the conduct of Australia's national sport.

The first case, which involved a hearing before a magistrate and the Full Court of the Supreme Court, took place in the second half of 1938 and arose out of what was described in evidence as a 'ringtail'. In March 1938, a horse that had been racing for a number of years in Rockhampton, 'Tommy', was investigated by the Rockhampton Jockey Club ('RJC') as information had come to it from Brisbane that 'Tommy' might not be the horse that was described in its registration papers.[127] 'Tommy' had something of a notorious existence in the area. He arrived as a two-year-old and was leased to his trainer, Hunter, in 1936. Concerned that too much interest was being shown in the horse, Hunter was apparently behind rumours that the horse had been bitten by a snake and died, an incident that was reported by the press, but which Hunter later denied.[128]

---

[124] *Richmond River Herald and Northern Districts Advertiser*, 2 June 1922, 3.

[125] It is unclear from the report whether the defendant was the owner or trainer, or was both.

[126] *Richmond River Express and Casino Kyogle Advertiser*, 5 June 1922, 3.

[127] *Morning Bulletin* (Rockhampton), 1 October 1938, 13.

[128] See the evidence to the RJC Enquiry, 12–13 April 1938, *Morning Bulletin* (Rockhampton), 13 April 1938, 6–7; 14 April 1938, 12.

When Hunter subsequently nominated Tommy for entry to a race, this pre-cipitated the first 'Tommy' enquiry, with the RJC arranging for a hearing to determine whether 'Tommy' was in fact alive (or as Magistrate Kelly put it in the later trial, had risen from the dead).[129] The enquiry found that 'Tommy' was still alive but in the course of its investigation a stipendiary steward had sought information on the registration details of the horse from the Registrar of Racehorses, located in Sydney. The information was returned to the RJC where it seems to have been filed. In fact, a not-very detailed comparison between the registration details for Tommy held in Sydney, and the horse in Rockhampton called 'Tommy', would have revealed that the Rockhampton horse was not Tommy at all. In March 1938 it was recognised that 'Tommy' was not the horse he was thought to be[130] and when the real identity of 'Tommy' became known, the plaintiff, the owner of a horse that had run second to 'Tommy' in two of its recent wins in Rockhampton in January 1938, sued the RJC to recover the difference in prize money between first and second in the two races, as well as general damages, for £100.[131]

The pleaded causes of action were breach of contract and negligence. The neg-ligence claim was that, as counsel for the plaintiff put it in argument, the RJC had material (the registration) and did not use it to determine that 'Tommy' was a different horse to the one he was believed to be. If the RJC had acted carefully, with the knowledge it had, Tommy would have been disqualified well before the races in which plaintiff's horse ran.[132] Duty of care was central to defence coun-sel's argument. There could be no responsibility for negligence unless there was a duty to take care. The only relationship on which a duty could be based was the contract entered into when the plaintiff's horse was nominated for the races it entered.[133] Here the plaintiff's claim ran up against difficulties associated with suing an unincorporated voluntary association which need not concern us here but relevant for present purposes is defence counsel's linking of the scope of the duty of care in negligence to the contractual obligations of the parties. The duty of care was not owed in the air but in the context of an established matrix of rela-tionships between owner, trainer and organising body (both local and regional). But defence counsel did not rely merely on doctrinal arguments. The decision was one that would have an effect beyond the parties and the issues involved not just the RJC but the whole racing community so the decision would have 'far-reaching effect'.[134] Apart from claiming the enquiry, which was meant to satisfy

---

[129] *The Evening News* (Rockhampton), 1 October 1938, 2.
[130] Ibid.
[131] The case is extensively reported in the *Morning Bulletin* (Rockhampton), 30 September 1938, 14; 1 October 1938, 13; 4 October 1938, 10; 5 October 1938, 12; *The Evening News* (Rockhampton) 29 September 1938, 2; 30 September 1938, 2, 14; 1 October 1938, 2; 3 October 1938, 2; 4 October 1938, 2, 3.
[132] *Morning Bulletin* (Rockhampton), 1 October 1938, 13.
[133] Ibid., 5 October 1938, 12.
[134] Ibid.

the public interest, was a whitewash,[135] counsel for the plaintiff stressed only one allegation of negligence: the conduct and aftermath of the 1936 enquiry, arguing that the information that was obtained from that enquiry should have been used to determine Tommy's false identity. The magistrate found for the RJC, holding that there was no negligence and no evidence of breach of contract,[136] although in the absence of reasons it is impossible to know whether the finding on negligence was based on lack of duty or breach.

The plaintiff appealed to the Full Court of the Supreme Court where the respondent club's counsel was not called upon by the court in dismissing the appeal.[137] Counsel for the appellant argued for the duty of care to be based on the RJC's position as a regulator of racing: it had the power to control and supervise racing in the district and in exercising those powers had to act reasonably and without negligence. In response to a query by R.J. Douglas J as to the extent of any duty, counsel for the appellant replied that it was the duty of the club to ascertain whether the horse they were accepting was identical to the horse as described in the Register of Racehorses.[138] Despite a later attempt to limit the duty to the facts of the case – where the duty arose from the documents in the club's possession – the damage had been done. R.J. Douglas J thought it 'ridiculous to expect every racing club in Queensland to check up the particulars of every horse nominated with the Australian Registrar of Racing before allowing a horse to start.'[139] If the magistrate had found the club negligent it would have been unreasonable; in his view the real cause of action was contract rather than negligence (on which the appeal also failed). As soon as the case was determined by reference to a general duty on clubs it was inevitable the claim would fail: even for large racing clubs the task would be onerous and for smaller ones practically impossible given the difficulties of obtaining information. But while the case hardly heralded an expansion of the tort of negligence into the operations and machinations of the RJC, there was no suggestion that this kind of negligence action had no place in horse racing in Queensland (at least). Horse racing, with its wide public interest deriving from both sporting and financial considerations, and its long history of legislative intervention, was a quasi-public activity, and it is no surprise that both parties in the case sought to use broader policy arguments in support of their cases. Moreover, the claim in negligence in the Tommy case was for financial losses rather than for physical injury and property damage, situations where racing, trotting, greyhound and other organising recreational clubs clearly owed duties to competitors and spectators and had occasionally been found liable for breach of those

---

[135] Ibid.

[136] Ibid; *The Evening News* (Rockhampton), 4 October 1938, 2. Neither of these reports state the magistrate's formal finding but in the report of the Full Court decision these findings are noted: *Morning Bulletin* (Rockhampton), 3 December 1938, 9.

[137] *Morning Bulletin* (Rockhampton), 3 December 1938, 9; *Telegraph* (Brisbane), 2 December 1938, 6.

[138] *Telegraph* (Brisbane), 2 December 1938, 6.

[139] Ibid.

duties. While denying a breach of duty could mask the nuance required to deal with potential liability for different kinds of damage and for different functions exercised by the defendant – especially through inscrutable jury verdicts – this would not always be possible.

The final case in this section is an early example of the increasing subtlety of reasoning that would be required to adjudicate more (legally) complicated claims. It is hard not to feel sympathy for the plaintiff in *Sinclair v. Cleary*, decided in May 1946.[140] The case arose out of a race at Clifford Park in Toowoomba in March 1945. Apparently, the plaintiff's horse won the race and the plaintiff who had been watching was congratulated by a number of people in the adjoining stand.[141] However, it was soon brought to his attention that the number of his horse, 12, was not the number that the judge had placed in the semaphore for any of the first three placegetters (this being the usual way for the judge to advise of the placegetters in a race). The plaintiff testified that he heard a voice from the stand reserved for the racing club members, who he said was that of Cleary, chairman of the racing club, say 'No. 12 won'.[142] There was a public demonstration and general uproar, with cries of 'Protest', and 'Achates won' [the plaintiff's horse]. The plaintiff then approached Cleary, who put his fingers to his lips and said 'Keep quiet. I will fix this up.'[143] Cleary then intercepted the judge, Kenyon, who was on his way to the members stand and Kenyon later went back and altered the number of the second horse to that of Achates. Aghast, the plaintiff saw the secretary of the club and told him he wanted to lodge a protest and was advised to see Kirk, a stipendiary steward. Kirk, who the plaintiff said was very drunk, refused to accept the protest, presumably because under the rules governing the meeting the only ground for a protest was disqualification (which this was not). Two days later, the plaintiff was again at the track and was introduced to the judge, Kenyon, who confirmed that he had made a mistake and had told the racing committee this. Cleary then appeared and the plaintiff told him that if the favourite had won by the margin his horse had, 'you would have had to arrive at a settlement in order to avoid bloodshed', to which Cleary replied 'I believe we would.'[144] The plaintiff continued to suggest to Cleary that a settlement should be reached but this never happened, the club writing to the plaintiff to advise that it had no alternative but to accept the judge's placings.

The plaintiff sued the Toowoomba Turf Club (through its representative Cleary), its committee members, the presiding stewards, and the judge for the difference between the first and second horse prize money for the race as well as for the loss of a winning bet of £250.[145] The pleaded case was a

---

[140] [1946] St R Qd 74.
[141] *Warwick Daily News*, 14 May 1946, 4.
[142] *Truth* (Brisbane), 19 May 1946, 27.
[143] Ibid.
[144] Ibid.
[145] The complete statement of claim and defence are reported in *Warwick Daily News*, 14 May 1946, 4.

mixture of claims for breach of contract and negligence but at trial there were only two issues seriously argued: the liability of the club for the negligence of Kenyon, the judge, and the personal liability of the judge. An application by defendants' counsel for a non-suit to Macrossan CJ, sitting in the Toowoomba Civil Court, was successful; he rejected both arguments for liability. In his view, the argument that the club was liable for the negligence of the judge was based on what seems to be non-delegable duty reasoning: the club was under a duty to carefully determine the winner and could not escape liability by appointing someone else to perform that task. But when the rules by which the plaintiff had agreed to be bound when nominating his horse were considered this submission could not be accepted. The limited grounds of review of a judge's decision showed that the judge 'in relation to the competitors and in relation to the club, occupies an independent position and the club and its members cannot be made responsible for erroneous decisions of the judge made by him in the performance of an independent duty imposed on him by the rules'.[146] As the cases cited by counsel for the defendant indicate, this reasoning drew on two strands of cases. The first, more narrow, strand referred to a well-established common law rule that there could be no vicarious liability of an employer/principal where the employee/agent exercised an independent discretion. This strand applied to persons exercising, broadly, executive functions, and its roots lay in the complicated law surrounding the liability of the Crown for its servants and agents.[147] None of those rationales were applicable here: the Toowoomba Turf Club or its employees and agents were not exercising any kind of executive authority: it was regulating a recreational activity. The second, broader strand related to the control test and vicarious liability: the refusal to recognise vicarious liability was based on the inability of the employer to exercise any control over the employed person because of the special skill of that person.[148] This too was not in play: there was no suggestion that the role of judge required the exercise of a special skill which the other members of the committee (for example) might not have. Rather, the inability to interfere came from the rules of racing rather than the technical expertise of the judge. The denial of vicarious liability, then, was a not very convincing extension of the existing categories of independent discretion although perhaps it might have been justified on the general rules relating to vicarious liability and independent contractors.

---

[146] [1946] St R Qd 74, 77.

[147] Counsel cited *Enever v. R* (1906) 3 CLR 969, a case discussing the relationship between constables and the Crown.

[148] Counsel cited *Strangways-Lesmere v. Clayton* [1936] 2 KB 11, a decision of a trial judge finding a hospital not liable for the negligence of nurses in its employ as the negligence was in the course of their skilled work. The exclusion of skilled work from vicarious liability for employee nurses had been rejected by the English Court of Appeal in *Gold v. Essex County Council* [1942] 2 KB 293. The other case cited by counsel on this point, *Fowles v. Eastern and Australian Steamship Co. Ltd* [1916] 2 AC 556, turned on the special position of port pilots in maritime shipping at common law and under the applicable Queensland legislation.

The personal liability of the judge also gave rise to interesting questions. Embryonic forms of arguments that would appear in future cases of negligence causing pure economic loss can be discerned. Apart from the forlorn submission that there was no evidence of negligence ('there may be evidence of mistake but not negligence'!), counsel for the defendant submitted that Kenyon could not be liable 'as he had a care and duty to everyone on the racecourse'.[149] It is not clear whether this was an indeterminate liability argument or a version of the modern argument that duties owed to the public cannot give rise to private rights of actions but the former was taken on by counsel for the plaintiff: he submitted that 'where a person had a duty to perform in order to protect the investments of others he had a duty of care to perform'.[150] When Macrossan CJ asked for a case where an action had been brought for negligence in the absence of fraud (meaning in cases of financial loss), counsel could give none but pressed his point. Other such actions must have been settled out of court, but 'we claim that the judge owes a duty of care to those people associated with the races and those affected by his decision.'[151] In retrospect, this duty was clearly too broad; it was a paradigm case of indeterminate liability (although much less so in an era where the only legal gambling was on-course). But the consequences of denying that any duty could exist were put starkly by plaintiff's counsel:

> It is a most extraordinary position if a judge, outside a fraud, can give any decision he pleases and the only risk he would run would be to be dismissed by the turf club.[152]

There was no real answer to this: in response Macrossan CJ said simply: 'That is a risk of course.' The risk did not prevent him from denying the duty. Despite counsel's attempt to argue that the duty of care and liability in negligence were fluid principles and that 'having regard to the investments in relation to race meetings, just ground exists for the extension of the principle of duty of care to meet investments of this kind',[153] Macrossan CJ affirmed the orthodoxy that in the absence of fraud (which founded deceit) there was no general duty to take care by any person performing any act from the performance of which somebody else may in some way be directly or indirectly damnified. Relying on *Charlesworth on the Law of Negligence* (no edition cited), any duty was limited to physical injury and/or damage to property. Although the two English cases he cited in support of his view pre-dated *Donoghue v. Stevenson*, he thought there was nothing in the judgment of the House of Lords that extended liability beyond the two categories he had previously mentioned.[154]

---

[149] *Warwick Daily News*, 14 May 1946, 4.
[150] Ibid.
[151] Ibid.
[152] Ibid.
[153] [1946] St R Qd 74, 76.
[154] Ibid., 79.

Sinclair v. Cleary is a fascinating case on a number of levels. Legally, it raised a narrow, novel legal point: the liability of a judge at a race meeting for financial loss caused by negligence. In answering the narrow question, the broader question about the scope of liability in negligence for purely economic losses had to be addressed. While the fact that the claim failed is not irrelevant, the importance of the case lies in the necessity of Macrossan CJ having to deal with the issue in a new context. Within the confines of the setting – a lower trial court in a regional Queensland town – the legal point was taken seriously, the argument taking the best part of a day. While *Truth* may have characteristically overstated the importance of the case by saying it was an 'epic' decision and involved '[o]ne of the most sensational allegations ever made in relation to an Australian racecourse',[155] it was nonetheless indicative of the increasing complexity of interactions between law and recreational activities in Australia. And when legal eyes were cast on the administration of sporting events, what was seen was not always edifying. The Toowoomba Turf Club may have won the case, but seventy years on the claim that the club had no control over the judge borders on the farcical given what actually happened in the case. As the two cases discussed in this section have illustrated, racing, especially away from the big metropolitan clubs, was a small-scale affair run by a series of connected individuals within and without racing circles. In that sense, it was a very Australian affair, and when things went wrong the steely gaze of the law did not always make for happy viewing.

Racing and the Sport Plaintiff: *Caveat Praedator?*

This chapter has been concerned primarily with the potential *liability* of sporting and recreational participants and organisers. However, there were rare examples, again from horse racing, where organisers of racing claimed damages as plaintiffs for economic losses allegedly suffered as a result of another's tort. While the status of the plaintiff was not the determinative legal factor, the existence of these cases remind us of the place of horse racing as the pre-eminent economic recreational activity in Australia throughout the period of this study. It is appropriate to finish this chapter by considering two cases at both ends of the period of this study that illustrate the legal complexity of the interaction between racing and the law when racing interests used the law to protect this status.

The first case, *The Mentone Racing Club v. Victorian Railways Commissioner*, arose out of an erroneous notice placed in a number of metropolitan Melbourne railway stations that the defendant's race meeting scheduled for later that day had been postponed. The weather had been wet in the morning and the defendant argued that these notices (which were corrected two hours later) caused a lesser crowd to attend the meeting with consequent economic loss

---

[155] *Truth* (Brisbane), 19 May 1946, 27.

to the defendant.[156] The evidence revealed there had been a mix up between various employees of the defendant but there was no suggestion of malice or ill-will in making the statement that the meeting had been postponed. At trial in the Victorian County Court, Judge Chomley found for the defendant: in the absence of the words themselves being defamatory, 'malice' of some kind was required and it was not present on the facts. Any injury that arose was due to the authority attached to the defendant's statements but the basic principle was clear: 'No action would lie against a person who met another person in the street bound for the races, and told him that they had been postponed.'[157] The arguments for the plaintiff were fleshed out when Leo Cussen appeared for it in the appeal to the Full Court.[158] There were two strands: one related to an action for slander of title and the other to negligence. In the latter Cussen pushed a radical argument: 'A man negligently using a horse and cart and thereby injuring another is held liable – why should he not be held liable for negligently letting his tongue loose…'[159] The Full Court was unimpressed with these novel arguments that attempted to impose liability for damage caused by an honest but carelessly made statement that caused economic harm. Orthodoxy – that fraud or malice was required to make the statement actionable– was reasserted although the focus on liability for statements masked concerns about extending liability for negligent statements to purely economic losses. In hindsight, there was very little too in the facts that might have moved judicial hearts to find a way to allow recovery. While it is unclear from the facts whether the defendant paid for the provision of the rail services, either way the case was weak: if it was a free rider it took the burdens along with the benefits of the service being provided, and if it contracted for the services it was a proprietary profit-making racing organisation which in modern parlance was well capable of bargaining for protection from this kind of error.

A much more pressing argument for expanding the law was made in the well-known case of *Victoria Park Racing and Recreation Grounds Company Ltd v. Taylor* in 1937. Here the plaintiff racing company alleged the profitability of its enterprise was reduced by simultaneous broadcasts of its races on one of the three defendants' radio station, another defendant being Cyril Angles, the broadcaster. The third defendant, Taylor, owned property adjacent to the track on which a platform had been built to allow Angles an unrestricted view of the racecourse when broadcasting. As Richardson and Trabsky note, the case was important because it forced the courts to decide whether, and if so, how, they would deal with the challenge that broadcasting posed to the traditional

---

[156] In fact, the trial judge expressed considerable doubt as to the causal link between the notice and reduced crowd but ultimately did not need to decide the point: *The Australasian*, 23 November 1901, 16.

[157] *Age*, 19 November 1901, 5.

[158] (1902) 28 VLR 77.

[159] Ibid., 79–80.

organisation of racing in Australia.[160] But in answering that question wider questions about the role of off-course (SP) betting were at play given that broadcasting was seen as instrumental in increasing this kind of gambling (at the expense of the traditional race clubs). In this context, the broadcasting of races was only part of a wider concern about the transfer of racing information – scratchings, barrier draws, starting price odds, professional tips – to persons outside the racecourse so that off-course betting could take place.[161] Seen in this light, the case was as much about the legal regulation of racing as the legal regulation of technology.

Betting had been confined to racecourses in New South Wales since 1906 as a result of reforms prompted by evangelical concerns,[162] an unintended consequence of which was to increase crowds at racecourses. But the Great Depression combined with advances in telephone and broadcasting technology facilitated an increase in SP betting and a concomitant decrease in racecourse attendances, and broadcasting of races was identified by racing clubs as a key part of the success of SP bookmaking.[163] Concerns began to be expressed in press reports in the early 1930s. In the Brisbane *Courier-Mail* in July 1934, it was noted that a stand had been erected outside Ascot (Eagle Farm) racecourse in Brisbane to allow the broadcasting of the races by a B class licence broadcaster.[164] The article also referred to the commencement of 'official broadcasts' from the course but the presence of unofficial off-course broadcasters made it difficult for race clubs to negotiate deals: in the absence of exclusivity there was little for the race clubs to sell. There was in fact little race clubs could do to prevent information leaving the course. Where broadcasting equipment was used in breach of radio licensing laws prosecutions could be brought[165] but this was unavailable against licensed broadcasters. Shortly before the action was commenced, the Victoria Park Club began its campaign by changing the contractual conditions of entry of patrons to the racecourse so that it was a breach of contract for a patron to communicate any racing information to any person outside the course until five minutes after the conclusion of the race meeting.[166] While this was greater protection than could be achieved by the non-proprietary race clubs – who did not own the tracks on which they raced and were more circumscribed in the conditions they could impose[167] – it was only a partial

---

[160] M. Richardson and M. Trabsky, 'Radio and the technology of the common law in 1930s Australia: *Victoria Park Racing v. Taylor* revisited' (2011) 20 *GLR* 1020.

[161] See generally O'Hara, above n 73, 188–194.

[162] Ibid., 142–145.

[163] A. McCoy, 'Sport as modern mythology: SP bookmaking in New South Wales 1920–1979', in R. Cashman and M. McKernan (eds,), *Sport: Money, Morality and the Media* (UNSW Press, 1981) 39–40.

[164] *Courier-Mail* (Brisbane), 6 July 1934, 15. Radio licences were issued in two classes: Class A where licensees were funded by licence fees and Class B where licensees had to self-fund.

[165] *Newcastle Sun*, 28 January 1936, 9.

[166] Ibid., 18 February 1936, 2.

[167] *Courier-Mail* (Brisbane), 19 February 1936, 14.

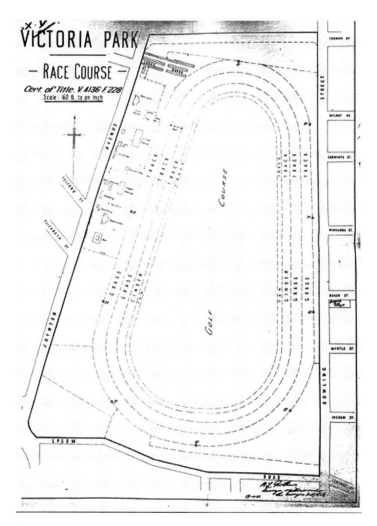

Figure 10.5 Victoria Park race course.
Source: NAA, A10071, 1936/76, Victoria Park Racing and Recreation Grounds
Company Limited v. Taylor, Appeal Book.

success;[168] as one newspaper noted, there was nothing to stop patrons from
passing on information once they had left the racetrack and this limited the
usefulness of the prohibition. As it correctly prophesied, the only effective remedy was an injunction against the broadcasters and until this was obtained 'their
efforts probably will not be of much avail'.[169] This did not stop other attempts to
rein in the broadcasters' power: in February 1936 officials at the Harold Park
club in Sydney informed representatives of the broadcasting stations that they

---

[168] *Truth* (Sydney), 23 February 1936, 3.
[169] *Queensland Times*, 25 February 1936, 9.

would not be allowed use of the club's phone, the concern being that information was being passed to two class B broadcasters outside the track.[170]

The claim for an injunction that was commenced in March 1936 was thus
part of a wider campaign against the passing on of racing information without
authorisation.[171] While the Victoria Park Club was the nominal plaintiff, it had
the support of many other racing clubs in Australia.[172] But as the case was waiting to go to trial, the question of race broadcasting remained in the public eye
for other reasons. In July 1936, the report of the Royal Commission on Racing
and Gaming in Queensland was handed down. Concerned primarily with gambling, it recommended that representations should be made to Federal authorities regarding the prohibition of broadcasting races until after the last race
of the meeting and, more generally, that attempts should be made to prevent
racing information from leaving the racecourse 'as to give ears and almost racecourse vision to thousands of outside betters'.[173] The *Courier-Mail* recognised
that this latter ambition would require the support of the Federal Government
through its control of broadcasting, telephones and telegraphs and would justify the interest of the Premiers' Conference.[174] And in August 1936 the final
evidence of the Royal Commission on Police and Illicit Betting in New South
Wales was given before Commissioner Markell. The police officer in charge of
suppressing SP betting, Keefe, told the Commissioner that if the dissemination
of 'illegal knowledge and broadcasting of racing information' could be stopped,
SP betting would be reduced by 60–75 per cent.[175] On the other side, commercial broadcasters pointed out that broadcasting of races themselves was not the
problem. A spokesman for 4BC, one of the leading off-course broadcasters in
Brisbane, noted that in Queensland 98 per cent of receivers were in private
homes. If the object was to prevent SP betting, and if the dissemination of racing news and information was the problem, then it was this that should be
regulated rather than the broadcast of races. To merely suggest deferring race
broadcast description until after the race was run 'is like killing the flea to stop

---

[170] *Truth* (Sydney), 23 February 1936, 7.

[171] It was preceded by an amusing incident where a loud motor siren interrupted Angles'
broadcast of a race, apparently for the purpose of identifying the broadcast as being of a
race from Victoria Park. Defiantly, Angles commented on air that if the motorist thought he
was going to put him off his broadcast he was mistaken as '[i]t will take more than a motor
"tooter" to put me off': *SMH*, 29 February, 1936, 17.

[172] This was certainly the case for metropolitan Sydney and Brisbane clubs (*National Advocate*
(Bathurst), 20 March 1936, 4; *Morning Bulletin* (Rockhampton), 11 April 1936, 9; *Sunday
Mail* (Brisbane), 12 April 1936, 8). One newspaper suggested that all the clubs in Australia
had decided to stand behind the Victoria Park Club: *Courier-Mail* (Brisbane), 13 May, 1936,
13. Evidence given at trial suggested that within Sydney there were towers or lorrys around
Warwick Farm, Ascot, Canterbury, Roseberry and Rosehill racecourses: NAA, A10071,
1936/76, Victoria Park Racing and Recreation Grounds Company Limited v Taylor, Transcript,
Evidence of J Hood, 324.

[173] *Courier-Mail* (Brisbane), 23 July, 1936, 12. See also *Truth* (Brisbane), 19 July 1936, 1.

[174] Ibid.

[175] *The Canberra Times*, 22 August 1936, 1.

the elephant'.[176] In the background was also the South Australian model, where off-course betting was licensed and after some initial disagreement the broadcasting of races was allowed on the payment of a fee.[177]

It was into this sharp debate about betting that the arguments and the first instance decision took place in October/November 1936.[178] The doubts over the nature of any cause of action are evident in the long statement of claim (28 paras). The primary action seems to have been in nuisance although there was a ubiquitous catch-all statement that the defendants' acts 'constitute a breach of the plaintiff's rights'.[179] At trial, an action for infringement of copyright by the transmission of racing information from the track was also raised.[180] Early on it was accepted by the plaintiff's counsel that there was no decided case in its favour but that the law of nuisance was flexible and could be adapted to novel uses by an adjoining landowner. As a trial judge this did not appeal to Nicholas J who said he was bound by decisions of higher courts, because those (English) decisions held that the plaintiff's claim for an injunction must be founded on the infringement of some right of the plaintiff.[181] In nuisance, this needed to be some kind of right connected with the use and enjoyment of land. This was not what the plaintiff was complaining about: the land was as fit for racing after the broadcasts as it was before. When Nicholas J asked what the legal right was on which the plaintiff relied, he understood the reply to be an immunity from the loss the plaintiff suffered owing to the use of the land by the defendants. But Nicholas J could find no basis for such an immunity. There could be no claim for mere competition (i.e. the defendant taking away customers of the plaintiff); there was high authority that there was no proprietary interest in a view so that there was nothing preventing the plaintiffs from overlooking the racecourse by whatever means they chose; there was no evidence of a desire to injure the plaintiff so any tort based on intended harm had to fail; the defendants had not actively sought to prevent patrons attending race meetings; and the same reasoning precluded any action based on breach of a right of privacy.[182] Moreover, any attempt to use a wide general principle of liability for loss caused to another in the absence of lawful excuse was rejected: whatever the merits of the views of Pollock and Winfield they had to be read in light of the decided cases.[183] The

---

[176] *The Telegraph* (Brisbane), 23 July 1936, 12, and more generally O'Hara, above n 73, 188–190.

[177] *The Advertiser* (Adelaide), 15 February 1936, 19. The management at Cheltenham Park racecourse had initially (unsuccessfully) attempted to use increasingly larger canvas screens to block the view from outside the course.

[178] (1937) 37 SR (NSW) 322.

[179] A10071, above n 172, Statement of Claim, para. 22.

[180] As this was not a tort claim it is not discussed further. For discussion of the use of copyright in protecting racing information see C. Bond, '"A spectacle cannot be owned": A history of the uneasy relationship between copyright and sport in Australia' (2013) 8 *Australia and New Zealand Sports Law Journal* 1.

[181] (1937) 37 SR (NSW) 322, 337–338.

[182] Ibid., 339–341.

[183] Ibid., 342–343.

wider context too was recognised: if it was unfair that the defendants were taking advantage of the plaintiff's spectacle to make a profit:

> It may be that this branch of the defendants' activities, in view of the additional inducements which they offer for illegal betting and of the losses which they may be thought to cause to racing clubs, should be brought under the notice of Parliament or of the authority responsible for the issue of licences.[184]

That this was a distinct possibility was evidenced by the coincidental introduction on the same day as the judgment was handed down of the Racecourses Act Amendment Bill into the Queensland Parliament. The legislation provided that no place was to be used for the conveying of racing information at any time when a race meeting was being held (defined as starting half an hour before the starting time of the first race and ending when the last race was started). The information was wide-ranging, covering details of any race to take place (but not the race itself), scratchings, riders, starting barriers, betting odds, and adjustments to the weight carried by any horse.[185] When the bill was introduced a specific question was asked of the Premier, Forgan-Smith, as to the action the Government would take if a tower was erected near a racecourse for the purpose of broadcasting: he replied that the Governor in Council could declare it a 'place' within the meaning of the Act.[186] The reply illustrates the broadcasting issue at the forefront of the concerns about off course betting the Queensland Government was trying to address. While these concerns were in part about the health of racing clubs this was inextricably linked the question of off-course gambling. In this context, the limits on broadcasting attracted some strong support, both for pragmatic[187] and more high-minded[188] reasons. That broadcasting per se was not the target of the legislation is illustrated by a press report only three days after Royal Assent had been given to the racing amendment bill. The Queensland Cricket Association was attempting to prevent outside broadcasts of matches played at its ground as part of the MCC (England) tour of Australia in the summer of 1936/7. In what the *Sunday Mail* described as a 'Gilbertian' situation, hessian screens had been erected to block a number of differently located towers outside the ground but, as the article recognised, it was impossible to fence sufficiently high in every case to block outside views and in any case if the fence was too high 'they could get a balloon or an autogyro'.[189] Outside broadcasts were a problem not only for horse racing!

The background to the High Court decision is important because the majority judgments dismissing the appeal have sometimes been portrayed as

---

[184] Ibid., 343.
[185] *Racecourses Act and Other Amendments Act 1936* (Qld) s. 21.
[186] *SMH*, 27 November 1936, 14.
[187] For example, catching revenue from betting taxes that were lost in illegal off-course betting: *Daily Examiner* (Grafton), 16 December 1936, 4.
[188] *Courier-Mail* (Brisbane), 16 December 1936, 20.
[189] *Sunday Mail* (Brisbane), 6 December 1936, 35.

conservative and technical judgments unwilling to expand the law to deal with new circumstances. Richardson and Trabsky argue that the dispute between the majority (Latham CJ, Dixon and McTiernan JJ) and minority (Rich and Evatt JJ) was essentially over the preferable judicial method; for the majority 'the answer was straightforward: since the traditional doctrines did not apply to this novel situation, the law could not be used to govern this technology's operation'.[190] While this is a largely accurate summation of the majority reasoning, this method of legal reasoning also rests on a premise that wide questions of social policy are best left to the legislature rather than the courts. Given both the variety of arrangements within Australian jurisdictions as to how broadcasting and betting interacted, and the fact that legislative intervention at state level was in the air, there were grounds for adopting a more restrictive approach. Nor was the refusal to extend the law due to any dogmatic belief in the inability of judges to develop the law – both Latham CJ and McTiernan J agreed that the categories of nuisance were not closed[191] – but rather their concern was that what they were being asked to do went beyond the judicial function.

There was good reason for the majority's caution. As a nuisance case, *Victoria Park Racing v. Taylor* raised fundamental issues over the nature of the tort. The first was the extent to which damage to purely economic interests in the land could give rise to a cause of action in a tort which protected a plaintiff's proprietary interest in land. This was a core difference between majority and minority: Evatt J thought the plaintiff's profitable conduct of its business could not be dissociated from the land[192] while Dixon J argued that the substance of the claim went not to interference with the enjoyment of the land but with the profitable conduct of its business.[193] McTiernan J went further: 'It was not a legal right of the plaintiff always to be able to carry on its undertaking without loss of profits or not suffer any diminution in the value of its land… [t]he landowner took the risk of a change in the circumstances that had previously made the use profitable.'[194] As G.W. Paton recognised when commenting on the case in 1938, it was 'rather anomalous' to treat the case as one of interference given the lack of interference with the comfort and enjoyment of the racetrack.[195] But Evatt J was able to garner support for his view from a decision of the United States Supreme Court, *International News Service v. Associated Press*,[196] that found some kind of property right in the creation of 'news'. In his view, the defendant had 'reaped where it has not sown' and taken the harvest of those who had by broadcasting the races organised by the plaintiff. It was the interference with this right that Evatt J used as the basis for the claim in nuisance. Analytically, this right had

---

[190] Richardson and Trabsky, above n 160, 1024.
[191] (1937) 58 CLR 479, 493 (Latham CJ), 524 (McTiernan J).
[192] Ibid., 513.
[193] Ibid., 508.
[194] Ibid., 525.
[195] (1938) 16 *Canadian Bar Rev* 425, republished in (1938) 55 *SALJ* 449.
[196] 248 US 215 (1918).

nothing to do with the property the subject of a nuisance action, but, in effect, Evatt J found a proprietary right – the right to control access to information from activities conducted on land – and held that this was actually a right relating to land which could be protected in private nuisance. As Dixon J pointed out, English law had never 'thrown the protection of an injunction around all the intelligible elements of value'[197] so Evatt J created a piecemeal, limited proprietary right enforceable only in the limited context of an action for private nuisance, and only in limited circumstances, against a neighbour.[198] Paton also explored the argument that it was possible to find that there was some kind of proprietary right in the spectacle or entertainment that could be protected by injunction. He recognised that what was 'property' for the purposes of granting an injunction had been flexibly applied by the courts and that although a finding of property in a spectacle 'would not have been unwarranted', he ultimately rejected it given the conceptual uncertainties that had been created by stretching the meaning of property.[199]

The second, related, challenge to orthodoxy in private nuisance was the conduct that could constitute a private nuisance. The majority correctly noted English precedent that had consistently held there was no 'right to a view' and it was perfectly permissible to look over a neighbour's premises for whatever purpose one liked. Both Evatt and Rich JJ effectively ignored that authority and found that there was only a relative right to look out over a neighbour's land and that the building of a tower to spy on another went beyond the reciprocal rights and obligations the law required of landowners. It is clear Evatt J saw the defendant's conduct as reprehensible: the use of Taylor's bungalow was 'in an unreasonable and grotesque manner' and only 'an insufficiently disciplined desire for business profit and an almost reckless disregard for neighbours' could have resulted in the defendants causing the plaintiff loss.[200] If the right to overlook a neighbour's property was absolute this was completely irrelevant as English law had never recognised a doctrine of malicious abuse of rights and counsel for the defendants repeatedly argued, relying on *Bradford Corporation v. Pickles*,[201] that bad motive could not make an otherwise lawful exercise of property rights unlawful.[202] For Evatt J, the recognition of both business losses and the relativity of the right to a view allowed him to find a remedy. But there was one more element in Evatt J's cocktail of concepts that merged to allow a claim.

Much modern writing on the case has concerned its comments on privacy. For the majority, there was no general tort remedy for invasions of privacy although conduct infringing privacy might be actionable if it interfered with

---

[197] (1937) 58 CLR 479, 509.
[198] Cf. Evatt J's views in *Cowell v. Rosehill Racecourse Co. Ltd* (1937) 56 CLR 605, discussed above at 254–5.
[199] [1938] *SALJ* 449, 459.
[200] (1937) 58 CLR 479, 516, 522.
[201] [1895] AC 567.
[202] (1937) 58 CLR 479, 486, 489.

the use and enjoyment of land. Evatt J agreed, but used the fact that privacy was sometimes protected in private nuisance as ground to support his conclusion that a nuisance was established on the facts. The analogies were not especially convincing as the cases involved conduct that affected the enjoyment of people on or going to the land but coherence was not Evatt J's primary concern. In the spirit of Lord Atkin in *Donoghue v. Stevenson*, he adapted the law in line with 'altering social conditions and standards', one of which was the prospect of television as well as radio broadcasts.[203] This was innovative, even if Paton would have gone further, suggesting that the 'bold but necessary step' of recognising a right to privacy should have been taken in light of the challenges posed by modern technical innovations.[204] But Paton's invocation of Warren and Brandeis' famous article revealed another problem with using privacy as the basis for the claim in *Taylor*. Warren and Brandeis saw privacy as an aspect of a personality right and their concerns were primarily with intangible harm caused to the victim by unwarranted publicity or unwanted intrusion into private spaces.[205] These situations bore no relationship to the facts of *Taylor*, where the plaintiff was a corporate entity suing for loss of business profits.[206] It was asking a good deal of Australian courts in the 1930s to fashion a remedy for breach of privacy for appropriation of some kind of intangible property where there was very little English authority to support it.[207]

For the purposes of this study, two additional things are noteworthy about the case. The first is the almost complete lack of guidance from any English precedent. On the specific legal problem, there was simply no analogous case. Australian commentators noted that in England at that time only a few classic races were broadcast and then only the races themselves. Conversely, one writer said that in Australia 'no single race any day of the week all the year round seems to be regarded as too small to put "over the air".[208] The question continued to be topical between the argument and the handing down of the judgment in the High Court, with rumours spreading of action by the New South Wales Government to introduce legislation limiting race broadcasting[209] at the same time as there were more reports of unauthorised broadcasts taking place.[210] It was recognised too that the issue went beyond racing and affected

---

[203] Ibid., 521. Rich J shared similar concerns over television (505).

[204] (1938) 55 *SALJ* 449, 459.

[205] 'The right to privacy' (1890) 4 *Harv L Rev* 193.

[206] NSW, Parliament, *Report on the Law of Privacy*, Paper No 170, (1973), para. 12 (report prepared by W.L. Morison, Professor of Law at the University of Sydney).

[207] Even Percy Winfield, who advocated a tort of invasion of personal privacy, thought the existing law tolerably well protected the rights of privacy attached to property: 'Privacy' (1931) 47 *LQR* 23. See further J. McKeough, 'Horses and the law: the enduring legacy of *Victoria Park Racing*' in A. Kenyon, M. Richardson and S. Ricketson (eds.), *Landmarks in Australian Intellectual Property Law* (Cambridge University Press, 2009) 53, 68.

[208] *Chronicle* (Adelaide), 8 October 1936, 21; *SMH*, 21 January 1937, 8.

[209] *Morning Bulletin* (Rockhampton), 14 May 1937, 3; *Newcastle Morning Herald and Miners' Advocate* (Newcastle), 16 July 1937, 13.

[210] E.g. *Newcastle Morning Herald and Miners' Advocate*, 3 May 1937, 7.

all sports where patrons paid to enter.[211] As one newspaper put it, the question was 'sooner or later' bound to require a judicial ruling on questions which 'have not been dealt with anywhere else in the world.'[212] The Australian courts would make the first contribution to British common law development on a narrow question with extremely wide ranging consequences for sports in Australia and beyond.

The second notable aspect of the case was the social and political climate in which the case was decided. Broadcasting of races was a political issue with lobby groups to be found on both sides.[213] While Richardson and Trabsky may well be right in arguing that the majority judgments operated in a legal positivist tradition,[214] it is also true that the High Court was aware that its decision was unlikely to be the last word on the matter and that legislation (as in Queensland) would be passed to deal with the question. It would not have escaped Dixon J's notice that in *International News Service v. Associated Press*[215] Brandeis J (whom he cited) advocated a legislative rather than judicial solution to the problem. Even in the majority judgments, the inspiration may well have been American rather than traditional adherence to an English jurisprudence that said little on the problem. Evatt J, while he advocated for a judicial solution, was equally aware that there was a wider context than the common law at play here: he expressly noted that the systematic broadcasting of races made it almost impossible to police gaming legislation and although both the Federal and State governments could prohibit the broadcasting of races, the absence of legislation did not mean the practice was lawful.[216] The novelty of the facts, and the significantly different judicial responses, make the High Court decision one of the most interesting of this study.

The stakes were too high to be left with the High Court. It had long been predicted that the case would be decided in the Privy Council, a prophecy that came true when after a short delay the plaintiff announced it was seeking leave to appeal. In December 1937, the Racing Taxation Bill was introduced into the New South Wales Legislative Assembly. It contained nothing to deal with broadcasting and SP betting but this was because there was a case before the Privy Council regarding the broadcasting of races 'which would materially alter the situation.'[217] But if the legislators hoped the Privy Council would

---

[211] Evatt J used cricket as an example, saying the defendants' conduct was equivalent to erecting a stand outside a cricket ground for the sole purpose of allowing the public to watch the game at a price lower than that for which they could enter the ground: (1937) 58 CLR 479, 517. Cricket grounds already had to deal with this issue: 271 above.

[212] *Evening News* (Rockhampton), 14 February 1936, 6.

[213] Race clubs repeatedly requested legislative intervention (*The Australasian* (Melbourne), 28 August 1937, 47) but for a view supporting broadcasting and off course betting see *Newcastle Morning Herald and Miners' Advocate* (Newcastle), 21 July 1937, 9.

[214] Richardson and Trabsky, above n 160, 1031.

[215] 248 US 215 (1918).

[216] (1937) 58 CLR 479, 512.

[217] *Daily Advertiser* (Wagga Wagga), 8 December 1937, 8.

solve the problem their hopes were dashed. In January 1938, leave to appeal was surprisingly refused.[218] At least from the press reports, Sir William Jowitt for the appellant based his case largely on an infringement of privacy. There was no right of a landowner to absolute privacy but it was a 'complete fallacy' to say there was a right to unlimited overlooking in the other side. There was a danger, he said, of it being thought that because English law did not allow perfect privacy, 'anybody, by means of modern inventions like broadcasting and television, could steal – for it is little more – that which other people provide without the expense of organising the entertainment for themselves.'[219] Despite his submission that it was most desirable that the matter, which did not concern Australia exclusively, should be decided, Lord Russell on behalf of the Judicial Committee stated that leave would not be granted. His few comments suggest he did not see any claim in nuisance as neither the land nor anyone using it was affected.[220] The decision created uncertainty as to the future of racing[221] and led the chairman of the Rosehill Race Club to predict a large drop in prize money,[222] but the New South Wales broadcasters were keen to stress they wished to co-operate with race clubs over broadcasts,[223] perhaps conscious too that the New South Wales Government said shortly after the decision that it would give 'early consideration' to the position created by the Privy Council decision.[224] In a similar but less prescriptive vein as the Queensland legislation, the Gaming and Betting Amendment Act was passed in October which proscribed the passing on of any betting odds until the last race of the meeting had started.[225] But the broadcast of the races themselves was not banned or restricted. As Richardson and Trabsky suggest, once the legal position was settled Coasian bargaining[226] could take place between the race clubs and broadcasters albeit in the shadow of a commonly held view that the High Court and Privy Council decisions illustrated that 'law and equity appeared different propositions.'[227]

[218] (1938) 54 *LQR* 319, 320 (case note written by G.W. Paton).

[219] *SMH*, 21 January 1938, 11; *Courier-Mail* (Brisbane), 21 January 1938, 13.

[220] Ibid.

[221] *Courier-Mail*, 24 January 1938, 6.

[222] *SMH*, 22 January 1938, 14; *Truth* (Sydney), 23 January 1938, 39; *The Mercury* (Hobart), 24 January 1938, 6.

[223] *SMH*, 22 January 1938, 14; *National Advocate* (Bathurst), 22 January 1938, 1. But not everywhere – it seems the Privy Council decision encouraged the first outside broadcast in Perth: *WA* (Perth), 26 February 1938, 12. Longer term, there was a commercial incentive to bargain as the alternative arrangements for broadcasting off-course were themselves not inexpensive as owners of properties adjacent to metropolitan courses were paid about £250/year: Griffin-Foley, above n 78, 293.

[224] *Truth* (Sydney), 23 January 1938, 39.

[225] *Gaming and Betting Amendment Act 1938* (NSW) s. 2.

[226] Richardson and Trabsky, above n 160, 1034–1035, and R.H. Coase, 'The problem of social cost' (1960) 3 *Journal of Law and Economics*, 1.

[227] *Referee* (Sydney) 27 January 1938, 7.

Contrary to the expectations of the race clubs, it seems that private ordering proved workable for both parties,[228] perhaps because legislative attempts to
curtail SP betting proved largely ineffective.[229] When the Royal Commission
on Television (chaired by the same G.W. Paton who had advocated for the
introduction of a right to privacy to solve the problem) reported in 1954, it
recommended that differences between sporting bodies and television broadcasters over the televising of sporting events be left to private agreement with
recourse to arbitration in the case of disputes. Accordingly, the Broadcasting
and Television Bill 1956 made no reference to the subject.[230] However, fears that
this would lead to inadequate protection for sporting bodies from television
led to the question being reviewed. Evatt, now Leader of the Labor Opposition,
made it clear he held the same strong views as he had in 1937 by requesting that
protection be given to simultaneous radio broadcasting as was proposed to be
granted to television.[231] After further consultation with sporting bodies by the
Government minister responsible for the bill (Davidson, Postmaster General),
a clause was suggested which protected these bodies from both television and
radio broadcasts but this was ultimately rejected by the Menzies Government.
Broadcasts had only been included by sporting bodies as they thought it logical if television was covered so also should radio broadcasts but Davidson was
concerned that the existing practice of private agreement 'where a satisfactory
basis of agreement had been reached' should not be interfered with by the legislation.[232] The result was that the introduction of s. 88A into the Broadcasting
Act 1942 (Cth)[233] only limited the rights to televise sporting events (and even
then only from outside the ground) although, as in the Victoria Park dispute,
the private bargaining for broadcasters and sporting clubs took place in the
shadow of threatened legislative intervention.[234]

Conclusion

Although litigation rarely interceded into Australia's national pastime of recreational pleasure during the period of this study, this was not because law was
seen as excluded from these activities. For a start, there was no monolithic body

---

[228] As the race clubs themselves seem to have quickly realised; Griffin-Foley notes that the AJC
aligned itself with the broadcasters to seek modification of the NSW bill intended to place
restrictions on what could be broadcast: above n 78, 294.

[229] McCoy, above n 163, 45, argues that by 1940 SP bookmakers in hotels were operating as before
the passage of the 1938 Act.

[230] Commonwealth of Australia, *Parliamentary Debates*, House of Representatives, 19 April 1956,
1541 (Davidson).

[231] Ibid., 10 May 1956, 1984.

[232] Ibid., 14 June 1956, 3219.

[233] Broadcasting and Television Act 1956 (Cth) s. 49.

[234] Davidson stated that the protection granted to sporting bodies from television could be
extended to broadcasters if thought desirable: Commonwealth of Australia, *Parliamentary
Debates*, House of Representatives, 14 June 1956, 3220.

of activities that fell under the rubric of sport and recreation so any attempt at limitation would in practice have been untenable. The business component of horse racing made it the most likely to attract litigation and the historical record bears this out albeit that the numbers of cases remain small. Novel questions of law – the scope of an occupier's ability to withdraw a licence to be on land, of liability in nuisance and of the duty of care to avoid pure economic losses – were tested in the very diverse conditions of Australian racing, conditions that bore limited similarity to those of England. Outside of racing, while there are only very rare examples of litigation in golf and none in cricket and rugby, the commentary on cases from other parts of the world suggests Australians knew cases were coming and encouraged participants to take steps to avoid liability. While the absence of cases does not indicate liability was not recognised – one suspects informal settlements from cricket or golf balls breaking windows of nearby houses was common practice – it is nonetheless surprising to see the disconnect between abstract concerns over liability and the actual incidence of actions being brought. Conversely, the decision of the Full Court of the Supreme Court of Queensland in *Chatwood* represented a potentially more favourable, and perhaps realistic, approach to spectator liability in the modern sport of speedway where audiences were presumed to be more novices than aficionados of the sport.

More broadly, the place of liability rules in sport illustrates another component in determining the influence of English law in Australia. For the most part, there was never any doubt about the applicable law: where fault was alleged the common law of negligence would apply and results would depend on the application of that law to the facts. But there is more to this story than just the formal abstract rules of law. If the shadow of fault-based liability increasingly, if rhetorically, was cast over sport and recreational activities in Australia, the reluctance to bring cases at all and the very limited success for plaintiffs when they were brought suggests a reluctance to subject this aspect of Australian society to standards externally imposed and, in actual litigation, with the benefit of hindsight.

11

Conclusion

The argument in this book is that tort law as applied in Australia in the first half of the twentieth century contained elements of dynamism and innovation. It was not independent of the English common law of tort of which it was part but it in its application to Australian conditions it developed in ways that were not necessarily mirrored in England. While the scale of any Australian exceptionalism should not be overstated, it undersells the intellectual achievements of an earlier Australian legal profession if Australian tort law is seen simply as uncritically accepting everything that happened in the mother country.

Two general themes may be identified from the preceding analysis that underpin the nature of dynamism and innovation of tort law in Australia. The first is the prevalence of jury trials in tort actions, something that continued – unlike in England – during the entire period of this study. Apart from fashioning the manner in which appellate courts considered substantive issues, archival and newspaper reports also allow for the arguments before and decisions of trial courts to be explored and for the decision-making of juries to be unpacked. Substantive legal arguments before juries not infrequently gave way to non-legal asides, matters that legal practitioners recognised were influential in determining the jury's ultimate answer on the legal questions. In some areas, such as claims for negligently inflicted psychiatric harm and in defamation cases, the legal rules promulgated by Australian judges were influenced by the perceived fear that juries would be too sympathetic to plaintiffs if too much was left to them to decide. Conversely, the abrogation of the non-natural use question to judges in actions involving *Rylands v. Fletcher* demonstrates that judges thought that juries could too easily misunderstand legal concepts in a defendant's favour. The complicated and multi-faceted interaction between questions of law (judge), questions of fact (jury) and appellate review of jury verdicts formed an important context in which decisions about tort law were made during the period of this study.[1]

The second theme is that the Australian environment played a key role in how the judges, and on occasion legislatures, fashioned the application of the British

---

[1] M. Lunney, 'Common practice, breach of duty and jury trials: the history of *Mercer v. Commissioner for Road Transport and Tramways* (1936)' (2017) 44 *Aus Bar Rev* 144.

common law in Australia. This might seem a trite observation but is worth making because of the limited recognition given to previous generations of Australian lawyers who successfully did it. The most extensive example relates to liability for fire, but in fields as far apart as sport and recreation and political discourse tort law was applied and developed in light of the consequences decisions would have for the Australian community it regulated. It is difficult to believe, for example, that judgements over whether a licence could be revoked in breach of contract so as to make the licensee a trespasser (*Naylor, Cowell*) or whether fair comment lay for comment on facts published on a privileged occasion (*Givens*) were not affected by contemporary issues over undesirables on racecourses and the vitriolic political debate surrounding conscription.

Whether the argument of the book is seen as convincing depends in part on how one views the relation between a legal rule and its application. Even if the argument relies solely on formal legal rules, there is plenty of evidence throughout the preceding chapters of Australian judges having to develop, clarify and at times create new rules to deal with the cases before them. As argued in Chapter 2, the cultural, intellectual and legal restraints under which they operated prevented these innovations from being seen for what they were. But beyond the formal rules, the manner in which Australian judges applied British common law gave that law an Australian character. It was not a character that conflicted with British common law because by definition the common law was seen to apply uniformly throughout the Empire. Australian lawyers too identified with a British common law; they would have been shocked to discover their efforts were contributing to an alternate Australian common law. In practice, however, as long as protestations of independence were muted, what happened as a result of applying the uniform principles was a matter that could be dismissed because of the diversity of the Empire. While this was a sensible position to take at a formal level, it masks the diversity and innovation of what was happening 'on the ground' in various parts of the Empire. For example, Sir Samuel Griffith's frequent reference to the importance of the Australian context in determining the application of the common law rules illustrates both a recognition of the practical limitations of the unity principle and a willingness to derogate where Australian conditions so required. At least in tort law, it is difficult to see Sir Owen Dixon's description of Griffith as having 'a legal mind of the Austinian age, representing the thoughts and learning of a period which had gone'[2]; rather we see Griffith the consequentalist, mixing his analytical jurisprudence with the needs of the new federation which he had done so much to create. Key judicial figures within this study – Isaacs, Evatt, Cussen – can be analysed in the same way. Equally, however, the challenge to common law rules in application can be seen in lower court decisions now available to the legal historian through the wider accessibility of newspaper reports during

---

[2] Address upon retiring from office of Chief Justice of the High Court of Australia, 13 April 1964 (1964) 110 CLR viii, ix.

the period of this study. Far from revealing a static, studied acceptance of rules derived from England, the record reveals a rich history of contest, ambiguity and resolution across a wide variety of courts and tribunals in Australia.

There is no doubt that the generalisation that Australian tort law largely conformed, in form and in practice, with the tort law that applied in England during the period of this study is accurate. But generalisations by nature are crude and blunt and the Australian legal profession who interacted with their common law of tort did so in distinct and innovative ways for which they have not always been given credit. If this book has caused a rethink of their contribution, it has achieved its aim.

Index

Addison, Charles G., 92
agency, liability for acts of third parties
    and, 97
Allen v. *Flood*, 36
Anderson v. *Commissioner of Railways*,
    164–165
'applied' legal history, 11–12
Australian Labor Party, 48, 52, 54, 55, 59,
    63–65, 69, 137, 142
    Political Labour League, 52–55

Baalman, John, 30
Bailey v. *Truth and Sportsman Ltd*, 72–74
Bailey, Kenneth, 25–26
Baker v. *Queensland Newspapers Pty Ltd*, 63–65,
    68, 77–78, 80
Barker v. *Herbert*, 98
Barnes v. *The Commonwealth*, 128–129, 130
Barry, Sir John, 44
Beven, Thomas, 91–92, 97, 114, 116, 204
Beyer v. *Drews*, 239
Black v. *Christchurch Finance Co.*, 218, 219
Blackburn, Maurice, 122–123
Bourhill (or Hay) v. *Young*, 136, 139, 143
Bradford Corporation v. *Pickles*, 273
Bradley, Captain William, 140
Brandeis, Louis, 274
Britain Steamship Company Limited v. *The
    King*, 174
British race patriotism, 6, 8, 9, 21–23, 29
Broadcasting Act 1942 (Cth), 277
Broadcasting Act 1956 (Cth), 44
Broadcasting and Television Act 1956
    (Cth), 277
broadcasting of horse racing, 277
Brodie v. *Singleton Shire Council*, 152, 156
Brown v. *The Mount Barker Soldiers Hospital
    Inc.*, 123–124

Brown, Jethro, 26–27
Browne v. *McKinley*, 71
Bugge v. *Brown*, 211, 212, 215–216, 217
Bunyan v. *Jordan*, 124–128, 129, 130, 131, 132,
    133, 144
Burnie Port Authority v. *General Jones Pty Ltd*, 230
business reputation, action for damage to, 35–37

Cambridge Water Co Ltd v. *Eastern Counties
    Leather plc*, 214
Cameron v. *Consolidated Press Ltd*, 65–67, 68
Canavan v. *Syme & Co.*, 55–59
Careless Use of Fires Act 1912 (NSW), 230
Castle v. *St Augustine Links*, 242
Chatwood v. *National Speedways Ltd*, 244–246,
    247, 248, 278
Chester v. *Council of the Municipality of
    Waverley*, 129–136, 137, 139, 141, 142,
    143, 144–145
Claims Against the Commonwealth Act 1902
    (Cth), 166
Clark, Manning, 10, 30–31
Collins v. *Commonwealth of Australia*, 224
Colonial Laws Validity Act 1865, 1
Commissioner of Railways v. *Wise Bros Pty Ltd*,
    224–226, 227
common law
    British ignoring of Australian contributions,
        21, 45, 47
    British interest in Australian contributions,
        136, 231
    judicial adaptation to Australian
        environment, 1–2, 279–280
    jury trial prevalence in Australia, 279
    'universality' in Empire, 2, 19, 29, 30,
        255, 280
Compensation to Relatives Act 1897 (NSW), 137
conscription, 52, 55–59

constitutional law, 11

Coptic, MV, collision with HMAS *Adelaide*, 169

Cottrell v. *Allen*, 205

Country Party, 66

Court of Appeal for the State of New York, 38

Cowell v. *The Rosehill Racecourse Co. Ltd*, 253–256

Craig v. *Parker*, 204–205, 212

cricket, 241, 242, 243

Criminal Code Act 1899 (Qld), 32

'cultural cringe', 1, 10–11, 12, 14–16, 21

Curlewis, H.R., 29

Curtin, John, 22

Cussen, Sir Leo, 8, 40, 43, 56, 57, 62–63, 68, 70, 71–72, 73, 74, 93, 96, 266, 280

Daly v. *The Commissioner of Railways*, 117–118

Davidson v. *Walker*, 167

Dawkins v. *Lord Paulet*, 47

decline of British influence, 3–4

defamation
absolute privilege, 47–50
codification of common law, 32
group defamation, 55–59
intention to refer to plaintiff, 45–47
judicial distaste for commercial press, 79–82
libel/slander distinction, 33–34
political reputation and free speech, 59–68
professional status of politics, 62–66
qualified privilege, 37–42, 58–59
based on self-defence, 74–76
and fair comment, 69–74, 76–82
radio broadcasting, 47
special damage requirement, 34–37
unintentional, 46

Defamation Act 1889 (Qld), 32, 33

Defamation Act 1895 (Tas), 32

Defamation Act 1912 (NSW), 40–41

Dennis v. *Victorian Railway Commissioners*, 157–161, 164

Dixon, Sir Owen, 8, 17, 46–47, 48, 62, 73–74, 88, 102, 106, 109–110, 127, 170, 171–172, 175, 176, 177, 178, 179–182, 184–186, 187, 188, 189, 218, 254, 255, 272, 273, 275, 280

Donoghue v. *Stevenson*, 105, 120, 126, 133, 264, 274

Downing, Reg, 140, 141, 142, 143

Doyle v. *McIntosh*, 52–55

dual national loyalties, 2, 16–17
community of interest and community of culture, 20–21
in law schools, 23–27

Dulieu v. *White*, 119, 120, 121, 123

Duncan v. *Cammell Laird & Co. Ltd*, 180–181, 186–188

English Court of Appeal, 22, 35, 130, 133, 176, 180, 220, 232, 247, 252

Entick v. *Carrington*, 172

Esery v. *North Coast National A and I Society*, 257–258

Evans and Wife v. *Finn*, 166–168

Evans v. *Municipality of Redfern*, 153

Evatt, Herbert Vere, 8, 48, 81, 82, 121, 128, 133–136, 137, 139, 140, 143, 145, 218, 253, 254, 255, 272–274, 275, 277, 280

Filliter v. *Phippard*, 206, 208

fire, 199–231
Australian natural environment, 227–229
legislation, 229–230
liability for failure to abate, 203
liability of occupiers for fires lit by licencees, 207–210
liability of occupiers for independent contractors, 217–219
non-natural use, 209, 211, 212, 213–214, 219–226, 227
strict v. fault-based liability, 199–215, 226–227, 230–231
vicarious responsibility for negligence, 215–216

Fires (Metropolis) Act 1774 (UK), 205, 206, 209, 226

Fitzpatrick, Brian, 10

Foley v. *Hall*, 37

Forrester v. *Tyrrell*, 43

Francis v. *Cockrell*, 256n. 112

Friedmann, Wolfgang, 13–14

gambling, effect on driving tort litigation, 266–267

Gaming and Betting Amendment Act 1938 (NSW), 276

Gibbons v. *Duffell*, 47–48

Giles v. *Walker*, 232

Givens v. *David Syme & Co.*, 69–72, 73, 74

Godhard v. *James Inglis & Co. Ltd*, 45

golf, 239–240, 242–243

Goodhart, A.L., 233, 247
Goodsell v. *Moore*, 241–242
government liability
    Crown immunity, 147, 150, 157
    military activities, 166–191. *See also*
        Shaw Savill and Albion Co. Ltd v.
        Commonwealth
    railway fires, 156–165
    roads, 147–156
        legislation in New South Wales, 152–153,
        154, 156
Gray, Hamish, 30
Griffith, Sir Samuel, 8, 11, 16, 32–34,
    36, 38, 41–42, 45–46, 60, 93–94,
    96, 149, 150–152, 156, 160–161,
    163, 208–210, 231, 233, 280

Hall v. *Brooklands Auto Racing Club*, 244,
    247–248, 256
Hall-Gibbs Mercantile Agency v. *Dun*, 34–37
Hambrook v. *Stokes Bros Pty Ltd*, 119–120, 121,
    122, 125, 126, 127, 130, 131, 139, 141, 145
Hancock, Keith, 2, 3, 17–19, 25, 31
Hargrave v. *Goldman*, 203, 225, 233
Harney, E.A., 21
Havelberg v. *Brown*, 200–203, 225, 234
Hazelwood v. *Webber*, 225–226, 227, 228, 230
Higgins, Henry Bournes, 24
High Court
    authority over state Supreme Courts, 3
    creation of, 3
    WWII patriotic conformity to English
        decisions, 21–22
highway immunity, 152–156
Holman v. *Sunday Times*, 76–77
Holman, William, 52, 55, 76
Holmes, Oliver Wendell, 47, 76
House of Lords
    Australian criticism of, 16
    authority over Australia, 22, 28
    precedents from, 36, 45–47, 94, 106, 107,
        136, 139, 187, 188, 226, 255, 264
Howe v. *Lees*, 41–42
Hoyt's Pty Ltd v. *O'Connor*, 99–108, 110
Hughes, W.M., 52, 69–70
Hulton v. *Jones*, 45–47, 57
Hurst v. *Picture Theatres Ltd*, 252–253,
    254–256

Imperial Federation League, 24
independent Australian Britons, 17–23

International News Service v. *Associated Press*,
    272, 275
Isaacs, Sir Isaac, 8, 16–17, 20, 41, 57–58, 60–61,
    94, 95, 96, 99, 102, 104–105, 106–108,
    110, 145, 163, 208, 209–210, 211, 212,
    215, 233, 280

Janvier v. *Sweeney*, 121, 125
JC Williamson Ltd v. *Lukey*, 253
Johnson v. *The Commonwealth*, 120–122, 125,
    126, 129
Jones v. *Festiniog Railway Co.*, 206
Jordan, Sir Frederick, 8, 48, 49–50, 81, 124–128,
    131–132, 133, 135, 145, 220–222, 224–
    225, 252–253, 254
Judiciary Act 1903 (Cth), 169

Kellett v. *Cowan*, 203–204
Kercher, Bruce, 7

Landa, Abram, 137–138, 139, 141, 143, 146
Landau, N., 136, 137
Lang v. *Willis*, 67–68
*Law Reform (Miscellaneous Provisions) Act
    1944* (NSW), 137, 142–143
Law Reform (Miscellaneous Provisions) Bill
    1943, 140–142
Law Reform (Torts) Bill 1942, 138–139
Lawson, F.H., 20
Lee v. *Wilson and Mackinnon*, 46–47
Local Government Act 1906 (NSW), 152–153,
    154, 156
London County Council v. *Great Eastern
    Railway Company*, 162
Lothian v. *Rickards*, 85–87, 89, 91, 93–97, 98, 107
Luntz, Harold, 12

Macintosh v. *Dun*, 37–42
Mair, Alexander, 138
Mangena v. *Wright*, 74
Manning, Sir Henry Edward, 140–141,
    142–143
Mattinson v. *Coote*, 214–215
McCarty v. *Leeming*, 223, 224
McCauley v. *John Fairfax and Sons Ltd*, 79
McDonald v. *Dickson*, 205
McDonald, Ramsay, 25
McKell, William, 137, 139, 141, 142
McLoughlin v. *O'Brian*, 133
Meldrum v. *Australian Broadcasting Co.
    Ltd*, 43–45

Mentone Racing Club v. *Victorian Railways Commissioner*, 265–266
Miller v. *McKeon*, 148–150, 151, 152, 156
Moore, Harrison, 24–25
motor vehicle accidents, 6
Mowlds v. *Ferguson*, 49–50
Musgrove v. *Pandelis*, 220
Mutch v. *McIntosh*, 52–55

nationalist historiography, 10–11
Naylor v. *Canterbury Park Racecourse Co. Ltd*, 250–253, 254, 255
negligence
  liability for conduct of third party, 85–110
  nervous shock, 111–146
    and gender, 144–145
    importance of impact, 116–118
  third party, 84–110
Newstead v. *London Express Newspaper Limited*, 47
nuisance, 98, 103, 148, 166–167, 213–214, 231–232, 234, 242, 270–274, 276, 278
nuisance', 217

occupier, liability for acts of children, 97–98
Odgers, William Blake, 33, 70
Osborne v. *Sparke*, 231–234
Owens v. *Liverpool Corporation*, 133, 139

Packer, Sir Frank, 78
parents, liability for acts of children, 109
Parsons, Ross, 22
Paton, G.W., 13, 14, 20, 27–29, 135, 272, 273, 274, 277
Peden, Sir John, 23
Penton v. *Calwell*, 74–76, 78–79
Pett v. *Sims Paving and Road Construction Co. Pty Ltd*, 212–214, 226
Phillips, A.A., 15
Pollock, Sir Frederick, 33, 89–91, 94, 96–97, 270
Pratten v. *The Labour Daily Ltd*, 62–63, 68
Prattis v. *Council of Municipality of Bexley*, 97–98
prickly pear, liability for spread of, 235
privacy, 273–274
Privy Council
  Australian criticism of, 16–17
  authority over Australia, 1, 8, 19, 22, 123
  cases appealed to, 39–42, 95, 108, 111, 112–115, 118, 119, 128, 145, 152, 209, 216, 255, 275–276

  precedents from, 94, 110, 154, 155, 218
  sensitivity to local tort law variation, 19
Prout v. *Stacey*, 211

Racecourses Act and Other Amendments Act 1936 (Qld), 271
Railways Act 1890 (Vic), 159
Ratcliffe v. *Evans*, 35
Re Polemis, Furniss and Withy, 119, 120, 121, 123, 126, 133, 134, 142
Rea v. *Balmain New Ferry Company*, 115–116
Read v. *J Lyons & Co. Ltd*, 226
Redmond, J.A., 44
Richards v. *Baker*, 136
Rickards v. *Lothian*, 110, 209, 213
Rohan v. *Municipality of St Peters*, 154–156
Round Table, 23–25
Royal Commission on Police and Illicit Betting in New South Wales, 269
Royal Commission on Racing and Gaming in Queensland, 269
Royal Commission on Television, 277
rugby union, 243
Rylands v. *Fletcher*, 200, 203, 204, 205, 206, 207, 208, 209, 210, 211, 212, 213, 214, 217, 218, 219, 221, 223, 224, 225, 226, 227, 228, 230, 231, 234, 279

Salmond, John, 26, 28, 43, 74, 134, 212, 213, 214
Savige v. *News Limited*, 80
Sealey v. *The Commissioner of Railways*, 116–117
Sedleigh Denfield v. *O'Callaghan*, 225
Sermon v. *Commissioner of Railways*, 161–164
Shaw Savill and Albion Co. Ltd v. *Commonwealth*, 168–190
  duty to take care, 171–172, 174–175, 177, 179, 181, 185
  justiciability, 169–170, 172–173, 174–175, 177, 179–180, 189
  negligence, 168, 171, 173, 174, 175–176, 178, 179, 180, 181, 184–186, 189, 190
  public immunity interest for evidence, 177–178
  public interest immunity for evidence, 180–181, 182–184
  secrecy of evidence, 177–178, 180–181, 182–184, 187
Sinclair v. *Cleary*, 262–265
Slatyer v. *Daily Telegraph*, 59–68

Smith v. *Leurs*, 108–110

Smith v. *London and South Western Railway*, 119, 159

Smith v. *Ministry of Defence*, 177

Smith's Newspapers Ltd v. *Becker*, 81

socialism as a defamatory term, 59–68

sport
    actions against broadcasters, 266–277
    actions against fellow competitors, 238–241
    actions against non-competitors, 238
    actions against organisers, 241–265
    actions by organisers, 265–277
    boating, 238, 241–242
    cricket, 241, 242, 243
    cultural importance of, 236
    cycling, 238, 239
    golf, 239–240, 242–243
    horse racing, 238–239
        actions by horse owners for economic loss, 259–265
        actions by horse owners for injury, 257–258
        actions by jockeys, 258–259
        actions by organisers, 265–277
        actions by spectators, 256
        trespass, 249–256
    rugby, 243–244
    speedway, 244–249

Subiaco Municipal Council v. *Walmsley*, 108

Sugerman, Bernard, 29

Thompson v. *Gosney*, 219

Telegraph Newspaper Co Ltd v. *Bedford*, 42, 82

Thompson v. *Truth and Sportsman Ltd*, 80–81

Thompson v. *Truth and Sportsman Ltd (No. 1)*, 79

Tolmer v. *Darling*, 223–224

trade protection societies, 33–42

transnational study of private law, 6–7

trespass to land, 256

Turberville v. *Stamp*, 203, 204, 212

Victoria Park Racing and Recreation Grounds Company Ltd v. *Taylor*, 266–276

Victorian Railway Commissioners v. *Campbell*, 160–161, 164

Victorian Railway Commissioners v. *Coultas*, 28, 111–115, 117, 119, 121, 127, 138
    avoiding limits of, 114–116, 117–118, 121, 122, 123–124, 132
    criticism of decision, 112–114, 122
    judicial rejection of, 135
    judicial sidelining of, 126, 128–130
    overcome by legislation in New South Wales, 137–144
    overcome by legislation in South Australia, 136
    overcome by legislation in Victoria, 122–123

Victorian Woollen and Cloth Manufacturing Co Ltd v. *Board of Land and Works*, 159

Wardle v. *McInnes*, 217–219, 227

Warren, Samuel, 274

Wason v. *Walter*, 71, 74

Watego v. *Byron Shire Council*, 211

Watson v. *South Australian Trotting Inc.*, 258

Webber v. *Hazelwood*, 219–223, 225

weed control, 231–235

Weld-Blundell v. *Stephens*, 106, 107

Wenbam v. *Council of the Municipality of Lane Cove*, 151

Western Australian Criminal Code, 32

Whinfield v. *Lands Purchase Management Board of Victoria and State Rivers and Water Supply Commission of Victoria*, 207–210, 217, 220, 221

Whitfield v. *Turner*, 211

Whitford v. *Clarke*, 68

Wilkinson v. *Downton*, 121, 122, 126, 127, 128

Windeyer, Sir Victor, 29, 234

Winfield, Sir Henry Percy, 28, 134, 137, 270

Wireless Telegraphy Act 1905–1919 (Cth), 251

Woinarksi, Severin, 20

Wood v. *Leadbitter*, 251, 252

workplace accidents, 6

Young v. *Tilley*, 205–207, 209, 210

MAX TEMESCU is an illustrator and writer
who received his Bachelor of Fine Arts from
Washington University in St. Louis. Since
graduating in 2013, his work has appeared
in a number of publications and platforms
including *Field & Stream*, *Popular Science*,
Wired, and *Adult Swim*. He currently resides
in New York City where he does freelance
work in graphic design.

TemescuArt.com